BOUNDED**MISSIONS**

CRAIG L. ARCENEAUX

BOUNDED MISSIONS

**MILITARY REGIMES AND
DEMOCRATIZATION IN THE
SOUTHERN CONE AND BRAZIL**

THE PENNSYLVANIA STATE UNIVERSITY PRESS
UNIVERSITY PARK, PENNSYLVANIA

Library of Congress Cataloging-in-Publication Data

Arceneaux, Craig L., 1965–
    Bounded missions : military regimes and democratization in the Southern
Cone and Brazil / Craig L. Arceneaux.

    p.   cm.
    Originally presented as the author's thesis (Ph. D.—University of California,
Riverside, 1997).
    Includes bibliographical references and index.
    ISBN 0-271-02103-9 (cloth : acid-free paper)
    1. South America—Armed Forces—Political activity. 2. Civil-military
relations—South America. 3. Military government—South America.
    4. Democratization—
South America.
    I. Title.

    JL1856.C58 A73 2001
    322'.5'09809045—dc21

                                                                    00-57136

It is the policy of The Pennsylvania State University Press to use acid-free paper for
the first printing of all clothbound books. Publications on uncoated stock satisfy
the minimum requirements of American National Standard for Information
Sciences—Permanence of Paper for Printed Library Materials, ANSI Z39.48–1992.

CONTENTS

Preface / vii

Abbreviations / xi

1 Introduction: An Institutional Approach to Military Rule and Transition Control / 1

2 Political Alienation and Balanced Transition in the *Revolución Argentina* / 31

3 Institutional Aggrandizement and Controlled Transition in Pinochet's Chile / 71

4 The Argentine *Proceso:* Politicization and Regime Collapse / 109

5 Brazil: Institutional Accommodation and Controlled Transition / 143

6 Institutional Accommodation, a Lack of Strategy Coordination, and Balanced Transition in Uruguay / 183

7 Conclusion: From Transition Control to Democratization / 223

References / 235

Index / 255

PREFACE

"What is the meaning of it, Watson? What object is served by this circle of misery and violence and fear? It must tend to some end, or else our universe is ruled by chance, which is unthinkable. But what end? There is the great standing perennial problem to which human reason is as far from an answer as ever."

—Sir Arthur Conan Doyle in
    "The Adventure of the Cardboard Box"

Misery, violence, and fear characterize the atmosphere that prevailed in the societies of the Southern Cone and Brazil during their most recent experiences with military rule. Early political studies, the seminal example of which is and continues to be Samuel Huntington's *Political Order in Changing Societies*, argued that the antidote to this state of affairs rested in strong institutions to provide order. The paradigm was simple: institutions provide the order necessary for the political and economic development that engenders peace and harmony within societies. That order is good and ought to be pursued was an explicit normative component of the research agenda. Misery and disorder stand on one side of the continuum, while harmony and order stand on the other. But the cases of the Southern Cone and Brazil prove otherwise. It was not the lack of institutions, but rather the arrangement of institutions that charted the political history of these countries while under military rule. Institutional regularities guided governments in these countries in the same manner that Western democracies submit to institutions. The institutions were undeniably more pliable than those found in Western democracies (and their malleability varied from case to case), but they did ultimately play the decisive role in the outcome of military rule. Moreover, as evidenced by this research, there was an unambiguous effort to respect and strengthen them. These militaries broke the institutional rules of the game when they took power, but they found that they could not dispense with the institutions themselves.

Given the brutality so often associated with military rule, an institutional approach to this form of governance can only be unsettling. There is comfort in the association between a lack of institutionalization and violence—we are wont to hold that humans are naturally compassionate and just, and that it is the environment of disorder that steers some to malevolence. But the reality is that institutions are not inherently good or evil. Therein rests the goal of this study—to extend the institutional paradigm to what might be considered a least likely case (military regimes), and thus demonstrate the ubiquity of institutions and the strength of the approach. To the question of why institutions, in some cases, produce evil—I leave this "great standing perennial problem" to the philosophers.

Support from a number of sources made this work possible. From the Department of Political Science at the University of California, Riverside, I received generous support while this work was in its early stages as a dissertation. A dissertation fellowship (1994–95) from the University of California Institute on Global Conflict and Cooperation in San Diego funded research at Stanford University, the Hoover Institution, and the University of Texas, and supported a trip to Buenos Aires, Argentina. A grant from the University of California, Riverside Academic Senate (1995) was also helpful in this regard, and Carlos G. Vélez-Ibáñez, dean of the College of Humanities, Arts, and Social Sciences at the time, was instrumental in assuring accommodations for me at Stanford University. Janet Moores and Esperanza Garcia from the Interlibrary Loans Department at UC Riverside went beyond the line of duty in their efforts to obtain numerous books and documents for me. Deborah Norden, Wendy Hunter, Bruce Wright, Frederick Nunn, and Sam Fitch all provided helpful comments. I thank Michael Desch and Randall Collins for the time they offered as dissertation committee members. A special debt of gratitude is reserved for David Pion-Berlin, who served as my dissertation chair and played an integral part in the development of this study from its earliest stages. His contribution to this work and my intellectual development as a graduate student could perhaps best be conveyed by my three-year-old daughter, who would characterize it as "big as a house." I also must give due regard to the anonymous reviewers at Penn State University Press. One in particular was essential to the transition of this work from dissertation to polished book. Sandy Thatcher and his staff smoothed the publication process with timely and unambiguous communications. This book also benefited from the superb copyediting of Andrew Lewis.

Chapter 4 is reprinted from the *Bulletin of Latin American Research* 16:1, Craig Arceneaux, "Institutional Design, Military Rule, and Regime

Transition in Argentina (1976–1983): An Extension of the Remmer Thesis," Copyright 1997, with the kind permission of Elsevier Science Ltd., The Boulevard, Langford Lane, Kidlington 0X5 1G5, UK3.

As I reflect on the time that has passed during the development of this book, the names of many other individuals who in one way or another encouraged, influenced, or cheered me come to mind. Ron Arceneaux, Casey Flanagan, David Geiser, David Largent, Vince Parker, and Joe Tullius had some sort of impact, the quality and effects of which I am still trying to determine, but I am certain the good outweighed the bad. My daughter Danielle, who is younger than the thoughts that inspired this book, has grown to be an inspiration herself for me and will continue to be so. My wife, Kathryn, stood supportive and patient throughout. It is to her that I dedicate this book and every moment spent on it.

ABBREVIATIONS

AD	Alianza Democrática (Democratic Alliance) — Chile
AD	Aliança Democrática (Democratic Alliance) — Brazil
AERP	Assessoria Especial de Relações Públicas (Special Advisory Staff on Public Relations)
ANCAP	Administración Nacional de Combustibles, Alcohol y Portland (National Administration of Fuel, Alcohol and Portland)
ANTEL	Ente de las Telecomunicaciones (Bureau of Telecommunications)
ARENA	Aliança Nacional Renovadora (National Renovating Alliance)
CAL	Comisión de Asesoramiento Legislativo (Legislative Consultation Commission)
CAEM	Centro de Altos Estudios Militares (Center of High Military Studies)
CES	Consejo de Económico y Social (Economic and Social Council)
CGE	Confederación General Económica (General Economic Confederation)
CGT	Confederación General de Trabajo (General Confederation of Labor)
CGT-Brasil	Confederación General de Trabajo-Brasil (General Confederation of Labor-Brazil)

CNI	Central Nacional de Inteligencia (Intelligence National Center)
COAJ	Comité Asesor de la Junta de Gobierno (Advisory Committee of the Governing Junta)
COAP	Comité Asesor Presidencial (Presidential Advisory Committee)
CODELCO	Corporación Nacional del Cobre de Chile (National Corporation of Chilean Copper)
COMASPO	Comisión de Asuntos Políticos (Commission on Political Affairs)
CONARA	Comisión Nacional de la Reforma Administrativa (National Commission on Administrative Reform)
CONACYT	Consejo Nacional de Ciencia y Técnica (National Council of Science and Technique)
CONADE	Consejo Nacional de Desarrollo (National Development Council)
CONAREPA	Comisión Nacional de Responsabilidad Patrimonial (National Commission of Patrimonial Responsibility)
CONASE	Consejo Nacional de Seguridad (National Security Council)
CORFO	Corporación de Fomento de la Producción (Chilean Corporation for the Promotion of Production)
COSENA	Consejo de Seguridad Nacional (National Security Council)
CPC	Confederación de Producción y Comercio (Confederation of Production and Commerce)
DINA	Dirección Nacional de Inteligencia (National Directorate of Intelligence)
DL	Decree law
DSI	Divisão de Informação e Segurança (Division of Security and Information)
ECI	*equipo de compatibilización interfuerzas* (interservice harmonization team)
EMP	Estado Mayor Presidencial (Presidential General Staff)
ESEDENA	Escuela de Seguridad y Defensa Nacional (College of Security and National Defense)
ESG	Escola Superior de Guerra (National War College)
ESMACO	Estado Mayor Conjunto (Joint Chiefs of Staff)
GAN	"gran acuerdo nacional" (great national accord)
IBAD	Instituto Brasileiro de Ação Democrática (Brazilian Institute for Democratic Action)

IMES	Instituto Militar de Estudios Superiores (Military Institute of Higher Studies)
IMF	International Monetary Fund
IPES	Instituto de Pesquisas e Estudos Sociais (Institute for Research and Social Studies)
JCJ	Junta de Commandantes en Jefe (Junta of Commanders in Chief)
JOG	Junta de Oficiales Generales (Junta of Generals)
MDB	Movimiento Democrático Brasileiro (Brazilian Democratic Movement)
MID	Movimiento de Integración y Desarrollo (Movement for Integration and Development)
NSC	National Security Council
NSD	National Security Doctrine
ODEPLAN	Oficina Nacional de Planificación (Office of National Economic Planning)
ONEMI	Oficina Nacional de Emergencia (National Office of Emergency)
PADA	Personal de Asesoramiento Designado por el Area (Consultation Staffs Designated by Area)
PDP	Partido Demócrata Progresista (Progressive Democratic Party)
PDS	Partido Democrático Social (Democratic Social Party)
PFL	Partido da Frente Liberal (Party of the Liberal Front)
PMDB	Partido do Movimiento Democrático Brasileiro (Party of the Brazilian Democratic Movement)
SENDET	Secretaría Ejecutiva Nacional de Detenidos (National Executive Secretary of Prisoners)
SEPLACODI	Secretaría de Planeamiento, Coordinación and Difusión (Secretary of Planning, Coordination, and Dissemination)
SGP	Secretaría General de la Presidencia (Secretary-General of the President)
SID	Servicio de Inteligencia de la Defensa (Defense Intelligence Service)
SIDE	Secretaría de Informaciones de Estado (State Secretary of Information)
SNI	Serviço Nacional de Informações (National Information Service)
SRA	Sociedad Rural Argentina (Argentine Rural Society)
STF	Supremo Tribunal Federal (Supreme Court)

UCRP   Unión Cívica Radical del Pueblo
UDN   União Democrática Nacional (National Democratic Union)
UTE   Administración General de las Usinas y Teléfonos del
            Estado (National Power Generation and Transmission
            Company)

1

Introduction: An Institutional Approach to Military Rule and Transition Control

Military rule played a prominent role in the history of Latin America, and its legacy continues to hound the fledgling democracies of the region. Although its specter has withdrawn from the area, it would be naive to discount the possibility of its reappearance. We should expect some countries to consolidate civilian rule, others to falter, and still others to fall somewhere in between (Huntington 1991). Even in the unlikely event that military rule disappears from the region, the subject would remain important not only for its historical interest, but also for its disparate legacies.

In Chile, the military has scorned threats to prosecute its members for human rights violations. Its political allies from the Pinochet era continue to protects its interests. And it still maintains a great deal of autonomy in its internal affairs. In Brazil the armed forces were unable to leave behind a lasting constitution like the Chilean military, but they were able to protect their interests and enforce their prerogatives during the 1988 constitutional reforms. Moreover, the Brazilian military essentially bred a new generation of politicians during its twenty-one-year rule and severely disrupted the development of the party system. In both countries there remains a strong positive impression of the military regimes—a finding that does not ease democratic consolidation. The Uruguayan military had less success in its attempt to establish a new political order, but it did prescribe the expected victor in the first presidential elections, avoided human rights inquiries, and has kept civilian control over the military at less than ideal levels. The Argentine armed forces of 1973 had less success controlling the transition to civilian rule, but this military was simply wounded and soon recovered to force its interests on a debilitated Peronist government. Finally, the Argentine armed forces of 1983 exerted the least amount of transition control and subsequent influence. Scarred by a "dirty war" against its own people, an economic crisis of its own making, and a crushing defeat in the Malvinas Islands, the Argentine military was unable to prevent the opposition politicians from drafting the rules of the new democratic regime, which included effective civilian control of the armed forces.

These legacies are testimony to the significance of military rule for present-day politics in Latin America. What remains unclear is why some militaries were able to exert greater control than others over the transition to democracy. The intuitive answers to this question serve only to deepen the mystery. The depth of democratic experience does not seem relevant. The militaries of Chile and Uruguay exerted high levels of control over the transition, although these were the countries with the greatest length of democratic rule before their respective military takeovers. Economic health does not seem relevant either. Chile endured a severe crisis from 1982 to 1985, but the Pinochet regime still managed to control the transition, and Brazil exhibited a high level of control even while falling into a deep economic crisis. Meanwhile, both Uruguay and the Argentine regime of 1966 to 1973 were enjoying modest prosperity even as control over the transition began to slip. Nor does the level of social unrest seem relevant. The protests preceding the collapse of the 1976–83 Argentine regime appear quite mild when compared to the *diretas ja* rallies in Brazil, the 1982–85 National Days of Protest in Chile, the marches at the obelisk in Uruguay, or the *cordobazo* in 1966–73 Argentina.

Seeking an explanation for why some militaries more than others controlled the transition to civilian rule in factors such as the depth of democratic experience, the economy, or the level of social unrest fails to take into account regime characteristics. Looking outside the regime, to its environment, for the factors governing regime change and transition control ignores how regime leaders were able to translate "environmental successes" such as the defeat of subversive groups or economic growth into political capital to support transition control, or how they were able to prevent "environmental failures" such as social protest or economic decline from undermining their regimes.

Does this mean that transition control depends upon the acumen, imprudence, or whim of regime leaders? If this were the case, it would be impossible to formulate a predictive model of transition control. We can avoid a skid toward description by recognizing that it simply is not the case that regime leaders act in a vacuum. On the contrary, we need look no further than the regime institutions themselves for indications to what regime leaders are likely to prefer and how they are likely to strategize on the issue of transition. Institutions instill goals, embolden or weaken, and thus largely determine the capacity of regime leaders to control a transition. The key to our puzzle thus lies in specifying which institutions determine this capacity and precisely how they do it.

The model I develop in this study is oriented toward the military regime—I justify this regime-specific approach below. The model rests upon two institution-dependent factors that in my view determine the capacity of regime leaders to control a transition. The first is military unity; the second is strategy coordination to allow for coherent political and economic agendas. The first factor, a united military, provides the regime with a stable basis of support. Without military unity, government officials cannot face society with the coherence and fortitude required to answer societal demands and create linkages to societal groups, nor are they able to effectively fend off opposition proposals or criticisms. They are either reluctant to act for fear of irritating one military faction or another, or find that any actions they do take are analyzed in the context of factional preferences and inevitably serve only to heighten animosity in the services.

By providing government officials with a stable basis of support, military unity alone tells us much about regime durability. But a durable regime is not necessarily a successful one. A regime may be able to defend itself from political opposition and last for some time, but transition control demands that a regime take the offensive and institute a coherent political and economic agenda. A regime must therefore be able to coordinate a strategy to take advantage of the opportunity to accumulate political capital and linkages that is simply *afforded* by military unity.

Such a strategy requires a regime to accomplish two purposes. First, it must walk a fine line between unchecked military involvement in government, which may serve to politicize the military and create disunity, and disregard of the military institution, which may serve to alienate the military and lead it to withdraw its support. Second, it must cultivate linkages with important economic and social groups and accumulate political capital with a significant portion of society. No government, no matter the coercive resources at its disposal, can successfully rule as a completely autonomous agent.[1] I argue that strategy coordination, like military unity, finds its chief determinants over time within regime institutions.

The model highlights important similarities among the cases under study. The most united militaries were found in the military regimes of Chile and Brazil, both of which also successfully developed strategy coordination. In consequence, both were able to achieve the highest level of transition control, that of a *controlled transition*. Uruguay and Argentina 1966–73 (the *Revolución Argentina*) also found relatively united militaries as their support base, but neither was able to develop strategy coordination. This led them to a lower level of transition control, that of a *balanced transition*. Finally, Argentina 1976–83 (the *Proceso*) had neither the advantage of military unity nor that of strategy coordination. In consequence, government officials were unable to exert much influence over the transition and the regime collapsed. (I consider the combination of military disunity and strategy coordination to be untenable in so far as military unity is a necessary condition for strategy coordination.)

The institutions that determine the level of transition control are in place well before the actual transition. In this sense, the future of transition control is written long before the actual withdrawal from rule begins. Most military rulers would have little difficulty with this argument because most military regimes define themselves as regimes of exception. Ruling militaries characterize intervention as a mission forced on them by disruptive forces such as subversion, political deadlock in government, or economic crisis. The military intervenes in government for any of a number of technical reasons—to gain more complete control over the antisubversive struggle; to reorganize electoral rules, political parties, or intergovernmental relations; or to discipline, reorganize, or revitalize certain economic sectors. The promise of a new regime—one that perfects representation and opens the door for economic development, political stability, and morality—is broadcast in government proclamations and public announcements. Transition control is thus a phenomenon that finds its roots at the very beginning of military rule. One cannot understand transition control without a detailed examination of the period of military rule that preceded it. Specifically, one must examine the mission the military set for itself and its success in

1. The unrefined link between autonomy and capacity was an early error made by statist theorists. For a discussion of this criticism, see Weiss 1998, 14–40.

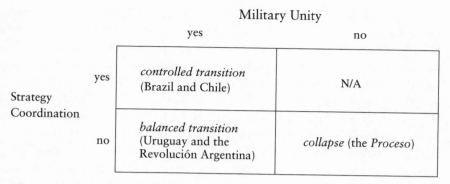

Figure 1   Determinants of Transition Control

completing that mission. And as I argue, the capacity of a military to complete its mission is largely determined by regime institutions.

The approach to military rule as a mission, a temporary engagement, is supported both empirically and theoretically. Empirically, Nordlinger (1977, 138–47) has noted that most military regimes do not last long, and withdraw from rule voluntarily. There are two theoretical explanations for this. First, most militaries retain a sizable faction that views governance as outside military expertise, but accepts intervention as a necessary measure in the face of disorder (Luttwak 1968). These officers exert pressure on the military regime to define its mission clearly and even to set a timetable for completion. Second, democracy and civilian rule are the dominant ideologies of the second half of the twentieth century. This is especially the case in Latin America, where most countries tailored their constitutions and political traditions after the liberal ideals of the American and French Revolutions. This makes it very difficult for a military to justify its rule as anything but temporary (Przeworski 1986). Rouquié (1986, 110–11) writes:

> In fact, military regimes are only really legitimized by their future. If elected governments have legitimacy by virtue of their origin, de facto governments have legitimacy only by the way they exercise power, and almost, one might say, by the performance they ultimately accomplish. The past may be used to justify the arrival of the military in power, but customary references to political and social chaos, to the vacuum of power, and to menaces of every kind, still reflect objectives that must eventually be attained or outcomes that must finally be avoided. The military regime, therefore, always lives for the future. It is, in essence, transitory.

An inquiry into the period of military rule sheds light on how transition control is determined. Military unity and strategy coordination have already been introduced as the determining factors for transition control. But we can deepen our understanding of transition control when we recognize that unity and strategy coordination can be produced (or undermined) in different ways. Different institutional configurations may produce similar results. Controlled transitions occurred in both Chile and Brazil, but as I explain below, in Chile the institutional configuration allowed regime factions to be suppressed, whereas in Brazil institutions were organized such that regime factions were accommodated. These same distinctions also characterized the process by which each military regime developed strategy coordination. Uruguay and Argentina 1966–73 were able to sustain a balanced transition in the absence of strategy coordination because their militaries were united, but again we find significant differences behind this similarity in outcome. Here, Uruguay resembles Brazil in that in both cases military unity was sustained through accommodation. But a different institutional configuration drove Argentina 1966–73, one which led its government to disregard input from the armed forces. In its relations with the military, the *Revolución* government failed not by politicizing the armed forces, but by alienating them. Military unity survived even while regime unity (government-military relations) diminished over time. Finally, the Argentine *Proceso* stands alone, in that it was the only case afflicted by military disunity. Here, regime institutions were such that military politicization became essentially inevitable, as did transition by collapse.

Institutions thus stand center stage in the dynamics of military rule and transition control. When a military intervenes in government to establish a new political and economic order, it carves its future in the governing institutions it establishes. Its mission is bounded from the start either to its advantage or to its disadvantage, as well as to the advantage or disadvantage of those governed.

Military Rule in Latin America and the Study of Institutions

Military Rule and Military Studies

In the nineteenth century, most countries in Latin America found rival *caudillos* battling at the local level for their own personal gain. The vacuum of authority left in the wake of the independence wars, along with general economic devastation, the proliferation of arms, and the heightened political expectations of the middle and lower classes did little to foster national unity. When a semblance of order was produced, it was more often founded upon the sword than upon legitimate authority. Another competitor, another armed band, another civil war, invariably loomed on the horizon. It thus comes as little surprise that the masters of military power also found themselves in positions of political power.

The rise at the turn of the century of a military class with a corporate identity produced calls for professionalization in order to secure distinction, pride, and expertise for the military as an institution (Nunn 1983). Military professionals, espousing their newfound values, looked with disdain on the politically charged and undisciplined behavior of the *caudillos*. Alliances with economic interests opposed to the uncertainty of military rule strengthened civilian rule in many countries. But the underdeveloped socioeconomic environment and political institutions which sheltered traditional interests created an environment in which political friction was endemic, a friction that often penetrated the barracks as politicians manipulated promotions, assignments, and retirements to curry favor. As constitutionally sanctioned guardians of the state, the armed forces developed a deep sense of distrust toward civilian politicians that further contributed to their general sense of "antipolitics" (Loveman and Davies 1997). Ironically, officers came to believe that they could only safeguard their professional, presumably apolitical, values and maintain political stability by becoming more involved in governance. Militaries acted as "moderators," or "guardians" of their regimes (Nordlinger 1977). They constructed boundaries of political action and tinkered with government personnel, removing those who dared trespass outside the imposed confines of action and inserting more trustworthy individuals. The imposition of outright military regimes in which the armed forces expressly assumed responsibility for government policy was not uncommon, and appeared to be the emerging norm by the 1970s.

Analysts could not, and did not, overlook the phenomenon of military rule. Nonetheless, early investigations tended to examine only its causes and consequences and ignored military rule itself as a subject worth studying in its own right. Perhaps driven by a normative concern with democracy, they viewed military rule as an aberration. Modernization theorists (e.g., Lerner 1958, Lipset 1960, and Cutright 1963) dismissed military rule as a transitory digression on the road to democracy, and dependency theorists (e.g., Baran 1957, Frank 1967, and Cardoso and Falleto 1979) saw military rule as a perversion caused by the international capitalist system. Huntington (1968) suggested that military rule was not necessarily aberrant because certain conditions conducive to it (weak civilian institutions) were in fact the norm in many countries. Important studies on the military as a political actor soon followed (e.g., Schmitter 1973, O'Donnell 1973, and Nordlinger 1977). Nonetheless, in most studies the armed forces were considered a dependent variable of sorts, a sort of "black box" which would change its behavior as environmental conditions changed.[2] The composition of the middle class, the strength of civilian institutions, and the level of economic development, political culture, or subversive threat were all used to explain differences in military rule (Horowitz 1985). Important exceptions to this approach were the examinations of military professionalism and the impact of national security doctrine (e.g., Abrahamsson 1972, Janowitz and Little 1974, Stepan 1971, and Arriagada 1986). But although such studies did open the black box, they largely centered on processes that occurred before military rule and how these processes influenced military rule. The dynamics and internal machinations of military rule remained essentially unexamined.

Current scholars are more apt to accept military rule as a subject worthy of study in and of itself (Pion-Berlin 1995). Stepan (1988) investigates the role of security apparatuses and their tie to military factionalism, and Arriagada (1991) gives a detailed examination of the Chilean military regime and the mechanisms used by Pinochet to consolidate power. Other works include Masterson 1991, which examines military politicization and its impact on military rule in Peru, and Remmer 1991a, which notes how the institutional variation of military regimes affects regime durability.

I follow those who approach military rule as a subject worthy of study in and of itself. Military intervention brings to center stage perhaps the most autonomous and certainly the most powerful (in terms of the capacity to threaten physical force) institution in a society. Entrants to the armed forces encounter a socialization process that isolates them from society and imbues them with the values of the military as a corporate entity (Janowitz 1960). In this sense Huntington (1957) rightly speaks of a "military mind" or, to use a more contemporaneous term, "worldview." Given that militaries have both this distinct mentality and control over the means of physical compulsion, it is surprising that earlier scholars looked to environmental factors to explain military rule. When a military assumes power, it and it

2. Huntington (1968, 221) argues: "As society changes, so does the role of the military ... the more backward a society is, the more progressive the role of the military; the more advanced a society becomes, the more conservative and reactionary becomes the role of its military." Similarly, Finer (1988) associates changes in political culture with the likelihood for military intervention.

alone decides what goals to pursue, which social sectors to incorporate as accomplices, how to arrange power within the new regime, and how to design the lines of authority between the government and the armed services. Economic conditions, social structure, political legacies, and culture will influence these decisions, but the decisions themselves are made by officers within the framework of the worldview of the particular armed forces under study. It is in this sense that one can confidently argue that the study of military rule ought to begin first and foremost with the military itself.

Institutional Theory in Social Science

Institutions shape politics in a number of ways.[3] For example, they determine the availability of the policy instruments that the state can use to extend its influence (Katzenstein 1978), and they demarcate the location of "veto points" through which individuals or groups can reach into the policy process and obstruct it (Immergut 1992). But institutions do more than simply constrain or empower actors in the pursuit of some goal, as rational choice approaches to institutions argue. Institutions influence not only strategy formation, but also goal and preference formation (Thelen and Steinmo 1992, 7–10). As Skowronek (1995, 94) notes:

> Different institutions may give more or less play to individual interest, but the distinctive criteria of institutional action are official duty and legitimate authority. Called upon to account for their actions or to explain their decisions, incumbents have no recourse but to repair to their job descriptions. Thus, institutions do not simply constrain or channel the actions of self-interested individuals, they prescribe actions, construct motives, and assert legitimacy. That is indeed how institutions perpetuate the objectives or purposes instilled in them at their founding; that is what lies at the heart of their staying power.

Thus institutions are "neither neutral reflections of exogenous environmental forces nor neutral arenas for the performances of individuals driven

---

3. The "new institutionalism" in social science actually signifies the rise of a number of competing institutional approaches. Surveys of these approaches can be found in Ethington and McDonagh 1995 and Hall and Taylor 1996. My approach most closely approximates the "historical institutionalist" approach advocated in Steinmo, Thelen, and Longstreth 1992. Other important historical institutionalist works include March and Olsen 1989, Dunlavy 1993, Hattam 1993, and Steinmo 1993.

by exogenous preferences and expectations" (March and Olsen 1984, 742). In its widest definitional breadth (most often accepted in sociological studies), "institution" has been defined as "a social order or pattern that has attained a certain state or property" (Jepperson 1991, 145). (Thus the United States Congress, the California Department of Rehabilitation, the free market, marriage, and the handshake are all institutions.) Accordingly, state institutions are only a subset of all institutions. But my study is concerned only with those in the state and assumes that they are the most consequential. Granted, if regime institutions are grossly out of tune with the most powerful social institutions (e.g., the dominant culture, religion, or economic order), they may be forced to yield to the pressures that these can bring to bear. But there is seldom a bright line of opposition between regime institutions and all the rest, mainly because the institutions outside government often have mixed agendas, especially in societies that value both democracy and order. The government, by drawing on the immense store of resources at its disposal (propaganda, socialization processes, material incentives, and threats of violence), can usually manipulate these values and play these nongovernmental institutions off against each other.[4] The military government in Brazil, for example, was able to deflect demands for democratization for twenty-one years with a style of rule that combined the promotion of economic development with repression and guided liberalization.

The concentration on regime institutions still opens a multitude of institutions to investigation. Ikenberry (1988a) differentiates three levels of institutional structure relevant to the regime. At the first level, one finds "the administrative, legislative, and regulatory rules that guide the adjudication of conflict." This level has its most direct effect through the machinations of the policy process. At the second level, one finds the institutions that refer to the centralization and dispersion of power among state organizations. Here one recognizes the distribution of resources, relative capacities, and other comparative attributes of such state organizations as the legislature, administrative agencies, and the president. Finally, at the third and most encompassing level, one finds the norms that define state-society relations. Here one examines the fit between regime policy and social norms, and the relative capacity of society and the regime to impose norms on each other. This final level goes beyond regime institutions proper, but it is useful to a schematic of regime institutions insofar as it defines a particular function of regime institutions, that of integrating or establishing social norms

4. The best exposition of why we ought to take the state seriously as a political actor in its own right is found in Skocpol 1985.

to ensure that the regime is viewed as legitimate. For my purposes, I locate at this level all those regime institutions directed toward creating linkages with groups in society (e.g., consultative groups, representative bodies, and educational facilities that intermingle regime and social elites).

My concern with regime change and the influence of variation in institutional design leads me to center my analysis on the second level—the level concerning the centralization and dispersion of power among state organizations. Nonetheless, a complete analysis must maneuver through all three. Administrative processes (level 1) open "veto points" to certain state organizations and thus help to define their relative capacity and affect the overall durability and authority of the regime. And the ability of the regime to create institutional linkages with social groups to coordinate or impose new social norms (level 3) is integral to the acquisition of legitimacy. Events at this level reverberate back into the regime, in so far as the relative capacity of different components of the regime to forge societal links affects the dispersion of power among state organizations. As I document in the case study, the rise of Pinochet within what originated as a more collegial military government was largely dependent upon his superior ability to forge links with important groups in society.

The contention that regime institutions themselves determine regime change demands that we explain the source of institutional dynamics. Many institutionalists accept Stephen Krasner's (1984) use of punctuated equilibrium theory to explain institutional change.[5] This approach emphasizes the sunken costs of institutions, the motivation of those gaining from a given institution to perpetuate its existence, and the embeddedness of institutions within other resistant institutions. All of these factors increase the resiliency of institutions, even those which have grown inefficient or outmoded, and even in the face of outside pressures for change or dissolution. Institutional change thus occurs episodically, only in the context of crises, such as war or economic collapse. At these "critical junctures" institutions grow more fragile as immediate solutions, perhaps blocked by existing institutions, are demanded. New institutions more conducive to the demands of the crisis develop and embed themselves in the state structure. These institutions persist even after the crisis that brought them into being has dissolved, and the process begins anew.

The contribution of the punctuated equilibrium approach is its recognition of the path dependency of institutional dynamics. Institutions do not

---

5. Punctuated equilibrium is an evolutionary theory originally developed by paleontologists Niles Eldredge and Stephen Jay Gould.

wax and wane in accord with efficient outcomes. Those "shadows of the past" embodied in institutions loom as ever-present constraints on decisions (Ikenberry 1988b). Nonetheless, the approach actually pulls us away from an institutional explanation. Thelen and Steinmo (1992, 15) write:

> The problem with [punctuated equilibrium theory] is that institutions explain everything until they explain nothing. Institutions are an independent variable and explain political outcomes in periods of stability, but when they break down, they become the dependent variable, whose shape is determined by the political conflicts that such institutional breakdown unleashes. Put somewhat differently, at the moment of institutional breakdown, the logic of the argument is reversed from "Institutions shape politics" to "Politics shape institutions."

Orren and Skowronek (1993) note that the problem rests in the assumption that order is the basis of normal politics.[6] An institution is defined by its output of standards and regulations. But this does not mean that a regime acts as a coherent source of order. A regime consists of numerous institutions in the three levels defined above, and there is no reason to presume that these institutions exist in harmony. Consider that political institutions have been created at different moments in history, that they embody different social interests (or combinations thereof) or different levels of autonomy from society, and that, insofar as they are *political* institutions, they endeavor to control the behavior of individuals and other institutions (Orren and Skowronek 1993). Tension, contradiction, and confrontation are thus much more characteristic of the normal regime than is order. The picture is of course not one of chaos, but rather of disorder at the margins. And it is in these areas of disorder that institutional change can be initiated: "As political actors, inside and outside of institutions, manipulate, elaborate, and oppose the norms and procedures at hand to achieve their ends, they amplify the dissonances inherent in the institutional organization of political space. In this way, the intercurrence of different ordering arrangements becomes the medium of change through time" (Orren and Skowronek 1996). Thus even dramatic institutional changes, such as regime

6. Rational choice theorists, in their unremitting search for the equilibrium produced by institutions (e.g., Shepsle 1986), suffer from the same presumption of order. The rational choice approach also tends to analyze institutions in isolation and thus misses institutional interaction, which often has a greater bearing on political outcomes than does the simple relationship between individuals and a single institution (Orren and Skowronek 1996).

change, can begin well before they are discernible and begin to affect every-day politics. Minor movements over time by one institution can reverberate throughout the regime, strengthening or weakening other institutions. Just as trickles of water, gusts of wind, and temperature changes can over time contribute to a massive landslide, so too can multiple minor institutional pushes and pulls contribute to sudden institutional change. Orren and Skowronek refer to the argument that institutional intercurrence is the source of institutional change as the "multiple order thesis."

The multiple order thesis leads analysts to emphasize institutions over actors when explaining political outcomes. The capacity of political actors to design institutions to their liking is constrained by the enormity of the task, by the often unpredictable consequences of successful minor changes to institutions, and by the institutional settings in which their efforts are initiated.[7] Even Pinochet, who deftly manipulated institution building to his liking, found that the institutions he himself had presided over ultimately directed him to leave government in order to ensure their own survival.

Given the dynamics of institutional interaction described in the multiple order thesis and the three levels on which institutions exist, an analyst investigating regime change must make a meticulous examination of the institutional composition of the regime and maneuver through institutions at all three levels over time to uncover the sources of regime change. This approach complements my argument that military rule ought to be approached as a mission, and that transition control is determined long before the actual transition from military rule to democracy occurs.

Transition Control in the Military Regime

According to an oft-cited definition, the transition from authoritarian rule to democracy begins "the moment that authoritarian rulers (or, more often, a fraction thereof) announce their intention to extend significantly the sphere of protected individual and group rights—and are believed" (O'Donnell and Schmitter 1986, 10). The extension of rights, commonly noted as liberalization, is then accompanied by certain procedural practices of democratization that lead to elections. The moment democratically elected public officials assume government duties, transition ends and

---

7. Rational choice theorists tend to take a more relaxed approach and assume that actors are unhindered in their capacity to dismantle and create institutions. See Elster and Slagstad 1988. The complexities of institutional design are further discussed in the Conclusion.

democratic consolidation begins.[8] How an authoritarian regime exits from government is referred to as the mode of transition.[9] Transition control, one mode of transition, can be divided into three categories: collapse, balanced transition, and controlled transition.[10] Collapse can occur as either the result of a severe internal crisis or from military defeat. This type of transition involves a rupture with a completely discredited and delegitimized authoritarian regime. A balanced transition involves a nearly equal level of control over the transition by the authoritarian incumbents and a democratic opposition. The authoritarian leaders and opposition negotiate, and both find some advantages in the outcome. Finally, in a controlled transition the authoritarians retain considerable control over the transition. Liberalization and democratization are basically independent choices of the authoritarian regime. And although authoritarian control is likely to wane over time, there remain important continuities in the political institutions, elites, and practices found in the immediate post-authoritarian regime (Share and Mainwaring 1986, 178–79; Valenzuela 1992).

The three categories of transition control are best thought of as lying on a continuum. Valenzuela (1992) criticizes the use of a continuum, arguing that a more clearly delineated schema would be more useful. He proposes that a controlled transition (he uses the term "transaction") be defined by

8. Most studies take democratic consolidation to mean the consolidation of political democracy, or procedural democracy. See Mainwaring 1992, 296–98 and Schmitter and Karl 1991.

9. That this exit can occur along several dimensions has not been lost in the literature. Beyond the dimension of transition control, researchers have defined "mode" wholly or partly in terms of compromise vs. force strategies of transition actors (Schmitter and Karl 1991), the unity vs. disunity of opposition elites (Higley and Burton 1989), authoritarian elites with attitudes tolerant toward democracy vs. less tolerant authoritarians (Valenzuela 1992), democratic transitions initiated by government ("top-down") vs. democratic transitions initiated by society ("bottom-up") (Zhang 1994), presence vs. absence of economic crisis (Ekiert 1991), gradual vs. rapid transition (Dahl 1971; Viola and Mainwaring 1985), and finally, the sequence of contestation and participation (Dahl 1971). Making matters even more complex are the studies that define a plethora of transition modes upon various dimensions, so much so that they approach description (Morlino 1987, Stepan 1986). Karen Remmer's (1991b) warning that failure to establish a solid theoretical approach to democratic transition would result in an endless proliferation of propositions and variables seems to have been borne out here. For a discussion of these dimensions, see Arceneaux 1997, 17–29.

10. This tripartite distinction is commensurate with the terminology used in Share and Mainwaring 1986 (collapse, extrication, and transaction) and Huntington 1991 (replacement, transplacement, and transformation). For a review of different typologies that center on the control dimension of transition and an argument for the three-fold distinction, see Mainwaring 1992, 317–26. His basic argument is that typologies with over three distinctions lose parsimony, whereas two-fold typologies, such as *reforma* vs. *ruptura* (Linz 1981) or consensual vs. nonconsensual (Share 1987), cannot account for the large amount of middle cases.

whether the formal rules of the authoritarian regime are broken (presumably, the distinction between collapse and the others is already clear). Although theoretically appealing, the Valenzuela proposal would be difficult in practice. First, one would have to define what constitutes the authoritarian regime's formal rules and when they are considered broken. Are all the rules of the authoritarian regime to be held in equal regard? To do so, one would have to disregard one of the most fundamental strategies of negotiation—overemphasis and the inflation of demands in the expectation that some will be rejected. It does not take much to assume that most authoritarian regimes have a "hierarchy of formal rules" and little incentive to protect fervently those on the lower rungs. Second, the notion that transition involves the negotiation of individual rules is misleading. More often entire government institutions are negotiated, and government institutions are sets of rules. What then do we consider the breaking of a formal rule? If unrepresentative electoral laws imposed by the authoritarians are made only slightly more representative, has a rule been broken? If an authoritarian imposed national security council is reorganized so that five of nine, rather than six of nine are military officers, has a rule been broken? Clearly, one would be hard-pressed to document a controlled transition given the standards Valenzuela sets.

The focus on transition control rather than transition *per se* is important. O'Donnell and Schmitter's landmark *Transitions from Authoritarian Rule* (1986) focuses on factors internal to authoritarian regimes to explain transition, arguing that the movement toward democracy results from dynamics in this area. Important scholarship since has reacted by recognizing factors outside the regime to explain transition. These studies have amassed an impressive array of explanatory variables such as economic development (Burkhart and Lewis-Beck 1994), development of the working class (Rueschemeyer, Stephens, and Stephens 1992), labor union pressure (Munck 1998), international diffusion effects (Starr 1991), global leadership by democratic states (Modelsky and Perry 1991), pressures from foreign actors (Whitehead 1996), civil society (Diamond 1999), and geography (Midlarsky 1995). My reaction to this debate is that we need to disaggregate our approach to democratization—the move to democratize and the mode of transition can be separated analytically for the purposes of gauging the relative impacts of factors external to and internal to an authoritarian regime.[11] I argue that while transition *per se* is influenced by

---

11. Remmer (1992/93) disaggregates democractization and recognizes the variation in causal forces as she analyzes the factors behind the impetus to democratize, the process of democratization, and the persistence of the democratization wave in Latin America.

both sets of factors (although I am inclined to grant greater emphasis to internal factors), the determinants of transition control are more deeply rooted within regime institutions. One can recognize clusters of democratic transitions over time, in Southern Europe, South America, Central America, Eastern Europe, or Africa, and one might rightly identify the debt crisis, the spread of democratic ideology, opposition movements, or some other "external" factor as a significant impetus. But one must also recognize that within these clusters of transitions, significant variations in transition control occurred. There is no doubt that the debt crisis affected the military governments of Brazil, Uruguay, and Argentina, but the fact remains that these regimes experienced transitions marked by control, balance, and collapse, respectively. Hence transition control signifies an interesting point of divergence within cases of democratization. Studies that limit themselves to the study of transition alone miss these variations in transition control, a factor that significantly affects democratic consolidation.

There are few studies on the causes of control. Donald Share argues that a controlled transition "is likely to be successfully implemented from relatively strong and secure authoritarian regimes, and not in regimes that fear for their survival" (1987, 544). Similarly, in an examination of South American transitions Hélgio Trindade notes that "the more far-reaching the changes which had taken place in the structure of society, the more the end of the authoritarian regime tended to take the form of a negotiated transition" (1991, 301).[12] These researchers are implying that authoritarian regimes that enact a controlled transition withdraw by choice, whereas authoritarian regimes that undergo a balanced transition or collapse withdraw by necessity (Share and Mainwaring 1986).

Working with these thoughts on strength and security and transition control, we can infer the following: "The stronger and more secure an authoritarian regime, the greater the level of transition control." Incorporating the aforementioned levels of control, this proposition holds that the strongest and most secure regimes will conduct a controlled transition, less strong and secure regimes will experience a balanced transition, and the weakest and most insecure regimes will withdraw by collapse.

The linkage between strength and security on one hand and transition control on the other is intuitively appealing and, at first glance, simple— almost too simple. But the real analytical task comes in the attempt to specify how strength and security are achieved. Huntington (1991, 110–21) and Linz and Stepan (1996, 55–65) approach this question, but neither

---

12. Matsushita (1987) gives a similar argument.

provides a sufficient analysis. Huntington explicitly associates regime type with transition control, but the association he purports is actually very weak.[13] Linz and Stepan examine how prior regime type influences likely paths to democratic transition, but the paths they define overlap so much (two categories are labeled "other regime-specific paths") and the possible outcomes within each are so open-ended that they demonstrate little more than the truism that a wide variety of outcomes are possible in any given regime type. Munck answers this problem by arguing that we should concentrate our efforts at a lower level of abstraction and subordinate the concept of transition control to regime type (1994, 365).[14] An example of this strategy comes from Bratton and van de Walle's (1994) study of patrimonial regimes in Africa. They distinguish six forms of patrimonial rule and note how the institutional configuration of each affects transition mode, including the dimension of control. The scholarship that recognizes how sultanistic regimes tend to generate mass movements and often lead to collapse can also be placed within this perspective (Goodwin and Skocpol 1989; Chehabi and Linz 1998).

The approach focusing on factors internal to the regime itself makes sense. By definition, different regimes organize power differently, and we should expect this to lead to a diversity in the obstacles to be overcome by regime leaders in their pursuit of strength and security.[15] For example, succession crises are peculiar to personalistic regimes and mobilization is important in totalitarian regimes. Appreciating these differences helps clarify why transition control varies within regime type.

Turning to the military regime, I argue that one must focus first and foremost on the role of military unity to assess strength and security accurately. This reasoning comes from the recognition that all professional

13. Huntington divides his regimes into four types: one-party, personal, military, and racial-oligarchic. The majority of his cases are either one-party or military regimes, and he finds that they are almost equally likely to experience transformation (controlled transition) or transplacement (balanced transition). As recognized in Munck 1994, 160: "If these two frequently encountered modes of transition are considered together, no clear pattern distinguishing military regimes from one-party systems is established. If these two modes of transition are separated, still no clear pattern emerges. Five of eleven one-party systems had transitions through transformation, as opposed to four through transplacement, and eight of sixteen military regimes had transitions through transformation, as opposed to five through transplacement. The strongest conclusion is that transitions through replacement are rare (six out of thirty-five)."

14. Lawson (1993) makes a similar argument.

15. Recognizing how different authoritarian regimes organize power differently, Geddes (1999) is able to explain why authoritarian breakdown varies among military regimes, personalist regimes, and one-party regimes.

militaries have the defense of state security as their paramount concern. To ensure security, a military fosters values of order and hierarchy within the institution. In the military worldview only a well-disciplined unit is able to protect the interests of the state effectively. Because of this recognized need for order and hierarchy, unity within the institution is a central value (Huntington 1957, 59–79). When a military seizes the reins of government, the novelty of the situation raises new issues and the division between the military as institution and the military as government becomes a central concern, one that may cause fissures within the armed forces (Finer 1988, 173–78; Stepan 1986, 72–78). Thus the maintenance of unity becomes integral to the continuance of military rule insofar as the military associates unity with the effective fulfillment of its primary role, state security.

The task then, for an institutional approach, is to ask how variations in the institutional organization of military regimes account for variations in military unity and in the capacity of the regime to develop strength and security. One widely cited distinction among military regimes is the extent to which military personnel supplant civilian officials in government (Finer 1988, 149–86; Ricci and Fitch 1990; Welch 1987). Another distinction comes from the recognition that while some military regimes are ruled collectively by a junta, others place a single officer at the pinnacle of power (Finer 1988, 257–61). Remmer (1991a) crosses "fusion of military and government roles" and "concentration of authority" and relates them to regime durability. In an analysis of South American military regimes, she finds that "oligarchic" (low fusion, low concentration) and "sultanistic" (high fusion, high concentration) regimes last substantially longer than "monarchic" (low fusion, high concentration) and "feudal" (high fusion, low concentration) regimes. Her explanation is that certain institutional arrangements forge regime unity better than others, and that unified regimes are best able to weather political crises.

Remmer's interest in regime unity focuses on the relationship between the military-as-institution and the military-as-government. While this relationship is ultimately very important to my approach, my model begins with the more confined concern over unity within the military institution alone. Because of this, I find the indicator used to measure fusion, the number (and significance) of government roles filled by military officers, to be too narrow an indicator for illustrating how the creation of a military regime affects the military institution. What is important is the extent to which the military is made to identify with the future of the regime. The more closely the future of the government is tied to the future of the military, the more the armed forces will view themselves as invested within the regime. Role supplantation is a significant indicator of this, but it alone cannot capture the manifold means by which investment can be cultivated (or undermined). In Chile, the direct involvement of military officers in government actually decreased over time as Pinochet circumscribed the power of his fellow service commanders and placed more civilians in the cabinet. Nonetheless, the identification of the military with the government remained strong. This was primarily due to how Pinochet defined regime institutions. They were the products of a successful war against subversion and any attacks upon them signified attacks upon this war against subversion and, ultimately, the principles of the military. The historical institutionalist approach informs this refinement of investment with its central tenet that institutions significantly influence the formation of preferences and expectations in political actors.

The case of Uruguay also highlights the importance of institutional definition as well as role displacement. Here the military regime was more civilianized than militarized and regime investment was low for the military. But one should also recognize that this was a regime that found it difficult to define institutions without acknowledging the future involvement of the traditional political parties. Argentina 1976–83 indicates that it is not only the extent of military involvement in government, but also what officers do while in these roles that is important. The fact that Argentine officers not only thoroughly penetrated government, but also engaged in notorious human rights abuses and extensive corruption must be recognized as a contributor to regime investment. The prospect of transition introduced threats at both the corporate and individual levels for these officers. And although in Brazil, like in Uruguay, neither military involvement in government nor regime investment was high, what investment there was (especially at the individual level) decreased as the repressive sectors of the military lost power. Finally, in the *Revolución* one cannot disregard the effect on the military as Onganía continuously pointed to the military as just one in a set of pillars upon which the regime rested. This added to the low level of regime investment created by the lack of officers in government.

For the above reasons, I argue that it is better that I use the more nuanced indicator of regime investment. Remmer has demonstrated how fusion, or role displacement, can help predict regime durability, but for my purposes, which involve a deep inquiry into the quality as well as quantity of rule, regime investment provides greater insight. Returning to the enterprise of investigating how regime characteristics affect military unity, we can begin by recognizing that two sets of factors affect unity in militaries: the social background and personality of personnel, and the immediate social situation (Janowitz and Little 1974, 96). The first set of factors is irrelevant to military unity after military intervention. The homogenization of military personnel that occurs through recruiting procedures before enlistment and through indoctrination after enlistment (Abrahamsson 1972) should remain constant. On the other hand, the assumption of government duties represents a dramatic change in the immediate social situation of the military. This change forces the military to confront two new problems that have seemingly contradictory solutions (Ricci and Fitch 1990). The first problem, the potential for division between the military as government and the military as institution, calls for a strong linkage between the government and the military. On the other hand, the second problem, the potential for the politicization of the military, means that this same strong linkage eases the transfer of political debate into the military hierarchy. Remmer's insightful analysis provides the basis for explaining how regime institutions affect military unity (Remmer 1991a, 39–42).

The greater the military's investment in the regime, the greater the need for concentrated authority so that government crises do not become crises for the military as an institution. Such regimes, exemplified in this study by Chile, strengthen ties between the military and government, but quell military politicization by centralizing power and repressing dissent. Conversely, the combination of high regime investment and a dispersion of authority, as was found in the Argentine *Proceso,* allows the military to be flooded with political debate without any mechanisms for control. For regime investment to be low, there must be a dispersion of government authority within the armed forces to maintain a linkage between the military and government, but significant military involvement in government should only occur at the highest ranks. If there are serious military factions, they can be persuaded to negotiate compromises as their leaders are incorporated into government institutions. Such representation serves to reduce conflict and uncertainty among different military groups. Brazil and Uruguay owed their military unity to this scenario. On the other hand, if low investment and a concentration of authority define a regime, a stark divide is created between the military and the government. The divide dulls the growth of politicization, in so far as military officers are denied the opportunity to participate in governance and find their behavior firmly restrained by the military hierarchy. But this comes at the cost of alienation within the military toward government. The armed forces grow reluctant to support a government that denies their input, especially as this government faces difficult economic, political, or social problems. Indeed, this alienation often spurs greater military unity as the institution bonds in its definition of a common problem—an overly insulated government. Hence, under the *Revolución* regime, even while the divide between the military and Onganía (and later Levingston) deepened, the military stood quite united in their opposition to government-military relations. The army commander, be it Pistarini, Alsogaray, or Lanusse, typically could count on the backing of the army and the support of the other services. Like similar cases in Rojas Pinilla's Colombia or Pérez Jiménez's Venezuela, in this sort of scenario we often find that the military begins to dissociate itself from the regime and reach out to society to aid the fall of the regime. In so far as its efforts reduce regime strength, a controlled transition becomes less likely, but in so far as it dissociates itself from the regime and faces society as a united institution, it is able to impose some conditions and salvage a balanced transition.

The combination of regime investment and the concentration of authority thus provides the institutional determinants for military unity in the military regime. Combination is the key here, for when viewed in isolation, these institutional features may mislead analysis. Regime investment alone does tell us much about the character of military rule and the motivation of the military toward transition. Militaries with high regime investment have a greater reluctance to withdraw from rule. O'Donnell and Schmitter note that the more a military is directly involved in government, the more likely it is that the military will view the transition process as involving corporate interests (1986, 34). Also, the greater the involvement, the more likely it is that the military will have used its time in power to benefit the military as an institution.[16] Thus transition becomes a threat to these gains. Finally, Krasner (1988) gives a theoretical basis to regime investment. He notes that both the extent to which institutions define individual actors (investment does this as the officers' corporate identity merges with government interests) and the number of linkages an institution has with other institutions (by linking the military and government, institutional linkages are increased) have a positive relation with institutional intransigence. Hence, in both Chile and the *Proceso,* there was a reluctance to withdraw, while the option was more palatable in Uruguay, Brazil, and the *Revolución,* especially when the government faced growing economic, political, and social problems. But the critical difference between Chile and the *Proceso* rested in the concentration of authority, as noted.

The devastating combination of regime investment and a dispersion of

---

16. Using military expenditures as an indicator, Remmer (1991a, 193–97) notes that military claims on political resources increase when military and government roles are fused.

authority in the *Proceso* created both disunity and the subsequent inability to rule with any effectiveness, as well as a reluctance to withdraw from rule. When the relatively uninvested militaries of the *Revolución* and Uruguay recognized their inability to govern effectively and the damage inflicted on the military institution, withdrawal was an option. But the leadership of the *Proceso* pressed on in the face of failure. Cavarozzi captures this entrapping resoluteness when he writes in reference to the *Proceso*: "When confronted with obstacles, the Argentine military seemingly blindly pushed ahead anyway" (1992a, 222). It is this obstinacy that makes collapse all the more likely for such regimes.[17]

On the other hand, in Chile regime investment did not have the same detrimental effects. First, one should recognize that regime investment is only devastating in the face of failure, and the concentration of power in Pinochet's hands allowed the Chilean regime to avoid the disunity that initiated the collapse of the *Proceso*. But when faced with transition, institutional combinations such as those found in Chile allowed the regime to more closely approach a unitary rational actor model. Nonetheless, the lingering effects of regime investment are highlighted by the Chilean case, where Pinochet withdrew with some reluctance after regime elites persuaded him to do so.

Military unity thus provides an important base of analysis for the dynamics of military rule and can significantly contribute to the durability of a military regime, as it did in Uruguay. But a durable regime is not necessarily a regime capable of enacting a controlled transition, as was also the case in Uruguay, where the regime lasted some twelve years but still managed only a balanced transition. A regime may be durable so long as conflict is quelled among regime elites and there exists no viable opposition. But transition has its own exigencies. As democracy begins to appear as a viable alternative, social actors become less likely to support the regime (Przeworski 1986, 51–53). And because the liberalization involved in the initiation of transition feeds upon itself and is inherently unstable (Przeworski 1991, 54–66), democracy usually becomes a viable alternative for many. Finer (1988, 282) illuminates the skill needed for a controlled transition,

---

17. This obstinacy is not surprising for an invested military. The sharp distinction most officers draw with civilians, and the disdain upon which they eye their disorderly, subversive-prone behavior, creates a strong in-group/out-group distinction for them. All this increases the defensiveness of military personnel. The more they become invested, the more determined they become to make the government work. They cannot defray responsibility. For the in-group/out-group distinction and how threats increase group cohesion, see Simmel 1955.

and how this skill must be directed toward both society and the military institution: "To control the government tightly ... involves rigging elections, favouring one party over another, etc.; and so the military's freedom of action is limited, and its claim to political neutrality tarnished. On the other hand, to control too loosely may lead to what they always fear—the return of their political enemies or the dismantling of their handiwork. Elements in the armed services will begin to press for a return to direct rule."

Thus the regime must not only maintain unity, but also be capable of designing a strategy to deal with this growing opposition and to contain military insecurities. This point has already been recognized in the literature by Garretón (1989), who argues that it is not enough for military regimes to be effective crisis managers; they must also propose a viable "foundational" project to guide rule. Munck (1998) identifies a similar process in his recognition that authoritarian regimes must confront the task of "constitutional definition." Similarly, Stepan (1985) discusses "defensive" and "offensive" projects. Only with an effective "foundational," "defining," or "offensive" project can a regime elicit support. Without a program that clarifies regime intentions in a variety of policy areas, groups in society will grow wary and fear granting support to a regime that may not be to their benefit. Growing social isolation will strengthen those military factions favoring withdrawal from rule under a minimum of conditions and swell the ranks of social opposition groups less willing to compromise. The creation of political and economic programs (and their acceptance within both the military and significant social groups) is the product of strategy coordination. Note that while military unity centers on the military as an institution, strategy coordination centers on the efforts of government.

The process by which government officials are able to devise a strategy can be partially illuminated with work by Kingdon (1984), who discusses three independent "streams" of processes involved in policymaking: problems, policies, and politics. Agenda setting, the first stage of the policy process in which government officials identify the problems they intend to confront, occurs when these three streams are "coupled." The processes are conceived of as streams because they "flow" relatively independently of each other. Moreover, each stream can act as the primary precipitant of agenda setting. The conception is one in which problems search for accommodating policies and politics, policies search for accommodating problems and politics, and the political climate favors some problems and policies but not others.

Coupling is not an automatic process. Two potential obstacles stand in its way: overloading and unpredictability. Overloading occurs when policymakers are faced with numerous and diverse problems and policies. As a result, "their attention drifts away to other, more manageable subjects" (Kingdon 1984, 185). Unpredictability refers to a policymakers' inability to forge a desired coupling. The more policymakers suspect that their policies or defined problems will be used or answered in a manner that they oppose further down the policy process, the less likely they are to act. Policymakers fear "setting in motion an unmanageable chain of events that might produce a result not to their liking" (185).

An institutional approach to program creation (the "foundational project") and the avoidance of problems such as overloading and unpredictability leads the researcher to inquire into how institutions either translate diffuse ideologies into political strategies or forge consensual strategies through mechanisms such as decision rules within the ruling group. The simple availability of ideas does not guarantee the rise of a coherent political program. Golbery's *Geopolítica do Brasil* and every other text inspired by the national security doctrine which served as a basis for political and economic policies in Brazil were readily available to the Uruguayan military government. But only in Brazil, with its more complete system of indoctrination for both military and civilian elite groups, was the national security doctrine able to serve as the basis for a viable political and economic program. In this sense, the generation of ideas within a country can be analyzed from an institutional perspective.[18]

Decision rules are also required for the development of a foundational project. This is especially a problem when there is a dispersion of authority, where collegial rule can lead to excessive log-rolling and even stalemate (Ramseyer and Rosenbluth 1995). The answer is again provided by a comparison between Brazil and Uruguay. In both, a group of superior officers were recognized government authorities. Nonetheless, in Brazil it was understood that one officer, designated as president, would be delegated power over daily decision-making and let alone so long as he did not trespass outside set policy boundaries. In Uruguay, the president was no more than a puppet, and collegial rule was extended to the most mundane of decisions. The impact was chronic delays in the decision-making process that lowered confidence in the regime and thereby instilled a more reaction-based approach to policymaking. The inability to coordinate initiative

---

18. Weir (1992) refers to the concept of "bounded innovation" to explain how institutions set both opportunities and boundaries for conceptual innovation. Also see King 1992 and Hall 1992.

hampered the coupling process described by Kingdon and impeded movements to take advantage of environmental successes or to guard against environmental crises. The result in Uruguay was a regime that simply muddled along, led by leaders able to agree that they should rule, but not what they should do while they rule. They thus failed to accumulate political credit for environmental successes and incurred damage from environmental crises. This placed them in a weak position at the start of transition, but the unity engendered by regime institutions allowed the Uruguayan military rulers to confront the democratic opposition with a united front and to institute a balanced transition.

To investigate the importance of strategy coordination, I trace the efforts in each case under study to develop a defining political and economic program. The Chilean and Brazilian governments successfully reached out to both society and the military institution to control their input into policymaking and make use of what expertise each had to offer. Uruguay, Argentina 1966–73, and Argentina 1976–83 all failed to develop strategy coordination. In Uruguay, the government did find success in its relations with the military institution (it walked the line between politicization and alienation), but was unable to successfully reach out to society. In the *Revolución* and the *Proceso*, we found governments that were unable to link themselves either to the military institution or to important groups within society.

The framework for the analysis of transition control is set. Two variables, military unity and strategy coordination allow us to predict transition control. Only with military unity and strategy coordination can a government accumulate political credit from environmental successes and have the chance to insulate itself from lethal damages from environmental crises.

Methodology and Case Selection

The following hypotheses can be drawn from the framework discussed above:

H^1: A military regime with military unity and strategy coordination is likely to effect a controlled transition.

H^2: A military regime with military unity but no strategy coordination is likely to transfer power in a balanced transition.

H^3: A military regime with neither military unity nor strategy coordination is likely to collapse.

As noted above, I consider the fourth combination, that of no military unity, but strategy coordination, impossible, since strategy coordination requires military unity.[19] To test these hypotheses, I use the comparable cases strategy (Lijphart 1971; Skocpol and Somers 1980). The cases of Chile (1973–89) and Brazil (1964–85) are used to test H^1, Uruguay (1973–85) and Argentina (1966–73) are used to test H^2, and Argentina (1976–83) is used to test H^3.

The cases represent a suitable test because although similar in many ways, they run the gamut on the independent and dependent variables. Each regime was led by a highly professionalized military that placed a priority on economic development and national security. Moreover, in each regime the military intervened as rulers rather than as moderators or guardians. That is, each intervened with the intention of long-term military rule to complete their mission. Also, these countries are similar in their levels of development and in their histories of colonialism. And unlike military rule and transition in Central America, pressure from foreign actors did not play an overly significant role. Finally, because of the time overlap among the cases, most were faced with similar international shocks, such as the oil crises and the debt crisis. When the institutional differences of the cases are set against these general similarities, one can better isolate the influence of institutions.

The comparable cases strategy is an appropriate method given the characteristics of the study. The model is best viewed as one that specifies a more combinatorial rather than aggregate approach. That is, it is the interaction between regime investment and concentration of authority, and in turn the interaction between military unity and strategy coordination, rather than simply the additive effects of these sets of variables that influences transition control. Such interaction is best captured with a comparable cases strategy (Ragin 1987, 23–44). Also, studies involving only a small number of cases are best examined with the comparable cases strategy (Ragin 1987, 9–13). Furthermore, research thus far in the field of democratic transitions has stressed case-specific attributes such as uncertainty, voluntarism, and *fortuna*. The comparable cases strategy is particularly helpful here insofar as it maintains sensitivity to particular cases as well as to the specification of testable and generalizable relationships (Ragin 1987, 20–44).

Because my case selection matches the comparable cases strategy, we

---

19. A regime in which the military and other societal actors can interact successfully in the midst of military disunity cannot be considered a military regime.

should have confidence that a number of potential alternative explanations are controlled for, and that the hypothesized relationships are not spurious. Our confidence should increase even more when it is recognized that the models are based upon many previously tested relationships. This follows from the Bayesian view of probability, which states that our confidence in hypothesized relationships ought to increase if these hypotheses are based upon previously formulated theories (George and McKeown 1985, 31).

The analysis of each case begins with an examination of those institutional influences upon military unity identified by the model—concentration of authority and regime investment. Because strategy coordination is ultimately indicated by the success found in formulating and implementing a coherent political and economic program, the efforts of each regime in these areas are closely scrutinized. Finally, the level of transition control exerted is documented. The *Revolución Argentina* opens the case studies in Chapter 2. Here, we see that while regime institutions did not contribute to factional growth and thus allowed for military unity, they did produce alienation toward the government, and thus undermined strategy coordination. This frustration within the military institution led it to re-intervene in government in order to guide the withdrawal from rule on its own. Because of the lack of political or economic success under the regime (and the inability to take advantage of what economic success there was), a controlled transition became untenable. Nonetheless, the sustained military unity allowed for a balanced transition to be salvaged.

In Chapter 3 we move to the Pinochet regime in Chile. Like the *Revolución*, here we found a government that tended to concentrate power in a single individual, but with different results because of the existence of regime investment and the success found in developing strategy coordination. I document how Pinochet deftly aggrandized institutions in such a way that he was able to suppress factional growth within the armed forces to maintain military unity, cultivate regime investment and his own concentration of power, and reach out to society to establish the linkages necessary for his political and economic programs. Notwithstanding the originating role played by Pinochet, this was ultimately a transition guided by institutions. Although Pinochet stood at the root of the Chilean military regime, these same regime institutions would in the end direct him to leave office. In this sense, Pinochet was undone by his own success. Nonetheless, this was a controlled transition in that the very same institutions that dislodged Pinochet also protected many of the prerogatives of the military regime to the detriment of its civilian opponents.

Chapter 4 returns us to Argentina for an analysis of the *Proceso* regime. Regime investment was high here, as in Chile, but unlike in Chile, authority was dispersed rather than concentrated. The military services divvied up government institutions and packed them with officers. Lacking defined lines of authority and responsibility to allocate decision-making, several high-ranking officers quickly emerged to contend for leadership in the formulation of political and economic programs. Their disputes both indicated and cultivated politicization in the armed forces, and the disparate, often contradictory, messages they sent only served to undermine any possible alliances with societal groups. Strategy coordination was clearly nonexistent. For the *Proceso,* the detrimental effects of regime institutions did not stop with a politicized military and the inability to introduce political and economic strategies. Because of the high level of regime investment, regime leaders essentially fell into a state of denial when faced with these problems. Even as failure seemingly grew apparent to all but the regime leaders, the government pressed on until it collapsed.

The Brazilian military regime, in Chapter 5, introduces the second case of a controlled transition. While suppression was the dominant regime characteristic in Chile, in Brazil accommodation was more prevalent. Low regime investment and a dispersion of authority allowed the leaders of regime factions to be incorporated into government. Recognizing that their leaders were guaranteed some level of input, this helped reduce the anxieties of factional supporters in the services as they looked across the divide between the military institution and the government. In Brazil, past institutionalized interactions between civilian and military elites significantly aided the development of strategy coordination. As in Chile, here we again see how institutions tend to develop strength independently of actors, insofar as the civilian-controlled legislature exerted greater influence over time. Nonetheless, the success of the regime gave its institutions the political capital necessary to control the transition, even as the Figuerido government seemed to weaken.

It is interesting to compare the Uruguayan case to Brazil and the *Revolución*. As in Brazil, the Uruguayan military regime used a dispersion of authority and low regime investment to accommodate factions and maintain military unity. But in the end, Uruguay looked more like the *Revolución,* as the regime found that it could do no better than a balanced transition. Both of these regimes owed their destiny to the lack of strategy coordination. The comparison between Uruguay and the *Revolución* is interesting because the cases illustrate the two-sided effort behind strategy coordination. Specifically, while the *Revolución* failed first in its relations with the military,[20] the Uruguayan military regime failed in its relations with society. The Uruguay military institution stood behind the regime for twelve years without exhibiting levels of politicization or alienation sufficient to undermine it. Rather, this regime found the roots of its failure in its relations with society. Even with moderate economic success and modest political goals, the Uruguayan regime was unable to cultivate political capital with society and ultimately faced a legitimacy crisis that was its undoing. Nevertheless, the military unity fostered by regime institutions allowed for a balanced transition.

The case studies are designed to illustrate the variety of military rule, and the significance of the institutional sources of this variety to transition control. Surprisingly, that there is variety in transition control seems to be a point of contention. Ricci and Fitch (1990, 68) are quite right when they argue that the "contradictions between military government and the military institution are fundamental and inescapable." But the fact is, the "fundamental contradictions" recognized by Ricci and Fitch (e.g., a lack of political skills, difficulties resolving conflicts, and legitimacy problems) are addressed by military regimes with different levels of success, and this can make the difference between two years of rule and twenty. Similarly, Farcau (1996) is correct to recognize the effects of government on military factionalism and presents a valuable study of the Brazilian regime. But in the final analysis, this regime lasted twenty-one years and its effects continue to reverberate through Brazilian politics. The more interesting inquiry is therefore not how this regime was shaken by factionalism, but how it was able to address this factionalism better than other regimes.

Other researchers have taken the opposite approach and placed the bar too low in their assessments of military rule. The *Proceso*, an exemplary case of regime failure, has been interpreted as having successfully guarded its interests such that the military remains a dominant force in Argentina politics (McSherry 1997). Such analyses miss the distinction of military rule and the transition from this type of authoritarian rule. Unlike other actors that have placed themselves in government (e.g., sultanistic rulers or communist parties), the military can look to its democratic successors and legitimately argue that it has a role to play in the new regime (Pion-Berlin 1992).[21]

20. This is not to suggest that the *Revolución* found success in its relations with society. It certainly did not. The point is that the prospect of forging links with society was made moot by the failure in government-military relations.

21. Also, what might appear to be military obstructions of civilian oversight can sometimes be better explained as instances where civilians simply lacked the expertise (rather than power) to legitimately impress their interests. For an example, see Pion-Berlin's (1998, 141–78) analysis of the failure of defense reform in Argentina.

My reaction is to emphasize that the variations in the impact of military rule has been too great to ignore. Some military regimes have failed miserably, while others have found significant levels of success in their intent to shape the party system, electoral system, representative system, economic program, lines of debate, or other facets of the successor civilian regime. Let us not be misled by the facts that even a controlled transition is likely to feature some setbacks for the military and that even a collapsed military is likely to retain some prerogatives.

2

Political Alienation and Balanced Transition in the *Revolución Argentina*

It is a pity, Onganía does not accept advice,
but turns to us when subversion springs up.
—Comment by a lower-ranking officer
    just after the *cordobazo*

The vast majority of Argentines welcomed the bloodless military *golpe* that removed President Arturo Umberto Illia on June 28, 1966. Likewise, the concentration of power granted to retired General Juan Carlos Onganía was accepted as a reasonable response to growing economic instability and the fragility of Argentine democracy, which rested upon an "impossible game" that excluded the popular Peronist *Justicialista* Party from higher elective offices.[1] But the political credit extended to the new regime would be squandered as Onganía stubbornly and unsuccessfully attempted to institutionalize a corporatist solution upon the Argentine economic and political landscape. Unable to suppress opposition in the armed forces, he would do no better than a stalemate in his relations with the military. Economic policy was ceded to liberals supported by the military while Onganía attempted to project corporatism from the Ministry of the Interior. In this way, Onganía created an "impossible task," insofar as the economic policy of the regime

---

1. On the consent of the general population and the events leading to the coup, see Castello 1986.

established a set of winners and losers that did not coincide with the corporatist political policies Onganía was trying to promote.[2] Specifically,
liberal economic policies favored international and large business, while
the corporatist program expected support from small and medium-sized
national businesses, agriculture, and labor. Thus, although Onganía had
the opportunity to cultivate regime support, his political lenses diverted
him from a potential support base.

At the outset, one might argue that the failure of Onganía's policies
was the result of his poor political judgment, that corporatism had little
chance of survival in historically liberal Argentina. Although the liberal tradition was a formidable barrier, I wish to stress the significance of regime
institutions in the failure of the *Revolución Argentina*. The case of Chile
illustrates the sensibility of this perspective. Before the Pinochet regime,
import-substitution policies and a network of state patronage saturated
Chile and were rarely questioned by any of the dominant political actors.
If, as I argue in Chapter 3, it was regime institutions that allowed Pinochet to dismantle this state and install liberalism as the dominant ideology in Chile, we ought not allow the barrier presented by liberalism in
Argentina to preclude an institutional explanation for the failure of corporatism under Onganía. In fact, some conditions did favor corporatism.
Perón had already demonstrated that liberalism could be effectively challenged; the Catholic Church stood as a potential partner; nationalist currents ran strong in the armed forces; and Spain, Portugal, and to some
extent Peru existed as concrete models. Thus I argue that just as regime
institutions emboldened Pinochet and allowed his political and economic
programs to succeed, in Argentina regime institutions enfeebled the political and economic programs of Onganía and made it likelier that they
would fail.

The ultimate explanation for the failure of *Revolución Argentina* rests
in the relations between the government and the military. There was a concentration of power in the presidency and a low level of regime investment.
Following the model, this means that the regime lacked institutions to
bridge the military and government. With this institutional combination,
the military acts as the primary pillar of rule, but stands far apart from
the regime. The ruler lacks the linkages to the military such as the powers
to promote, reassign, and retire personnel, which descend deep into the

2. The "impossible task" can be likened to the "impossible game" identified by O'Donnell
(1972). The impossible game found the military repeatedly holding elections after intervention
in hopes that the working class would be drawn from Peronism by some centrist party.

military hierarchy, or the ability to award government positions that offer prestige and double salaries. On the other hand, the military is apt to view itself as an outsider over time. It is viewed as responsible for the regime, but it is granted little, if any, decisional input. This may not be a problem when the economy is robust and the regime is popular, but when difficulties arise and the regime founders, the military is likely to grow frustrated. Shut out from imposing its policy solutions, the military is likely to grow alienated and withdraw its support from the regime. Lacking investment in rule, the military does not find the decision to withdraw this support particularly difficult.

The *Revolución Argentina:* Military Unity at the Cost of Alienation

The *Revolución Argentina,* the brazen title given to the 1966–73 regime by the armed forces, found retired General Juan Carlos Onganía at its helm from June 29, 1966, to June 8, 1970. General Roberto Marcelo Levingston followed and ruled from June 18, 1970, to March 23, 1971. General Alejandro Agustín Lanusse assumed the presidency on March 26, 1971, and relinquished power to a civilian government on May 24, 1973.

The institutions of the *Revolución Argentina* were challenged over time. Under Levingston the service commanders attempted to secure a legislative role in order to have greater input into the workings of government. Levingston's reluctance to acquiesce preserved the design presided over by Onganía, but it also preserved the alienation toward his administration. The continuing tension between Levingston and the armed forces led Lanusse to reintroduce the military into government. He retained the position of army commander and accorded the other service commanders a greater role in important policy decisions. The move to reduce military alienation came too late, insofar as military rule was largely discredited by this time, and Lanusse assumed the presidency with military withdrawal as a priority.

The Concentration of Authority

The June 28, 1966, *golpe* placed in power the Junta Revolucionaria, which consisted of the commanders in chief of the armed forces. Within one day, Lieutenant General Pascual Pistarini, Admiral Benigno Varela, and Brigadier General Teodoro Alvarez published foundational documents of the new regime, appointed Onganía president, and dissolved the Junta. The rapid movement of events added to the concentration of authority established in the foundational documents.

The *Acta de la Revolución Argentina* and three annexes comprised the foundational documents of the regime.[3] In fourteen articles, the *Acta* announced the removal of the president, the vice president, all governors and vice governors, the national and all provincial legislatures, the replacement of all members of the Corte Suprema de Justicia and the attorney general, and the dissolution of all political parties (articles 2–5). The *Acta* also authorized the appointment of Onganía as president (article 11) and dissolved the Junta at the moment he was sworn in (article 14). The first annex, *Mensaje de la Junta Revolucionaria al Pueblo Argentino,* simply described the environment of economic and political instability that justified the *golpe,* but provided no explicit guidelines for the regime.

The second annex, *Estatuto de la Revolución Argentina,* was meant to establish the institutional framework of the regime. Consisting of only ten articles, the document (in articles 1 and 5) placed all constitutionally mandated executive and legislative power in the President of the Nation, less constitutional articles 45, 51, and 52, which dealt with congressional oversight of the judiciary. The document also established that the provincial governors would govern at the pleasure of the president (article 9), and that the president would determine the composition of the executive cabinet and its functions (article 2) and have the authority to convoke permanent or transitory consultative bodies (article 6). It further stated that the National Constitution would remain in force only insofar as it did not conflict with the *Estatuto* (article 3). It is important to note what the *Estatuto* did not contain—provisions for presidential succession. Article 10 read: "In case of incapacity or death of the president, his successor will be designated in common agreement by the commanders in chief of the armed forces." Thus, so long as Onganía remained healthy, the foundational documents sanctioned his rule (Fayt 1971, 155).

The third annex to the *Acta, Objetivos Políticos,* was meant to establish guidelines for the regime and was divided into two sections, general objective and specific objectives. The general objective was summarized in a haughty paragraph which included calls for "the consolidation of spiritual and moral values ... the elimination of the profound causes of economic stagnation ... and the reestablishment of an authentic representative democracy in which order prevails in the law." The specific objectives were divided into foreign policy, internal policy, economic policy, labor policy,

3. These documents can be found in Selser 1986a, 319–33.

social welfare policy, and security policy. Each area received no more than a few sentences, enumerated goals that few would oppose, and gave no indication how these goals would be achieved.[4]

While in power, the Junta promulgated just nine decrees. Only one of these decrees signified an effort to have any real influence in the subsequent government (decree 8/66, which named provincial intervenors). The other eight simply sanctioned the dismissals of government officials or further empowered the president. Overall, the hasty transfer of power left Onganía in a position of great authority. Onganía was unencumbered by the dissolved Junta Revolucionaria and faced neither explicit guidelines for his government nor a legislative legacy from the Junta. Few could question that he was in complete control of the government (Alvarez 1966).

Onganía's authority extended throughout the Argentine political system; and despite the praise he would give to provincial diversity and empowerment, he effectively destroyed federalism (Lousteau Heguy 1966, 72). The most obvious encroachment on federalism came from article 9 of the *Estatuto,* which allowed the president to appoint governors who would assume executive and legislative powers granted by their respective provincial constitutions. The appointees served more as administrators of the federal government than as representatives of their provinces (Botana, Braun, and Floria 1973, 51–57). Provincial autonomy was further undermined with the division of the country into eight regions under law 16,964. Some of these regions divided existing provinces.[5] A *junta de gobernadores* managed each region and coordinated among the provinces developmental policies designed by the federal government. These bodies also formulated suggestions for developmental policy.[6] Each *junta de gobernadores* consisted of the governors of the provinces in the region in question and a regional delegate appointed by the president. The regional delegate was directly subordinate to the secretary of government in the Ministry of the Interior and would convoke and coordinate meetings, act as the official representative of the body before federal institutions, and was meant to assure continuity

4. For example, the section under security policy simply stated: "To achieve the complete capacity necessary to assure procurement of the objectives in the other areas." In economic policy, the specific goals included "the elimination of the profound causes that have led the country to its present stagnation," "the establishment of the bases and conditions to allow for a great economic expansion," and "the guarantee of greater access to more goods and services."

5. For a list of the provinces that constituted each region, see de Dromi 1988, 2:463.

6. For an example, see "Acta de la primera reunión de la Junta de Gobernadores de la Region de Desarrollo de la Patagonia," March 10, 1967 (Ushuaia: Secretaría de Prensa de la Presidencia de la Nación).

in the junta (de Dromi 1988, 1:464). A final mechanism for greater centralization came through the purse. Pírez documents how the *Revolución Argentina* reversed a decentralizing trend that had started in 1947. Under the regime, provincial control over public spending decreased 11.4 percent and federal control increased 14.6 percent (1986, 44–45).

Within the federal government, the legislature and judiciary were removed as counterbalances to the executive. Although members of Congress were dismissed and their powers transferred to the president, many of their staff members remained in government so that their expertise in processing legislation could be utilized. Decree 74/66 authorized the president to appoint an intervenor to exercise the powers of the presidents of both chambers of Congress (de Dromi 1988, 2:364). In this way, the congressional staff system remained at the disposal of the executive. Some staff members were uprooted and transferred to the Secretaría General for the more immediate use of the president (Roth 1980, 100).

The judiciary was reorganized only at the top. Onganía appointed new members to the Corte Suprema de Justicia and the attorney general, but the principle of immovability held for all lower magistrates. In fact, the autonomy of the lower courts was somewhat increased. The authority to remove judges had belonged to Congress. With Congress dissolved, under article 8 of the *Estatuto* that power was transferred to the judiciary itself, which was to exercise this authority through peer juries (de Dromi 1988, 1:367–70). Purges were also limited in the provinces. Under article 9 of the *Estatuto*, the provincial governors were allowed a one-time purge of the local *tribunal superior* at the time of their appointment. Afterwards, any guarantees of immovability established in the provincial constitution would hold.

The incomplete purge of the judiciary had a significant impact. The subservience of the higher courts was not matched at the lower levels (only members of the Corte Suprema were made to swear on the *Estatuto* before the constitution). The "rebellion of the court" highlighted the rift in May 1968, when some lower courts found that the government had not had the authority to close certain news magazines (Fayt 1971, 165; Bra 1985, 31–38). Nonetheless, the structure of the judicial system ultimately tilted power toward the government; the decision was overturned when it reached the Corte Suprema. Another ruling that highlighted the ultimate power of Onganía was the August 1968 Corte Suprema ruling that the president could dismiss the service commanders.[7] In sum, the higher levels

7. The question posed to the court was "Can Onganía dismiss the commanders that gave him power?" By deciding in favor of Onganía, the court settled the ambiguity found in the foundational documents on the power of the commanders in chief. On this issue, see

of the judiciary were subservient to the executive (LADH 1969, 12–14), but not the lower ones (Botana, Braun, and Floria 1973, 286–90).

Final authority was thus unquestionably placed in the executive during the tenure of the *Revolución Argentina*. And like the other branches of government, the executive was not left unblemished under the new regime. The new Law of Ministers,[8] called for by article 2 of the *Estatuto,* reduced the number of ministerial positions from eight to five and redesigned the distribution of secretariats. The ministries and their respective secretariats were the Ministry of the Interior (Government, Culture and Education, and Justice and Communications); the Ministry of Foreign Relations and Religion; the Ministry of Economy and Labor (Agriculture and Livestock, Finance, Industry and Commerce, Energy and Mining, Labor, and Public Works and Transportation); the Ministry of Defense (the service commanders were secretaries of their respective forces); and the Ministry of Social Welfare (Community Assistance and Promotion, Social Security, and Public Health and Housing).[9] The law gave the ministers the power to formulate policy and national strategy, and the power of implementation was soon delegated to the secretaries.[10] Only the ministers were entrusted as permanent cabinet members. Secretaries and service commanders could attend cabinet meetings only at the request of the president (Fayt 1971, 153).

The Law of Ministers also created a new bureaucracy, the Presidencia de la Nación, to ensure presidential dominance. Four separate bodies composed this bureaucracy. The Secretaría General acted much like a military general staff. It was expected to provide technical and legal advice, to inform the president on government activities, and to perform bookkeeping and accounting duties (Fayt 1971, 153). It also filtered policies as they passed to the president. This was especially the case when Héctor Repetto led the staff (Potash 1996, 273–74). Those policies it deemed to be of greater political significance or those policies which touched upon constitutional issues were sent to the president for more detailed examination. Those policies it considered more routine were signed off by the president with little to no consideration (Roth 1980, 98–99). A second body, the

---

"Cuestiones militares," *Primera Plana,* December 13, 1966, p. 11. On the court decision, see "El verdadero golpe de Alsogaray," ibid., September 3, 1968, pp. 13–15.

8. Law 16,956 (September 23, 1966).

9. Law 18,416 (October 20, 1969) added the ministers of public works and services (Public Works and Transportation; Energy, Communications, Hydroelectric Resources), Culture and Education, and Justice (Procuration of the Treasury; Justice). It also added the Secretariat of Foreign Business to the Ministry of Economy and Labor.

10. Decree 2870/66 (October 19, 1966).

Casa Militar, managed security, transportation, feeding, housing, communications, and other logistical concerns. Another body, the Secretaría de
Prensa, controlled communication with the media. Finally, the Secretaría
Privada acted as the president's personal secretary. The chiefs of the first
three bodies were accorded secretarial status in the government.

One of the first actions of the Presidencia de la Nación was the creation
of the Sistema de Planeamiento y Acción para el Desarrollo y la Seguridad
under laws 16,970 (October 6, 1966), which created the Consejo Nacional
de Seguridad (CONASE), and 16,964 (September 30, 1966), which reorganized the Consejo Nacional de Desarrollo (CONADE). General Osiris
Villegas deeply influenced the Sistema after he was appointed secretary of
CONASE (Lázara 1988, 157). General Villegas's faithful adherence to
national security doctrine clearly emerged in the Sistema, which was meant
to closely coordinate economic development and national security, giving
the armed forces an institutional input to decision-making and purportedly
purging politics from what was viewed as essentially technocratic work
(Smith 1989, 54–55). While CONADE was responsible for elaborating
plans on the basis of objectives provided by the government, CONASE was
to harmonize these plans with security concerns (Fayt 1971, 154).[11]

The specific functions of CONADE included formulating policy and
national strategy on long-term development; integrating economic and
social policies with defense policy in relation to development; imparting
directives and norms to sectoral and regional authorities responsible for
medium- and short-term development policies; and coordinating its actions
with CONASE. All ministers were permanent members, the service commanders and secretaries of state were nonpermanent members, and the
president presided directly over the body (de Dromi 1988, 1:457).

CONASE was expected to plan policies and strategy related to security;
impart directives to authorities responsible for security; establish security
zones and oversee the high administration of these zones; integrate internal,
foreign, economic, and defense policy with security affairs; and coordinate
its actions with CONADE. To complete its functions, CONASE was authorized to demand facts, statistics, and other information directly from
national ministers, commanders in chief, secretaries of state, provincial and
territorial governors, municipal *intendentes*, public bodies, and private
entities. CONASE had two main subunits below it—the secretarial staff,
which would act as a working/study group, and the Comisión Nacional de

---

11. These objectives and the responsibilities of the two institutions were initially formulated under the "Directiva para el planeamiento de la acción de gobierno" (Buenos Aires:
Secretaría de Prensa de la Presidencia de la Nación, August 4, 1966).

Zonas de Seguridad, which would advise, inform, coordinate, and administer all work. Both civilians and military personnel were found in these two organizations. CONASE included the ministers and service commanders as permanent members, and the chief of the Central Nacional de Inteligencia (CNI—the principal intelligence agency) and all secretaries of state as nonpermanent members. Like CONADE, CONASE was directly subordinate to the president (de Dromi 1988, 1:458).

Later, a third institution would work with CONADE and CONASE— the Consejo Nacional de Ciencia y Técnica (CONACYT), which was created to formulate, promote, and coordinate state policies in matters of science and technology.[12] Its immediate duties were to formulate national scientific and technical policy, to relate this policy to security and development, and to coordinate its activities with CONADE and CONASE. Like CONADE it had the ministers as its permanent members, and the service commanders and secretaries of state as its nonpermanent members. Although the president presided over it, CONACYT also had a working secretary, who was commissioned as a secretary of state and was assisted by the Consejo Nacional Asesor, which consisted of public and private entities dedicated to science and technology (de Dromi 1988, 1:458–59).

The structure of the executive provided Onganía with multiple direct lines of authority that extended not only to the ministers but also directly to many secretaries who had no superior ministry. But the octopus-like extension of his authority may have been a disadvantage insofar as the lack of a more defined hierarchy prevented him from exercising total control in these areas. The flood of information he was forced to contend with probably contributed to the devolution of some authority toward the ministers. Roberto Roth, who worked as the legal and technical subsecretary in the Ministry of Economy and Labor describes the policymaking process: "The dissolution of Congress produced a phenomenon in public administration. Each national agency was transformed into a little congress in its own area, and began to propose legislation in its own particular sphere of action. The proposals ascended up the hierarchy and arrived at the office of the President with the signature of the minister, who added his signature and converted it into law. Simple" (1980, 99).

Perina (1983, 174) also describes the autonomy granted to government agencies and notes that cabinet meetings to debate specific policies were usually held only for policies expected to arouse popular resistance.

In sum, although authority was concentrated, it is also important to

---

12. Established under law 18,020 (December 24, 1968).

note the devolution of authority in daily decision-making. Nonetheless, this attribute is more a qualification than a repudiation of the concentration of authority under the *Revolución Argentina*. Where he determined it necessary, Onganía made his authority clear.

Low Regime Investment

Differences within the Argentine armed forces over the role of the military in politics had deepened in the decade before the 1966 *golpe*. After the 1955 fall of Perón, two notable factions formed in the military. Although both were fervently anti-Peronist, they favored different strategies to eradicate the movement. The *colorados* favored an outright military dictatorship, whereas the *azules* pointed to the Aramburu (1955–58) administration to emphasize the problems military rule causes for the armed forces. The *azules* argued that the Peronists could only be defeated if the military concentrated on its purely professional duties in national security to combat the more revolutionary elements of Peronism. Beginning in 1962–63, the two factions met each other in a number of armed skirmishes that ultimately saw the *azules* emerge dominant. Led by General Onganía, the *azules* oversaw the 1963 elections that brought Illia to power (Potash 1996, 1–117).

More than economic decline, the reluctance of the Illia administration to confront the still-powerful Peronist movement and the victories expected by the Justicialistas in the 1967 elections inspired the 1966 golpe (Floria 1983, 80–82). Onganía, having grown in popularity both in society and in the armed forces as a symbol of professionalism, was viewed as a natural choice for president.[13]

By the time of the *golpe,* the ideas of national security doctrine largely filled the chasm between the *azules* and *colorados* (Snow 1972). When the Junta Revolucionaria chose Onganía, he accepted on the condition that they return to the barracks and be limited to an advisory role (Castello 1986). For Onganía, *azul* professionalism still had a role in a regime empowered by a military *golpe*. In his first address to the armed forces, he alluded to the division of labor he envisioned for the regime: "The armed forces have initiated the revolutionary process; the production of the acts that give clear satisfaction to the great needs of the country now corresponds to the

---

13. Illia forced Onganía to resign when he appointed an officer inferior to him to the position of secretary of war, a post above army commander in the government. Onganía and Illia had clashed over a number of issues, most notably Illia's decision not to send troops in support of the U.S. invasion of the Dominican Republic (Castello 1986).

national government."[14] The evidence suggests that most of his former *azul* compatriots and others in the high command did not share his sentiments.[15] General Julio Alsogaray was originally placed as secretary-general and worked with his team of colonels to reorganize the Presidencia de la Nación to conform to military criteria. Although he did enact some changes at the higher levels of the bureaucracy, he was soon returned to strictly military duties by Onganía and replaced by an old friend of Onganía, retired general Héctor Repetto (Roth 1980, 97–98). The only real legacy from the initial drive toward greater military participation in government was the appointment of retired officers as governors by the Junta Revolucionaria. When Onganía did replace governors, he usually did so with retired military personnel as well.[16]

The state corporations represented the only other area of significant military participation, and here too only retired personnel were used. Given the sizable corporatist and nationalist factions in the armed forces (Smith 1989, 66–72), the use of retired personnel could not be reasonably considered an exertion of influence by the predominantly liberal high command. Indeed, the placement of retired officers in state businesses linked the military to the public sector, and actually increased nationalist sentiments in the armed forces (Perina 1983, 151).

The high command had hoped that the Sistema de Planeamiento y Acción para el Desarrollo y la Seguridad would institutionalize military participation in policy decisions. But the service commanders were permanent members only in CONASE, and Onganía normally ignored this body (Smith 1989, 54). Likewise, although CONADE personnel could be found in each ministry, the body was understaffed and underfunded as long as it was under liberal control.[17] The high command was simply too quick to

14. "Discurso del Presidente de la Nación en la comida de comradería de las fuerzas armadas" (Buenos Aires: Secretaría de Prensa de la Presidencia de la Nación, July 6, 1966).

15. The high command of the Argentine armed forces consisted of the service commanders; the chiefs of staff of the services; the chief of staff for coordination; the chief of the President's Military Household; the commanders of the First, Second, Third, and Fourth Army Corps; the commandants of the military institutes; the director of the National Gendarmerie; the admirals commanding the Atlantic Fleet, the Puerto Belgrano Naval Area, and the Navy Air Arm; and the air force commanders of the Combat Wing, the commandant of the Air Institute, and the air quartermaster general.

16. Onganía also stayed true to the distribution of power among the governorships established by the Junta. In September 1967, eleven governors were army personnel, four were navy, and four were air force. The apportionment of important provinces was also recognized: Córdoba went to the air force, Santa Fe went to the navy, and Buenos Aires went to the army. "Las tendencias del gobierno," *Primera Plana*, September 26, 1968, p. 11.

17. "Un cuarto y nuevo Conade," *Primera Plana*, November 26, 1968, pp. 13–16.

assume that Onganía would accept the presidency as a delegate of the armed forces (Smith 1989, 66–67). The hasty transfer gave them no time to understand Onganía's actual motives,[18] and the vagueness of the foundational documents allowed him to manipulate their meaning so that the military was virtually shut out of the decision-making process. Early tensions were manifest in a September 1966 private meeting, when the high command presented to Onganía its first complaints about the limited role accorded to it (Rowe 1966a). Onganía would be more frank in his position on military participation by the end of the year, when he executed a major cabinet change and only invited comments from superior officers weeks later.[19]

The result was an overwhelmingly civilian government, and little upon which to build regime investment for the military. Outside of Onganía himself, retired general Repetto, and the three service commanders, who acted as the secretaries of their respective forces in the Ministry of Defense, there were only four military representatives in high federal positions. And none of these officers could be considered an agent of the liberals in the high command. One was the already noted secretary of CONASE, General Osiris Villegas. Even here, the placement of an officer as secretary in a security council is understandable, and Villegas's stature as a military intellectual lent substantial credence to his appointment. Another was retired general Eduardo Señorans, who was an old friend of Onganía and was appointed director of the Secretaría de Informaciones de Estado (SIDE), the intelligence-gathering apparatus of the president. Significantly, the responsibility for identifying subversives was given to SIDE rather than to the CNI, the logical choice as the central intelligence apparatus. This was done in order to contain the power of Villegas, an active officer and, though a strong proponent of the national security doctrine and thus not an ally of the liberals in the high command, one who did not share the corporatist thoughts of Onganía to the same extent as Señorans (Selser 1986b, 292–93). Third, retired general Guillermo Borda served time as minister of the interior after a December 1966 cabinet reshuffle, but he was a recognized nationalist. Finally, retired general Francisco Imaz was appointed as minister of the interior in June 1969, but his appointment was not done at the insistence of the military. His Peronist history made many in the armed

18. Rowe (1966a) notes that although Onganía was popular at the time of the coup, little was known about his ideological standing. This is not surprising, since Onganía became popular precisely because of his *legalista*, or essentially nonpolitical, stance.
19. "Sobre relevos y cambios de guardia," *Primera Plana*, January 17, 1967, p. 19.

forces suspicious, and by this time, the government had become so unpopular that the military was opposed to the placement of any officers in government.[20]

The low regime investment interfered with the extension of Onganía's authority. While authority was indisputably concentrated in Onganía in the government, the same could not be said about his position in the armed forces. On the one hand, he was commander in chief of the armed forces and was not afraid to display his power by dismissing a service commander. He also had a great deal of control over the military courts[21] and effectively controlled repression at least to the May 1969 *cordobazo,* as well as successfully ignoring advice from the military. He was deliberately slow in meeting with the service commanders, and when he did, he avoided references to political, economic, or social issues.[22] On the other hand, he did not have governmental positions to dole out in order to win over supporters or contain opponents, and his control over military promotions, assignments, and retirements dwindled over time.[23] Indeed, it was common knowledge that the minister of defense was more an administrator for the service commanders than vice versa.[24] The lack of significant patronistic ties to the armed forces below the level of service commander made it difficult for Onganía to establish himself as the definitive center of power. While the government bureaucracy at his disposal allowed him to face society as its undisputed leader, he lacked the institutional wherewithal to extend authority through the armed forces. The disregard he showed toward the military institution over time whittled away what little regime investment there may have been and contributed to military alienation.

20. "Un gabinete cuestionado," *Primera Plana,* June 17, 1969, pp. 10–14; "Question Mark over Onganía," *Latin America,* June 20, 1969.

21. "Tribunales militares: organización y competencia," *Vigencia,* September/October 1969, pp. 12–14.

22. "Primer planteo militar al Presidente Onganía?" *Panorama,* September 1967, p. 25.

23. In the army, Onganía was limited to a list provided by the Junta Superior de Calificaciones de Ejército, which consisted of the commander in chief, the chief of the general staff, and all division commanders. Onganía's influence over this body was still significant in late 1967, most likely as a result of the dismissal of army commander Pistarini in December 1966 after public disagreements with Onganía over promotions and retirements (see "Historia de ascensos y conspiraciones," *Primera Plana,* November 14, 1967, p. 14). By the following year, his influence had dropped considerably ("Las designaciones en el ejército," ibid., September 17, 1968, pp. 14–15).

24. The first minister of defense, Antonio Lanusse, resigned in recognition of his own powerlessness after the army decided not to purchase a shipment of tanks from the United States that he had worked hard to secure. "Onganía y los militares," *Primera Plana,* March 12, 1968, pp. 12–13.

Economic Success and Political Failure under Onganía:
The Pitfalls of a Lack of Strategy Coordination

The *Revolución Argentina* presents us with a puzzle. Most economic indicators displayed a fairly healthy economy, yet the regime failed to generate political support. How is it that the regime could be successful economically yet so unsuccessful politically? The answer lies within the political institutions of the regime and how these institutions failed Onganía in his quest to consolidate authority.

Normally, one would expect a regime to build on economic success to create political support. The problem was that the economic success Argentina experienced did not represent success for Onganía's economic program and thus rewarded groups not included in his political program. Onganía had entered office with economic and political programs steeped in corporatism. Unable to consolidate authority in his primary support base, the armed forces, he was forced to concede power to liberal opponents of his plans. He did so by ceding the Ministry of Economy and Labor. Retreating to the Ministry of the Interior, Onganía's corporatist allies faced an impossible task: they would have to cultivate political support for corporatism while liberals implemented economic policies that harmed small and medium-sized national business, agriculture, and labor—all potential supporters of corporatism. The resultant schizophrenia doomed the regime. Groups that benefited materially under the regime found it difficult to support because it offered them an uncertain future. On the other hand, groups that could have expected to benefit under corporatism faced liberal policies implemented by the very same government that had promised them a better future. In consequence, the regime found itself surrounded only by opponents or by potential supporters who found it most reasonable to remain neutral. So when the regime faced a crisis, in the form of the *cordobazo* of May 1969, it found that it had no supporters to which it could turn.

The lack of strategy coordination explains the schizophrenia in the *Revolución Argentina*. Military rulers set upon concentrated authority and low regime investment (such as Onganía, Rojas Pinilla in Colombia, or Pérez Jiménez in Venezuela) are in a precarious situation. The ruler owes his position to the armed forces and thus relies upon them as his central support base. But the formal divide between military and government roles means that he cannot manipulate superior officers with government positions or significantly influence a wide range of promotions, assignments, and retirements in the officer corps. Meanwhile, the armed forces are reluctant supporters. They are held responsible for a government in which they are granted little, if any, say. This alienates them and opens them to alliances with government opponents. Onganía found himself unable to contain military dissatisfaction with his rule, thus allowing the military to reach out to the liberal opponents of the government, whom it viewed as better equipped to solve the immediate problems faced by the regime. But as government leader, Onganía did have some authority and thus was able to retain his corporatist program in the Ministry of the Interior. Regime institutions thus led to the impossible task, and ultimately to the demise of the regime itself.

Economic Policy under the Revolución Argentina: *Failure within Success*

In his first address, Onganía announced that "the country will know very soon my plan of government" and declared that his government would be "homogeneous in its conception of the national interest."[25] The *golpe* had taken place sooner than Onganía had desired. He had asked army commander Pistarini to hold off the action until after he devised a political plan and secured government personnel, but his co-conspirators and his perception of the events around him compelled Pistarini to act (Castello 1986, 24).[26] As noted, this hasty transfer of power allowed Onganía to concentrate considerable authority. But it also meant that he was pressed to organize a government team. In economic policy this meant that personnel were recruited without proper discretion and that there was no time to lobby important economic actors on the desired economic policy. The consequent lack of clarity in policy opened the political space necessary for liberal critics of the economic program to pressure the armed forces for support and usurp control over economic policy. Impaired by low regime investment, Onganía was powerless to stop the liberal pressure.

In the first six months of the *Revolución Argentina,* the economic team was clearly more nationalist than liberal. The minister of economy and labor, Jorge Nestor Salimei, was a member of the Confederación General Económica (CGE), a coalition of small and medium-sized businesses. Salimei

25. "Mensaje del Teniente General Onganía, al pueblo de la República, con motivo de asumir la Presidencia de la Nación" (Buenos Aires: Secretaría de Prensa de la Presidencia de la Nación, June 30, 1966).

26. The primary organizers of the *golpe* were Generals Pascual Pistarini, Alejandro Lanusse, Osiris Villegas, Cándido López, Alcides López Aufranc, and Von Stecher; retired generals Francisco Imaz and Eduardo Señorans; and Colonels Guevara, and Alfonso Alsogaray. General Julio Alsogaray also played a fundamental role, having been authorized to organize a group outside of the military institution to elaborate *golpe* plans. The action was essentially an army *golpe* (Fayt 1971, 41).

placed other moderate nationalists in the Secretariats of Finance (Francisco R. Aguilar), Industry and Commerce (Rodolfo Galimberti), and Agriculture (Adolfo Raggio). More radical nationalists were placed in the Banco Central, where bank president Felipe Tami led a cohesive group of academic technocrats. The Tami group had high credentials from its links to the Instituto Torcuato Di Tella, and their affiliation to sectors within the Catholic Church no doubt caught the eye of Onganía when he welcomed them into his government. But the Catholic sectors with which they consorted were among the more progressive, and the group endorsed policies recommended by the Economic Commission for Latin America in the United Nations. For these reasons, the group soon found themselves shunned and accused of "leftism" not only by liberal critics, but also within the economic team (Niosi 1974, 172; Smith 1989, 57).

Early on, it seemed that a moderate nationalist network of supporters might be forthcoming from society. After Onganía's inaugural address, the Sociedad Rural Argentina (SRA) noted in its annual record: "The opinion of the SRA on the address of the President is very good" (Niosi 1974, 156). Salimei and Onganía welcomed the CGE in government meetings, and the organization expressed its pleasure to be involved in government policy.[27] Even the Peronist-dominated Confederación General de Trabajo (CGT), the principal union confederation, showed collaborationist tendencies. The organization applauded the fall of the Radical Illia government, and in the absence of Péron, local leader Augusto Vandor saw collaboration as a means to wrest control from Péron (Anzorena 1988, 15).

Despite the nationalist orientation of the economic team, economic policy showed little signs of coherence (Niosi 1974, 146). One government aide explicitly recognized this as he explained the regime's difficulties in securing a loan just after the *golpe:* "There can be no question of approaching (any lending source) until we can present them with an economic plan. But we have no plan, because of the inability of business and military backers of the Government to get together."[28] Many business leaders grew suspicious of the government's economic plans early on when the government dodged a clearly defined relationship with business and labor, despite the liberal tone of the foundational documents and some government pronouncements.[29] Government declarations that seemed to place the blame

27. "Temas económicos analizaron Onganía y los empresarios," *La Nación,* August 24, 1966, p. 5.
28. "Onganía's Backers Divided by Economic Crisis," *New York Times,* July 21, 1966, p. 5, Late city edition.
29. "Las primeras fricciones," *Primera Plana,* July 19, 1966, pp. 14–15.

for recent inflationary trends on business rather than labor raised red flags for business. For example, the government sided with labor in wage negotiations and promised to look into "monopolistic practices and the entire retailing system" in the effort to curtail inflation.[30]

An important obstacle to the nationalist push of the government came from the liberal proponent Alvaro Alsogaray, a former minister of the economy and brother of army corps commander Julio Alsogaray. Onganía had attempted to defray these intentions by appeasing (and distancing) him with the ambassadorship to the United States. But Alsogaray proved to be just as damaging there, undermining the economic team early on by declaring to U.S. officials promises of a strictly liberal Argentine economic policy (Selser 1986a, 239). And when the government finally did secure a loan in September through the World Bank, Alsogaray used his personal connections to have it withdrawn at the last minute.[31] Aggravated by such actions, growing criticisms, and constant dismissals of their suggestions, the Tami group resigned *en masse* in November (Selser 1986a, 213–20, 235–40).

In the face of the liberal attack, only the more liberal-appearing features of the moderate nationalist program were pursued. Thus the government became fixated on administrative rationalization, an idea shared with the liberals. The government's inflexible moves to downsize port facilities in October and the railroad system in November resulted in severe labor unrest that made headlines through the end of the year. Likewise, the imperious shutdown of numerous sugar mills in Tucumán to reduce the flow of government subsidies was done with little thought of the consequences. The move left thousands unemployed and initiated economic decline and political protests that would leave the region ripe for the spread of the *cordobazo* (Anzorena 1988, 25–26).

The unrest caused by the government actions brought out the more repressive features of the regime, which further alarmed many liberal critics, who became convinced of the potential for the emergence of an authoritarian corporatist state. Government attacks against university autonomy and violent reactions to subsequent student protests intensified these fears. The consequent alienation of business leaders and growing unrest disturbed

30. "Argentine Rulers Vow Price Curbs," *New York Times,* August 14, 1966, p. 26, Late city edition. Also see "Inquietudes de los gremios en la presidencia," *La Nación,* September 8, 1966, p. 1. The nationalist tint of the government also worried many international businesses. See "Catholics Assail Argentine Action," *New York Times,* August 7, 1966, p. 19, Late city edition.

31. "Argentine Regime Divided on Loans," *New York Times,* September 18, 1966, p. 27, Late city edition.

the armed forces.[32] Military pressure worked to end nationalist influence in economic policy in December 1966, when the government initiated a cabinet reshuffle that expelled Salimei and much his staff and opened the Ministry of Economy and Labor to the liberals (Potash 1996, 207–8).

A tactical error by Onganía also fortified the liberals. He had forced the resignation of Pistarini over promotion decisions earlier in December and appointed Julio Alsogaray in his place, who was known to have greater political interests than Pistarini and strong connections to the liberals.[33] In all likelihood, Onganía simply did not feel powerful enough to dismiss two of the principal organizers of the *golpe*. Thus, as a result of his attempt to extend his authority into the military, Onganía found himself facing a more politically concerned army commander (Potash 1996, 209).

The appointment of Adalbert Krieger Vasena as the new minister of economy and labor relieved much of the pressure business leaders and military officers had placed on Onganía.[34] But the concession meant an abdication of the nationalist program in economic policy. Soon Krieger extended his authority over CONADE, the last outpost of the nationalists. He legitimized rejections of CONADE suggestions by calling attention to the superior expertise available in the ministry.[35] By March 1967, the government had its first coherent economic program. The program centered on inflation, which was linked, not only to excessive budgets and the public debt, but also to inefficiencies in the collection of taxes and the delivery of government services and salaries and the inflationary expectations caused by erratic policy. The export of nontraditional manufactures was encouraged, and foreign investment was accepted as an important contributor to economic growth. The overall plan was designed to instill business confidence, increase economic efficiency by reducing advantages previously given to less profitable businesses, and reorient state participation in the economy toward the supervision of infrastructure development, collective bargaining, and credit allocation (Perina 1983, 98–120; Smith 1989, 74–84).[36]

The policy enacted under Krieger represented a dramatic turn. As late as November, Onganía had pointed to agricultural exports as a key to economic growth insofar as the earnings could be used to spur industrialization, and intimated that the exchange controls on agricultural exports

32. "Officers in Argentina Grumble at Failures of Onganía Regime," *New York Times*, August 21, 1966, p. 29, Late city edition.
33. "Ejército: algo más que traslados," *Primera Plana*, December 13, 1966, pp. 12–14.
34. "Gobierno: ahora o nunca," *Primera Plana*, January 3, 1967, pp. 12–14.
35. "Gobierno: la oposición interna," *Primera Plana*, April 11, 1967, pp. 12–13.
36. The "Krieger Strategy" is outlined in "La nueva paridad del dólar ha sido fijada en 350 pesos," *La Nación*, March 14, 1967, p. 1.

would be liberalized ("Mensaje" 1966, 20, 22).[37] But the Krieger plan favored nontraditional manufacturing exports, and in fact placed export taxes on many traditional agricultural exports to check domestic prices (Perina 1983, 101). Second, while expanding on how the resources for industrial investment would be acquired, Onganía had maintained that even more than agricultural exports, "national savings will have to put forth the greatest part of this investment" ("Mensaje" 1966, 30). The Krieger plan canceled this hope and created a deep dependence on foreign investment, as indicated by the 40 percent devaluation of the *peso* in March 1967 (Smith 1989, 80). Another turnabout from the November message was the call for tariff reductions contingent on reciprocity ("Mensaje" 1966, 23). Under Krieger, tariff reductions were applied generously to whatever goods were considered important to industrial expansion (de Dromi 1988, 2:405). Finally, whereas Salimei had assured labor organizations that he would not freeze wages, Krieger was to do just that (Bra 1985, 23, 28).

More evidence that Onganía did not fully support the liberals placed in the Ministry of Economy and Labor comes from his reactions to the new economic policy. While the economic policy sought to prevent workers from exerting their influence, Onganía called for an official dialogue to secure labor support for the government and boldly pronounced: "The revolution is being done for the workers and although there are some that look at me with a grim face, that does not have importance. It is necessary that you put trust in all the measures adopted for the goodwill of the workers." The statement was seen as an explicit move against the liberals.[38] Another notable response to the liberal plan was Onganía's reaction to the proposal for greater administrative rationalization. Krieger proposed a Comité Central de Expertos to manage the downsizing, but Onganía instead placed in control the secretary-general of the president, Héctor Repetto, a recognized nationalist. Repetto responded by shelving the Comité Central idea and allowing each ministry to establish its own plan, an obvious move to curtail the downsizing.[39] Indeed, by March 1969, only 6,000 of the 800,000 total bureaucrats had been released (Fayt 1971, 170).

The Salimei expulsion brought forth not only a change in policy, but also a change of groups represented in the economic team. Whereas the SRA and CGE had been dominant under Salimei, under Krieger they were

---

37. In this paragraph, "Mensaje" refers to "Mensaje al país del Presidente de la Nación Teniente General Juan Carlos Onganía" (Buenos Aires: Secretaría de Prensa de la Presidencia de la Nación, November 7, 1966).

38. "Gobierno: la lucha por el poder," *Primera Plana*, September 12, 1967, pp. 12–13.

39. "Racionalización: ahora o nunca," *Primera Plana*, October 24, 1967, pp. 12–14.

shunned in favor of the ACIEL (Asociación Coordinadora de Instituciones Empresarios Libres), a grouping of larger businesses with international connections (Niosi 1974, 156–73).

The Krieger plan found significant success. The price increase rate fell from 21 percent in 1967 to 4 percent in 1968. GDP increased 2 percent in 1967, 5 percent in 1968, and 7 percent in the first half of 1969. The deficit fell 13.2 percent in 1967 and 12.6 percent in 1968, for a total reduction of 52.8 percent over the 1966–70 period. Tax collection increased 30.6 percent from 1966 to 1970. And in export policy, nontraditional exports increased 63 percent in U.S. dollars. Finally, the classification of the *peso* as a "solid currency" by the IMF brought prestige to the Krieger plan (Niosi 1974, 147; Perina 1983, 109–17).

Despite this success, not all groups gained under the plan. Labor saw real salaries fall 8 percent from 1966 to mid-1969, and unemployment wavered around 7–9 percent. Overall, the outer provinces suffered under denationalization because foreign investment flowed mainly to the capital region, and domestic investment was not enough to supplant the government exodus (Pírez 1986, 47–49). Furthermore, exchange controls and new land taxes adversely affected agricultural production. Small and medium-sized domestic businesses were also hurt. Credit was restricted,[40] and for some producers the devalued *peso* and lower tariffs combined to reduce access to foreign goods and increase competition from foreign interests. In general, Krieger drew the support of large urban business (both national and those associated with foreign interests), international finance and industry, the military, a majority of professionals that worked in the modern sector, and the technocrats. Clear losers under Krieger were small and medium-sized businesses, outer provincial economic interests, and agricultural producers (Perina 1983, 152). In sum, there was a potential support base for the regime, but the regime failed to cultivate it.

The failure to cultivate support led to the week-long explosion of civil unrest known as the *cordobazo*. The event exposed the isolation of the regime and placed the economic program in complete disrepute. The economic losers under the program had rebelled, and the economic winners preferred to remain neutral rather than display support, then withdraw their confidence. To understand how this happened, it is necessary to discuss the political program of the regime and its incongruence with the economic program.

40. Law 16,898 (July 8, 1966) gave the *Banco Central* jurisdiction over all credit cooperatives. It used this authority to restrict credit access and direct it toward larger businesses (Niosi 1974, 152–53).

The Impossible Task: Political Corporatism under Economic Liberalism

The lack of strategy coordination failed the *Revolución Argentina*. Onganía entered government with a team of corporatist officials. But because he was unable to consolidate authority over the armed forces, he also found himself unable to implement his corporatist plans. It was the armed forces that compelled him to surrender economic policy to the liberals, and it was their persistent pressure that kept the corporatists in check thereafter. Unable to consolidate authority within the regime, he could only look to potential supporters in society for help. But here he faced an impossible task, for the potential supporters were those very groups that were most harmed by the economic policies of the regime, and thus were quite unlikely to place their trust in him. The consequent lack of any clear political program frustrated the military. Because Onganía had no mechanisms to contain this frustration, and in fact furthered this frustration with his disregard of military concerns, the military moved to outright opposition and overthrew him.

As a devoted traditional Catholic, Onganía had a natural affinity for corporatist thought. As an officer, he regularly attended religious retreats known as *cursos de Cristianidad* with civilians and other officers. These retreats stressed the relevance of Catholic doctrine to all areas of life. When Onganía sought recruits for his government, he looked to those he had met in the *cursos*. Influential *cursillistas* placed in government included Salimei, Señorans, Interior Minister Martínez Paz, and Interior Undersecretary José M. Saravia, Jr. (Selser 1986b, 11–18). Under the authority of Onganía, government members organized their own *cursos* to dialogue with like-minded officers, businessmen, professors, and professionals in a semi-secret environment (Sáenz Quesada 1986). Another group partial to corporatism tapped by Onganía was the Ateneo de la República, a semi-clandestine club charged by its strongest critics with having fascist and elitist tendencies. At the height of its influence, the Ateneo had at least fifteen members in government, the most important of whom were Guillermo Borda (minister of the interior), Mario Díaz Colodrero (secretary of government), Nicanor Costa Méndez (minister of foreign relations and religion),[41] and the president of the Ateneo, Mario Amadeo (ambassador to Brazil) (Selser 1986a, 26–50).

Onganía's corporatist inclination is demonstrated not only by these associations but also by numerous actions just after the *golpe* that broke

---

41. Costa Méndez would later move to the liberal camp. See "Se busca un caudillo para la oposición," *Panorama*, January 1968, pp. 20–21.

with political liberalism and hinted at corporatist thought. When asked about the future of political parties in October 1966, Onganía answered cryptically: "Concerning the organization of political parties, I can tell you that this will be achieved upon new bases, in liberty, in authentic liberty, that is to say, with order and security."[42] Persistent rumors concerning the establishment of community organizations to channel participation and act as the cornerstone of the new regime immediately followed the *golpe* (Rowe 1966b, 7; Selser 1986a, 223–24). The creation of the Secretariat for the Promotion and Assistance of the Community in the Ministry of Social Welfare and statements by Interior Minister Martínez Paz[43] gave credence to these rumors, but no explicit plans were put forth at this time. Indeed, the regime began its rule without clearly defined political plans.[44]

The foundational documents of the regime originally presented a clear political mission. Heavily influenced by Alvaro Alsogaray, the documents initially called for the restoration of liberal democracy and a monetarist-based commitment to the free market. A president would be imposed by the military, but would only be empowered to pass decree laws, with the expectation that the measures would be reviewed by a future congress. But Onganía had his aids tone down the references to a restoration of democracy in the documents before they were published and insisted that all government measures be considered laws. The publication of *Objetivos Políticos* was delayed two weeks while it was edited to one-quarter its original size (Potash 1996, 195–97).

Onganía could get away with the revisions because many officers remained leery of political parties, and because there were still significant nationalist factions in the armed forces. Nonetheless, the primary concern of the commanding officers was order and stability (O'Donnell 1988, 61), and the corporatist intimations of the Onganía administration seemed to be jeopardizing it. In addition to the concerns of the military over the impact of nationalist economic actions on both domestic and foreign business leaders, Onganía also ordered the Interior Ministry to intervene in the universities to contain Marxist and other anti-corporatist divisive thought (Anzorena 1988, 23). As a security measure, the military originally supported the action. But the level of protest and damaging international

42. "Dirigiosé Onganía a la prensa interior," *La Nación,* October 30, 1966, p. 2.
43. "In consequence of the dissolution of political parties, the government will promote the participation of citizens in the daily political life of the country across organizations based in the community, through which an authentic and effective representative democracy will be arranged." "Dirigiosé al país el Dr. Martínez Paz," *La Nación,* September 8, 1966, p. 1.
44. "Las escasas definiciones," *Primera Plana,* July 12, 1966, pp. 12–13.

exposure led the military to withdraw its support, even to the point of calling for the restoration of university autonomy.[45] The message from the armed forces was clear: do something to restore order in the country and allow for stable economic growth. The armed forces sent this very message in September of 1966 (Potash 1996, 207–8). And with the replacement of Pistarini by Alsogaray in December, Onganía faced not only a military concerned with the disorder produced by corporatism but also an army commander with a liberal disposition.

It is not difficult to see why Onganía conceded economic policy to the liberals in the face of military pressure. The country faced urgent economic problems. Nationalist inclinations repelled domestic and international investment, and international aid seemed contingent on assurances of economic liberalism. The fact that the economic crisis forced 40 percent of the army to be placed on a two-week furlough in July heightened the political immediacy of the crisis.[46] Onganía did not have the military support necessary to defeat the opposition to his nationalist plans in the economic sphere and found in liberalism a quick answer to the concerns of the military. Krieger Vasena was appointed with these problems clearly in mind. He had recognized international connections and was well respected in the international financial community (Smith 1989, 74).

The cabinet shuffle maintained corporatist influence in the Interior Ministry and Ministry of Social Welfare (Potash 1996, 210–11). A more moderate nationalist, retired general Guillermo Borda, replaced Interior Minister Martínez Paz (Smith 1989, 59). But Borda's historic Peronist linkages stood in contrast to the new economic policy, and the move was viewed as an explicit concession to the Peronists (Roth 1980, 224). Borda and Secretary of Government Díaz Colodrero moved quickly to initiate a dialogue with politicians and labor to gain their support, even while stressing that the government had no plans to withdraw in the near future.[47] But the CGT expressed greater concern over the impending implementation of the Krieger plan and issued a *plan de acción* that called for a series of nationwide work stoppages in February (Anzorena 1988, 28–30). The imminent threat of disorder brought military pressure in favor of the liberals. In a CONASE meeting, Secretary Osiris Villegas drafted a measure to freeze the funds of some CGT affiliated unions and threaten further

45. "Officers in Argentina Grumble at Failures of Onganía Regime," *New York Times,* August 21, 1966, p. 29, Late city edition.
46. "Onganía's Backers Divided by Economic Crisis," *New York Times,* July 21, 1966, p. 5, Late city edition.
47. "Gobierno: otro pozo de aire," *Primera Plana,* January 24, 1967, pp. 12–13.

seizures as well as outright repression of any popular mobilizations by the CGT. Borda and Díaz Colodrero debated the measure and received only a small concession. The final draft would include the statement: "The *Revolución Argentina* was not enacted against the working class."[48] But the military's threat worked—the CGT withdrew its plan, and the dialogue was broken.

By this time, the split in the government between the corporatists and liberals was clear to everyone.[49] Onganía attempted to mollify union concerns over the new economic program with his *Tres Tiempos* (three phases) doctrine in March 1967. The doctrine divided the *Revolución Argentina* into three phases. First, there would be an economic phase, in which government policy would promote rapid economic development and allow the country to compete more effectively in the international economy. A social phase would follow, during which dialogue and significant social policies would be implemented to lay the foundational for the political phase, when the institutions for an authentic republican democracy would be set.[50] The doctrine was a clear message to the workers that they would simply have to wait out the present economic program, and that their inclusion would come at some future time. The doctrine did buy Onganía some time. While the Congreso General Confederal of the CGT gave strong support to a resolution that rejected any long-term participationist plans with the government in May, the Consejo de los 20 faction did extend a tacit truce and relative calm ensued (Raggio 1986, 112–13).[51]

Through 1967, Onganía was able to consolidate power under the tide of a growing economy, but the regime remained without a clear political program.[52] Alvaro Alsogaray attempted to gain the upper hand with a September speech in Washington, D.C., that stressed the profound democratic nature of Argentina and called the regime a "political pause." Díaz Colodrero angrily responded that "the *Revolución Argentina* is not a simple parenthesis but an outcome and point of departure from a process that should achieve objectives of authentic representation.... We must rule out the electoral process in the short run" (Bra 1985, 29–30). At the same time, Onganía was making moves that seemed to point toward a corporatist

48. "Gobierno-CGT: la ruptura," *Primera Plana*, February 21, 1967, pp. 12–13.
49. "La tensa etapa de las indefiniciones," *Panorama*, March 1967, pp. 4–6; "El mercado de las ideas en el gobierno," ibid., May 1967, pp. 6–7.
50. For the introduction of this doctrine, see the Onganía speech reproduced in *La Nación*, March 29, 1967.
51. "Gobierno: la lucha por el poder," *Primera Plana*, September 12, 1967, pp. 12–13.
52. "Onganía More Firmly in the Saddle," *Latin America*, September 22, 1967, pp. 167–68; "El general va ganando batallas," *Panorama*, December 1967, pp. 20–21.

solution. In widely publicized visits, a number of European corporatist intellectuals were invited to Argentine universities under the auspices of the Interior Ministry and were expected to discuss developmental plans with Onganía.[53] Likewise, when asked in late August about the economic program, Onganía simply answered, "This is a stage," and reaffirmed the commitment of the *Revolución* to the workers.[54] Nonetheless, Onganía remained ambivalent before the armed forces. In a single speech to the army high command in October he emphasized the long-term nature of the regime's plans, declared that "the whole world knows me, and in no way can one say that I am a corporatist," and announced that "traditional liberalism is finished in Argentina and will not be established."[55]

The political indecisiveness was wearing thin on the unions, especially in the context of economic liberalism (Sáenz Quesada 1986).[56] One of the last straws came at the turn of the year. In September 1967, Secretary of Labor San Sebastián met with a dozen potential participationist union leaders and promised higher wages as an enticement to dialogue. All plans were crushed in January 1968, when Krieger undercut San Sebastián by refusing to grant the increases.[57] Ironically, Onganía would reach the peak of his power during this time in spite of these government divisions. Economic growth placated many in society, and the consequent strength of the liberals in government blocked the development of alliances between the corporatists in government and the unions, and thus weakened unified protest.[58]

The frustration of both the corporatists and unions to forge an alliance led each group to take a more independent, forceful strategy.[59] The labor movement indicated its complete distrust of government promises for a future of closer collaboration when it elected Raimundo Ongaro to lead the CGT in March 1968 (Sáenz Quesada 1986, 75). As leader of the 62 Organizaciones faction, Ongaro was the most outspoken nonparticipationist figure in the CGT. The movement to the opposition camp by labor had been preceded by similar moves by Peronist politicians after Perón made his opposition clear in June 1967. Recognizing the alienation of potential

53. "Gobierno: ha nacido el plan político?" *Primera Plana*, September 19, 1967, pp. 12–14.
54. "Gobierno: la lucha por el poder," *Primera Plana*, September 12, 1967, pp. 12–13.
55. "Onganía y la lucha por el poder," *Primera Plana*, October 24, 1967, pp. 14–15.
56. "Sindicalismo: participación o contradicción?" *Panorama*, October 1967, pp. 22–23.
57. "Gobierno: divide y reinarás," *Primera Plana*, February 6, 1968, pp. 12–13.
58. "El general va ganando batallas," *Panorama*, December 1967, pp. 20–21; "Opposition to Onganía Still Disunited," *Latin America*, November 24, 1967, pp. 242–43.
59. "Peronists Tire of Discussion," *Latin America*, December 15, 1967, pp. 269–70.

regime allies, the corporatists within government became more outspoken on their position in 1968.[60]

Onganía renewed the corporatist push on March 5 with a sudden strong reaction to the need for a political program. In a speech at Los Olivos, he announced that "the pillars of the *Revolución* are the military and labor." Onganía then called a meeting of over two hundred high government officials and officers to admonish them for the lack of a political program, call for a clarification and deepening of the *Revolución,* and request the resignation of any official who did not fully support him (Bra 1985, 37). Finally, he met with the service commanders to request individual lists of all secretaries and ministers that they would like removed.[61] The action was entirely out of tune with the political environment surrounding the regime. The Ongaro election confirmed that labor had no desire to act as a pillar to the regime, and the military had no desire to act as a pillar alongside the Peronist-dominated CGT. Onganía soon illustrated the imprudence of his decision to request removal lists from the commanders by shelving their suggestions when he received them. At this point, the regime seemed totally devoid of sound political leadership. The economy was still growing, and that portion of the business sector that was prospering supported the regime as long as Krieger's position was secure. The opportunity to cultivate their support was there, but Onganía ignored it.[62]

Onganía continued his push for corporatism at the annual governors' meeting in Alta Gracia on April 1. His address was considered the clearest definition thus far on the political plans of the regime.[63] In it, Onganía stated that the representative sectors of the community ought to prepare to take part in government, and that this participation would develop at the municipal level first, then would be extended to the provincial and national levels. He went on to declare that "the process, when the conditions present themselves, should culminate in an advisory council that will concern itself with economic and social aspects of interests to the community." Absent in the exposition were any references to political parties, electoral competition, or legislative duties for the proposed social and economic councils.[64]

60. "Gobierno: divide y reinarás," *Primera Plana,* February 6, 1968, pp. 12–13.

61. "Nationalists Getting the Upper Hand?" *Latin America,* March 15, 1968, p. 15; "Gobierno: que se propone Onganía?" *Primera Plana,* March 19, 1968, pp. 12–13; "Gobierno: el difícil tiempo nuevo," ibid., March 26, 1968, pp. 12–13.

62. "El gobierno hostigado," *Primera Plana,* April 9, 1968, pp. 12–13.

63. "Con voz, o con voz y voto," *Panorama,* May 1968, pp. 4–5.

64. "Discurso del Presidencia de la Nación al inaugurar la Reunión de Gobernadores de Provincias en Alta Gracia" (Buenos Aires: Secretaria de Prensa de la Presidencia de la Nación, April 1, 1968).

A more caustic endorsement of corporatism came from Interior Minister Borda in a well-publicized speech to the Foreign Press Association on April 24 (Potash 1996, 230–32). Borda also suggested social and economic councils, but added a sharp criticism of liberal democracy. He lauded worker participation programs in certain state businesses, arguing that it pointed to "the loss of the mentality of pressure groups and the abandonment of the idea of action in the service of particular interests," and in urging the extension of such participation, proclaimed that "this participation is born from the concept of social organization, which opposes the individualist idea, which only envisages the state-citizen relationship."[65]

Reports that Onganía had sanctioned the speech angered Alsogaray, who increased his criticisms of the lack of military input in the government (Potash 1996, 228).[66] In response to questions from the press in May, he avoided references of direct support for Onganía. When asked if the army backed the president, he responded, "the army is in line with the other two armed forces inside the objectives of the *Revolución Argentina*." And when asked if the foundational documents disqualify liberalism and favor corporatism, communitarianism, or any other form of government, Alsogaray retorted, "The document of the *Revolución Argentina* is of a marked anti-totalitarian tendency. All of it is based in immanently democratic concepts."[67] The display of distancing unleashed the greatest wave of *golpe* rumors since the start of the Onganía government (Perina 1983, 186; Lanusse 1977, 62–64).[68]

In an attempt to reestablish authority, Onganía relieved all three service commanders in August. The dismissals should not be interpreted as evidence of strength on the part of Onganía. Alsogaray was due to retire at the end of the year, and many officers favored his replacement, Alejandro Lanusse, believing that he would press the military's political interests more forcefully in government.[69] Indeed, Alsogaray did not display the depth of his disagreement with Onganía until after he left his position.[70] A true show

65. The speech can be found in *Cinco discursos y una revolución*, by Publicaciones Movimiento Humanista de Derecho (Buenos Aires: Publicaciones Movimiento Humanista de Derecho, 1968), pp. 7–11.
66. "Onganía-Alsogaray: una cierta sonrisa," *Primera Plana*, May 14, 1968, pp. 13–14; "The Crisis Recedes—for the Moment," *Latin America*, May 31, 1968.
67. "Alsogaray ratificó la unidad de las fuerzas armadas," *La Nación*, May 23, 1968, p. 1.
68. "Gobierno, 1—ejército, 1," *Primera Plana*, May 25, 1968, pp. 13–15.
69. "Onganía y los militares," *Primera Plana*, March 12, 1968, pp. 12–13.
70. Like Onganía, Alsogaray was deeply influenced by the 1962–63 *azul-colorado* feud, and greatly feared the politicization of the armed forces. "La trayectoria del poder," *Primera Plana*, September 10, 1968, p. 12.

of strength would have been a purge of the armed forces that went beyond the very peak of the hierarchy, but as noted, Onganía lacked the authority and, more important, the legitimacy. He simply did not have the political standing to reach very far into the military. The reactions of the armed forces toward Onganía indicated unity and alienation, rather than fragmentation and politicization. It is not surprising that the vast majority of military-based criticisms on the lack of a political program or on the moves toward corporatism came from retired officers (Fayt 1971, 164). Likewise, the most visible jailed political critics of the regime were retired officers (de Dromi 1988, 2:421).

The retirements inspired Onganía. At this time, he fully expected to rule for at least ten more years, stating in August: "Nothing can be further from the thinking of the *Revolución* than the search for political exits. The dissolution of hundreds of political parties is an irrevocable fact" (Anzorena 1988, 47). And in what O'Donnell views as a watershed event, in December Onganía called for the restoration of collective bargaining by the end of 1969, thus completely alienating the large and international businesses that had offered tacit support because of the autonomy granted to Krieger (O'Donnell 1988, 157). For many, the solidification of the corporatist push came at the annual governors' meeting on May 6, 1969, where Onganía repeated and further detailed his calls for economic and social advisory councils, which he expected to be in place by the end of the year.[71] In light of the events of the past year, few doubted that the councils meant the death of political parties and liberal democracy in Argentina. This led Arturo Frondizi of the Movimiento de Integración y Desarrollo (MID), Ricardo Balbín of the Unión Cívica Radical del Pueblo (UCRP), and Horacio Thedy of the Partido Demócrata Progresista (PDP) to join the Justicialistas and Illia's Radicales in the party opposition. The "wait and see" strategy of these parties was officially over, leaving Onganía isolated from every major political party (de Dromi 1988, 2:483). In addition to this growing opposition, many individuals were drawn to the guerrilla groups that gained prominence at this time (Ollier 1988, 83).

The stage was now set for the fall of Onganía. His inability to consolidate control in the armed forces had led to the division of the administration between the liberals and corporatists and ultimately left him with no supporters. The uncertainty caused by the lack of a clear political program produced reluctant support from winners under the economic program, but the more overt moves toward corporatism led to their complete withdrawal

---

71. "Onganía: La caza de aliados," *Primera Plana,* May 13, 1969, pp. 8–11.

of support. The political parties had the same reaction. Labor stood to gain from the corporatist move, but could not bring itself to trust a government that thus far had offered only liberal economics. The institutions that had failed Onganía in his quest to exert authority over the armed forces redoubled his problems because these institutions also failed to offer the armed forces any official venue to express their grievances.

The social explosion known as the *cordobazo* represented the beginning of the end for Onganía. Preceded by violent student protests in Corrientes, Resistencia, and Rosario in mid-May, the *cordobazo* erupted on May 29 in the city of Córdoba in the midst of protests headed by students and unions against the policies of Governor Carlos Caballero. Caballero was the first governor to institute the economic and social councils called for by Onganía, and Borda viewed the province as a corporatist showcase (Potash 1996, 247; Anzorena 1988, 52). The unrest spread through Corrientes, Rosario, and Tucumán and lasted nearly one week.[72]

After the *cordobazo,* two facts were clear to all in Argentina: Onganía was thoroughly isolated from all groups in society, and his rule was based on nothing more than the threat of repression. The military was well aware of this and had no desire to act as a medium of repression in support of an unpopular regime (Smith 1989, 154–57; Perina 1983, 202–4). A lower-ranking officer noted just after the *cordobazo:* "It is a pity, Onganía does not accept advice, but turns to us when subversion springs up."[73]

Under pressure from the military, Onganía did institute a cabinet change, but it represented more a change of personnel than a change of policy, and the military widely criticized it (Fayt 1971, 187). Krieger himself chose the new minister of economy and labor, Diego Pastore, and the new interior minister, Francisco Imaz, was a recognized nationalist with Peronist links.[74] Likewise, Onganía remained steadfast in his commitment to a corporatist solution (O'Donnell 1988, 175). In an address at the Colegio Militar in July, he blindly declared: "We are now allowed to initiate the social period, which will consolidate the human content of the *Revolución,* and has as its principle objective the protection of the efforts of workers." And in September, he reaffirmed his commitment to the establishment of social

---

72. On the *cordobazo,* see Delich 1974 and Smith 1989. On the events leading to the *cordobazo,* see "La semana trágica de Juan Carlos Onganía," *Primera Plana,* May 27, 1969, pp. 11–18.

73. "Gobierno: un gabinete cuestionado," *Primera Plana,* June 17, 1969, pp. 10–14. On the growth of political violence during this time, see Gillespie 1982.

74. "Dropping the Pilot," *Latin America,* June 13, 1969, p. 185; "Question Mark over Onganía," ibid., June 20, 1969, pp. 194–95.

and economic councils.[75] Finally, CONADE proposals suggesting a more nationalistic economic program led large businesses to become yet more critical (O'Donnell 1988, 181).[76]

In his account, Lanusse claims that by the end of 1969 the high command was committed to a prompt political exit and that the Army General Staff began work on a number of documents that called for political liberalization, the recognition of political parties, and elections with no proscriptions (Lanusse 1977, 56–59). Also, Lanusse began to meet with superior officers to discuss greater military participation in government to ensure these goals (Lanusse 1977, 81–82). The army commander further fortified his position through his influence over the round of promotions, retirements, and assignments at the end of the year.[77]

By April 1970, the armed forces were prepared to force their proposal for a political exit. When Arturo Frondizi, one of the last party leaders to join the opposition, gave a scathing public attack of the regime on April 22, the military knew that the isolation of the regime had reached its most critical point (Potash 1996, 279). On April 28, the Army General Staff released a comprehensive document critical of the lack of a political plan, and on May 11, Lanusse met with Onganía to suggest that he meet with all superior officers and clarify his political intentions (Lanusse 1977, 87–90). Onganía agreed and called a meeting for May 27. To the dismay of the superior officers present, Onganía used the opportunity to outline in detail his plan for a corporatist regime. The regime would consist of three hierarchical chains of appointed councils that would run from the municipal to the provincial to the national level, where each would culminate in a national confederation. There would be a labor confederation, a business confederation, and a confederation of professionals and technicians (Potash 1996, 284–88). The response of the high command was overwhelmingly negative (de Dromi 1988, 2:355; Lanusse 1977, 102).

If the corporatist moves were not enough, the kidnapping and murder of retired general Pedro Aramburu on May 29 was the final blow for the military. Aramburu had been viewed as the last individual capable of reestablishing the link between the *Revolución* and society. To many, his kidnapping represented the breakdown of all authority. Onganía simply

75. For the July address, see "Onganía habló ayer a las fuerzas armadas," *La Nación,* July 8, 1969, p. 1. For the September address, see "No existen previsiones para el tiempo político," ibid., September 12, 1969, p. 1.

76. "Anunció el CONADE el Plan de Desarrollo," *La Nación,* February 20, 1970, p. 1; "Analiza la Unión Industrial el Plan de Desarrollo," ibid., April 24, 1970, p. 9.

77. "Amnesty and Purge," *Latin America,* December 5, 1969, p. 392.

made things worse when he announced the murder of Aramburu on June 2. In the TV and radio broadcast, Onganía spoke of the spread of subversion and said that the government had been "powerless to provide for the complete security of all its inhabitants, powerless to administer rapid and effective justice, and powerless to neutralize the propaganda that through a few modes of dissemination persistently works for its discredit" (Sáenz Quesada 1986, 81). Gone was the grandeur of a regime that had valiantly assumed rule to dispose of politics and restore pride in the *patria*. It was too much for the armed forces. Onganía was overthrown six days later.[78]

Levingston, Lanusse, and Balanced Transition

Military unity, when combined with a level of military alienation that undermines strategy coordination, raises the probability of an internal *golpe* and can be expected to lead to a balanced transition. Because military alienation weakens the government, it can do little more than wear at any political credit initially granted to the regime. As such, the regime is unlikely to allow for credible threats or to aid the cultivation of outside support. Without these capabilities, the government is unlikely to impose many political conditions on the successor regime as it withdraws from rule. But the lack of regime investment can save the regime from collapse—it leaves officers more open to withdrawal before the situation grows much worse. Officers can return to the barracks with the rationale that failure actually rested outside the institution of the military.

The *Revolución Argentina* corroborates these predictions. Onganía was unable to gain the support of the armed forces and thus was unable to pursue his economic and political programs effectively. The growing alienation of the Argentine military led it to overthrow Onganía. Much to the dismay of the armed forces, however, Onganía's replacement, Levingston, acted quite similarly to Onganía. The army commander, Lanusse, desired greater military input, but Levingston guarded the low regime investment developed under his predecessor. Lanusse responded by assuming the presidency himself, as army commander. The Lanusse tenure shows the cumulative impact of low regime investment. Because the military had been essentially excluded from government and thus saw little stake in its continuance, Lanusse was able to dissolve the *Revolución* with little resistance.

---

78. "La Junta de Commandantes destituyó á Onganía y asumió el gobierno," *La Nación,* June 9, 1970, p. 1.

Levingston: More of the Same

General Roberto M. Levingston seemed to be the perfect candidate for president. Navy commander Pedro J. Gnavi had worked with him in SIDE, air force commander Carlos A. Rey had worked with him in the Joint General Staff, and Lanusse had been his superior at the Escuela Superior de Guerra. These personal connections, plus the fact that Levingston had never held a command position, led the service commanders to believe that they had chosen a reliable and compliant president to lead the return to civilian rule (Lanusse 1977, 145–47).

The same day the Junta de Commandantes installed Levingston as president, June 18, they also announced that the government would draft a plan to withdraw from rule without delay.[79] The Junta had already redirected the *Revolución* with the passage of decree 46/70 (*Las Políticas Nacionales*) the previous day. The decree was an attempt to save the dignity of the armed forces as it retreated from the lofty goals laid out in the *Acta* and its annexes. One hundred and sixty objectives were listed in this decree,[80] but they were described as guiding principles, and not as steps in a concrete plan to be completed before a political transition (Botana, Braun, and Floria 1973, 87–89). To supervise Levingston during the anticipated transition, the Junta altered article 5 of the *Estatuto* to grant itself input on legislation of "significant transcendence" (*significativa transcendencia*).[81] If a law or decree was of significant transcendence, the minister or secretary of the ministry concerned was to send it to the secretary-general, who was in turn to transfer it to the general staff of each force. The general staffs were then to send it to their respective commanders, each of whom was then to meet with the other service commanders and the president and vote on the bill. If there was a tie, a decree would receive ten further days of discussion, and a law would receive thirty. If the impasse remained, the president would cast the deciding vote (Lanusse 1977, 166–67).

The confidence placed in Levingston by the Junta was swiftly dampened. In his inaugural speech, Levingston claimed the "total and exclusive

79. "General Levingston, I Presume," *Latin America*, June 19, 1970, pp. 193–94.

80. For example: to respect the dignity of man, to assure the liberty of expression, to aid population growth and its regional distribution, to establish an adequate health system, and to assure the development of the national economy (de Dromi 1988, 2:338–39).

81. "The laws and decrees of significance to the objectives of the *Revolución Argentina* will require the previous consent and agreement of the *Junta de Commandantes en Jefe* ..." (Perina 1983, 205). The day before appointing Levingston (June 17), the Junta passed law 18,713, which gave both the Junta and the president the authority to deem a bill of significant transcendence.

responsibility for executive acts," thereby rejecting Junta supervision of executive decrees, whether of significant transcendence or not (Lanusse 1977, 149). And in a dinner with senior officers on July 7, Levingston stated that "the political exit will occur when the fundamental objectives of the *Revolución* have been achieved ... the process will not be short" (Fayt 1971, 205).

Appointments made by Levingston also did little to demonstrate a commitment to transition. At first, the liberal-nationalist split was maintained, and the bent of the administration was unclear.[82] But Levingston quickly moved to undermine those liberal appointments that he did concede. His most significant move came in the Interior Ministry, where the air force had imposed retired air force general Eduardo McLoughlin, a visible proponent of dialogue and speedy political transition. Levingston responded to the pressure to democratize with the creation of two new institutions in the Interior Ministry to handle the transition, the subsecretary of political affairs and the director-general of policy, and appointed Enrique Gilardi and Roberto Meoli to those posts. Gilardi worked aggressively to check moves by McLoughlin to open discussions with party leaders, declaring that party leaders were not valid interlocutors for dialogue because all parties had been legally dissolved.[83]

Levingston made his lack of commitment to transition clear in an address on September 29, in which he subordinated political progress to social and economic progress, called for new party forces, and announced his desire for constitutional reform: "The party structures in force to 1966 are of the past.... [The reopening of political activity] will accompany the strengthening and deepening of the revolutionary process in the economic-social area across a time that, one estimates, will be approximately four to five years.... The instrumentation of the political plan will bring about a formula that neutralizes political atomization and eases the channeling of opinion in great and new party forces."[84] Through October, Levingston followed these statements with complementary actions. His refusal to recognize the traditional political parties, his calls to begin dialogue with

82. "What Sort of Government?" *Latin America,* July 10, 1970, pp. 220–21. When Onganía was removed, many government officials delayed their decision to resign until after they discovered who his successor would be. In this way, many appointment opportunities passed from the Junta to Levingston when he assumed office. See "Estímase que hoy habrá otras designaciones," *La Nación,* June 22, 1970, p. 12.

83. "Levingston's Fate," *Latin America,* October 16, 1970, p. 336; "Díalogo sobre el futuro político," *La Nación,* August 26, 1970, p. 1.

84. "Levingston refirióse á la reapertura política," *La Nación,* September 30, 1970, p. 1. Also see Fayt 1971, 207.

nonparty social leaders over a political plan, and his references to an *oficialista* "party of the *Revolución*" led McLoughlin to resign his position as interior minister, and the liberal-leaning Moyano Llerena, to resign his position as minister of economy and labor (Smith 1989, 178). The appointments of Cordón Aguirre as interior minister and Aldo Ferrer as minister of economy and labor were explicit moves to "deepen the *Revolución.*" Levingston planned to boost government support with populist economic policies, and to redirect political participation from the traditional political parties (Sáenz Quesada 1989, 5). Late October saw a flurry of populist policy pronouncements, including wage increases, greater government participation in workers' affairs, unemployment security measures, and a proposal for a National Bank of Development to assist small and medium-sized traditional businesses.[85] Ferrer led what he called the *"argentinización* of the economy" by, among other actions, stimulating internal demand through wage increases and government expenditures, and redirecting bank credit toward domestic firms (Smith 1989, 170–73).

The move actually did have some success in steering economic gains toward workers, small and medium-sized businesses, and agriculture. The CGT, CGE, and SRA all found themselves advantaged (Perina 1983, 156–57). But it was too late to gain political capital from economic success. The economic gains were not enough to cover losses sustained over the previous five years, and the political parties were uniting in the face of aggressive government criticisms (Sáenz Quesada 1989, 6).[86] This party action culminated on November 11 with *La Hora del Pueblo,* a document published by the Radicals, moderate Peronists, and numerous small parties that called for immediate elections without proscriptions.[87] The document was not radical. Many in the military shared these sentiments contained in the document and saw in that an opportunity for dialogue. Nonetheless, Levingston vilified it as disruptive and demagogic. His response led to an increase in political violence that further irritated the armed forces (Perina 1983, 290; Anzorena 1988, 149–52). Moreover, Levingston again moved to distance the Junta from important policy decisions. A press release from a meeting at the Colegio Militar on November 25 noted that Levingston had told the officers that the military "has access to the legislative process dealing with problems of significant transcendence, unless this implies an

85. "Formuló anuncios el General Levingston," *La Nación,* October 27, 1970, p. 1.
86. "Declaraciones sobre el último discurso de General Levingston," *La Nación,* October 3, 1970, p. 5.
87. For text, see "Agrupaciones políticos dieron una declaración," *La Nación,* November 12, 1970, p. 6. Also see Sáenz Quesada 1989, 40–44.

absolute interference with the necessary liberty of executive action."[88] Further movement away from military input came in December, when Lanusse sent the army's proposal for a political plan to Levingston. Interior Minister Cordón accepted the proposal offhandedly, stating that the government had over fifty such proposals, and that the army proposal, as well as the expected navy and air force proposals, would simply be considered along with the others.[89]

The key event leading to the fall of Levingston was the social upheaval in Córdoba known as the *viborazo*. Statements made in Levingston's presence by the newly appointed governor, the extremist catholic nationalist José Camilo Uriburu, set off the *viborazo* on March 7. Uriburu likened all student and union protesters to subversives, compared them to a "poisonous snake (*víbora*) of one hundred heads," and asked that God give him the honor of beheading this snake (Ollier 1988, 84). The statements ignited unrest throughout Córdoba, but it was the reluctance of the military to put down the unrest that made their opposition to Levingston clear (Sáenz Quesada 1989, 6; Potash 1996, 348–53).[90] Levingston was dismissed on March 23.

As with Onganía, it was institutions that failed Levingston. His political and economic programs were at odds with those dominant in the armed forces (not to mention the fact that this was an armed forces tiring of rule), and the institutional arrangement provided no means to cultivate support. The result was again an alienated military. Levingston needed a military that was prepared to enforce his rule through repression, and that he did not have.

Lanusse: Confronting Narrowed Options

With the dismissal of Levingston, the Junta de Comandantes established itself as the center of government. Under an amendment to the *Estatuto*, the chairmanship of the Junta, a two-year position that rotated among the service commanders, was accorded the authority granted to the president of the nation under article 5 of the *Estatuto*. As chairman, Lanusse assumed the presidency, and although the position was due to be rotated to air force commander Rey in March 1973, Rey waived his rotation to allow for greater continuity during the transition (and to deflect air force

88. "Reuniones militares," *Primera Plana*, November 25, 1970, pp. 14–17.
89. "Plan político," *Primera Plana*, December 1, 1970, pp. 14–16.
90. "El volcán político: temblor en Buenos Aires, llamas en Córdoba," *Panorama*, March 16, 1971, pp. 8–10.

responsibility for anything that might go wrong). Overall, the result was a collegial government. Although Lanusse was required to gain the approval of only one other Junta member on issues of significant transcendence, in actuality he sought unanimity for all issues he regarded as important (Potash 1996, 361–62). The detrimental institutional design developed first under Onganía was disposed of, but its effects were to overwhelm Lanusse nevertheless.

The Junta publicly expressed its commitment to political transition in an official document released April 2, 1971.[91] In this document, the Junta established as its general mission "to create in the political arena the conditions that allow for the reestablishment of the constitutional order in a period of approximately three years and that assure the continuity of the effort to achieve the objectives of the *Revolución Argentina.*" This mission statement sent a mixed message. The objectives of the *Revolución* were declared to be still valid, but the military was willing to relinquish direct control over their pursuit. To this end, Lanusse sought to draw all significant political party and sectoral leaders into a "gran acuerdo nacional" (great national accord, or GAN). Under the GAN all the political parties were to agree to reject violence and accept democratic procedures, formulate a common set of goals to be achieved, and select a candidate to preside over a transitional government. Movement toward the GAN was initiated with the establishment of the Comisión Coordinadora del Plan Político, which consisted of both military representatives from each service and civilians, and which coordinated work on constitutional reform and new statutes on political parties and electoral laws.[92] Lanusse soon made it clear that unlike his predecessors, political planning would take priority over economic objectives.[93]

The audacious objectives set out in the GAN were never to be met. The political parties recognized that participation would grant legitimacy to the crippled regime and diminish their own standing in the public eye. Thus began a progressive decline in regime expectations and conditions for political transition. The alienation experienced in the armed forces led

91. *Directiva de la Junta de Comandantes en Jefe para el Ministro del Interior: bases del plan político* (Buenos Aires: Secretaría General de la Presidencia de la Nación, April 2, 1971).

92. "Reunión constitutiva de la comisión política," *La Nación,* April 16, 1971, p. 1.

93. Indeed, under Lanusse no clear winners or losers emerged in economic policymaking. In the attempt not to alienate any economic group, the regime designed its economic policy to maintain the status quo, which gave it an ad hoc character (Perina 1983, 158–59). Toward this end, the powerful Ministry of Economics was dismantled and many of its secretarial positions were raised to ministerial status (Botana, Braun, and Floria 1973, 126).

many officers to press for withdrawal under minimal conditions, and the inability to cultivate political credit left the regime with very little support in society. Lanusse himself recognized the enduring impact of institutional design when he succeeded Levingston: "His fall placed me in the Presidency of the Nation. But, when I arrived at the *Revolución Argentina,* it had already passed to loneliness, through two stages. And in this way I arrived weakened of power, because the structure which supported me was weakened, confused, and disoriented" (Lanusse 1977, 192).

His call for a "gran acuerdo nacional" having been rejected, Lanusse had to find another way to bring the *Revolución Argentina* to a peaceful end. He could have threatened an internal *golpe.* Government leaders proposing a transition can often force the incoming opposition to accept their conditions on the manner of the transition by threatening a reversion to authoritarianism under regime hard-liners if those conditions are not met (O'Donnell and Schmitter 1986, 24–25). This option was closed to Lanusse, even if he had wanted to use it, when hard-liners attempted their own nationalist *golpe* in October 1971. By putting it down Lanusse placed himself solidly with those officers who favored elections and transition as the only viable sources of regime legitimacy (O'Donnell 1988, 244–46; Smith 1989, 193).[94] Lanusse's second card was the possibility that he might run for president in the upcoming elections. He refused to deny this possibility in hopes that he could use a guarantee not to run as a bargaining chip to extract concessions from the parties (Potash 1996, 398–99). But by July 1972, it was clear that they were ignoring his possible candidacy, and that it was doing nothing more than causing unease in the military. In a July 7 public address, Lanusse announced candidacy requirements that disqualified incumbents, effectively disqualifying himself. The speech also marked a move in regime strategy from dialogue over transition conditions to manipulation of the electoral laws to prevent a Peronist victory in the March 1973 elections (Sáenz Quesada 1989, 20). Perón himself could not meet the residency requirement, and with the establishment of a second round in the presidential and senatorial elections, it was expected that non-Peronist parties would eventually ally and defeat the Peronists.[95]

By late 1972 it was clear that GAN was dead. In its place, a document

94. "Victory or Death, We Surrender," *Latin America,* October 15, 1971, pp. 332–33.

95. The new electoral regulations were part of a set of constitutional changes introduced by the outgoing regime. The constitutional revisions were not real signs of strength in the Lanusse government. Under pressure from the Corte Suprema, the changes were declared provisional unless validated by a constitutional commission by 1976 (de Dromi 1988, 2:359).

of *cinco puntos,* or five points, was issued in February 1973. Unable to dilute Peronist influence through the GAN, and wary of a Peronist victory in the March elections, the regime hoped that the *cinco puntos* would handcuff any successor government. Drafted in the army and sanctioned by the Junta, the document

1. assured all concerned that the military was committed to an electoral process and would accept the outcome, demanding only that all participants accept the constitution and related legislation;
2. pledged the next government to support republican institutions;
3. demanded that the stability and independence of the judiciary be respected;
4. warned against indiscriminate and total amnesties for guerrillas;
5. insisted on cabinet participation by the military to facilitate supervision of national security.[96]

The electoral manipulation failed. The Peronist candidate for president, Héctor Cámpora, won an overwhelming victory. The *cinco puntos* document was summarily ignored. On May 27, just two days after assuming power, the Cámpora government declared an amnesty for hundreds of political prisoners and overhauled the Corte Suprema (Fraga 1988, 39–40). The new government also dismissed the service commanders. The most junior major general, Jorge R. Carcagno, was appointed army commander, thereby forcing a complete overhaul of the army high command. A similar move in the navy in December would force the retirements of seven senior admirals.

This looks like a transition by collapse. But the turn to the armed forces in mid-1974 after the failure of the civilian police to reverse the rising political violence indicates progressive weakness on the part of the government, and an escalating strength on the part of the armed forces (Fraga 1988).[97] Moreover, the reentry of the armed forces into government within three years indicates that the Peronist government never came close to consolidating the new regime. The *Revolución Argentina* thus falls somewhat closer to balanced transition than collapse on the scale of transition control. More alienated than politicized, the armed forces recovered quickly from the damage done to them by the institutions of the *Revolución Argentina.*

96. The document can be found in Fraga 1988, 49.
97. "Memories Are Made of This," *Latin America,* June 7, 1974, pp. 179–80; "History Repeats Itself," ibid., November 29, 1974, pp. 373–74.

Conclusion

The *Revolución Argentina* was marked by military unity and a lack of strategy coordination. Sheltered from government, the military hierarchy remained strong. Moreover, the refusal by Onganía to accept input from the highest ranks, and his relentless pursuit of a corporatist program that only served to disrupt public order and reduce support from significant economic groups, gave the officers a unifying concern. The resulting alienation made it difficult for Onganía to formulate and implement coherent economic and political programs. Although the *cursillistas* crossed the civil-military divide, this group was far too exclusive to build on, and simply could not play the foundational role played in Brazil by the Escola Superior de Guerra. Hence, Onganía found it difficult to convince the armed forces to support his political and economic strategies and lacked the power to impose them by force. The puzzling schizophrenia of the regime (liberal economics and corporatist politics) is explained by this peculiar combination of military unity and lack of strategy coordination.

The inability to control the linkage between the government and the military points to a lack of strategy coordination. Thus, even when the regime found some economic success, it was unable to convert it into political capital. Because an alienated military is not necessarily a divided military, the armed forces were able to intervene in government again in a relatively coherent manner. The Levingston tenure replayed the problems of the Onganía period and led the military to assume direct control under Lanusse. At the head of a regime drained of legitimacy and supported by a wearied military, Lanusse slowly relented to opposition demands. The armed forces were wounded, but they did not collapse. Their increased involvement in security affairs under the subsequent Peronist government would set the stage for a more devastating experience with rule from 1976 to 1983.

3

Institutional Aggrandizement and Controlled Transition in Pinochet's Chile

One can develop a dialogue and search
for consensus [with the opposition], but
our course has been plotted—we are the
armed forces and we are going to follow
it to the end.
—Augusto Pinochet

September 11, 1973, marked the beginning of a period of profound political, economic, and cultural change in Chile. For the next seventeen years, the Chilean armed forces were to govern under a regime that not only effectively repressed its opponents but also cultivated genuine support within society. Led by Augusto Pinochet Ugarte, the regime defied the worldwide wave of democratic transitions in the early 1980s even as it confronted a deep economic crisis. Transition in Chile would not occur until 1990, just as planned under the constitution Pinochet had designed. And the democracy that finally emerged from this transition would be covered with Pinochet's fingerprints.

Military unity and strategy coordination characterized the Chilean military regime. Because the institutional design was such that authority was concentrated in the hands of one man and regime investment was high, factions could be suppressed. As predicted by the model, the regime successfully instituted a controlled transition. It set the rules for transition, and the democracy that emerged worked within the institutions the regime had designed. Indeed, it was these institutions that not only made the controlled transition possible, but also allowed Pinochet to maintain the loyalty of the armed forces and to forge a level of stability and certainty in the regime which led its supporters to view it as reliable, especially when compared to its opposition through the mid-1980s.

The Pinochet Regime:
Forging Military Unity Through Suppression

The regime that immediately followed the September 1973 *golpe* that overthrew Allende's Unidad Popular government is best described as collegial. Power was located in the governing Junta de Gobierno and distributed among the army, navy, air force, and Carabinero (Chile's national police force) commanders, each of whom were accorded control over specific cabinet positions. As I have argued, a dispersion of authority in a situation likely to spur regime investment is inherently unstable (as illustrated by the *Proceso* regime in Argentina). But the regime was able to survive because the high level of perceived subversive threat that followed the *golpe* induced military unity, and because many in society had virulently opposed the Unidad Popular government and thus welcomed short-term military rule. By the time the influence of these factors had diminished, Pinochet was well on his way to concentrating power, and by 1978 his supremacy within the regime was unquestionable.

Although this discussion centers on the institutional character of the Pinochet regime, it is important to recognize a characteristic of the Chilean armed forces that facilitated Pinochet's emergence, namely, the historical, social, and political isolation of the Chilean armed forces, especially in comparison to other more interventionist South American militaries. Before 1973, Chile had not approached military rule since the dictatorship of Carlos Ibáñez (1924–31), and interactions with civilians through consultative groups or educational training was practically nonexistent (Nunn 1976). A second feature of the Chilean armed forces that facilitated the emergence of Pinochet (as well as regime investment) was that most officers, and an increasing number of generals, had been trained in the Cold War anti-Marxist tradition. When combined with the isolation of the military, this meant that officers were easily aroused by Pinochet's anticommunist rhetoric (Remmer 1991a, 122–23).

The Concentration of Authority

The concentration of authority in Pinochet's hands is a story of institutional aggrandizement—Pinochet used institutional positions at hand to gain access to other institutions and in this way concentrated authority. This institutional aggrandizement occurred in four steps as Pinochet moved from army commander, to president of the Junta, to president of the republic, and finally, to generalissimo of the armed forces.

Pinochet's limited role in the *golpe* disadvantaged him at the outset in relation to the air force and navy commanders.[1] Air force commander Gustavo Leigh immediately emerged as a potential leader and attracted civilian advisers such as Jaime Guzman. Indeed, it was Leigh who originally established a commission to study constitutional reform. But Leigh's weakness lay in the pluralistic organization of his branch. He encouraged discussion among his generals and allowed a relatively democratic decision-making process to exist at the higher levels. This pluralism weakened him, especially when Pinochet moved to reestablish "absolute obedience" in the army hierarchy. The navy commander, José Torino Merino, was simply taken aback by the autocratic Pinochet and easily overawed (O'Brien and Roddick 1983, 47–48). These factors, as well as the institutional weight accorded to the army by the perception of a subversive threat (Varas 1982, 51), allowed Pinochet to assume the presidency of the Junta de Gobierno.[2] Nonetheless, Pinochet originally assumed the position under the pretext that it would rotate among the service commanders. Not yet strong enough to dominate the regime, he expressed equality with his colleagues in an early press conference: "There was, in reality, a gentleman's agreement. I have no pretension to direct the junta while it lasts. What we will do is rotate. Now it is me, tomorrow it will be Admiral Merino, then General Leigh and after General Mendoza. I don't want to appear to be an irreplaceable person. I have no aspiration but to serve my country" (cited in Valenzuela 1991, 27). At the time, domination would not have been possible. Any move to concentrate power demanded that Pinochet first and foremost assure the loyalty of what would be his primary institutional base of power throughout the regime—the army.

1. Despite Pinochet's argument to the contrary in his book, *El Día Decisivo* (The decisive day), the historical record shows that although Pinochet did not oppose intervention, the navy and air force actually initiated the September *golpe*, with the aid of less senior generals of the army (the *golpe* began in the navy home port of Valparaiso). See Arriagada 1991, 94–101 and O'Brien and Roddick 1983, 37–41.

2. DL27 (September 24, 1973).

In the period immediately following the *golpe,* many senior army officers came forward to express their political beliefs (Arriagada 1991, 102–4). The army hierarchy was weak at this time because the army initiative for the *golpe* had not come from its commander, Pinochet.[3] DL33 (September 21, 1973) helped Pinochet reestablish his authority. This law gave each of the service commanders one year of extraordinary powers over promotions and retirements for the purpose of purging officers associated with the previous government. Within eight months, Pinochet retired six division generals and five brigadier generals, and essentially freed the army of *constitucionalistas.*[4] But the temporary status of this measure demanded that he institutionalize his dominance over the army in other ways. The Consejo de Generales had long played a significant role in the army (Arriagada 1991, 138–41), and although it had given Pinochet a free hand to see the army through the transition period following the *golpe,* in time the generals could be expected to reassert control.

The generals' power had rested in the Officers' Assessment and Appeals Board, which gave them significant control over promotions and retirements. DL33 suspended the traditional functions of the Board and limited the generals to "serving as a consultative body only." Soon, Pinochet established a new body under DL220 (December 24, 1973), the Officers' Extraordinary Assessment Board, to contain the influence of the Consejo de Generales. This Extraordinary Board was entrusted with proposing promotions for colonels and generals, and the Consejo de Generales was limited to rejecting or accepting these proposals. The procedural regulations governing the Extraordinary Board failed to specify a quorum or rules for convening, stipulating only that the army commander was authorized to call a session. In this way, the body allowed Pinochet to usurp powers previously held by the Consejo de Generales. The generals reluctantly accepted the procedure as an emergency measure, but it was later incorporated into the armed forces personnel regulations in January 1977 (Arriagada 1991, 141–45).

DL220 also allowed the army commander to retire colonels, lieutenant colonels, and majors under "special circumstances." Equally important was DL624 (August 26, 1974). This measure removed all outside discretion from promotion and retirement decisions.[5] Moreover, the decree also

3. Arriagada (1991, 95) lists the following generals as probable instigators (1973 seniority rank in parentheses): Major Generals Manuel Torres (5), Ernsto Baeza (6), and Oscar Bonilla (7); and Brigadier Generals Carlos Forestier (19), Arturo Viveros (20), Sergio Nuño (21), Sergio Arellano (22), and Javier Palacios (24).

4. "Chile: General Post," *Latin America,* May 17, 1974, pp. 148–49.

5. Traditionally, outside branches would be given minority representation on appeals boards.

contained a stipulation that all officers with thirty years in service or three years at any set rank submit a letter of resignation, which, if not accepted, would be left pending indefinitely. Because army regulations required all colonels to serve four years at that rank before they could be promoted (five years after 1979), the stipulation effectively meant that no officer could be promoted to general without first submitting his resignation, and that all generals would serve knowing that they could be retired at any moment.[6]

Over time, Pinochet's control over the army increased as officers near his cohort retired. By 1980, twenty-three of thirty-eight generals had commission dates ten years or more after Pinochet's 1937 commission. The age difference had a substantial psychological impact, insofar as newly promoted generals were reluctant to question the decisions of an officer who had been commanding troops at the time of their enlistment. Pinochet's dominance was also extended as he increased the size of the corps of generals and created new prestigious positions within it. With a greater scope of opportunity, officers found themselves eager to demonstrate loyalty and cater to the desires of the individual who controlled their future—Pinochet.

The revisions to army personnel regulations that concentrated authority in Pinochet's hands have been well documented (Arriagada 1991, 123–69). In the period just after the *golpe,* purges and repression of officers known to have collaborated with the Allende government helped Pinochet establish his authority.[7] But it was Pinochet's legalistic maneuvers that secured his dominance in the army. Initial changes drew criticism from the generals, but the perceived subversive threat and their fear that a weakened army hierarchy would give the advantage to air force commander Leigh muted their reactions.[8] And by the time these fears diminished, Pinochet loyalists filled the army ranks.

Securing control of the army allowed Pinochet to concentrate on dominating the Junta. At first he had to deal with a government structure that accorded specific government functions to each military branch. The navy took responsibility for economic affairs, the air force had responsibility for social affairs, the Carabineros had responsibility for agricultural affairs,

6. Arriagada (1991, 145–49) stresses the career instability of officers as a significant contributor to Pinochet's concentration of authority. Another example was a regulation that allowed Pinochet to call any officer into temporary retirement, which, if it lasted longer than three years would result in full retirement. Because all officers assigned to government posts were placed in temporary retirement, at any given time Pinochet had a number of officers uncertain whether they would be called back into active service or retired.

7. "La otra repressión," *Análisis,* April 25, 1988, pp. 33–36.

8. "Chile: Who Rules?" *Latin America,* January 9, 1976, pp. 9–10.

and the army was expected to provide political leadership and lead the subversive struggle. Pinochet realized early on that because military officers inexperienced in rule permeated the regime, consultative committees would be playing a significant role in government, and power would rest in the control of these committees (Valenzuela 1991, 40).

By October 6, 1973, Pinochet organized a consultative committee consisting of army officers. Other Junta members soon recognized the need for such a committee and decided the following month that Pinochet's committee would be used to organize a consultative committee for the Junta itself. Navy, air force, and Carabinero officers as well as civilians were added to create the Comité Asesor de la Junta de Gobierno (COAJ) (Huneeus 1988, 102). To deal with the government workload, the COAJ was divided into five departments: Interior, Foreign Relations, Social Policy, Economics, and Legislation (a juridical division). Junta members were equally empowered to call on the COAJ for advice in their respective areas of responsibility.[9] Nonetheless, because the COAJ was simply an enlargement of a Pinochet committee, army officers dominated the organization.

Already advantaged by the dominance of his appointees, Pinochet began to court all COAJ members, meeting with them often and gaining their trust. Pinochet attracted COAJ members because of their concern over the policymaking process, which they viewed as cumbersome and inefficient when compared to the strong presidential tradition of Chile (Valenzuela 1991, 36). In early 1974 they implemented a campaign to centralize power. They pushed references to Pinochet as "general of the people" in the media, convinced him to stop wearing his impersonal dark sunglasses, dressed up his office, and orchestrated more public appearances. The culmination of this campaign was the lobby for DL527 (June 26, 1974), or The Statute of the Governmental Junta, which reorganized the regime to place greater power in the hands of Pinochet (Cavallo Castro et al. 1990, 29–31).

This small legal step gave Pinochet the foothold required for institutional aggrandizement. Whereas executive and legislative power had previously rested in the Junta as a corporate body, DL527 placed executive power in the hands of the president of the Junta and legislative power in the Junta itself. In addition, the president of the Junta was granted the title "Supreme Chief of the Nation." The stipulation that their tenure could be terminated only through "death, resignation, or any kind of total disability of the incumbent" advantaged all Junta members. But because this stipulation also

---

9. DL460 (May 13, 1974) formally created COAJ. On its early organization, see "El equipo militar," *El Mercurio,* May 2, 1983, p. D2.

applied to the "Supreme Chief," this meant that the Junta could not dismiss him. And the failure of the decree to establish a set tenure for Pinochet increased his autonomy even further.

Leigh stated that the Junta accepted DL527 because the economic, political, and social crisis facing the country required a greater centralization of power.[10] Skillful bargaining also facilitated its passage. Pinochet's concession of Junta unanimity as a requisite to pass legislation weakened executive power, but because he remained a member of the Junta, this same rule granted him veto power over legislation. And although ministers, ambassadors, *intendentes*, and governors were appointed with the "concurrence of the Governing Junta," they held their posts at the pleasure of Pinochet. Finally, previous to the decree, the incongruity between a Junta member's responsibility and relevant cabinet positions hindered each member's authority over his respective areas of responsibility. In a move that facilitated the passage of DL527, the navy received responsibility for the Ministries of Finance, the Economy, and the Central Bank, the air force received responsibility for the Ministries of Education, Housing, and Health, the Carabineros received responsibility for the Ministries of Agriculture and Land Colonization, and the army received responsibility for the Ministries of Defense, the Interior, and Foreign Relations (Arriagada 1991, 16). This was to change, however, for over time, Pinochet weakened the power of the cabinet and placed civilians and army officers in positions previously held by officers of the other three branches.

Pinochet's continued dominance of the COAJ allowed him to dominate legislation. With both the COAJ and the ministers reporting primarily to him, Pinochet determined which laws the ministers would be permitted to present to the Junta. Given that this legislation was in areas in which the ministers had a great deal of expertise and the Junta members very little, Pinochet essentially determined which legislation would become law (Valenzuela 1991, 38). Leigh recognized the connection between Pinochet's dominance of the COAJ and legislation and insisted that he be allowed to appoint more members to important positions. Implementing a technique that he would utilize throughout his rule, Pinochet agreed with Leigh but failed to act on the suggestion (Cavallo Castro et al. 1990, 26–27). An expectant Leigh thus waited as Pinochet consolidated power yet further.

Monopolization of the executive allowed Pinochet to control another institution, the Comisión Nacional de la Reforma Administrativa (CONARA), which worked to decentralize the administration by delegating some

---

10. "Las descrepancias de Leigh," *Ercilla,* July 26, 1978, pp. 8–11.

responsibilities to the regional *intendentes* and governors. The Junta readily accepted decentralization as a response to the centralization that occurred under Allende. But this action ultimately concentrated greater power in Pinochet because such officials held office at his pleasure (Vergara 1982, 91).

Pinochet's first major move after DL527 was DL807 (December 16, 1974), which granted him the title "President of the Republic." The title created distance between Pinochet and the Junta and set him among past Chilean chiefs of state, thereby allowing him to cultivate "retroactive legitimacy" for his authority. Another important step came from DL966 (April 1975), which granted Pinochet full authority over ministerial appointments. But again, it was his control of information through consultative committees that assured his concentration of power. In 1976, DL991 created a legislative commission for each branch, but the COAJ, and Pinochet, remained dominant. In fact, the legislative division of the COAJ was used to create the Secretaría Legislativa for the Junta and coordinate the branch commissions. By 1977, Pinochet established the Estado Mayor Presidencial (EMP) to formalize his control. This body was to act as a "permanent consultant, at the national level, to the president of the republic in all areas of political management of the state and to coordinate information of a consultative character that the chief of state gives to other public organs." All administrative bodies of the state were obligated to give all information or records, as well as technical or administrative aid, requested by the EMP on behalf of the president of the republic. Although the COAJ continued to exist as a member of the EMP and retained its autonomy as consultant to the Junta, the EMP usurped much of its control over information.[11]

By 1977, Pinochet had established his dominance over both the army and the Junta. Nonetheless, his control over the armed forces was incomplete. The centralization of repression under the Secretaría Ejecutiva Nacional de Detenidos (SENDET) in December 1973 and the Dirección Nacional de Inteligencia (DINA) in June 1974 had provided one medium of control early on.[12] Just after the *golpe*, the intelligence and repressive agencies of each military branch worked independently, and repression depended greatly upon local military leaders (Fruhling 1983). SENDET and DINA centralized the repressive activity of the state and undermined the power

11. For an excellent overview of policymaking before 1980, see "Los hombres del Presidente," *El Mercurio,* July 6, 1980, pp. D1–2.

12. The creation of DINA (DL521) relegated SENDET to administrative duties (for example: the holding and identification of prisoners; the collection of statistical information on prisoners; and the dispersion of or information related to aid for financially troubled family members of prisoners). For a sympathetic but informative discussion, see "Así es 'Tres Alamos,'" *Que Pasa,* February 19, 1976, pp. 28–35.

of local military commanders.[13] At the same time, "DINA emerged as the legal and institutional manifestation of the army's security apparatus over all the others" (Arriagada 1991, 17). Although answerable to the Junta as a whole, the dominance of army personnel in DINA allowed Pinochet to control it. With power over the state security apparatus, Pinochet not only extended his control over society but also used the apparatus to collect incriminatory information on and act against rival officers.[14] The August 1977 replacement of DINA by the CNI to assuage international human rights concerns was cosmetic, and in fact formalized Pinochet's existing control by placing the agency under the authority of the minister of the interior (who retained his post at the pleasure of Pinochet).[15]

But despite the power over the armed forces he had because he controlled the security apparatus, Pinochet still lacked one power that every Chilean president had had under the democratic regime—the power to dismiss service commanders. In 1978, this would change when Pinochet gathered all his institutional weight to retire General Leigh.

The 1978 *consulta,* a veritable plebiscite on the Pinochet presidency, reignited Leigh's criticisms of Pinochet. The *consulta* asked the Chilean electorate to express support for President Pinochet in the face of international human rights probes (the ballot read "in the face of international aggression"). Pinochet angered Leigh because he had called the *consulta* without informing the Junta. Leigh saw human rights issues as a concern to be addressed by the Junta. Pinochet answered that as the executive he had two responsibilities—to exercise the normal responsibilities of the executive, and to oversee the development of discretionary faculties. He argued that this second responsibility empowers the executive to find solutions to national problems not found in existing legislation, and to make decisions for the good of the country as he saw fit.[16] The success of the *consulta* thus legitimated a further extension of Pinochet's authority to "discretionary faculties"—an extension of authority that would later be formalized under the constitution of 1980.

Leigh criticized the power grab and called for greater clarity in the allocation of executive, judicial, and legislative powers.[17] Recognizing that the

13. "Honeymoon Over," *Latin America,* January 25, 1975.

14. The "mysterious" deaths of rivals General Oscar Bonilla, Brigadier General Augusto Lutz, and retired General Carlos Prats were likely the work of DINA. For other instances of repression of military officers, see "La otra represión," *Análisis,* April 25, 1988, pp. 33–36.

15. "Fancy Wrapper," *Latin America Political Report,* August 19, 1977, pp. 254–55.

16. "Contra viento y marea," *Hoy,* January 4, 1978, pp. 8–11.

17. "El triunfo de Pinochet," *Hoy,* January 11, 1978, pp. 8–12; "El poder y la libertad," *Hoy,* May 11, 1978, p. 10.

institutional aggrandizement by Pinochet was unlikely to be curtailed, the one-time hard-liner spoke of the need for withdrawal and a credible timetable. When he made these calls in an Italian magazine, Pinochet cried sedition and found the opportunity to oust him from office. As executive, Pinochet first called a meeting of the Council of Ministers to condemn Leigh's statements. Notably, this group of ministers was the first whose entire membership had been appointed by Pinochet, the majority having just arrived in the March 1978 cabinet reorganization (Huneeus and Olave 1987, 137). Armed with this political capital, Pinochet then had the Junta declare Leigh "totally unable to continue performing his duties," and dismissed him using implied powers granted under the Statute of the Governing Junta (DL527) (Arriagada 1991, 36–37).[18] Ten generals retired in solidarity with Leigh, and another eight were forced to retire when the general below them in seniority, Fernando Matthei, was promoted to commander. The result was a completely revamped air force high command, filled with Pinochet allies.[19]

Soon after Leigh's dismissal, Pinochet began to act as the commander in chief of the armed forces, and proclaimed in his annual 1979 presidential address: "The high commanders are responsible for informing their subordinates about matters of government, an obligation that has been assumed by the President of the Republic, in his capacity as Generalissimo of the Armed Forces and the Forces of Order" (translated in Arriagada 1991, 37). From that moment on, the authority of Pinochet was clear. He was commander of the army, president of the republic, and commander of the armed forces. The constitution of 1980 would only formalize the power that was already in his hands. As before, the power grab would be institutionalized later, but once again it was the previous institutional aggrandizement that made such a power grab possible.[20]

Forging Regime Investment

Upon seizing office, the Chilean military began to reform the civilian government. Keeping with the legalistic tradition in Chile, the Junta churned out decrees to authorize these changes in government. Through 1975 the military government decreed an average of 548 new laws annually. Compare this to the 1938–58 average of 346. Many of the Junta's laws were directed

18. Also see "Las discrepancias de Leigh," and "Razones de retiro," in *Ercilla*, July 26, 1978, pp. 8–13.
19. "Pinochet tiene su propio freno," *Ercilla*, August 2, 1978, pp. 8–11.
20. For case studies illustrative of Pinochet's concentration of power, see Chaparro N. and Cumplido C. 1982.

toward administrative changes as it sought to dismantle the massive state created under the Frei and Allende governments. DL6 (September 19, 1973) declared all public services to be under a state of reorganization, and CONARA was created to reorganize and trim government. Thus, while from 1938 to 1958 only 7 percent of Chilean laws dealt with administration, through 1975 this percentage stood at 32 percent.[21] But to accomplish these changes the military had to assume control first and foremost at the peak of government.

DL1, issued the day of the *golpe,* placed executive, legislative, and constituent power in the Junta. Although this decree also formally preserved the judiciary, and DL128 (November 12, 1973) stated that "the judicial power will exercise its functions in the form and with the independence and powers that are established in the constitution," in reality the judiciary complacently allowed itself to be undermined. Article 86 of the 1925 constitution gave the Supreme Court "directive, correctional, and economic supervision" over "all the tribunals of the nation." But the court allowed army and navy Tribunales Militares de Tiempo de Guerra to try cases outside their discretion. These tribunals were even delegated the authority to hear military abuse cases, and responded with a paltry conviction rate of 4.7 percent for the 1973–84 period.[22] The courts themselves became notorious for rejecting petitions to investigate the disappeared and stood idle as the right of habeas corpus was repeatedly violated.[23] And when some courts boldly ruled against the legality of some relatively unimportant decrees, the Junta responded with DL788 (December 2, 1974), which declared that all previous decrees of the Junta were to be considered amendments to the constitution. Finally, the military ensured its dominance over the judiciary by dismissing the Constitutional Tribunal, a body charged with mediating constitutional disputes between the executive and legislature, and by ensuring the complacency of the comptroller general, who in Chile is charged with certifying the constitutionality of government actions.[24]

21. Statistics from "Variaciones de la nueva legalidad Chilena," *Mensaje,* September 1976, pp. 409–14.

22. Of course, most instances of abuse were never even brought to trial. See "La curiosa justicia militar," *Análisis,* September 24, 1984, pp. 27–31.

23. "El poder judicial y las garantias individuales," *Mensaje,* July 1976, pp. 292–301. For an overview of compliant actions by Supreme Court presidents, see "Presidencia de la Corte Suprema y régimen militar," ibid., June 1984, pp. 237–44.

24. "La Contoralía General de la República y las garantías individuales," *Mensaje,* September 1976, pp. 415–25. When Pinochet ordered the 1978 *consulta,* the comptroller general argued that he needed the approval of the Junta. Pinochet responded by replacing him. See "Contra viento y marea," *Hoy,* January 4, 1978, pp. 8–11. For an overview of the duties of the comptroller general, see Iturriaga Ruiz 1983.

The legislative participation of the military extended beyond the branch commanders. The legislative commissions created in 1976 under DL991 consisted of five or six individuals each, and about half were usually military (Huneeus and Olave 1987, 143). As noted, these commissions had little influence on regime policy. Nonetheless, they did draw about ten senior officers into government each year.

Actual regime policy was set in the executive as a result of Pinochet's noted dominance of consultative committees. At first, policy was formed primarily in the cabinet, which included military personnel throughout the regime. From 1973 to 1987, 169 individuals found themselves in cabinet positions. Ninety-five (56.2 percent) of these individuals were military personnel, while 74 were civilians (43.8 percent). Of course, these numbers mask changes over time—military cabinet participation decreased from 67 percent in the 1973–78 period, to 58 percent in the 1978–83 period, and to 31 percent in the 1983–87 period (Huneeus and Olave 1987, 134–35). But the decrease should not be interpreted as a sign of decreasing military participation in government, a move that might decrease regime investment. Rather, it was a sign of greater consolidation by Pinochet. Pinochet's most trusted confidants remained military, but over time they were less likely to be found in the cabinet, and more likely to be found in his personal consultative committees. Indeed, after 1980, cabinet members became more likely to begin statements with "I am personally of the opinion" rather than speaking in the name of the president, thus demonstrating a deterioration of their political capital.[25] By shifting the locus of important policy decisions to his committees, Pinochet retained the support of important officers but kept them out of the public eye to ensure that none of them would seek to become a rival.

Consultative committee changes beyond those already mentioned continued as Pinochet consolidated his power. In December 1981, the COAJ was renamed the Comité Asesor Presidencial (COAP) when it was merged with CONARA, thereby deleting all references to the Junta. In January 1983 COAP was then merged with the EMP to become the Secretaría General de la Presidencia (SGP). The SGP remained the most powerful institution under Pinochet through the remainder of the regime. Under law 18,201, the SGP was charged with "counseling [the president] in the exercise of his administrative and co-legislative functions, and in other cases in which it is required, providing him with the information necessary for the adoption of the decisions he advances." To fulfill its duty, the organization

25. "Los hombres del Presidente," *Que Pasa,* January 1985, pp. 8–11.

was given broad powers. It could obtain "all information and records that it deems necessary" from "all ministers, servants, and organs of the civil administration of the state, their business, societies, or institutions that have the support, participation, or representation of the state." All information requested was to be turned over "opportunely," and when information was requested from a ministry, the order was given directly to the minister under the heading "by the order of the President of the Republic."

Under the secretary-general himself, three management chiefs divided the labor of the SGP. The first management chief concentrated on executive functions and prepared candidate lists for minister, subsecretary, ambassador, and other high-level positions. The second management chief concentrated on legislative functions and reviewed laws before they were delivered to the Junta for approval. The third management chief led the División de Estudios, which united officers and civilians for the study of specific issues that did not correspond to the expertise found in the technical ministries. In 1988, eighty-seven individuals, most of them military, worked under the SGP, and in practice many more were involved in "comisiónes de servicios" as temporary consultants (Huneeus 1988, 101–6).

The placement of military confidants in powerful but low-profile positions was characteristic of Pinochet's centralized rule. Officers were found throughout government, but direct military participation was subordinated to the concentration of authority so that Pinochet could both avoid politicization in the armed forces and maintain a strong link to it. Hence, the decrease in high-profile military involvement in government did little to diminish regime investment. Indeed, the approach to military participation allowed Pinochet to employ a variety of Machiavellian instruments to assure his dominance over both the military and government, and to cultivate in officers their own personal stake in the regime (Remmer 1991a, 113–50; Valenzuela 1991, 30–35). For example, appointments to positions as university rectors, ambassadors, mayors, subsecretaries, diplomats, and administrators of state corporations provided political prestige and often extra income, and thus were used as carrots for officers. Pinochet was especially adept at placing retired officers in these positions to maintain yet another linkage with the military while avoiding its politicization (Huneeus and Olave 1987, 151–55). Second, he frequently rotated officers in government to keep them from accumulating political status. Also, his requirement that officers take temporary leaves of absence drew them back to the service to ensure advancement there. The leave requirement also ensured that officers in government answered to the government hierarchy first rather than to their immediate military superiors. Similarly, he placed officers from different branches in the same bureaucracy also to isolated them from their branch peers. Finally, he used classic divide-and-rule tactics to maintain his authority. To undercut ministerial power, he placed officers as subsecretaries under the most important civilian-held cabinet positions (e.g., economics, finance, and foreign relations) but gave them longer terms of office. He did the same with military *intendentes* and governors. These officials retained their command positions, but Pinochet created vice command positions to deal with the load of both military and government duties. This practice allowed him to reward his appointees by giving them prestigious command positions and at the same time to hinder their accumulation of power.[26] To summarize, even with officers schooled in political science, economics, international relations, and law at the Academia de Guerra, a government source could note in 1985: "To explain (an officer's) position, one must not look to their studies but to their loyalty to Pinochet."[27]

The significance is thus—regime investment, when combined with a concentration of power, is not necessarily equated with politicization. With the aforementioned techniques, Pinochet demonstrated that the potential for politicization when officers are placed in government could be neutralized, while the positive aspect of participation (for the regime), regime investment, could be enriched. The skill with which Pinochet infused the government with officers explains why when *El Mercurio* (the dominant newspaper in Chile) ran a tenth-anniversary story on the most influential political figures in the unabashedly *military* regime, only two of the nine individuals mentioned were military.[28]

Indeed, the military domination of government should not lead us to neglect the important, albeit secondary, role played by some civilians. This was especially the case in economic policy, where from 1975 to 1984 a group known as the Chicago Boys acquired a relatively free hand to implement their neoliberal economic policy (the Chicago Boys were so named

26. See "Safe in the Saddle," *Latin America*, May 7, 1976, pp. 141–42. A final example of divide and rule tactics was the overlap of bureaucratic responsibilities. For example, in 1976 ODEPLAN, CONARA, COAJ, and the Ministry of Health all studied health policy. See "La operación salud … y cómo cambió en el camino," *Que Pasa*, January 29, 1976, pp. 30–34.

27. "La economía con uniforme," *Que Pasa*, March 1985, pp. 12–14.

28. "Sus figuras y su historia," *El Mercurio*, September 11, 1983, p. D2. The list excluded Pinochet. The two officers were Colonel Ernesto Videla, an important actor in the Beagle Channel dispute with Argentina, and General Santiago Sinclair, the president's secretary general at the time. Notably, Sinclair was included not so much in his own right, but as a representative of "all those military consultants that have exercised, *in spite of their anonymity,* a decisive influence on the President" (emphasis mine).

because of their links to the University of Chicago, which many of them attended. For details, see Valdés 1989). Nonetheless, their role was strictly subsidiary. As I note below, they gained power only insofar as Pinochet associated them with his consolidation of authority. When their policies began to fail, he diluted their influence. Other than the Chicago Boys, civilians were allowed to dominate some technical bureaucracies (the Ministries of Justice, Education, Health, and Housing) simply because of their expertise. In the political realm, civilian participation was strictly advisory, and usually ceremonial. The most visible was the Consejo de Estado, which consisted of former presidents and government officials, "distinguished" citizens, and retired generals. This body was charged with counsel over legislation. DL575 (July 10, 1974) created the Consejos Regionales de Desarrollo and the Comités Asesores de los Gobernadores Provinciales to provide the *intendentes* and governors, respectively, with civilian consultants, and DL1289 (December 12, 1975) did the same for mayors (who themselves were often civilians) with the creation of Consejos de Desarrollo Comunal (Sanders 1978, 3).

A 1988 study by Huneeus illustrates military infusion under the Pinochet regime. Huneeus divides top government posts into political, economic, and technical sectors (the president and Junta are excluded). Of the 102 total posts in the political sector, 71 (69.6 percent) were filled with officers and 31 (30.4 percent) with civilians. In the economic sector, 43 individuals filled 49 posts. Twenty-four (56.3 percent) were military, and 19 (44.4 percent) were civilians.[29] Only in the technical sector, where 83 individuals filled 86 posts did the civilians dominate. Only 20 (24.1 percent) of these individuals were officers. The gravity of this military involvement is indicated by the effect that participation in government had on the military. For example, in 1988, 24 of the 57 commanders of regiments or schools doubled as governors. Also, in 1985, 35 percent of active-duty generals held government posts, and in May 1988 this figure rose to 44 percent (Remmer 1991a, 132).

In sum, military personnel permeated the Pinochet regime. Nonetheless, one should acknowledge that military involvement was subordinated to Pinochet's concentration of authority. While military participation in government often tends to politicize the forces, when it is combined with a concentration of authority this participation can be molded so that politicization is neutralized, while a linkage to the military remains.

---

29. A discussion of military participation in the economic sector can be found in "La economía con uniforme," *Que Pasa,* March 1985, pp. 12–14.

Strategy Coordination, Political Success, and the Founding of New Economic Agendas

The Development of a Viable Political Program

The constitution of 1980 represented the establishment of a clearly defined political program for the Pinochet regime. This raises the question of why the regime waited seven years to establish one. To answer that the regime first needed to subdue society would be inaccurate. The regime had society under control by 1974, and repression actually decreased over time. The answer lies in the gradual establishment of military unity and, more important, strategy coordination under the auspices of Pinochet. Before their establishment, Chile looked like most military regimes—factions grappled for power and the regime lacked a clear political program because no faction was strong enough to impose its own.

The first reference to a political program can be found in DL1, issued on the day of the *golpe*. In it the regime defined as its objective the "restoration of Chilean values, justice, and the broken institutionality." Many groups who had supported the intervention expected the call for restoration rather than fundamental changes and long-term rule. This call was echoed in unofficial talk among army generals who envisioned military rule only to November 4, 1976, the date Allende's tenure was set to expire (Cavallo Castro et al. 1990, 12–13). As noted, this period saw Leigh's rise as an early potential leader, and many superior army officers moved forward to express their political beliefs.

The probability of long-term rule became more apparent by early 1974.[30] In March, the regime made its first attempt at a long-term political program with the publications of *La Imagen de un Chile Nuevo* and *Declaración de Principios del Gobierno de Chile*.[31] Nonetheless, both documents did more to muddle than illuminate. The first calls for the establishment of an effective social democracy, the eradication of poverty, and the projection of Chilean culture and politico-economic thought internationally. It presents a vision of a new Chilean culture based on solidarity, equality, fraternity, and the freedom for all to develop their potential and asserts that such a culture would allow the pursuit of these objectives under a new constitution. It claims that the call for a new constitution transcends previous calls for reform, but it also explains that the mission of the armed forces is to "restore the enduring values of our nationality" and insists that political

30. "Honeymoon Over," *Latin America*, January 25, 1974.
31. *La Imagen* can be found in *El Mercurio*, March 10, 1974, pp. 40–41; *Declaración de Principios* can be found in ibid., March 13, 1974, pp. 21, 23.

parties are not to be abolished but only to remain in recess. More important, the document is vague on issues of political institutionalization and policy. The only references to institutionalization are found in declarations on the virtues of administrative decentralization and a commitment to organizing youth, women's, business, neighborhood, and other social groups under the Ministry of the Interior. Moreover, *La Imagen* stresses that the fundamental organizing base would not be a political organization but a societal organization—the family. The document attempts to define government policy in sections devoted to industry, fishing, mining, forestry, agriculture, housing, education, labor, social security, and social organization. But each passage simply reiterates the call for depoliticization in government so that all individuals can realize their own potential. Finally, the fact that all this is covered in a document that fills just over one newspaper page illustrates the lack of definition.

The *Declaración de Principios,* issued just three days later, goes beyond the calls found in DL1 and *La Imagen*. Reconstruction explicitly replaces restoration as the operative expression. A "change in the mentality of Chileans" is touted as a central goal, as are new institutions based on decentralization, a "technified" society ruled by rationality rather than ideology, and the depoliticization and autonomization of intermediary groups to allow for true social participation. But the document still leaves the regime without a clear political program. The document advances the portentous statement that "the armed forces' management of government is not set to a timetable, because the work of moral, institutional, and material reconstruction requires a profound and prolonged action." But it then adds, "Nonetheless, although the time is not set, the Junta will opportunely hand over political power to those the people elect through universal, free, secret, and informed suffrage." The document then moves back to the hard line, stating that after elections, "the armed forces will then assume the role of institutional participation that the new constitution assigns to it," and "charge itself with the duty of national security, in the broad sense this concept has in the present era." This duty is held to entail "the inspiration of a new and grand civil-military movement." Notably, the document concludes with an obvious concession to military nationalists in the face of growing economic liberalization. Economic growth is marked as a central goal, which "must be accompanied by constant action on the part of the state to transform this wealth into social progress."[32]

---

32. On the *Declaración de Principios,* also see "Consideraciones sobre la Declaración de Principios del Gobierno de Chile," *Mensaje,* May 1976, 164–70.

The ambiguity in the political program promoted at this time is illustrated by the continued hopes of the Christian Democrats, who had supported the *golpe* in the expectation of short-term rule. After the publications of *La Imagen* and *Declaración de Principios,* the party issued an official statement recognizing the government as "a military dictatorship of indefinite duration, whose mission is to create a new political, economic, and social order for Chile," but still called for cooperation with it, defining as its strategy the "achievement of an understanding of political forces and social democrats *with the armed forces* for the restoration of democracy" (emphasis mine) (Ortega Frei 1992, 50). Faced with an undefined political regime, the Christian Democrats would maintain their faith in short-term rule through 1974 as they continued to press the government to clarify its political intentions. By January 1975, party president Patricio Aylwin would even concede that although a "time of dictatorship" may be necessary, he could not imagine it lasting over five years.[33]

Another move toward institutionalization came in late 1975.[34] A new document, *Objetivo Nacional de Chile,* was published that proposed norms of action to implement the goals specified in *Declaración de Principios.* But the document did little more than introduce the nebulous idea of "admissible ideological pluralism" and reiterated the values of a technified society. Late 1975 also saw the creation of the legislative commissions under the Junta and the Consejo de Estado, but as noted, these institutions had little power. Nonetheless, the expectation that these changes marked the beginning of greater institutionalization helped to produce a temporary image of stability.[35]

By 1976 it was obvious that the regime was unable to promulgate a clear political program, and that debate over such a program was growing within the regime (Garretón 1989, 137). The consequent vacuum led the military to institute the national security doctrine as a political ideology. The doctrine had worked to unify the military, so the thought was that it could be extended to society. It would complement the economic shock treatment enacted in April 1975, which shattered economic groups and atomized society, and would legitimate long-term military rule. The three *actas constitucionales* decreed in September 1976 represented the manifestation of national security as a political ideology. *Acta* no. 2 (*acta* no. 1 established the Consejo de Estado in December 1975) decreed that the

33. The progressive alienation of the Christian Democrats through 1975 is documented in "El Partido Democrática Cristiano y la dictadura militar," *Chile-America* 4 (1975): 4–7.

34. "Novedades políticas e institucionales," *Que Pasa,* January 8, 1976, pp. 6–7.

35. "Rewriting the Constitution," *Latin America,* July 16, 1977, pp. 222–23.

actas have authority over the constitution and placed sovereignty "essentially in the nation," but qualified this placement with the assertion that sovereignty "is exercised in observance of the *actas constitucionales* of the Junta de Gobierno and all provisions which have been or may be enacted under it." It also reiterates the values originally expounded in *Declaración de Principios. Acta* no. 3 abolished the chapter on constitutional guarantees in the constitution of 1925 and sanctioned new rights and duties. Basic rights of life, liberty, and expression were guaranteed, but were highly qualified by national security concerns, such as the prohibition of all doctrines deemed contrary to the family or the regime, or that propose violence or are founded upon the principle of class struggle. The national security status of the regime is most visible in *Acta* no. 4, which established various regimes of emergency under which the rights granted by the previous *acta* could be suspended, and broadened the emergency powers of the state.[36]

The *actas constitucionales* were a military solution to the recognized lack of a political program. They effectively abrogated basic constitutional rights and legalized the restrictive activity not only of the national government but also of *intendentes*, governors, and municipal leaders (MacHale 1979). Situating the *actas* as amendments to the constitution interfered with the work of the constitutional commission (an entirely civilian group), as did the references to a new constitution.

The extensive powers accorded to the state under the *actas* increased the isolation of the regime as it became obvious to many civilian supporters that they would play at best a subsidiary role in it. The Christian Democrats became even more aware of this as it saw a final purge of its members who had remained in government.[37] By March 1977, the regime reached the peak of its isolation with DL1697, which ordered the dissolution of all parties currently in recess. The decree placed even the right-wing parties under the same legal status as Allende's Unidad Popular. With his strongest criticism of political parties yet, Pinochet stated that it was "necessary to put an end to traditional political parties" and went on to herald the *actas* as the basis of the future regime and the Consejo de Estado as an imminent legislative base. "Political parties," continued Pinochet, "will come to be currents of opinion that only influence through the moral quality of their members and the seriousness of their doctrinaire proposals and practices,

---

36. *Constitutional Acts Proclaimed by the Government of Chile* (Santiago: Junta de Gobierno, 1976). For a contemporary analysis, see "Actas Constitucionales del 11 de Septiembre de 1976," *Mensaje*, October 1976, pp. 463–65.

37. "Wishful Thinking," *Latin America Political Report,* February 11, 1976; "Pride Goes Before a Fall," ibid., March 18, 1977, pp. 81–82.

and not as groups that illegitimately seek to hold power to their own particular benefit."[38] Three members of the constitutional commission resigned
to protest the now undeniable move away from the restorative character of
DL1 (Maira 1988, 20).

Soon criticism from previously supportive civilian groups, political parties, the United States and other governments, and the Catholic Church
engulfed the regime. The increased criticism from the Church especially
upset the navy, as the most conservative and Catholic branch. Consequent
moves by the navy to distance itself from the human rights abuses being
committed by the regime seemed to preface a major division in the armed
forces.[39] But by this time, Pinochet's authority was fairly well concentrated.
The institutions that would allow for stable military rule were not quite in
place, but what was in place effectively allowed him to review the situation
and take the initiative to resolve it. He did this on July 9, 1977, at Chacarillas, in a speech that would be considered the first real political program of
the regime.[40]

The Chacarillas speech set a three-stage timetable for the establishment
of new institutions and withdrawal. The first stage, recuperation, would see
the promulgation of new *actas constitucionales* and a high military presence in government. The second stage, transition, would begin in 1981 and
see greater government participation by civilians. A new legislative chamber would consist of individuals appointed by the Junta to represent
regions or regional organizations (two-thirds of all members) and prominent citizens appointed by the president (one-third of all members). This
legislature would have the power to draft laws and ask for revisions of
existing laws through the presidency, but the Junta would have veto power
over any matter viewed as a national security threat. The Junta would
retain constituent power, and the president would retain executive power.
The final stage, consolidation, would begin in December 1985 and would
see the popular election of those legislative members previously appointed
by the Junta (the traditional political parties would remain banned). The
legislature would then elect one of its own to the presidency for a six-year
term. This period would also see the promulgation of a new constitution.
The next president would then be popularly elected in December 1991 in a
new democracy described as authoritarian, protective, integrative, technical,

38. "Cámara legislativa incluirá integrantes de generación popular," *El Mercurio*, March
19, 1977, p. A1.
39. "Tea and Sympathy," *Latin America Political Report*, July 17, 1977, pp. 213–14.
40. "Etapas y fechas en vía institucional," *Hoy*, July 13, 1977, pp. 10–11.

and as allowing for authentic social participation. This new regime was labeled the New Institutionality (Sanders 1978).

The New Institutionality Pinochet called for at Chacarillas marked a break with the *actas* and their idea that national security could serve as a political ideology (Garretón 1978). The move saved the regime from its increasing isolation and responded to calls for democracy. But what was important here was that the move came from Pinochet alone. The Junta was never consulted.[41] Had Pinochet not emerged as the dominant player in the government to initiate strategy coordination toward society just as he had toward the military, the regime would have remained isolated, consigned to propagate its alienating national security doctrine as a political ideology.

Remmer (1980), who meticulously describes the demobilization of society, accurately summarizes the 1973–78 period. She notes how the steady erosion of internal and external support paralleled demobilization and presents a bleak future for the regime. Of course the regime successfully pressed on for twelve more years and recovered much of the support it had lost. Hindsight presents us with a greater understanding of what really happened. Demobilization did weaken and isolate the Chilean regime of 1978, but the Chilean regime of 1978 was also a different regime than that which had ruled for the previous five years. Knowing what we know now, we can see that it was an error to project the future of the regime based upon its past actions. In 1978 the regime truly became the Pinochet regime, and at that moment gained the institutional basis for strategy coordination that would allow it to rule with confidence for twelve more years.

Hence, 1978 marked the emergence of strategy coordination, under the direction of Pinochet. With the *consulta* having further consolidated his authority, Pinochet made another move to monopolize the emergent political program. In a presidential discourse on April 5, 1978, he announced that the phase of transition would not be governed by *actas*.[42] Instead, the timetable for the completion of the new constitution would be advanced. Hindsight again allows us to analyze what was really happening. We know that the Chacarillas plan was never implemented, and that it was most likely a move to sidetrack calls for democratization as well as to deflect the increased pressure from the United States in reaction to the Letelier assassination (Arriagada 1991, 33). The real political significance of Chacarillas

---

41. "Los primeros cuatro años," *Hoy,* September 7, 1977, pp. 10–11.
42. "Verdad y realidad en la creación de una Nueva Institucionalidad política," *Realidad,* September 1979, pp. 35–44.

was as an indicator of the emergent consolidation by Pinochet. And when this consolidation seemed assured after the *consulta,* Pinochet replaced the Chacarillas plan with the proposal for a new constitution.

The Chacarillas plan was born under a regime in crisis. Indeed, the Chacarillas plan ultimately would have undermined Pinochet. It called for a new president in December 1985, and thereby created uncertainty as to who would fill this role. This would have undoubtedly increased factional-ism in the armed forces as officers looked to other potential leaders. The new constitution, an unfinished document, would arise from the newly developed institutions and allow Pinochet to implement his own personal political program. Again, with hindsight we can document the dismissal of Chacarillas as a political program. Just three months after the speech at Chacarillas, Pinochet was asked if he would aspire to the presidency when the time came. He answered, "When the moment arrives, I will already be so old, that I do not believe that I will be a candidate for President of the Republic."[43] Knowing that Pinochet would later attempt to extend his pres-idency to 1997, we must infer that Pinochet was not thinking of December 1985 as "the moment." Finally, the death of Chacarillas became abundantly clear in April 1979 when Pinochet denied its essence, the establishment of a timetable. He asserted: "We have never established timetables, only goals for the present management of government, since the work to complete is profound and involves a change in the beaten and choked mentality of the social body."[44]

Indeed, Chacarillas again reared its head in the original draft of the constitution, but Pinochet promptly removed it. The constitutional com-mission had finished its work in October 1978.[45] The draft then went to the Consejo de Estado for review. When it left this body in June 1980, the constitution called for a transition period of five years. During this time, Pinochet would continue as president, and a legislative body consisting of deputies appointed by the Junta and senators appointed by Pinochet would be established. After the transition period, general elections would be held for president and all the legislative seats. But this proposal never made it past the Pinochet-dominated Junta or Pinochet himself. Instead, the final draft called for a transition period of eight years, with Pinochet as presi-dent, after which a plebiscite would be called to legitimate his rule for an additional eight years. Thus the vision of civilian rule by 1985 was replaced

43. "Avances en el proceso," *Hoy,* October 1, 1977, p. 8.

44. "Aclaraciones y clase magistral," *Hoy,* April 11, 1979, pp. 6–8.

45. For an overview of the constitutional commission, see "Primicias de la nueva Consti-tución," *Ercilla,* August 23, 1978, pp. 8–12; also see Bertelsen Repetto 1988.

with the prospect of a Pinochet presidency that would last until 1997 (Huneeus 1985, 48).

The constitution of 1980 was passed in a September 11, 1980, plebiscite and fixed the direction that Pinochet's strategy coordination was to take. Because the document allowed Pinochet to remain as army commander even if he lost the 1988 plebiscite, the loyalty of army officers was assured well into the future (Huneeus 1988, 98). The diminished role of the Junta under the new constitution led some to view it as creating an even more authoritarian regime.[46] The twenty-nine transitory articles that would be in effect during the transition period confirmed these suspicions. For example, transitory article no. 24 allowed the president to suspend individual rights and specifically granted him the powers to place arrestees in unofficial detention centers, to restrict the right of assembly, and to exile citizens when "a state of danger of disturbing the eternal peace" was declared. Unsurprisingly, such a declaration was made through supreme decree 359 on March 11, 1981, the date the constitution went into effect.[47] Criticism of the constitution is best summed by the Grupo de los 24, a group of opposition lawyers organized to critique the constitution:

> The new constitution rejects representative government, ignores the natural and exclusive right for people to govern themselves, denies ideological pluralism, establishes a political and militaristic regime, implants a true presidential caesar, minimizes the parliament, transforms the constitutional tribunal to a bureaucratic organism more powerful than Congress and lacking popular representation, authorizes the unlimited power of the armed forces, subordinates the validity of fundamental human rights to the arbitration of government and identifies itself, economically, with the individualistic capitalism of the free market.[48]

From 1981 to 1989 Pinochet was to rule over a regime that was entirely under his command. Four main areas composed the hierarchy beneath him: the economy, civil administration, military political power, and the armed forces. Under the economic hierarchy, one found the Ministry of the Economy, the Ministry of Finance, the Central Bank, CORFO, CODELCO, and

---

46. "El ideal es la democracia," *Hoy*, January 10, 1979, pp. 15–17.

47. "Disposición vigesimocuarta transitoria," *Mensaje*, July 1981, pp. 320–23. For a summary of each transitory article, see Rickard and Brown 1988.

48. "La nueva Constitución: opinion del 'Grupo de los 24," *Mensaje*, May 1981, pp. 171–73. For a thorough discussion of the constitution, see Maira 1988.

ODEPLAN. The civil administrative hierarchy (military personnel were present, but not dominant here) contained the remaining ministries under the Cabinet Council. Here, the Ministry of the Interior acted as a super-ministry with both administrative and policy-oriented sectors beneath it. Under the administrative sector one found the governors, the Consejos de Desarrollo Regionales, mayors, and the Consejos de Dessarrollo Comunales. Under the policy-oriented sector, one found ONEMI, the Human Rights Commission, the Secretariat of National Employment, the Secretariat of Social Development, and the ministries. The military political power hierarchy was Pinochet's true power base and was divided into four sectors. The intelligence sector contained the SGP with its executive, juridical, and working-group divisions. The CNI, the chiefs of the emergency zones, the attorney general, and the *tribunales militares* comprised the repressive sector. The General Secretariat of the Government organized the final two sectors, the propaganda sector and the sector designed for political organization. Under the former, one found the National Director of Social Communications, the Presidential Secretariat of the Press, the Department of External Dissemination, the Department of the Press, the World Agency, National Radio, National TV, and the Department of the Nation. Under the latter, the Directorate of Civilian Organizations organized the Secretariats of Youth, Women, Workers, and Religion. Finally, in the armed forces hierarchy Pinochet placed himself as commander in chief.[49]

The constitution of 1980 thus sanctified the political program that had been developing slowly but surely under the regime—Pinochet would rule, and he would rule absolutely.

Political Management During the 1982–85 Economic Crisis

Economics was consistently subordinated to politics under the Pinochet regime. An examination of the changes in the economic program allows us to view Pinochet's direction of strategy coordination in progress. The neoliberal program of the Chicago Boys, initiated by the shock treatment of April 1975, was allowed to continue only as long as it advantaged Pinochet. Ironically, the Chicago Boys had their strongest connections in the navy at the time of the *golpe* (O'Brien and Roddick 1983, 37–53). Navy commander Merino had authority over economic policy at this time and

---

49. An excellent chart of the hierarchy under Pinochet can be found in "Así gobierna Pinochet," *Análisis*, August 15, 1988, pp. 4–7.

coordinated their ascent. But because the early effects of the economic program were so devastating, Merino shied away from accepting responsibility for their appointment (Arriagada 1991, 20). By the time the program began to show positive effects in 1977, Pinochet was in a position to identify himself with the policy and take credit for its success. He found acceptance of the Chicago Boys easy because they served his political interests. The implementation of market discipline atomized society and broke the back of labor, and thereby complemented the power he had gained as chief of the security apparatus. Likewise, the economic policies undermined General Leigh's plans to cultivate support among labor groups (Zapata 1979).[50] And although the program alienated traditionally powerful business sectors advantaged by import substitution policies, neoliberalism allowed Pinochet to draw new allies from the financial sector and nontraditional exporters (Silva 1993).

Neoliberalism had a tremendous impact. From 1973 to 1981, the number of state businesses decreased from 533 to 12. In the public sector, employment was reduced by 25 percent. Also, the state reduced its role as a financial intermediary. In 1970 the Banco de Estado controlled 51.9 percent of investments (note that this measure predates the statizing policies of the Allende government), but by 1981 it controlled only 26.4 percent. Finally, by 1979, tariffs were set at a uniform 10 percent in a country previously recognized as a rigid adherent to import substitution policies (Fernández Jilberto and Polle 1988; Walton 1985). These policies produced irreversible changes in the Chilean economy and society and yielded enough advantages to foster support for Pinochet.[51] But by late 1981, the economy began to sour. In November the government intervened in eight financial institutions that had made use of support credit from the Banco de Estado, and by the end of the year, the current account deficit stood at U.S.$4.8 billion. The crisis worsened in January, when the government intervened in five banks, liquidated three, and took direct supervision over two. These ten banks represented 64 percent of private capital reserves. The financial crisis soon translated into rising unemployment, which rose from 8.1 percent in September 1981, to 15.9 percent in March 1982, and held at 19.9 percent in June and November of 1992. The impact was especially

50. Leigh himself expressed this in an interview. See "El ideal es democracia," *Hoy,* January 10, 1979, pp. 15–17.

51. For a sympathetic examination of economic policy to 1979 by regime supporters, see "Política económica: 1973–1979," *Realidad,* October 1979, pp. 23–30. For a more objective analysis, see Andrés Fontaine 1993 and Foxley 1983.

devastating in some sectors. From July to December 1982, the unemployment rate stood at an incredible 62 percent for construction and at 30.1 percent for industry (Huneeus 1985, 53).

The regime's inability to anticipate the crisis drew widespread criticism from the business community and thus threatened the societal linkages that were key to strategy coordination.[52] But at first, these criticisms were of little significance in the absence of a viable opposition. Pinochet realized his position of strength and soon raised the stakes with an April 1982 cabinet shuffle that increased the presence of hard-liners.[53] The message was clear: support existing policy, or be prepared for a resurgence of anticapitalist nationalism. In the past, such aggressive moves had worked to subdue the business sector because it lacked an alternative program. This void can be traced to the pre-1973 experiences of businesses. Before Allende, many businesses thrived off a state that regularly intervened in the market on their behalf. But the Allende government transformed the definition of an interventionist government so that intervention became equated with the threat to private property. The deeply entrenched interventionist economic program of Chilean business was suddenly unacceptable. This inability of the business community to formulate another coherent economic program in the wake of the *golpe* had opened the space needed for the Chicago Boys (Campero 1984, 127–33).

Pinochet was betting on a quick economic recovery. But rather than economic recovery, Pinochet soon found that he faced a politically recovered business sector. Over time, neoliberal ideas gained some favor in previously protected businesses. This was partly because many of those businesses most in need of intervention or opposed to neoliberalism had already failed under the new program. But the ability of many surviving businesses to accept the new economic program made them central actors in socioeconomic development, a role that historically had been monopolized by parties or workers (Campero 1984, 299). The growth of this approval led the previously protectionist businesses to develop a coherent economic program known as pragmatic neoliberalism. The program called for high exchange rates, justifiable protection from unfair competition, a reflationary monetary policy, low interest rates, debt relief, a more inclusive policymaking process, and sectoral policies to aid export promotion, construction projects, and

52. "The Craftsmen Move Up the Military Ladder," *Latin American Regional Reports: Southern Cone*, November 14, 1981, p. 4; "Businessmen Angry about Handling of Fiscal Deficit," *Latin American Weekly Report*, April 9, 1982.

53. "Military Men Threaten Chicago Boys," *Latin American Weekly Report*, April 23, 1982, p. 5.

agricultural development. United under the Confederation of Production and Commerce (CPC), many of these businesses were suddenly prepared to go beyond criticism and move into the opposition with their new economic program (Silva 1993, 550).

Through 1982 and into 1983, Pinochet's support was clearly ebbing. In June 1982, business confidence was further shaken when the regime reneged on a promise and devalued the *peso*. By early 1983, the crisis had clearly reached the middle classes. Growing political protests and criticisms from former right-wing politicians led one foreign newsmagazine to conclude, "The President has never looked so unstable as he does at the moment."[54] The signal that the economic crisis had truly become a political crisis came on May 11, 1983, when the Confederation of Copper Workers organized a massive protest that was joined by groups calling for political change. A second National Day of Protest occurred on June 14. Pinochet remained defiant with subtle calls for a civil-military party to support the regime and the passage of a number of populist measures.[55] July 1983 would see the revival of party opposition, when the Christian Democrats, the Radicals, a sector of the Socialist Party, and two other political parties formed Alianza Democrática (AD) to coordinate their opposition.

July 1983 also saw the rise of veiled threats from the CPC that they would join the opposition if their economic program were not accepted. It was now clear to Pinochet that the business sector could no longer be bullied. He would have to restore his societal linkages if he were to maintain strategy coordination. A three-pronged strategy followed. On one front, he increased the repression of labor and the social movements involved in the monthly National Days of Protest. On another front, he permitted partial liberalization, which allowed the middle classes to express their beliefs more freely in the press and heightened political activity in student federations and professional groups (Huneeus 1985). Moreover, the government drew the AD into an official dialogue, ostensibly to negotiate a transition. But the partial liberalization served to increase infighting among the parties as they sought to reestablish their bases, and the dialogue was a charade from the start. Just over one month after supposedly granting the new interior minister Sergio Jarpa authority to meet with the parties, Pinochet declared, "One can develop a dialogue and search for consensus [with the opposition], but our course has been plotted — we are the armed forces and we are

---

54. "Speculation Mounts over Pinochet," *Latin American Weekly Report,* February 11, 1983, p. 2.

55. "Pinochet Digs in His Heels," *Latin American Weekly Report,* June 10, 1983, p. 7; "Pinochet's Greatest Test," ibid., June 17, 1983, p. 5.

going to follow it to the end."[56] Nonetheless, the AD retained its faith in the dialogue until November 1984.

On the final front, Pinochet appeased the newly invigorated business sector with policies that conformed to their pragmatic neoliberal agenda. The April 1984 cabinet changes initiated these concessions. Luís Escobar and Modesto Collados, two recognized pragmatic neoliberals, assumed the portfolios of Finance and the Economy, and were allowed to implement the new program. Collados soon routinized triennial meetings with members of the CPC, and in May 1984, the Social and Economic Council was established as a new advisory body under Pinochet and filled with leaders of peak business associations. The business sector was also granted greater access to the legislative commissions under the Junta, and was allowed to participate when the National Commissions for Commerce and Industry were created in the Ministry of the Economy in early 1986 (Silva 1993, 552–55).

The plan worked to near perfection. On November 6, 1984, Pinochet declared a state of siege, effectively ending both the dialogue and the partial liberalization. The action infuriated all political parties and allowed the AD to increase its cooperation with parties to the left and right in talks sponsored by the Church. The result of this widened cooperation came in August 1985 with the *Acuerdo Nacional para la Transición a la Plena Democracia*. The accord pronounced a commitment to democracy, attempted to define the type of democracy valued by the signatories, and called for a number of immediate measures to ease the transition (e.g., the formulation of electoral registers and an electoral law, ending the states of exception, and the legalization of party activity). At first, the document seemed to present a real threat to the regime. It had the strong backing of the Church, and General Matthei spoke favorably of it (Ortega Frei 1992, 277–92). But it soon became clear that the document was all bark and no bite. The parties had grasped the strength of the regime and drafted the document as a sign of moderation. Its signatories refused to support the document with popular pressure and even filled it with basic guarantees for the economic program. Lacking both negative and positive incentives, the reinvigorated regime ignored the *Acuerdo Nacional*. The Left-Center split soon resurfaced, when the former argued that the document did not contain a great enough rupture with the regime. The reemerging split provided just the opportunity that the government was looking for, and it pointed to this split as an indicator of vagueness in the document, which it summarily

56. "El camino está trazado y FF.AA lo harán cumplir," *El Mercurio*, October 4, 1983.

rejected in December 1985. The pragmatic neoliberal business sector, potentially tempted by the economic concessions in the accord, found the regime's decision easy to accept. Continuing divisions in the parties made the opposition an uncertain alternative. And with a regime now committed to its policies, the business sector had no reason to oppose it.

The parties' response was to return to a strategy of popular mobilization. But the protests had lost their momentum, and the growing violence associated with them was alienating the middle classes. The result was clear—Pinochet was victorious. His support base was reestablished among the business classes, and he even managed to deflect the repression associated with the protests onto the Carabineros and use this to increase his control over them.[57]

Many studies look to party infighting as the source of the failure to capitalize on the economic crisis (for example, Livermore 1988, Loveman 1986, Oxhorn 1994, and Ortega Frei 1992). In sum, a divided opposition provided an uncertain and thus nonviable alternative, which led the business classes, the military, and eventually some in the middle classes to accept the Pinochet regime as their only hope for stability. But such society-centered analyses miss the integral role that institutions played in allowing the Pinochet regime to survive the crisis. The judgment of an alternative is inherently relative, and thus depends upon the status of the regime. Even at the peak of the crisis, Pinochet was able to maintain army unity and thus present an image of stability (Agüero 1988). Also indicative of regime stability was the character of the party divisions, which were more tactical than goal oriented. That is, although most parties could agree on the end of the regime as a goal, they diverged over how to utilize popular mobilization, negotiation, and the placation of the business sector. If the Pinochet regime had been weak and collapse had seemed imminent, unity on goals would have been more important than unity on tactics and the opposition would have found it easier to present a united front. Finally, the tools accorded by the institutions surrounding Pinochet played an integral role during the crisis in so far as his domination of them gave him great flexibility in redirecting regime policy. Although Pinochet originally refused to budge from the neoliberal program, when it became obvious that only a change to pragmatic neoliberalism would maintain a support base in society, the appropriate changes were made. Also, because the regime institutions

---

57. "Carabineros de Chile," *Mensaje*, November 1984, pp. 418–23. In August 1985 Pinochet forced Merino to retire because of Carabinero complicity in the March 1985 murders of three communists and gave the CNI a greater oversight role over Carabinero activities. See "Carabinero: la nueva etapa," *El Mercurio*, August 11, 1985, p. D1.

conferred such a fundamental role to Pinochet, he was able to present himself as the quintessential chief of state, and thereby above and beyond the economic crisis—which was defined as a governmental problem and attributed to the bureaucrats involved in day-to-day policymaking. Thus the economic crisis was portrayed not a crisis of the regime, but a crisis of policy, easily resolved with the appropriate reshuffling of bureaucrats.[58]

Controlled Transition in Chile

In the final stages of the formulation of the constitution of 1980, the Junta as well as his own advisers convinced Pinochet to include a provision calling for a 1988 plebiscite to determine the presidency for the following eight years. At the time, this seemed to be a safe strategy to increase regime legitimacy. Pinochet had won a 1978 plebiscite, the constitution itself was slated for plebiscite, and popular opposition to the regime on a grand scale had yet to occur (Agüero 1991). But the 1982–85 opposition movement changed things. Although liberalization during this period was limited, it initiated a learning process that would lead to a unified opposition strategy—to play within the rules of the game established by the regime and incrementally work toward democracy. With the 1988 plebiscite looming in the future, the opposition set aside most of their differences and collectively concentrated on the plebiscite as a medium for democratic transition. This strategy was formally geared toward the plebiscite on February 2, 1988, when thirteen opposition parties signed the "Agreement for the NO" (Garretón 1991).

Following constitutional provisions, the Junta named a candidate on August 30, 1988, and set the plebiscite date for October 5. Although there was some internal opposition, few were surprised to learn that Pinochet had been nominated. In what was generally considered a free and fair election, NO won with a vote total of 54.7 percent to the YES total of 43 percent.[59]

Pinochet seemed surprised by the outcome. There were reports that he had planned to declare an emergency and overturn the election, but the

58. Huneeus (1985) makes this point and cites a 1983 poll in which 55.5 percent of respondents refer to "the government in general" as responsible for the crisis while only 4 percent refer to "Pinochet directly."

59. For an overview of the 1988 plebiscite, see International Commission of the Latin American Studies Association to Observe the Chilean Plebiscite, "The Chilean Plebiscite: A First Step Toward Redemocratization," *LASA Forum* (Winter 1989).

Junta and right-wing civilian leaders persuaded him not to. Pinochet finally admitted that he had lost the battle, but he was determined not to lose the war. By the end of 1989, open elections for president and the two chambers of Congress would be held, but Pinochet would do his best to conserve the limited democracy called for by the constitution of 1980 (Arriagada 1992).

Pinochet's strategy from the plebiscite loss of October 1988 to the transfer of power in March 1990 can be divided into three areas: the extrication of government personnel, the *leyes de amarre* (the binding laws), and the constitutional reform battle. Although Pinochet found success in each of these areas, it is interesting to note that relatively greater success was found in the extrication of government personnel and the *leyes de amarre* than in the constitutional reform battle. These differences can be directly linked to the importance of institutions to the regime. Specifically, the development of the former two could be contained largely within the government apparatus. On the other hand, constitutional reform played itself out more in the public arena, and thus opened itself up to greater societal influence.

As noted, the Pinochet regime was a military regime in the fullest sense of the term. The imminent retreat of the military high command from top government posts demanded the extrication of military personnel at the lower levels of government. Here, Pinochet wasted little time exercising his legal right to request resignations from government officeholders (Tomic 1988, 288).[60] The extrication of military personnel created a new support base for Pinochet. Thousands of soldiers who had been trained to govern were deprived of their positions, and thus could personally identify with the blow dealt to Pinochet by his defeat at the polls. This cultivated a nationalist hard-line current in the Chilean forces. This current would provide Pinochet the allies he would need against the opposition even after he withdrew from office and would solidify his strength with respect to the other services.[61]

In the effort to release civilian government officials who wished to campaign in the upcoming election, Pinochet faced a problem created by his own constitution (articles 44 and 46), which prohibited government officials from running for office for two years after their resignation. Now that Pinochet was not assured of winning the presidency, this provision would hamper his attempt to contain the opposition. To overcome this obstacle,

60. Also see "Presidente Pinochet designó a siete intendentes civiles," *El Mercurio,* November 18, 1988, p. A1; "Designados 28 nuevos gobernadores," ibid., December 2, 1988, p. A1; "Jefe del Estado designó a 67 nuevos alcaldes," ibid., December 29, 1988, p. A1.

61. For reports of the hardline junior military officers, see *Foreign Broadcast Information Service—Latin America,* December 28, 1988, p. 33; "Ejército expresan su malestar por ofensas a S.E.," *El Mercurio,* April 11, 1989, p. A1; and "Officers Issue a Second Document," *Latin American Weekly Review,* May 4, 1989, p. 5.

Pinochet simply had the Junta pass a measure that eliminated this provision for the upcoming election, thus allowing hundreds of government officials to run under right-wing parties.[62]

One more move in this area dealt with the Supreme Court justices. Although they would retain their positions in the transfer of government, many were growing old and Pinochet presumed that a younger crop would better ensure loyalty into the future. With this intent, Pinochet used the powers of the executive office to offer the sitting justices generous retirement packages so that he could replace them with younger judges sympathetic to him.[63]

Paralleling Pinochet's success in the extrication of government personnel was perhaps the most devious of his moves during the transition—the *leyes de amarre*.[64] We can broadly include in this class all those laws promulgated by the Pinochet regime with little or no negotiation that were designed to restrict the actions of the incoming government. For example, state corporations were privatized to limit government leverage in the economy, tenure was amplified in the public sector to restrict appointments, and some government expenditures were bound into the future (Angell and Pollack 1990; Huneeus 1997; Joaquín Brunner 1990).[65]

Many of the restrictions were written into the constitutional organic laws, which require a supermajority of four-sevenths in the Congress to reform. For instance: the Central Bank Organic Law transferred many economic policy powers from the president to the Central Bank Committee; the Congressional Organic Law prohibited congressional investigations into government actions previous to March 11, 1990; the Political Parties Organic Law and the Electoral Organic Law gerrymandered districts against the left and established the binomial electoral system, which allocates two seats per district and requires a party to double the vote of the second place party to gain both seats and thereby checks single-party dominance in government; the Public Administration Organic Law decentralized policy implementation from the executive and debureaucratized government; and the Education Organic Law secured Pinochet supporters in university rector positions.

62. "Despachada ley sobre distritos y pactos electorales," *El Mercurio,* April 12, 1989, p. A1.

63. Ley de Jubilación (law 18,805); "Dos renuncias en la Corte Suprema," *El Mercurio,* August 10, 1989, p. A1.

64. Genaro Arriagada, "Un estado militar dentro del estado democrático," *La Epoca,* October 22, 1989.

65. Also see "Ricardo Lagos reiteró que se derogarán leyes 'arbitrarias,'" *El Mercurio,* August 13, 1989, p. C9; "Aylwin: 'seguir legislando es inaceptable,'" ibid., January 20, 1990.

But the most controversial of the organic laws was the Armed Forces Organic Law. During the constitutional reform negotiations, it was agreed that many of the issues surrounding the armed forces would be incorporated into an organic law, which would be drawn up in later negotiations. By October 1989, the political parties were surprised to learn that the Armed Forces Organic Law was being drafted without their consultation. Indeed, Patricio Aylwin stated that he had learned about the early draft of the law only by reading the newspaper.[66] By December, the Pinochet government agreed to listen to party concerns, and the Concertación de Partidos por la Democracia (a coalition of left and center parties) left the negotiations satisfied. But to their dismay, when the law was made public in January it contained unexpected changes that disregarded agreements reached in the negotiations.[67] The power of the president to remove the service commanders, for example, a primary concern of the Concertación since its inception, was missing from the finished version. Other provisions that increased the autonomy of the armed forces included the following: presidential power over retirements, promotions, or assignments of upper-level officers was confined to lists provided by the service commanders; the military budget was forbidden to drop below 1989 real levels; the service commanders were to formulate their respective budgets; and the president was to be considered the commander in chief only in time of war (during peace, this duty is divided among the service commanders).

Other government statutes designed to bind the hands of future democratic governments included the 1978 Amnesty Law, which prohibits the prosecution of human rights violations committed between September 11, 1973, and March 10, 1978. The armed forces were also empowered by a number of antiterrorist and security measures that granted broad faculties to the armed forces in antiterrorist actions and largely maintained the considerable jurisdiction of the military courts (Loveman 1991). Finally, Pinochet made a number of direct threats to the next government, which had the purpose of outlining the boundaries of what he considered to be appropriate civilian action in the area of civil-military relations. The clearest and most detailed of these threats was made on August 23, 1989, in a ceremony that celebrated the sixteenth anniversary of his becoming commander in chief. In his speech, Pinochet stressed that the new government would have to

66. "Aylwin criticó envío a la Junta de estatuto sobre fuerzas armadas," *El Mercurio,* October 19, 1989, p. C5.

67. "Se rompe la confianza," *Analisis,* January 22, 1990, p. 6.

1. respect the constitutional functions granted to the armed forces;
2. maintain the immovability of the service commanders;
3. ensure the prestige of the military institution and its security from political attacks;
4. prevent class struggle;
5. fully apply the law against terrorism;
6. respect the function of the National Security Council;
7. uphold the amnesty law;
8. refrain from meddling in defense policy, training instruction of military personnel, military jurisdiction, budgetary provisions, and the established system of promotions, retirements, and appointments.[68]

When Pinochet made these statements, he looked to the democratic opposition with all the authority accorded to the president of the republic and generalissimo of the armed forces, and he did so with the confidence that most of these stipulations were already covered in a legal web that would entangle the next government.[69]

Although the extrication of personnel and *leyes de amarre* worked in Pinochet's favor, he found less success in the battle to preserve the constitution. Immediately after the plebiscite loss, Pinochet was adamant in his assertion that there would be no changes to the constitution.[70] By November 17, Pinochet did mention that the constitution "as any human work, can be improved," but still rejected the opposition's primary reform demands.[71]

But Pinochet met resistance to his intransigence even within his own government and from right-wing politicians. The other members of the Junta indicated publicly that they might accept limited reforms. By December, the Renovación Nacional published a list of proposed reforms, and the Unión Demócrata Independiente followed suit in January (Geywitz 1991, 26–27, 32–34).[72] Pinochet still refused to budge, declaring in February: "We will

68. "Lo que esperan las FF.AA.," *Ercilla,* August 30, 1989, pp. 8–10.

69. Pinochet's position as generalissimo granted him the devoted respect of many in the armed forces, especially the army, during the transition. This was significant because the more obstinate Pinochet acted, the more regime opponents criticized him, and the more regime opponents criticized him, the more the army supported him in the face of such criticisms. In their view, criticizing Pinochet was the same as criticizing them. The peril of this situation for the opposition is obvious. See "Ejército expresa su malestar por ofensas a S.E.," *El Mercurio,* April 11, 1989, p. A1. For similar expressions from air force commander Merino, see "Aylwin es un obstáculo para transición pacífica," ibid., June 28, 1989, p. C4.

70. "Se cumplirán todos los pasos constitucionales," *El Mercurio,* October 10, 1988; "The Right to Coup," *Report on the Americas,* September/October 1988.

71. *Foreign Broadcast Information Service—Latin America,* November 18, 1988, p. 40.

72. "Hamilton pide acuerdo de la Junta y sectores políticos," *El Mercurio,* November 2, 1988, p. C2.

talk about constitutional reforms only when the various provisions of the constitution are fully in effect and we can fully appreciate both its good and bad aspects."[73] But with the above pressures and statements within his own administration that dialogue on constitutional reform might be forthcoming, Pinochet caved in and on March 11, 1989, the eighth anniversary of the constitution, outlined a number of reforms.[74] By late April, the government had proposed nineteen reforms. Viewing them as insufficient, the Concertación quickly rejected them. Pinochet reacted briskly, withdrawing the proposal and announcing the end to all dialogue on constitutional reform. At this point, reform adherents in the government again swung into action. General Matthei was the most outspoken Junta member, and Interior Minister Carlos Cáceres played an important role in mobilizing government personnel. Outside the government, Renovación Nacional leader Sergio Jarpa worked to bridge the gap between the Concertación and the government.[75]

In less than one month, negotiations were reopened, and a list of fifty-four reforms were drawn up for a July plebiscite. The more important reforms included an increase in the number of elected senators from twenty-six to thirty-eight; the elimination of article 8, which placed ideological limits on political activity; a restraint on the capacity of the National Security Council to express its opinion on policy only to the president and the Constitutional Tribunal;[76] the addition of one civilian (the comptroller general) to the National Security Council to balance the representation of civilians and military personnel; the incorporation into the constitution of international human rights treaties signed by Chile; and relaxation of the procedures for constitutional reform (Geywitz 1991). Supported by both the government and the Concertación, the plebiscite won a easy victory on July 30.

The constitutional reform battle is especially intriguing because of the role that government actors played in pressuring Pinochet. How was it that regime cleavages could play such an important role in a system designed to

---

73. *Foreign Broadcast Information Service—Latin America*, February 9, 1989, p. 43.

74. "Eventual reforma constitucional sería punto de discusión política," *El Mercurio*, November 16, 1988, p. C1; "Pinochet Says He Will Pick the Man," *Latin American Weekly Review*, March 9, 1989, pp. 4–5; "Pinochet ordenó estudiar cambios constitucionales," *El Mercurio*, March 12, 1989, p. A1.

75. "Opposition Rejects Reform Proposals," *Latin American Weekly Review*, May 18, 1989, p. 9; "General Matthei lamentó interupción de dialogo," *El Mercurio*, May 7, 1989, p. C3; "Constitution Will Be Reformed in July," *Latin American Weekly Review*, June 15, 1989, p. 3.

76. This body is entrusted with overseeing the sovereignty of the constitution and mediating constitutional conflicts among state organs. Of its seven members, three are appointed by the Supreme Court, two by the National Security Council, one (who must be a lawyer) by the president, and one by the senate. See Ribera Neumann 1987.

subordinate both military unity and strategy coordination to the authority of one man? Any response to this question must take into account the fact that the constitutional reform battle was not much of a defeat for Pinochet. The final reforms did not vary substantially from those he had proposed in April—the Concertación itself viewed them as far from path breaking (Geywitz 1991, 167–70). Indeed, one could argue that the reform process taken in its entirety was ultimately a victory for Pinochet to the extent that it helped legitimate the transition and isolate the radical Left (Cuevas Farren 1989). Recognizing this, the existence of cleavages becomes almost irrelevant because in the end, the Pinochet formula won out (of what significance are cleavages if they do not weaken the government?). We should also note that Pinochet's disappointment over the results of the plebiscite and his fear that a new government might undo seventeen years of work led to his bullheaded opposition to constitutional reform. Other government officials, recognizing constitutional reform as a prudent tactic, convinced him over time that reform would be to the advantage of his agenda in the longer run. In this sense, the cleavages were drawn only on a tactical basis and closed in a short time.

Notwithstanding these qualifications, the fact is that constitutional reform did trouble Pinochet. But this is consistent with the expectations that follow from a high level of regime investment. Moreover, of the three areas, constitutional reform best escaped the purview of government institutions. The magnitude and uncertainty surrounding the issue engendered debate within society. And the opposition, well staffed with intellectuals and constitutional scholars, was prepared to cultivate this debate and maintain popular interest in it. Issues engendered in the other two areas, such as judicial retirement proceedings, central bank autonomy, or the specifications of electoral laws, simply were not as interesting as the open idea of constitutional reform, and thus made it more difficult to rouse public pressure for negotiations over them. Thus, Pinochet was able to shelter such issues within the government where his institutional position would give him control.

Pinochet's success in extricating military personnel from government, passing the *leyes de amarre,* and containing constitutional reform, did well to guarantee that the March 11, 1990, inauguration of President Aylwin would be more a change of administrations than a change of systems. The Pinochet regime had promulgated 4,637 laws, which the new democracy had inherited.[77] The new democratic president, Patricio Aylwin, would have

---

77. "Màs de 4 mil leyes aprobó la Junta en 16 años de gobierno," *El Mercurio,* March 6, 1990, p. C3.

to face constitutional provisions that accorded the armed forces a role as "guarantors of the constitution" and imposed their presence through the powers granted to the National Security Council, the designated senators, and an organic law that legalized a great deal of autonomy for the military in political matters.[78] Legal reform was of course an alternative, but Pinochet ensured that it would not be viable by stipulating supermajorities (two-thirds for constitutional reform and four-sevenths to reform the organic laws), imposing the binomial electoral system with nine designated senators[79] to dampen the impact of parties able to garner overwhelming majorities of the vote, and placing supporters in the Supreme Court and Constitutional Tribunal. In 1990, democracy was reestablished in Chile, but a defiant and powerful Pinochet remained. Indeed, just after the transition Pinochet often appeared in public under a banner that read "misión cumplida."

Conclusion

The Chilean case features both military unity and strategy coordination. Military unity was largely the result of Pinochet's ability to create a solid hierarchically organized institutional apparatus with himself at the top, combined with his capacity to foster regime investment in the military through both the allocation of government positions and rhetoric that identified the military with regime institutions. While regime elites were less than unified in the years immediately following 1973, unity developed as Pinochet aggrandized institutions and used his authority to suppress dissent.

By 1978, it was clear that Pinochet was the leader of the regime, and the government could now work to develop strategy coordination. Political linkages to society were integral to the evolution of a political program, as indicated by both the involvement of right-wing constitutional scholars in the drafting of the 1980 constitution and the supportive role played during the transition by the Renovación Nacional and Unión Demócrata Independiente. Without such linkages, the regime would probably have remained mired in the national security ideology advanced by the *actas constitucionales*. The development of the economic program also illustrates the importance of societal linkages, and the capacity of Pinochet to manipulate these

78. For interpretations of the duties granted to the military by the constitution from the military's point of view, see Molina Johnson 1990 and Canessa Robert 1992.

79. Six were designated by Pinochet and three by the Supreme Court. See *Constitución Política de la República de Chile*, Article 45, p. 46.

linkages. The incorporation of the neoliberal economic policies formulated by the Chicago Boys allowed the regime to assert a coherent economic program of its own and set the parameters of debate for regime opponents. Most important, the program clearly identified with significant economic groups (indeed, it helped create them) in the form of the financial sector and nontraditional exporters. And when the economic program fell into crisis, the regime was able to successfully shift its linkage to the pragmatic neoliberal business sector, represented by the CPC. Only a military regime unharried by politicization or factionalism from the military institution, and with sufficient communication with societal groups could be expected to direct such a reorientation. The change in the economic program, like the origination of a coherent political program, was a clear indicator of strategy coordination.

4

The Argentine *Proceso:* Politicization and Regime Collapse

The struggle against subversion characterizes
and conditions all and each one of the
government measures adopted at all levels.
—General Albano Harguindeguy

In early 1976, Argentina could be described as nothing other
than chaotic. Political deadlock, a government judged legitimate by few, and rampant terrorist actions by right-wing
death squads and guerrilla groups had thrown the country
into upheaval. Given the circumstances, it should come as
no surprise that a significant number of social organizations,
political parties, and citizens welcomed military intervention. Although some of this support waned when the new
government announced plans for long-term military rule,
the opportunity to cultivate the remaining support base was
there. Nonetheless, in seven years the self-designated *Proceso de Reorganización Nacional* would find itself riddled
with internal cleavages and completely isolated from society. Inept and stubborn, the regime would withdraw from
rule in a collapse.

I argue that the skid toward collapse can be explained by
the institutional design of the *Proceso* regime. With institutions that fed regime investment and dispersed government
authority, the *Proceso* quickly fell victim to military disunity. Thoroughly politicized, the regime found that strategy coordination remained a distant goal, as did controlled

transition. And because of regime investment, this regime could not be satisfied with a balanced transition. Incapable of a controlled transition, and averse to a balanced transition, the regime pressed on until its disunity became overwhelming and pushed it toward collapse. For the *Proceso*, the Malvinas invasion, which was supposed to have rallied the Argentine people to support the extension of the regime well into the future, epitomized this obstinacy. Although the sound defeat in the Malvinas was the immediate cause of the collapse of the regime, this analysis will show that the fate of the *Proceso* was fixed much earlier by the design of regime institutions.

The dispersion of authority and level of regime investment in the *Proceso* were reflected in the institutional roots of military disunity and politicization, which effectively foreclosed all possibility of strategy coordination. Military leaders fought among themselves, shunned societal input, and ultimately found themselves unable to establish a political project or to implement a coherent economic program. Although failure in these areas was obvious, the investment of the regime encouraged it to press on. This inability to face failure led to the collapse of the regime, which even as it was collapsing remained completely isolated from society and preoccupied with the still-unresolved issue of military unity.

The *Proceso*: Disunity Through Politicization

There was little institutional change during the *Proceso*. Army, navy, and air force personnel filled and partitioned government offices at all levels and were equally represented in the supreme organ of the regime, the Junta Militar. The August 1978 designation of the president as a "fourth man," separate from the Junta Militar, did increase the authority of this office, but the balance of power was already so heavily tilted toward the Junta Militar that this increase did little to reverse the overall dispersion of authority. The only real movement from the collegial rule, the three-month withdrawal from the Junta Militar by the air force and navy after the June 1982 Malvinas defeat, was too brief and too late to alter the trajectory of the regime significantly.

The Dispersion of Authority

The Argentine armed forces approached military rule in 1976 with the memory of the *Revolución Argentina* still fresh in their minds. The 1966–73 regime was yet another failure in the series of military interventions that had punctuated Argentine history. The solution, it was surmised, would be to divide the government among the services.[1] In this way, it was assumed, each would be equally responsible and thus more prone to compromise than conflict (Fontana 1987, 45–46).[2]

The *Estatuto para el Proceso de Reorganización Nacional* (March 24, 1976) and law 21,256 (*Reglamiento para el funcionamiento de la Junta Militar, Poder Ejecutivo Nacional y Comisión de Asesoramiento Legislativo*) comprised the foundational documents of the regime. These documents established three institutions to lead the *Proceso:* the Junta Militar, the Legislative Consultation Commission (Comisión de Asesoramiento Legislativo, or CAL), and the president. The Junta Militar consisted of the service commanders. It could not meet outside the presence of any member, and although regulations stated that decisions would require only a majority (unanimity only to appoint or remove the president), there was always a strong effort for unanimity (Fontana 1987, 30 n. 40). The CAL was created "to exercise powers of legislative consultation (to the president) as a representative of the armed forces."[3] To ensure that it represented the armed forces, each service was authorized to appoint three members from their own ranks to this nine-member body.

The president, of course, could not mirror the armed forces as the other two institutions did. The army initially secured that office for a member of their service by reasoning that as the most powerful service, this would best serve the "war against subversion." The army's institutional weight allowed it to hold the office through the entire *Proceso*. Nonetheless, the services divided the ministerial,[4] secretarial, and subsecretarial positions, as well as a number of administrative positions, of the executive branch, among themselves.

The constitution was used as a base from which to define the powers of each institution. The president was granted all the executive and legislative

1. During the *Proceso,* the high command constantly emphasized the lack of personalism in the regime. The following statement by army commander General Roberto Viola at a 1976 press conference is indicative: "The '*Proceso de Reorganización Nacional*' is the institutional response of the armed forces.... Consequently, it is devoid of any type of personalism" (Lazara 1988, 229).

2. Although each force came to view division as a medium for cooperation, navy commander Emilio Massera initially imposed the idea. When first approached on the idea of a *golpe* by the army in January 1976, Massera linked navy support to the equal division of government (Vásquez 1985, 20).

3. Article 3.3.2.1, law 21,256.

4. Initially, the army received Labor and Interior, the navy received Social Welfare and Foreign Relations, the air force received Justice and Defense, and civilians were appointed to Education and Economy.

powers authorized in the constitution, minus those powers related to military matters,[5] and minus the power to appoint Supreme Court members, the attorney general, and the general prosecutor of the Office of Administrative Investigations. The Junta Militar usurped all of these powers.

As a consultative body and not a legislative body proper, the CAL did not have the authority to legislate. Rather, the CAL would accept legislation and identify those pieces held to be of "transcendent significance." The body would deliberate on such legislation and had the authority to veto it when initiated by the president. In reality, the CAL was not the deliberative body described in the foundational documents. With their superior officers in the Junta Militar, the CAL was more of an extension of this body than an independent entity (Vásquez 1985, 47). Its role became essentially limited to establishing the order in which laws were promulgated.[6] But as an institution that placed more military personnel in government and found itself divided among the services, the body served to deepen the dispersion of authority along service lines.[7]

The Junta Militar, as called for by article 1 of the *Estatuto*, was the "supreme organ" of the *Proceso*. Although the president was invested with both executive and legislative powers, his subordination to the Junta Militar was designed to ensure that the equal representation of the armed forces would not be upset. The Junta Militar appointed the president and had the authority to dismiss him. Moreover, the Junta Militar's duty to "supervise the completion of the basic objectives and concurrent policies during the entirety of the *Proceso*"[8] entailed a strict oversight role over the president. The separation of the office of the president from the Junta Militar in August 1978[9] was matched with the creation of the Comité Militar. Consisting of the president and Junta Militar, it was given responsibility for all matters of national security and was designed to institutionalize consultation from the Junta Militar in this area. Finally, the Junta Militar itself was granted legislative roles through two processes—by the initiative of

5. The power to act as commander in chief of the armed forces, declare war, declare a state of siege, or supervise military promotions and assignments.

6. "Sin proyectos para la CAL," *La Opinión*, December 1976, p. 12.

7. Each service independently established the term of office for their CAL members, and its presidency (determined by the Junta Militar) was rotated annually (de Dromi 1988, 2:215).

8. Article 1.4.2, law 21,256. The "basic objectives" of the *Proceso* are listed under another document that I will discuss later.

9. Before this time, General Jorge Videla was both president and, as army commander, a member of the Junta Militar.

any one of its members, and in its role as arbitrator when the president and the CAL disagreed on policy.[10]

We can see that the institutional design called for by the foundational documents of the regime dispersed authority, primarily along service lines. While most governments might be ideally portrayed as a pyramid with a political leader at the peak, the *Proceso* could best be portrayed as three nearly equal pyramids, each of which independently extended deeply into the government and had as its peak a service commander in the Junta Militar. But there was also a sense in which authority was dispersed vertically, especially within the army. This occurred over time mainly as the result of internal repression.

In the negotiations before the *golpe,* General Luciano Benjamín (Third Army Corps commander) had army commander Jorge Videla agree to allocate extensive authority to the corps commanders after the *golpe* to assist the antisubversive campaign (Vásquez 1985, 28). Although the other two services also involved themselves, the army accepted primary responsibility, with the country divided into five zones each controlled by a corps commander. These zones were further divided and placed under the responsibility of infantry and cavalry brigade commanders, who in turn divided these subzones and placed them under regimental and battalion commanders. These officers had direct authority over about 340 fully staffed clandestine detention centers (Pion-Berlin 1989a, 102–3). Along with this repressive bureaucracy, the corps commanders were also granted the authority to establish special war councils (*consejos de guerra especiales estables*) to try cases involving violations of the antisubversive laws (de Dromi 1988, 2:234).[11]

Control by the Junta Militar over the repressive activities of the corps commanders was more formal than real.[12] To justify the unprecedented arrests and the decrees that allowed for these arrests, the government

10. For a contemporary report on the dominance of the Junta Militar, see "Argentina: Low Profile," *Latin American Weekly Review,* August 11, 1978, p. 246.

11. Laws 21,264 and 21,461. The authority of the councils was extended under laws 21,268 (covering the creation and transportation of arms or explosives) and 21,272 (covering crimes against military personnel). Equivalents to the army commanders in charge of repression in the navy and air force had the same authority. Also see "Créanse consejos de guerra y severas penas por atentados," *La Prensa,* March 25, 1976, p. 5.

12. This is not to imply that neither the members of the Junta Militar nor the president approved of repression, but that the precise application of repression was largely beyond their control. Their toleration of, and often direct involvement in, repression, however, is well-documented. See *El Libro de El Diario del Juicio* (Buenos Aires: Editorial Perfil, 1985).

Table 1   Presidents and *Junta* Members in the *Proceso*

President	Tenure
Jorge R. Videla	(March 1976–March 1981)
Roberto E. Viola	(March–December 1981)
Horacio Tomás Liendo (interim)	(November–December 1981)
Carlos A. Lacoste (interim)	(December 1981)
Leopoldo Galtieri	(December 1981–June 1982)
Reynaldo Bignone	(July 1982–December 1983)

Junta members*	Tenure
Jorge Videla, Emilio Massera, Orlando Agosti	(1976–1978)
Roberto Viola, Armando Lambruschini, Omar Graffigna	(1978–1981)
Leopoldo Galtieri, Jorge Anaya, Basilio Lami-Dozo	(1981–1982)
Cristino Nicolaides, Rubén Franco, Augusto Hughes	(1982–1983)

* Because members of the *Junta Militar* succeeded each other in accordance with their respective service regulations, turnover was slightly staggered among the force commanders. Each commander is grouped with those two commanders with whom he spent the greatest time in office. One important disjuncture that ought to be noted is that Galtieri's tenure began in December 1979.

constantly alluded to discretionary powers granted to the executive in a state of siege.[13] Legal procedures related to habeas corpus and norms of due process were ignored. These "discretionary powers" filtered down the hierarchy, deteriorating lines of responsibility and encouraging a sense of impunity in the security personnel. Moreover, the character of many of these laws was conducive to a vertical dispersion of authority. Because many of these repressive laws criminalized opinions, beliefs, and affinities rather than physical acts as crimes, they were readily open to interpretation at the lowest administrative levels (Groisman 1984; Spitta 1983, 80–82).[14] Thus, the corps commanders had both massive bureaucracies at their disposal and ample latitude to use their authority.[15]

The vertical dispersion of authority significantly influenced the *Proceso*. Still, the horizontal dispersion of authority along service lines was the greater obstacle for any moves toward a concentration of authority. The characterization of the regime as an *escalafonocracia* (government of the *escalafon militar*—the military promotion list) is accurate (Lazara 1988, 236). Because

13. The state of siege was in effect until October 28, 1983 (decree 2834/83).
14. For example, law 21,528 allowed the arrest of persons revealing a "rebellious position." See Groisman 1984, 67.
15. On the autonomy of the security forces, see "Argentina: Martial Airs," *Latin America*, April 16, 1976, pp. 125–26, and "Argentina: Deeds Speak Louder than Words," ibid., June 4, 1976, pp. 170–72.

of the explicit attempt to institutionally represent the armed forces, it is no surprise that the *Proceso* cannot be identified with any single individual. Across time, it was led by seven presidents and four juntas. Their rotation prohibited any movement toward a personalization of power.

Regime Investment

Upon taking power, the military moved quickly to replace civilian public officials with military officers. Like the dispersement of authority, this action was a direct response to the experience of the armed forces during the *Revolución Argentina,* when the military felt isolated from the government, yet was held responsible for its actions. The direct participation of the armed forces, it was assumed, would guarantee support for the government from the armed forces (Fontana 1987, 45–46).

The *Acta para el Proceso de Reorganización Nacional,* publicly issued on the day of the *golpe,* dismissed the president and executive staff, governors, vice governors, federal intervenors, the National Congress and the provincial congresses, the Supreme Court and the provincial superior tribunals, the general secretary of the nation, and the secretary of the treasury. It was the first move by the military to place its personnel in government. With the exception of the congressional branches, which were simply dissolved as institutions, and the courts, which were filled with sympathetic judges,[16] military personnel filled these posts under laws 21,273 and 21,257.

The distribution of government posts among active military personnel, retired military personnel, and civilians was weighted heavily toward the first. Just after the *golpe,* the members of the Junta Militar, the president, the cabinet, the secretaries and subsecretaries of the president, the members of CAL, intervenors in communication mediums and private businesses administered by the state, and union intervenors were active officers. Retired officers were mainly confined to provincial governorships, and civilians assumed roles chiefly as Supreme Court members, secretaries of state, mayors, and presidents of state businesses and banks.[17] Active military personnel

16. The judiciary was effectively neutralized as an institution until about the time of the Malvinas defeat in June 1982. See Groisman 1984 and Groisman 1987. Law 21,279 established the following hierarchy for judicial rulings to follow: (a) the "basic objectives" established by the Junta Militar; (b) the *Estatuto;* and (c) the National Constitution (de Dromi 1988, 2:209–10).

17. See "La cúpula cívico-militar," *Carta Política,* June 1976, p. 32. The article also notes that most civilians were economists, lawyers, businessmen (especially rural businessmen), and administrators with links to the 1962–63 and 1966–73 military governments. Notable was the lack of union or political leaders.

would remain dominant for the duration of the regime, although retired officers and civilians would make gains in some areas.[18]

Administrative posts held the greatest number of military personnel in government. Recalling the capacity of union organizations to mobilize politically, hundreds of military officers were stationed as federal intervenors in unions (Abós 1982, 7). And with strong nationalist sentiments in the military to maintain the size of the state, and the mutual distrust among the services which made each reluctant to allow privatization in the areas allocated to them, the number of military personnel in administrative positions was not greatly affected by the regime's neoliberal economic program.[19] Another indication of military involvement in administration is given by the Comisión Nacional de Responsabilidad Patrimonial (CONAREPA).[20] CONAREPA was tasked with, among other duties, collecting the assets of individuals and businesses guilty of corrupt activities or assisting subversion, and placing intervenors in charged businesses (de Dromi 1988, 2:237–42). Finally, thousands more military personnel participated in the daily politics of the regime through their service in the repressive apparatus.

The depth of military involvement is also illustrated by the involvement of superior officers in the policymaking process. While this process only involved dozens of officers and thus paled in comparison to the thousands involved in administration, the *quality* of the personnel was greater. That is, the policymaking process drew dozens of officers at the highest levels of each force into daily national politics and thereby increased the opportunity for factional growth at the peak of the armed forces. A discussion of the legislative process will clarify the insertion of military personnel in this area.

The president and the Junta Militar could initiate legislation.[21] The bill would then go to the CAL, which, in plenary session and within seventy-two hours, would establish whether or not the bill qualified as one of "transcendent significance." If it did not, the bill would be sanctioned and promulgated. If it did, it would be handed to one of the eight working sub-commissions of superior officers headed by a member of the CAL, which would coordinate a study of the bill with the relevant executive office(s).

---

18. After August 1978, the attempt was made to ensure that the president was a retired officer (Galtieri would be the exception). The presence of retired officers and civilians would peak during the abbreviated Viola presidency (see "El nuevo estilo de gobierno y los limites de realidad," *Vigencia*, May 1981).

19. I discuss the incongruence between the regime's neoliberal program and military interests in great detail later.

20. Established by decree 3245 (October 21, 1977).

21. The process for the formation and sanction of laws is dealt with in law 21,256, article 4.

The study would be limited to twenty days, save bills related to the budget or other "complex" bills, which would be given thirty days. After the study, the bill would go back to the floor of the CAL, which in plenary session would send a final decision to the president within seventy-two hours. If the president disagreed with the final decision of the CAL, the bill would be sent to the Junta Militar, whose determinations were final.

Although the Junta Militar played a significant role in the daily processing of legislation (both through its ability to initiate legislation and through its role as arbiter when the president and the CAL disagreed), care was taken to defer much of the debate to subsidiary levels in the Junta Militar to manufacture a veneer of harmony among the commanders. These subsidiary levels incorporated more superior officers into the daily politics of the regime and thus broadened the extent of military politicization.

Each service commander was equipped with an independent bureaucracy consisting of superior officers to which bills would be deferred the moment they were forwarded to the Junta Militar. Known as Consultation Staffs Designated by Area (Personal de Asesoramiento Designado por el Area, or PADA), each PADA essentially mirrored the president's cabinet and was coordinated by the secretary-general of the respective commander's force. When a bill was submitted to the Junta Militar, the secretary-general of each member would direct it to his PADA. In this way, bills would initially be considered independently by each force. Each PADA was authorized to call on military and civilian experts for advice. After independent consideration, an interservice harmonization team (*equipo de compatibilización interfuerzas*, or ECI) would be created from members of each service's PADA. The ECI would then harmonize the appraisals from each service and draft a final bill. Like the PADAs, the ECIs could call on military and civilian experts. The bill would then be returned to the secretaries-general, who would meet at least once a week to review bills. If the ECI failed to find agreement on any portion of the bill, or even on the fundamentals of the bill, it would be up to the secretaries-general to search for a consensus. Only if they failed in this task would the Junta Militar proper debate the bill. After the Junta Militar reached agreement, the secretary-general of the Junta Militar (a position rotated among the secretaries-general every two months) would forge the exact language of the bill.

The *Proceso* was a military government in the fullest sense of the term. In sum, regime investment for the Argentine military can be divided into three categories: corporate, material, and psychological. Having so thoroughly assumed responsibility for government, both in word through public proclamations and physically by placing military personnel in government positions, the reputation of the armed forces as a corporate body became inextricably linked to the success of government policy. Materially, the armed forces both as an institution through budget increases and individually through corruption (Spitta 1983), double salaries from government positions,[22] and "war booty" in the antisubversive campaign[23] reaped tremendous revenues. Finally, involvement in the antisubversive campaign tied many officers to the principles of the *Proceso*. Many officers virulently supported the regime in order to justify the atrocious acts of violence they committed in the dirty war. *Proceso* leaders were well aware of this psychological impact and therefore consciously rotated as many officers as possible into the repressive routine of the antisubversive campaign to "dirty" as many hands as possible (Pion-Berlin 1989a, 103; Dabat 1984, 136). Videla recognized the fusion between military and government roles from the start, stating: "The armed forces, as an institution, gave an institutional response to a crisis that was also institutional."[24]

The Steadfast Movement Toward Collapse

When the military leaders of the *Proceso* assumed the reins of government, they were granted a "passive" sense of legitimacy from society. The escalating economic crisis and the inability of the Peronist government to contain the rampant political violence had dampened social support for civilian rule. And when Ricardo Balbín, leader of the Unión Civica Radical, publicly admitted just eight days before the *golpe* that his party could offer no solutions to the deepening crisis, all viable civilian alternatives were lost. Entering office with a license to bring order and security back to the country, the armed forces were generally accepted by Argentine citizens as their last hope (Quiroga 1989, 41–42).

The military embraced the duty to eradicate subversion. Given the still heavy influence of national security doctrine,[25] Interior Minister General Albano Harguindeguy's announcement at a June 1976 meeting of provincial

22. Significantly, the Junta Militar originally communicated that the acceptance of a government office by a military officer was to be a unpaid act of service. See "La función pública es un acto de servicio," *La Prensa*, March 26, 1976, p. A1. Five years later, a law would be passed (22,480) prohibiting active and retired officers from accumulating governmental salaries. See "Modifícanse haberes del personal militar que ocupa cargos públicos," *La Prensa*, August 5, 1981, p. A1. Nonetheless, "double-dipping" would remain a reality.

23. Paoletti 1986 gives a thorough examination of this activity.

24. *Clarín*, May 26, 1976.

25. For a study of national security doctrine during the *Proceso*, see Pion-Berlin 1989a.

governors should come as no surprise: "The struggle against subversion characterizes and conditions all and each one of the government measures adopted at all levels" (Troncoso 1984, 1:42). With the influence of NSD, the armed forces were inclined to perceive subversion even after armed resistance to the regime (which was weak to begin with) had long waned. The following statement by the commander of the Third Army Corps, General Luciano Menéndez, in May 1979 is representative of numerous statements by higher officers: "Armed subversion is totally annihilated in the country; but, with respect to the other, the ideological, I do not venture to say that it has been eradicated in the university staffs, nor in our civic life, in associations, in neighborhoods, in the working environment. The ideologues are hidden and delinquent subversion can rise up again" (Troncoso 1984, 3:85–86). Indeed by late 1981, military journals continued to publish work under the national security doctrine framework, as exemplified by the title of a contemporaneous (July-August 1981) article in *Revista de la Escuela Superior de Guerra*: "Areas of Subversive Action: Political, Economic-Syndical, Religious, Cultural-Educative, Neighborhood, and Psychosocial."[26]

But the political plans of the military went further than the restoration of order.[27] Planning for the *golpe* had begun in November 1975.[28] By the time of the March 24, 1976, intervention, the armed forces were committed to ending the cycle of civilian and military government that had characterized Argentine politics since 1930. Yet as we shall see, the military could never move beyond its "antisubversive" assignment. The war against subversion unified the military, and any moves beyond it engendered factionalism. Such a formula for governance simply could not be sustained. Unable even to clarify its goals (much less effectively pursue them), the *Proceso* regime grew more and more isolated from society over time. The vicious circle was completed as the failure to organize a "successful" regime in any sense of the word intensified divisions within the armed forces.[29]

26. For other contemporary examples, see General Ramon Camps, "La subversión," *Revista de la Escuela Superior de Guerra*, no. 335.51 (July-August 1979), and "Los factores de la defensa nacional," *Geopolítica* 7:22 (June 1981).

27. One week after the *golpe*, Videla stated: "But it ought to be left clear that the events which occurred on the twenty-fourth of March did not only bring about the fall of a government. They signified, on the contrary, the definitive close of a historical cycle and the opening of another, whose fundamental characteristic will be given by the work to reorganize the nation, initiated with the authentic calling to service by the armed forces" (*Clarín*, March 31, 1976).

28. For an account of pre-*golpe* planning by the armed forces, see Vásquez 1985, 17–42.

29. Argentine military regimes have historically distinguished themselves by their concern with social approval. See Philip 1984. This strengthened the isolation-division circle during the *Proceso*.

Leadership changes and their impact on regime divisions highlight the chronology of the *Proceso*. Videla (1976–81) was able to sustain unity early in his term with the antisubversive campaign. Later, divisions began to rise over the economic plan and political goals. The rise of Viola in March 1981 represented an attempt by regime soft-liners to move toward a political opening and to dampen the harsh repercussions of the economic plan. Thwarted and contradicted by hard-liner moves, Viola was finally removed in December 1981 and replaced by the army commander, Leopoldo Galtieri. Attempting to consolidate a hard-line regime, Galtieri invaded the Malvinas Islands to shore up support. The disaster in the Malvinas assured the imminent withdrawal of the military in July 1982. Until the complete withdrawal in December 1983, division would continue at the highest levels with President Bignone assuming the role of soft-liner and the Junta Militar acting as a hard-line base during the transition.

According to the model, collegial rule and regime investment leads to politicization and prevents the regime from coordinating strategy, hindering the development of political and economic programs. The continuing effect of regime investment in the midst of these failures leads the regime to press on until it collapses. An overview of the history of the *Proceso*, with particular attention granted to the conflicts that enveloped the search for a political program and the difficulties surrounding the implementation of economic policy, confirms this model. Furthermore, once the *Proceso* had collapsed, the military, in complete disrepute for its defeat in the field and its failure to move beyond the antisubversive campaign, returned to this very theme to salvage any remaining semblance of unity as it returned to the barracks.

The Search for a Political Program

The desire to be more than an interim government between civilian rulers was announced in the originating documents of the *Proceso*, which were issued on March 26, 1976, the day of the *golpe*. As noted, the *Estatuto*, the *Acta*, and law 21,256 outlined the distribution of authority in the new regime. Another document, *La Proclama*, justified the intervention, pointing to the vacuum of power in the government, corruption, subversion, and economic decline. *El proposito y objetivos básicos del Proceso de Reorganización Nacional* delineated the basic goals of the *Proceso*. Here the regime established its fundamental statement of purpose:

> To restore the essential values that fundamentally serve in the integral management of the State, emphasizing the sense of morality,

perfection, and efficiency, indispensable for the reconstitution of the content and image of the Nation, to eradicate subversion and promote the economic development of national life based on the balanced and responsible participation of all the distinct sectors toward the goal of assuring the later restoration of a democratic, representative, and federal republic, adjusted to reality and the demands for solutions and progress of the Argentine people.

Nine basic objectives followed the fundamental statement of purpose:

1. the creation of political institutions independent of sectarianism, personalism, or other factions.
2. the strengthening of Christian values.
3. the strengthening of national security and the eradication of subversion and the conditions that facilitate it.
4. the establishment of legal and social order.
5. the establishment of socioeconomic conditions that permit the country and its citizens to realize their potential.
6. the establishment of well-being in productive work and equality of opportunity for all.
7. the establishment of harmonious relations among state, capital, and business.
8. the creation of an educational system in accord with the objectives, culture, and values of the Argentine nation.
9. the guarantee of self-determination in world arena.[30]

A sixth document, the *Bases para la intervención de las fuerzas armadas,* summarized the arguments in *La Proclama* and *El Proposito.* But the importance of this document is found in its fourth section, "Desarrollo del Proceso." This section states that the *Proceso* would develop in three phases. The first was the assumption of control. The second would be the reordering of institutions. The third phase would be one of consolidation, but exactly what "consolidation" meant, it was explicitly stated, would be explained at a later date.

The failure to define "consolidation" opened a door of debate that would challenge the regime for a coherent response. Few officers disagreed with the fundamental proposition or the basic objectives. But disagreement flourished as different regime members offered their ideas on exactly how

---

30. A copy of the document can be found in *La Prensa,* March 25, 1976, p. 1.

these objectives ought to be consolidated. The omission allowed officers to debate a host of questions, including: How long should the *Proceso* last? Should there be an interim civil or civil-military government? What role should the traditional political parties play? What marks the end of the subversive threat? What strategies best diminish subversion? And to what extent should the military institutionalize itself in the future democratic order? That factionalism can be linked to this legal ambiguity again demonstrates the consequence of institutions.

The first cleavages found President Videla facing off against fellow junta members Admiral Emilio Massera and General Genaro Díaz Bessone. Massera's main concern was how the concentration of power in Videla's hands affected his own personal aspirations. Although original agreements between the services called for a retired officer to hold the presidency, it was later agreed that it would be best to have the army commander retain the presidency during the antisubversive campaign. However, the air force and navy demanded that the retention of the presidency be considered a *situación de excepcionalidad*, subject to repeal in the event the subversive threat subsided (Fontana 1987, 47).

By early 1977, Massera began to lead navy assertions that subversion was subsiding, and therefore the *situación* ought to be repealed and a "fourth man" placed in the executive office. Massera's plan was to retire and assume the position of fourth man himself (de Dromi 1988, 2:205). Interestingly, Videla was able to stave off Massera with the tacit support of army hard-liners such as General Luciano Menéndez and General Carlos Suárez Mason, both of whom were corps commanders. Although their interests would later diverge greatly, both Videla and the hard-liners found advantages in the *situación* in early 1977. The *situación* gave Videla extensive powers as both army commander and president, and the hard-liners were accorded extraordinary powers as a result of the antisubversive campaign (Fontana 1987, 59–60, 137; Alvarez 1992).[31]

Massera made full use of the institutions accorded to him as he pursued his megalomaniacal dreams. His control of the Ministry of Foreign Relations allowed him to visit a number of countries in attempts both to bolster his international reputation as a leader of the *Proceso* and to meet with Argentine exiles he viewed as potential allies. Massera met with leaders of the Socialist International, right-wing Peronists, Frondizi *desarollistas*, disenchanted politicians, and anyone else who would listen to him (Vásquez

---

31. Many hard-liners also refused to confront Videla for fear of breaking military unity in the face of the subversive threat. See "El peso de la geometría," *Carta Política*, February 1977, pp. 7–9, and "Variaciones sobre un mismo tema," ibid., May 1978.

1985, 131–35). Illegal seizures of torture victims' goods at the notorious Navy Mechanics School paid for much of his campaign to assume the presidency (Paoletti 1986, 145–60). Massera's abject lack of principle was epitomized by the fact that while he fully supervised the torture center, outside the country he criticized human rights abuses in Argentina, placing full blame on the army to bolster the position of the navy.[32] Indeed, the repressive apparatus Massera controlled was an important tool in his drive for power. In February 1977, Massera had union leader Oscar Smith "disappeared" just before he was to consummate an important labor agreement with the Videla government, and in July 1977 he had the ambassador to Venezuela, Hidalgo Solá, "disappeared" as well. Solá was the first and most senior Radical Party member to cooperate with the Videla government, and was regarded as a potential interim presidential candidate.[33]

Massera's pressure to end the *situación* in 1977 was stepped up toward the end of the year, as he began publicly to question the dual role held by Videla.[34] But concern for army unity, and the unity spurred by the Beagle confrontation with Chile, led to the April 1978 decision of the Junta Militar to allow a retired Videla to retain the presidency in August of that year (Fontana 1987, 67–68).[35] Massera's failure to be appointed president was the beginning of the end for him. Retired in September 1978, he was left without an institutional position from which to influence the regime and slowly faded even as his criticisms of the regime intensified.

The other early threat to Videla came from General Díaz Bessone, an important power player in initiating the *golpe*. To appease his thirst for power, Videla allowed Díaz Bessone to create and head the Ministry of Planning in September 1976. The ministry was charged with drawing up the medium- and long-term plans of the regime. As a hard-line nationalist, Díaz Bessone would use the institution to criticize the neoliberal economic program of Martínez de Hoz and attempt to build a support base in agriculture and among primary sector producers.[36] The core of his political

32. "Argentina Navy Uses Rights Issue in Rift with Army," *Washington Post,* January 27, 1978, p. A20; "Argentina: Rocking the Boat," *Latin America Political Report,* March 3, 1978, pp. 68–69.

33. "Argentina: Another Near Miss," *Latin America,* February 25, 1977, p. 63; "Argentina: The Navy Way," ibid., July 29, 1977, pp. 225–26.

34. "Habló Massera en Puerto Belgrano," *La Nación,* August 4, 1977; *Confirmado,* September 1977.

35. On preliminary power consolidation by Videla, see "Argentina: Videla Alone," *Latin America Political Report,* January 13, 1978, pp. 14–15.

36. "Las claves del plan" *Redacción,* September 1976; "Un proyecto nacional," *La Opinión,* June 1977, pp. 9–10.

program was to establish *comisiones de modernización* to channel public participation in the regime. The *comisiones* would consist of individual citizens who represented the opinions and concerns of certain sectors and regions of the country. The proposal was an obvious attempt both to undermine political parties as alternative political channels and to bolster the power of Díaz Bessone by placing the commissions under the Ministry of Planning.[37]

The *comisiones de modernización* were part of Díaz Bessone's program outlined in *Proyecto Nacional*, a document drawn up in mid 1977 to act as the political plan of the *Proceso*. The document called for a military government for ten to twelve more years, and constitutional reform pending input from the *comisiones*. Although the Junta Militar approved the *Proyecto Nacional*, it was made clear that it would serve more as a general guideline than as a strict plan (Fontana 1987, 61). Constitutional reform was an intense subject of debate in the armed forces—many wanted a less gradual opening, and the traditional political parties were still viewed as valid interlocutors by many officers. Interestingly, Massera's push for a resolution to the fourth-man problem strengthened Videla and his more softline approach vis-à-vis Díaz Bessone. Even army hard-liners fell in behind him, realizing that any resolution of the fourth-man problem that did not favor Videla would weaken the army as a whole. Recognizing that his document and ministry would have little real influence, Díaz Bessone retired as minister of planning in December 1977.[38]

The fact that Massera and Díaz Bessone had fallen was no sign that Videla was consolidating the regime. Both had failed to impress their political projects on the regime, but both had succeeded in distracting Videla from advancing his own agenda. Radical Party leader Raúl Alfonsín illustrated the lack of regime consolidation in December 1977 when he implored the government "to unify its personnel, because it cannot have twelve voices of government, but only one" (Troncoso 984, 2:84). The stability of Videla depended upon army hard-liners, who supported him only as long as he followed a line they supported. Indeed, to remind Videla of his precarious situation, army hard-liners would often step up the repressive campaign to

37. "Mentas sobre una reforma," *La Opinión*, January 1977, p. 11; "Planeamiento: designaciones," ibid., January 1977, p. 11.

38. "Argentina: Videla Alone," *Latin America Political Report*, January 13, 1978, pp. 14–15. Perhaps the final straw came in December when Díaz Bessone announced he would draw up any plans to incorporate political parties, but was rebuked by Interior Minister Harguindeguy, who stated that party relations was clearly in his domain ("I am the voice of the government in this matter"). See "Un anuncio para el futuro," *La Opinión*, December 1977, p. 15, and "En nombre del gobierno," ibid., December 1977, pp. 12–13.

embarrass Videla as he made motions toward a political opening, or they would disappear his soft-line supporters.[39]

But the departures of Massera and Díaz Bessone did invigorate Videla in the short run. About March 1978, Videla announced that the "Period of Ordering" was nearing its end, and that a "creative stage" would begin and last roughly one year.[40] Videla's hope was to implement the political proposal designed by Secretary-General of the President José Villarreal and his subsecretary Ricardo Yofre, which emphasized civil-military dialogue and general elections within seven years (Vásquez 1985, 75–76). Videla's power seemed to be strengthened with his appointment as the "fourth man" in August 1978 and a ministerial reshuffle that largely favored him (Fontana 1987, 72).[41] But a late 1978 internal document titled "Report on the National Situation" clarified the reality of these moves. The pessimistic document stressed weak presidential authority, regime isolation, and the continued ill effects of military factionalism (Vásquez 1985, 94–103).

The departures of Massera and Díaz Bessone would not allow the regime to strengthen itself because the regime institutions that had allowed their intrusions remained. No sooner had they left than other obstacles to Videla's consolidation were raised, most notably by General Albano Harguindeguy. The friction between Videla and Harguindeguy was already apparent in 1977, when they clashed over the prospects of political opening (Troncoso 1984, vol. 2).[42] As interior minister, Harguindeguy saw himself as the central figure on the question of political opening. To check such aspirations, Videla had a new office created in the late 1978 ministerial reform, the adviser to the president on political reforms. The office was given to a civilian and specifically designed to initiate support from the political parties, a move that Harguindeguy had publicly criticized (Fontana 1987, 76–77, 81–82).

Videla's drive to implement the Villarreal-Yofre plan was soon dulled by the more arduous endeavor to draft a political proposal that united separate official proposals drawn up by each service between September 1977 and July 1978. An interservice commission had been formed to resolve

39. See "Argentina: Martial Airs," *Latin America,* April 16, 1976, pp. 125–26; "Argentina: Habeas Corpses," ibid., June 11, 1976, pp. 180–81; and "Argentina: Police Confusion," ibid., July 9, 1976, pp. 213–14. Also see "Argentina: A Knife at Videla's Throat," *Latin America Political Report,* April 22, 1977, pp. 113–14, and Vacs 1987, 26.

40. "Tras el Beagle, una transición decantadora," *La Opinión,* March 1978, pp. 10–12.

41. Also see "Argentina: Videla Tightens His Grip," *Latin America Political Report,* November 3, 1978, pp. 337–38, and "Argentina: The New Men," ibid., November 10, 1978, pp. 349–50.

42. Also see "Sin diálogo con los partidos," *La Opinión,* March 1977, p. 12.

the major points of disagreement, which included (1) whether or not to set a fixed date for transition; (2) whether or not to create an official party to represent the military; (3) whether or not to restructure the traditional parties; and (4) how much to open political activity. Through 1979, negotiations between the services continued. In regard to the political parties and political activity, the army under Videla took the soft line, desiring a loosening of political activity and dialogue with the political parties. The air force took an opposing position, and the navy the middle ground, although closer to the air force position. Harguindeguy distanced himself from the official army position and aligned himself closest to the navy position. In a number of public statements viewed favorably by the navy and air force commanders, he called for the restructuring of the political parties and constitutional reforms to institutionalize the military in government. Harguindeguy's actions weakened Videla's attempt to assert army hegemony and helped to lengthen the negotiations for the interservice political proposal. Indicative of the dispersion of authority, regime leaders reacted to the inability to resolve differences in June 1979 by inviting all active-duty generals, vice admirals, and brigadiers to join in the debate (Fontana 1987, 79–83). Meanwhile, the need for a political plan was becoming more urgent as the subversive threat dissipated and Argentine society demanded to know the specific intentions of the regime.[43] In part a response to government stagnation in this area and the softer position of the army under President Videla and army commander Viola, General Luciano Menéndez led an unsuccessful uprising from his garrison and called for the resignation of Viola. Forced to resign and imprisoned, the influential hard-liner declared: "I am convinced that the Argentine military is atypical, unconstitutional, and circumstantial, and that it ought to exercise power in the military style to find grand solutions; only this can justify its presence in power" (Troncoso 1984, 3:132–33).

The interservice political proposal was published under the title *Los bases políticos de las fuerzas armadas para el Proceso de Reorganización Nacional.*[44] It is significant that air force pressure led to a change in the title of the document from "Proposal" to "Bases." In sum, the document could not be considered a strict delineation of the political project of the regime (de Dromi 1988, 2:416). It failed to specify time frames for opening political and partisan activity, equivocated on questions of constitutional reform and the institutionalization of the armed forced in a future government,

43. "Las dudas del Presidente," *Redacción*, March 1979.
44. See text in *Clarín*, December 20, 1979.

and omitted any references to the creation of an official political party (Fontana 1987, 89). Concerned more with military factionalism than ideological clarification, the ritualistic publication of the document was indicative of military concerns rather than governmental concerns. Argentine society viewed it with dissatisfaction, and the lack of any real linkages between the regime and society remained.[45]

The only significant process initiated by *Los bases políticos* was the dialogue with social sectors and political parties.[46] Headed by Harguindeguy, the process lasted from March to September 1980. Officially boycotted by both the Peronists and Radicals, the participants consisted mainly of sympathetic political and economic groups, who met with Harguindeguy to voice their objections to the economic program (de Dromi 1988, 2:417; Troncoso 1984, vol. 4). Galtieri, a corps commander at this time, set the tone at the outset with his statement: "The political dialogue has begun. This does not mean that tomorrow there will be elections. The ballot boxes are well guarded and will remain well guarded" (Troncoso 1984, 4:47). Likewise, Harguindeguy maintained the pessimistic tone on military withdrawal at the conclusion of the dialogue, asserting, "Insofar as the objectives can be achieved in three years—something that seems particularly difficult to me—one could say that this would be the last military government. But if the objectives are not achieved, this would not be the last military government" (Troncoso 1984, 4:118).

While the armed forces remained politically ambivalent through 1980, their divisions became more public as a result of the deliberations to decide who would succeed Videla in March 1981 (Portantiero 1987, 268). Viola had been groomed for the office since he retired in December 1979, but opposition to him was strong from the navy and Galtieri, now army commander. But Galtieri found it difficult to shore up support within the army, having underestimated the allies Viola had gained during his years as army chief of staff and army commander. This led the naval commander, Armando Lambruschini, to reluctantly withdraw his opposition to General Viola out of fear of spurring greater disunity in the armed forces (Fontana 1987, 124).

With the rise of Viola, many assumed that the time of political definition had finally arrived (de Dromi 1988, 2:345). As army commander, Viola had originally pushed for an official political party, labeled the *Movimiento*

45. "En que consiste el plan político?" *Redacción,* January 1980.
46. Even the dialogue was surrounded by negotiations and conflict, especially over how much control the Junta Militar or president ought to exert over it and who would be appointed to the government team to lead it. See Fontana 1987, 85–86.

de Opinión Nacional, consisting of unions, provincial parties, and disillusioned members of the Peronist and Radical parties. But the idea lost support early on within the army for fear that it would "bring into existence a new Perón" (Vásquez 1985, 92–93; de Dromi 1988, 2:418). Viola thus saw political opening as the last hope for the regime to gain support in society and announced his desire for it in his inaugural address (de Dromi 1988, 2:203–6), but the public took that announcement with a grain of salt. Most realized that the dispersion of power undercut the power of the president and that there existed substantial opposition to political opening in the armed forces.[47] Although the political parties championed Viola's intentions, they were reluctant to place their support behind someone so precariously positioned (Fontana 1987, 133).[48]

Galtieri blocked or undermined every move made by Viola to initiate political opening (Pion-Berlin 1987, 217–18; Babini 1991). Galtieri had three advantages over Viola: he was an active officer and chief commander of his service; as a member of the Junta Militar he had more authority than Viola did; and as a member of a collective agency, he was spared the daily wear of an executive. Viola's only advantage lay in his limited ability to influence policy as chief administrator (Babini 1991). Galtieri laid the groundwork for his attack early, promoting Viola opponents and passing over his allies in the December 1980 army promotions. Of the five corps commanders, the only remaining Viola supporter was General José Villarreal. And lower in the army hierarchy, independents were noticeably chosen over Viola partisans.[49] The rise of Viola was thus more a cosmetic gain for soft-liners than a real one, as the consolidation gains made by Galtieri emboldened the hard-liners. Indeed, one month after his inauguration, the Junta Militar sent Viola a document, Orientations No. 2, in which it warned him to cease the political opening.

Junta members also began to remind Argentines publicly that power resides in the Junta Militar, and not the presidency, and to undermine moves by Viola (Fontana 1987, 128–32). In one of Viola's earliest attempts to demonstrate reconciliation with the Peronists, he publicly stated that the government would release Isabel Perón as a sign of good will. Nonetheless, Galtieri soon rebuked him by declaring that such an act would lead to a

47. "El nuevo estilo de gobierno y los limites de realidad," *Vigencia,* May 1981; "Exito del Proceso y estructura del poder," ibid., June 1981.
48. "Hay dudas sobre la democracia," *Redacción,* April 1981.
49. "Argentina: Right Wingers Move Up in Reshuffle of Army Command," *Latin American Weekly Review,* April 3, 1981, p. 10.

request for his resignation from the Junta Militar.[50] Also, in August 1981, Galtieri went to the United States and announced that Argentina would be willing to contribute troops to a multinational force being prepared to support the Camp David Accords, knowing that Viola had recently affirmed the opposite (de Dromi 1988, 2:346).

The major obstacle faced by Galtieri in his push to oust Viola came from Lambruschini, who opposed the move in fear that it would cause greater disunity in the armed forces. With the retirement of Lambruschini in mid-1981 and his replacement by Jorge Anaya, a long-time Galtieri associate and personal friend, Viola's ouster became inevitable (Fontana 1987, 140–41). Finally, in December 1981, Galtieri took advantage of a health emergency that Viola would later describe as minor to have him declared incapacitated and unfit for office. Galtieri himself then assumed the presidency. Under Galtieri, the absolute political isolation of the regime from society would become clear as he led Argentina to war, and the *Proceso* to collapse.

The Inability to Implement a Coherent Economic Policy

Economic policy during the *Proceso* was subordinated to the corporate and political interests of the military as a whole, as well as to the short-term material interests of each service in particular. The neoliberal-monetarist based agenda originally proposed by the minister of economics José Alfredo Martinez de Hoz was applied piecemeal, and the result was usually an ambiguous and often contradictory approach to economic policy that harmed nearly every economic sector. This is not to argue that a consistently applied neoliberal program would have engendered economic growth, stability, and wide support from all sectors, but that the lack of coherence prevented the regime from targeting *any* economic group as a support base. Although one might point to the financial sector as a beneficiary, even it was devastated by 1982 (Dabat 1984, 134).

For help with the ailing economy, the military looked to Martinez de Hoz. Martinez de Hoz had a long affiliation with conservative interests in the interior provinces. He had served as minister of the economy in Salta Province in the 1950s, worked for agricultural interest groups thereafter, and returned to government at the national level as secretary of agriculture

---

50. "Argentina's New President Facing Showdown with His Generals," *Latin American Weekly Review,* May 1, 1981, p. 1. Viola would later overcome such threats and release Isabel Perón. See "General Viola Wins a Breathing Space," *Latin American Weekly Review,* July 10, 1981, p. 2.

and later minister of the economy under President José María Guido (1962–63), who assumed the post after military pressure forced President Arturo Frondizi from power. Martinez de Hoz diagnosed the problems in the Argentine economy as the destructive results of populist policies. An oversized state, inefficient industries protected and subsidized by statepolicies, and a dangerously mobilized labor force that could extort wage increases were viewed as the culprits. Martinez de Hoz reasoned that these ills could be cured by a hefty dose of the free market. This would discipline Argentine businesses and workers and strengthen the competitive capacity of Argentine exports as inefficient industries rightly failed and the country worked to its true comparative advantage in agriculture.

It is important to recognize why the armed forces initially decided to accept the Martinez de Hoz program. Fontana notes that most military officers were impressed, not so much with the economic program of Martinez de Hoz *per se*, but with how the program could provide such simple answers to problems that in their view had long plagued Argentine society (Fontana 1987, 55). The overriding concern of the armed forces was subversion, which it linked to the growth of an immoral culture (Spitta 1983). Neoliberalism, by focusing on the growth of the populist state and the privileged access that certain business and labor groups had to it, answered the question of where this immorality had come from. It was the corporatist state that was immoral, and what was needed was the discipline of the free market. We can see then that the military accepted neoliberalism as a means to stabilize governability in Argentine society and as an attempt to redefine power relations (Canitrot 1980a). On the other hand, the Martinez de Hoz economic team valued neoliberalism as a goal in and of itself commensurate with economic growth and productivity (Fontana 1985). For example, while the economic team viewed the stimulation of agricultural growth in the interior as an adjustment toward Argentina's comparative advantage in the world market, military leaders were just as likely to view such development as a means to check subversive recruitment.[51] This disjuncture in the assumed purpose of neoliberalism would lead to conflict in day-to-day policymaking.

The institutional structure of the regime handicapped the economic team. The dispersion of authority increased the probability that any given policy would be the responsibility of one or more military sectors. The institutional hurdles faced by the economic team can be listed under three

---

51. "Contra la sectarización del poder y por el desarrollo del interior," *La Opinion,* July 1976.

headings: direct institutional confrontations; public criticisms; and independent implementation.

One direct institutional confrontation was between the economic team and the Ministry of Planning. As noted, the ministry served as a political base for General Díaz Bessone. Recognizing the overlap of this nationalist-led ministry with his own ministry, Martinez de Hoz expressed his disquiet early on.[52] A second institutional confrontation was inserted directly into the Ministry of Economics. Decrees 223 and 274 of April 1976 established the Secretaría de Estado de Programación y Coordinación Económica. This body was charged with studying the various economic proposals presented by domestic and foreign businesses to the state. The committee consisted of five members: each service appointed a member, the minister of labor appointed a member, and the minister of justice appointed a member (in the case of proposals presented by foreign businesses, an appointee from the Ministry of Foreign relations was added) (de Dromi 1988, 2:317–18). One more direct institutional confrontation was the interministerial commission that coordinated privatizations. It allowed the armed forces to filter privatization efforts (de Dromi 1988, 2:312).

Public criticisms also allowed military officers to impede the economic program. We can view this as an institutional obstacle insofar as the importance of the criticisms was determined by the institutional position of the officer making them. The first major criticisms of economic policy came from Junta Militar member Admiral Massera in October 1977, as he began to publicize a quasi-alliance with Frondizi *desarollistas*. Labor Minister General Horacio Liendo, who tied Martinez de Hoz's policies to labor unrest, followed suit.[53] Soon afterward, Massera would use the navy publication *La Gaceta Marinera* as a forum to criticize economic policy (Troncoso 1984, 2:78). Other institutional statements, such as the July 20, 1980, air force pronouncement on the importance of air force industries, can be viewed as veiled warnings to Martinez de Hoz (Troncoso 1984, 4:90). More obvious was General Oscar Bartolomé Gallino's (director of the military industrial complex Fabricaciones Militares) public assertion that economic policy in the *Proceso* depreciated the role that industry had played in the development of the country (Troncoso 1984, 5:27).[54]

52. "Gobierno, poder y monopolio de la fuerza," *La Opinión,* August 1976.

53. "Argentina: Musical Chairs," *Latin America,* October 28, 1977, pp. 334–35. Another example is Brigadier General (ret.) Acdel Vilas, who was incarcerated for his January 1978 criticisms (Troncoso 1984, 2:92, 97).

54. Contemporary reports of military unease over Martinez de Hoz's policies can be found in "Argentina: Lingering Discontent," in *Latin America Political Report,* February 9, 1979, and "Argentina: Whistling Up the Wind," ibid., February 23, 1979, pp. 60–61.

A third obstacle to the neoliberal Martinez de Hoz agenda was dependence of the economic team upon military actors to implement certain policies. The *Proceso* economy was a militarized economy, in that military officers administered nearly every public sector business, and officers (retired and active) were placed in most large businesses and banks as supervisors (Ferrer 1982, 113).

Given these institutional obstacles, it should be little surprise that military interests were able to block many neoliberal initiatives. Early on, Martinez de Hoz was able to withstand some military pressures because of the military incentive to limit infighting during the antisubversive campaign. Support from Videla was enough to embolden the economic team. Wage policy exemplifies this. In one of Díaz Bessone's first public pronouncements as the minister of planning, his November 1976 governmental guidelines for 1977, he called for salary increases in opposition to Martinez de Hoz's wishes to stabilize them.[55] Labor Minister General Liendo joined Díaz Bessone in leading such pressure. But success would have to wait until October 1978, when General Liendo would publicly embarrass Martinez de Hoz and lead army pressure to raise salaries.[56]

In other policy areas, the antisubversive drive led military leaders to weaken the economic team's suggestions. First, fears that unemployment would spur greater subversive activity led the military to attack policies that they feared would increase unemployment (Ferrer 1982, 110; Canitrot 1980b).[57] Second, many military leaders recognized the power that the Peronists held in Argentine society and argued that it would be necessary to establish some sort of alliance with its more right-wing sectors (Fontana 1985, 103). This argument was presented to Videla just a few days before the *golpe* by some thirty colonels. The influence of their argument can be found in the fact that unions were not dissolved during the *Proceso*, but frozen.[58] Indeed, from 1976 to 1977 Generals Viola and Carlos Dalla Tea met with labor leaders on a number of occasions in an attempt to establish some sort of collaboration (Pozzi 1988, 115). It was not until the November 1979 promulgation of the comprehensive repressive labor law 22,105 that one could argue that the military had a clear labor strategy (Abós

55. "Son otras las pautas políticas para 1977," *La Opinión*, November 1976.
56. "Argentina: Musical Chairs," *Latin America*, October 28, 1977, pp. 334–35. Ferrer 1981 provides the following figures on real salary levels expressed as percentages of 1974 salaries: 1975 (93); 1976 (65); 1977 (56); 1978 (52); 1979 (59); 1980 (68).
57. Also see "Argentina: Whistling Up the Wind," *Latin America*, February 23, 1979, pp. 60–61.
58. "Argentina: One Voice, Divided Counsels," *Latin America*, April 9, 1976, pp. 114–16. For a detailed analysis of labor relations under the *Proceso*, see Munck 1998.

1982, 63–68). But even it would fail to anchor the regime in a clear strategy, since in little over a year it would stand at odds with Viola's projected political opening.

Another current inimical to the economic team was the nationalist outlook that typified most military hard-liners. The nationalists viewed the economic team with suspicion from the start because of their international connections and "anti-industrial" comments (Fontana 1985, 104). The nationalist attack came in two forms. First, the nationalists criticized what they saw as the "irresponsible dismantling" of the state. It is important to note that the nationalists' concerns were not principally directed toward decreases in the military budget or the provision of raw and strategic materials (areas where the state was likely to be involved in production). On the contrary, the economic team called for increases in the military budget and accepted military participation in many areas of the economy. But the nationalists' concerns were broader than this, and they looked upon almost every privatization move made by the "internationalist and anti-industrial" economic team with distrust (Fontana 1985, 103–4).[59]

Other than this general animosity toward most privatizations, the nationalists also argued that the narrow standards of output and efficiency used by the economic team to decide where the state ought to direct resources failed to take into account larger issues of development, as in the case of state businesses that contributed to the development of border zones through job creation and the exploitation of local resources (Fontana 1985, 104). An important area of confrontation here was tariff reduction.[60] Although the economic team was cognizant of the armed forces' interests in protecting certain strategic and raw materials, it was largely taken by surprise by the intensity of military opposition to tariff reductions in areas such as automobiles and electronics (Spagnolo and Cismondi 1984, 55).

In other areas, the economic team failed to pursue its agenda because of its inability to control all aspects of the policy process. For instance, the Laws of Dispensability (21,260 and 21,274) were passed with the intention of reducing the total number of state employees. The laws held that public employees with subversive, partisan, or sectoral ties were subject to dismissal (de Dromi 1988, 2:394–95). Although hundreds were dismissed

59. "Argentina: Taking Up Arms Against the Free Market," *Latin American Weekly Review,* November 30, 1979, pp. 56–57.

60. Examining data from 1977, Spagnolo and Cismondi (1984, 55) note that tariff reductions affected finished goods much more than primary goods. At this time tariffs on primary products varied from 20 to 100 percent, while tariffs on finished goods varied from 0 to 20 percent.

under these laws, most were promptly replaced. As it turned out, the laws were used more as tools of domination by supervisors than as measures to decrease the overall level of employment (Spitta 1983, 83–84). Another example of difficulties in the policy process faced by the economic team was directly related to the division of authority among the three services. The portion of the state allotted to each service was essentially viewed as a measure of its power. This meant that any reduction in a given service's sector would be viewed by that sector as a reduction of its power vis-à-vis the other two services. Thus, argues Fontana, even when the military was disposed to accept privatization in certain areas, often it fought such measures simply because of the institutional arrangement of the regime (Fontana 1985, 106–7).

Opposed by some portion of the military wherever he turned, Martinez de Hoz found himself unable to apply his neoliberal plan consistently. Argentine policy was erratic in freeing prices, freezing wages, cutting fiscal policy, freeing trade, and stabilizing monetary policy (Ferrer 1981, 110–29). This fact was clearly drawn to the government's attention in August 1979, when twelve businessmen met with Videla to indicate the "need for a coherent policy in the economic sphere" (Troncoso 1984, 3:114). Similar reasoning can be found in a July 1980 statement issued by La Coordinadora de las Industrias de Productos Alimenticios: "After more than four years after being installed in power, the economic team still owes industry its opinion on the industrial plan toward which it wishes to arrive" (Troncoso 1984, 4:91). Many businesses were willing to accept the discipline of the free market as called for by the objectives outlined in the originating documents of the *Proceso*. In March 1979, the Movimiento Industrial Argentino (which consisted of 160 industrial business branches and federations) issued a statement that proposed "saving the philosophy and basic outline of the economic program announced in April 1976, with the implementation of concrete measures more in accordance with it." Likewise, in the same month the Consejo Empresario Argentino expressed its support for the actions of the government which carry out the objectives established by the *Proceso*—a clear message that the group viewed present government policy as deviant (Troncoso 1984, 3:67–69).

The erratic nature of economic policy was so consequential that even the sector which was supposed to be its main beneficiary, agriculture, grew increasingly critical. The only group to consistently grant support was the Sociedad Rural Argentina. But the regime received stinging criticisms from other agricultural groups, including the Federación Agraria Argentina, the Confederacion de Asociaciones Rurales del Centro y Litoral Oeste, the

Confederaciones Rurales Argentinas, the Confederación de Asociaciones Rurales de Buenos Aires y La Pampa, the Confederacion Intercooperativa Agropecueria Limitada, the Corporacion Argentina de Productores de Carnes, and the Consejo de Argentino del Lanar (Troncoso 1984).[61] After recognizing the incoherence in policy caused by the confrontation between the Martinez de Hoz agenda and military interests, one ought not be surprised by the conclusion drawn by Ferrer in his study of economic policy under Martinez de Hoz: "One of the greatest paradoxes of the Argentine experience is the difficulty in identifying its beneficiaries" (Ferrer 1981, 162).

The inability to implement a coherent policy had significant repercussions that added to the collapse of the economy. The neoliberal agenda counted on foreign investment as a dynamic for the economy.[62] But many international businesses lost confidence in the economy precisely because of the instability in policy and invested elsewhere (Spagnolo and Cismondi 1984, 57–58). And economic failure fed on itself as businesses went bankrupt and were absorbed by the largest creditors, the state banks. Indeed, the number of failed businesses absorbed by the state outstripped the number of state businesses privatized by the state, so that state involvement in the economy during the *Proceso* actually increased (Spitta 1983, 84; Ugalde 1984, 168–69). Moreover, the absorption of businesses was not without its own costs, so that the bankruptcies contributed to the deficit and further burdened fiscal policy.[63]

Martinez de Hoz and his economic team were replaced after the inauguration of President Viola in 1981. From Viola, to Galtieri, to Bignone, economic policy moved further away from strict neoliberalism. Nonetheless, the agenda sought by Martinez de Hoz remained at the center of debate. Moreover, by 1981 and especially with the overthrow of Viola, the damage was irreversible. Any political capital initially granted to the regime was expended as the economy fell into ruins, and the inability to target specific economic groups as beneficiaries of a coherent economic program meant that the regime had no linkages to society upon which to build. A crisis emerged, and the regime proved unable to weather it.

61. Other business groups which voiced their disgruntlement include La Asociacion de Bancos de Republica Argentina, Federacion Economica de la Provincia de BA, Convocatoria Nacional Empresaria, Unión Industrial de la Provincia de Buenos Aires El Movimiento de Integracion y Desarrollo de la Provincia de Buenos Aires, Centro de Industriales Siderúrgicos, Centro Argentino de Ingenieros, Centro Argentino de Ingenieros Agrónomos, Cámara Argentina de la Industria Frigorífica, and Asociación de Industrias Argentinas de Carnes (Troncoso 1984).

62. In August 1976, law 21,382 was passed to ease the infusion of foreign investment.

63. On this point, see the November 15, 1980, *La Prensa* editorial.

Galtieri, the Malvinas, and the Collapse of the Proceso

By the time Galtieri seized the reins of government, a sense of urgency surrounded the *Proceso*. Viola's move from the unpopular neoliberal policies of Economics Minister Martinez de Hoz failed to stifle economic decline. Union protests began to stir. And the political parties gave signs of active opposition with the creation of the Multipartidaria to coordinate planning. Lethargy and confusion had flooded the *Proceso*, and its leaders were becoming increasingly isolated from society.[64] The armed forces were in disarray over their inability to formulate a unified political program and frustration with economic decline.

For the military, withdrawal was not even considered as an option because of the high level of investment the military had in the regime. Transition would mean defeat for the military as an institution. For individual officers, transition would deprive them of material gains made under the regime and raise the specter of human rights investigations. The regime was driven to fight to the end

Against this background, Galtieri began to reach out to society in an almost populist manner, making several public appearances outside the major cities.[65] But it would be a mistake to interpret Galtieri's actions as an attempt to restore regime legitimacy. Simply put, the *Proceso* had grown too autonomous to be concerned with questions of legitimacy (Fontana 1986, 32). Overcoming social isolation was simply a means to alleviate what Galtieri saw as the more serious problem, the military disunity that had grown from politicization. Galtieri's plan was to implement a solid political program to unite the military. His strategy called for his popular election in 1984. His initial support base would come from the conservative parties in the country's interior. The election would pit him against the now-retired Massera, who had been wooing Peronist sectors independently and would pull in their support. To ensure his own popular appeal and election, Galtieri would stir the nationalist sentiments of the population with an invasion of the British-held Malvinas Islands, over which the Argentina claimed sovereignty. The action would further solidify Galtieri's position insofar as it would appease hard-line nationalists in the armed forces who had been pressing for a military adventure (Fontana 1986, 7),

64. For a contemporary comment, see "El primer mandamiento: reconstruir la República," *Vigencia*, December 1981, pp. 18–19.

65. "Argentina: Shaking Hands and Kissing Babies," *Latin American Weekly Review*, February 26, 1982, p. 6.

as well as pressure from Admiral Anaya, to whom Galtieri was indebted for his support in the Viola ouster (Wynia 1992, 96–97).

The April 2, 1982, invasion initiated the strategy, which soon seemed headed for success. Popular support for the regime rode the rising nationalist sentiment. The CGT-Brasil union, which had just led the first massive challenge to the regime in a March 30 protest, issued the "Primero la Patria" document, which announced the suspension of its *plan de lucha* as a sign of support. The political parties, likewise, were nearly unanimous in their support and those who refused to give support were ignored (Fontana 1987, 164–65).

But by the end of June, it was clear that the invasion was a disaster. Rather than unify the armed forces, the invasion exemplified the depth of the current division. Each force implemented military strategies that paralleled their political positions toward the war. The inability to coordinate military operations discouraged a strong response to the British and was an important factor in the defeat (de Dromi 1988, 354).

Accepting defeat, Galtieri, ignorant of the political situation that confronted him, moved strategically to shore up what support he could. His plan was to recognize defeat by a superior force with U.S. backing, and reassert Argentine sovereignty over the islands. He planned to make this announcement in a speech on June 15 from the presidential balcony of the Casa Rosada overlooking the Plaza de Mayo. A crowd gathered, not to hear his speech, but to protest. Galtieri was forced to address the public in an "unconvincing" television appearance.[66]

The Malvinas defeat had thus triggered the inevitable—the collapse of the *Proceso*. Passive obedience had irreversibly turned into active opposition. But this opposition should not be overemphasized. For although the military defeat assured collapse, civilian forces did not immediately take a strong offensive. One reason for this was the devastating affect that the *Proceso* had had on both civil and political society. The unions were intervened, and political parties and other political organizations had been dissolved. State-directed terror produced a culture of fear in the Argentine population with the murder and disappearance of an estimated 9,000 to 20,000 persons, the systematic use of torture, and what was essentially a criminal organization within the armed forces that sold babies borne to jailed suspects and looted the possessions of those arrested at home.[67]

66. "Military Defeat Hammers Last Nail into Galtieri's Political Coffin," *Latin American Weekly Review,* June 18, 1982, p. 1.

67. Centro de Investigaciones Sociales Sobre el Estado y la Administración, *Del colapso*

Moreover, because most political party leaders had adhered to official policy during the war, their credibility as a viable alternative was weakened in the aftermath of the defeat. Rather than take a more challenging offensive after the war, the Multipartidaria simply reissued its demand that the military withdraw from power after it had first resolved problems related to human rights abuses, corruption, and external debt, as well as the additional problems created by the Malvinas debacle (Fontana 1986, 14).

But the lack of a forceful opposition was not enough to allow the armed forces to avoid withdrawal. Divided more deeply than ever before, the only point on which the forces could agree was withdrawal from rule. The regime had muddled through failure in the political and economic spheres, but military defeat represented a failure in the area in which the armed forces had its greatest expertise. And the issue of who was responsible was of paramount importance for the armed forces. Galtieri, as president, army commander, and member of the Junta Militar, shouldered the greatest responsibility and was replaced as army commander by General Cristino Nicolaides on June 17. Filling the presidency soon became a matter of dispute among the forces, and the ultimate imposition of General Reynaldo Bignone led the navy and the air force to withdraw from the Junta Militar. On June 22 the army announced that it would assume total responsibility for the government and the transition.

As the army negotiated with the air force and navy to rejoin the Junta Militar, its own internal problems became more apparent. A highly nationalist group led by officers at the brigade level began to push for the removal of all higher officers in the army and demanded that all proposed investigations of human rights abuses be prohibited. Known as *brigadistas*, this group and other nationalist factions would have a significant effect on the transition and the regime's position on human rights violations (Fontana 1987, 171).[68]

By September 10, the high command of the air force and navy were replaced and the Junta Militar was reestablished. With the Junta Militar's

---

militar al triunfo de Alfonsín: claves de dieciocho meses de transición política, Cuadernos del Bimestre (Buenos Aires: CISEA, 1984), pp. 26–39. On the "culture of fear," see Corrandi, Fagen, and Garretón 1992.

68. For contemporary accounts of this group and other hardline factions, see "Internas militares," *La Prensa,* August 8, 1982, p. 1; "Las internas militares (II)," ibid., August 14, 1982, p. 1; "Bignone Seeks Reconciliation, but Argentine Government is Fragile," *Latin American Weekly Review,* July 2, 1982, pp. 1–2; "La 'interna' de los militares," *Redacción,* October 1982, pp. 10–12; and *Foreign Broadcast Information Service—Latin America,* June 22, 1982, p. B3.

ratification of a decision to withdraw from rule by the early months of 1984, the government made the move for a negotiated transition with the opposition. Bignone soon took on the role of the regime soft-liner, and the Junta Militar, being more open to pressures from the *brigadistas* and other nationalist groups, filled the hard-liner role.

Bignone attempted to launch the negotiations in mid-October with a publicized agenda for discussion that included human rights investigations, the Malvinas Islands, economic policy, the Chilean border dispute, and the composition of the new electoral regime. Confirming the continued division in the armed forces, the Junta Militar demanded that a number of other issues be added, the most important of which were the stability of judicial personnel, existing union and social legislation, and the constitutional presence of the armed forces in government.[69] The response of the parties was to reject the government's proposals unanimously[70] and call for a December 16 street protest. The union leadership followed with the call for a December 6 work stoppage. The work stoppage and the December 16 *marcha de la civilidad* were huge successes and marked the resurgence of civil society in Argentina.[71] At the same time, pressure from the lower ranks continued, as illustrated by a December 4 military ceremony for Malvinas veterans, in which hundreds of conscripts protested with shouts of "down with the Junta Militar" and booed attending officers.[72] Bolstered by these events, the opposition continued to answer government appeals for negotiations with mobilization (Cuevas Farren 1990, 91).

Over the next few months, the cleavage between Bignone and the Junta Militar widened as Bignone showed some concurrence with opposition demands and the Junta Militar remained intransigent. Although the division nearly led to the resignation of Bignone, the parties reacted to the hard-line position of the Junta Militar with dampened criticisms and demands and an agreement to negotiate. In these negotiations, the Junta Militar expected that they would be able to negotiate the institutional participation of the armed forces in the new regime, as well as restrictions on human rights investigations. But the parties publicly announced that they would reject any "commitments limiting the next government." In consequence,

69. For a complete list, see *Convicción*, November 12, 1982. Also see "El Proceso en su hora más nerviosa," *Redacción*, November 1982, pp. 10–13.

70. See statements in *La Nación*, November 23, 1982.

71. "El lento proceso de normalización sindical," *Redacción*, January 1983, p. 24.

72. "Argentine Strike Heralds Fresh Challenge to Bignone Regime," *Latin American Weekly Review*, December 10, 1982, p. 1.

the negotiations ended in March and led only to the setting of the date for elections (October 30, 1983) and the transfer of power (January 30, 1984) (Fontana 1986, 21–28).

Setting the date for elections marked the end of regime attempts to negotiate with the opposition. Although regime leaders then attempted to implement an alternative strategy of underground negotiations with likely election leaders and unions that largely failed (Cheresky 1985, 26),[73] for the most part regime leaders directed their efforts directly toward rebuilding military unity by concentrating on the issue which least divided the armed forces— the antisubversive campaign.

The first government action occurred with the April 28 publication of the *Documento final de la Junta Militar.* The polemical document stated that all disappeared persons ought to be considered dead, denied the existence of clandestine detention centers, and insisted that only God and history could judge the acts committed in the war against subversion.[74] Other government actions included a propaganda campaign that detailed plans by subversives to infiltrate the government and assassinate union and party leaders.[75]

That the attention given to the human rights issue was designed more to cultivate military unity than as an actual attempt to impose a limitation on the next regime is evidenced by the promulgation of the *Ley de Pacificación Nacional* (Law 22,924). Passed on September 23, the decree granted an amnesty for "subversive activities and excesses in its repression" committed between May 25, 1973, and June 17, 1982. Because the law was passed with the full recognition that the next government would revoke it, one can assume that it was intended primarily for internal consumption (Dabat 1984; Fontana 1987, 182). The irrelevance of the decree was soon established when it was pronounced unconstitutional in the courts even before the transition.[76]

Upon assuming office December 10, 1983,[77] the Alfonsín administration

73. "La tormenta del pacto militar-sindical," *Redacción,* May 1983, pp. 12–15.
74. Text in *Clarín,* April 29, 1983.
75. See reports in "La Junta trató las muertes de Cambiaso y de Periera Rossi," *La Nación,* May 20, 1983, and "Informe de la Junta sobre Montoneros," ibid., May 21, 1983. Also see "Los estertores del régimen autoritario," *Redacción,* July 1983, pp. 12–14.
76. *Foreign Broadcast Information Service—Latin America,* September 29, 1983, p. B4; ibid., October 3, 1983, p. B5.
77. Originally established for March 1984, then January 1984, the movement of this date further exemplifies the weakness of the military regime. While Bignone had once spoken of "a number of things which must be arranged before handing over power," it later became clear to him that he was in no position to negotiate. See *Foreign Broadcast Information Service— Latin America,* January 18, 1983, p. B1.

faced only a thin veneer of untenable threats and decrees. The new democracy would represent a clean break with the previous authoritarian regime, which had spent the previous seventeen months more shoring up military unity than placing limitations on the next regime.

Conclusion

The ill-fated institutional design of the *Proceso* led the regime to collapse. Collegial rule, when added to regime investment, gives the contenders for power within the regime the desire and the wherewithal to pursue independent agendas, which drive the regime toward stalemate. Strategy coordination becomes a distant goal when regime elites find themselves too busy fighting among themselves to reach out to society and create stable bases of support. The severe political and economic crises faced by the regime and its subsequent collapse were more the products of an institutional arrangement that bred a fatal combination of military disunity and investment than the inevitable outcomes of military rule.

The economic program implemented during the *Proceso* was not the neoliberal program originally envisioned by Martínez de Hoz. Again, this is not to argue that such a program would have necessarily led to economic success, but that the inconsistency of what was implemented eventually disadvantaged nearly every sector and left the regime with few supporters. The lack of support itself is significant, since confidence in an economy is normally a key to economic growth. This fact alone highlights the political roots of economic failure under the *Proceso*. And military interference in the economic program highlights the institutional character of these political roots.

In regard to the search for a political program, one might argue that any political program would have been doomed to failure because to the extent that military rule was accepted, it was solely as a short-term resolution to political disorder. But the evidence suggests otherwise. A number of groups moved forward to grant potential support to the regime. Most syndical organizations, a primary target of repression, endeavored to accommodate the regime in talks through mid-1977 (Pozzi 1988) and remained willing to dialogue through 1978 (Troncoso 1984, 2:112). During the Harguindeguy talks in mid-1980, a number of groups, while not expressing support for the regime, avoided outright opposition and waited for the regime to clarify its political goals.[78] Likewise, Viola received a significant amount of

---

78. "Los políticos se portan bien," *Redacción*, May 1980.

supportive statements from important economic and political groups (Troncoso 1984, vol. 4). Thus it stands to reason that the regime had the opportunity to gain support had it not promoted such uncertainty in society.[79]

The Argentine *Proceso* supports the predicted relationship between military disunity and the lack of strategy coordination on one hand, and collapse on the other. Politicization in the ranks and isolation from society were outstanding features of the *Proceso*. The regime failed to avoid political crises. Economic crisis was allowed to translate itself into political crisis. And when faced with failure that seemed abundantly clear to everyone else, the armed forces, guided by their level of investment, pressed on and led the *Proceso* to collapse.

79. The failure of the military to clarify its intentions and the "wait and see" attitude of civilians is described in "Propuesta militar para un Movimiento de Opinion?" *La Opinión*, June 1980, pp. 4–5.

5

Brazil: Institutional Accommodation and Controlled Transition

will promote a political opening, and
ill have anyone who dares to oppose it
iled and beaten.
─President João Baptista Figueiredo

April 1, 1964, brought the end of civilian rule in Brazil. In the next few days, populist President João Goulart would exile himself and the newly formed Revolutionary Supreme Command would set the framework for twenty-one years of military rule. Five military presidents would follow and effect a controlled change of the Brazilian economy and political system.

The executive dominance achieved under the military presidents belied the collegial style of rule that typified the regime. Movements toward personalization were severely restricted, and inputs from other superior officers were institutionalized at the highest levels. The Brazilian regime was marked by this dispersion of authority of rule, along with an initially low level of regime investment that decreased yet further over time. As such, the regime was generally able to avoid politicizing the military. Although this institutional arrangement allowed the regime to avoid a collapse, it was the existence of institutions that facilitated strategy coordination that allowed it to institute a controlled transition from 1982 to 1985.

The Brazilian Regime: The Institutional Foundations of
Military Unity and Strategy Coordination

The Brazilian regime was collegial in character and enjoyed a substantial
civilian presence throughout its tenure. Indeed, these traits increased over
time as the legislature was allotted greater power and civilians found themselves in more significant positions of authority. The Brazilian regime did
not have the advantages of the centralized Chilean regime, where Pinochet
could direct strategy and quite effectively suppress criticism. For the Brazilian regime, although collegiality (when combined with low regime investment) helped to alleviate the pressures that worked toward disunity, it also
inhibited economic planning and the setting of political agendas because
the political leaders lacked a concerted strategy to guide them. How regime
elites resolved their differences and reached consensus on economic and
political strategy thus becomes a significant point of inquiry.

The Dispersion of Authority

One can distinguish three dimensions along which authority was dispersed
in the Brazilian regime. The most significant was the distribution of executive authority among senior officers. Although at certain times the president may have seemed to wield unquestioned authority, over time it was
clear that each president ruled only with the approval of the senior officers
of the armed forces. A second dimension is found in the strict promotion,
retirement, and assignment regulations. Such regulations inhibited the
development of the military as a base of personal power. Finally, power was
also dispersed between the president and the legislature. Although this
dispersion was negligible at the outset of the regime, with power heavily
tilted toward the executive, after 1974 the legislature increasingly began to
develop as a viable alternative source of power within the regime.

At the outset of the regime it was clear that even though executive
authority would dominate, no single officer would be granted a monopoly
on power within the executive branch. Following constitutional procedures,
Chamber of Deputies president Ranieri Mazzilli replaced Goulart as provisional president on April 2, 1964, after the president of the senate declared
the office vacant. But at the same time, the senior service officers in Rio
de Janiero (army commander General Artur da Costa e Silva, naval commander Admiral Augusto Rademaker Grünewald, and air force chief of
staff Brigadier Francisco de Assis Correia de Melo) formed the Revolutionary Supreme Command and communicated to Mazzilli that they would

make all major decisions (Schneider 1971, 118–20). Committed to purging Brazilian politics of individuals associated with Goulart and other perceived subversives, the junta worked to draft a document to grant themselves the necessary powers. To do so, the four army field commanders, the chief of the army general staff Marshal Humberto Castelo Branco, and Secondary Commander Olympio Mourão Filho were invited to special neetings convened by the Revolutionary Supreme Command. The ultimate outcome was the Institutional Act and the selection of Castelo Branco to serve out Goulart's term.

The Institutional Act explained the Revolution, as the *golpe* was boldly labeled, and granted extraordinary powers to the Revolutionary Supreme Command and later to the new president. Among the most important of these powers were the authority to suspend political rights of citizens for up to ten years; the withdrawal of congressional immunity and the power to cancel all electoral mandates; the power to introduce constitutional amendments; the *decurso de prazo,* by which all bills designated as "urgent" were automatically passed if Congress fails to act on them within thirty days (thereby allowing a minority to filibuster executive bills into law); and near complete authority over the budgetary process and appropriation and the power to declare a state of siege.[1] While in control of the executive office, the Revolutionary Supreme Command directed a massive purge of politicians, bureaucrats, and military officers.

When Castelo Branco assumed office on April 15, he did so as all his successors would, as a delegate governing in the name of the armed forces (Coelho 1988, 153). As a precaution against a presidential power grab, military personnel were placed in political offices close to each president. The most important supervisory body was the National Security Council (NSC). This body consisted of all cabinet members, the president, the vice president, the chiefs of staff of the services, the chief of staff of the armed forces, the chiefs of the military and civilian households, and the director of the National Information Service (SNI—Serviço Nacional de Informações—the chief intelligence apparatus). Article 87 of the constitution established the NSC as the highest body to advise the president. And DL348 (January 9, 1968—also known as the National Security Law) formalized and clarified the powers of the NSC to study all policies related to national security. Under the influence of the national security doctrine, national security was interpreted to allow for the study of transport, industrial development, nuclear energy, labor unions, immigration, education,

---

1. The text of the Institutional Act can be found in Bemis 1964, 240–42.

and telecommunications.[2] Often, such studies would result in legislation produced under presidential initiative. Moreover, the NSC played a more direct role at the policy implementation stage. The body, in cooperation with the SNI, oversaw a Division of Security and Information (DSI) in each ministry to supervise all policy implementation related to its broadly defined notion of national security (Ronning and Keith 1976, 233).

The collegial character of the regime was clearly demonstrated when President Costa e Silva suffered a stroke in August 1969. The service commanders intervened to deny the presidential sash to the civilian vice president, Pedro Aleixo, as was called for by the constitution drafted under their auspices just two years earlier. The military hard-liners deeply distrusted Aleixo, thus the commanders opted to rule as a junta until a successor was chosen (Skidmore 1988, 95). Schneider describes the collegial decision-making process:

> The 118 army generals on active duty (as well as the sixty admirals and 61 air force general officers) were each to discuss the problems, goals, and priorities of the revolution with their subordinates and sound out sentiments on the succession question. On the basis of the top choices of each senior officer, generals of four star rank were to compile a list of the three preferred candidates of their commands. These were subsequently consolidated into a list for each service and finally narrowed down to a single choice for the Armed Forces. Thus, while the process of consultation would reach down to the level of colonels, the great electors would be the seven members of the High Command of the Armed Forces, a body which had never formally met since its creation several years before. In this system, suggested by the navy, the military ministers (who comprised the *junta*), the three service chiefs of staff, and the Chief of the Armed Forces General Staff constituted the final electoral college. (Schneider 1971, 298–99)

The process lasted over one month and a half and was notably contentious (Flynn 1978, 439).[3] Although constituted at the time to deal with the succession crisis, versions of the "military electoral college" effectively chose each of the subsequent presidents under the regime (Alves 1985, 106).

---

2. "Law No. 348," *Latin America*, January 19, 1968, p. 21.
3. Also see "Triumvirate in Brazil Keeping Policies of Stricken President," *New York Times*, September 4, 1969, p. 10, Late city edition.

Bacchus (1990, 33) notes the overall collegial character of decision-making under the regime: "Even while restricting decision-making authority to the most senior levels, consultation and adherence to the views of the majority far down the ranks was maintained, giving strength and some breadth of collective wisdom to the choices the seniors faced about national policy and strategy."

Nonetheless, the particular character of each president contributed to the level of the dispersion of authority. President Castelo Branco (1964–67) set the overall tone with his determination to avoid *caudillo* politics as president. His insistence that a clause be inserted into the Second Institutional Act (October 1965) to make him ineligible for a second term created the expectation that no president would work to succeed himself. Perhaps more important, he instituted regulations to guard against the personalization of promotions, retirements, and assignments in the armed forces. This curbed the growth of factions and increased the prestige of the presidency in the eyes of the military (Skidmore 1988, 63–65).

President Costa e Silva (1967–69) began the move toward the more hands-off approach in daily policymaking that President Emilio Garrastazú Médici (1969–74) would clearly institute. Médici divided his government into three spheres and placed "czars" in control of each. Army Minister General Orlando Geisel was placed in charge of military affairs, Finance Minister Antônio Delfim Neto was placed in charge of economic affairs, and Chief of the Civilian Household João Leitão de Abreu was placed in charge of political affairs (Skidmore 1988, 67, 108).[4] This political style came to an abrupt end under President Ernesto Geisel (1974–79), who took a much more direct role in policymaking.[5] He wrested control of economic policy from the Ministry of Finance with the creation of the Secretariat for Planning and presided over the newly created Council for Economic Development, which consisted of the ministers of finance, agriculture, industry, commerce, and the interior (Flynn 1978, 478–79). Geisel also excluded the high command from decision-making, and provoked its ire when he nominated Figueiredo as his successor without consulting it.

One might argue that the greater concentration of authority under Geisel marked a move away from collegial rule, with significant input only from his chief of the civilian household, General Golbery de Couto e Silva. Although this is partly correct, one should recognize that the move also

---

4. Under Médici, "special advisers" came to hold greater influence over the presidency. See "Ministers Must Toe the line," *Latin America*, March 6, 1970, pp. 74, 76.

5. "Political Reality," *Latin America*, January 10, 1975, p. 12.

highlighted the underlying collegial nature of the regime. That Geisel's independent actions threw the regime into its deepest crisis demonstrated the expectation within the armed forces that the regime be based upon collegial rule (Sanders 1981, 188; Dunbar 1979, 31–35).[6] Also, the argument represents a "snapshot" form of analysis, and thereby neglects the dynamics of the regime over time. As I discuss later, although Geisel was concentrating authority vis-à-vis the military, he was also setting the stage for power concessions to the legislature. Geisel concentrated power with the intent to disperse it.

Under President João Baptista Figueiredo, Geisel's decision-making style was brought to an end. Figueiredo's extension of authority to interministerial councils marked a return to decentralized decision-making. Likewise, multiple advisers with considerable power again surrounded the executive. Early on, the three most important were Chief of the Civilian Household Leitão de Abreu, Planning Minister Antônio Delfim Neto, and SNI Director Octavio Medeiros. The chief of the military household, General Rubens Ludwig, and the minister of justice, Ibrahim Abi Ackel, also played important roles (Wesson and Fleischer 1983, 75; Skidmore 1988, 212).

Strict promotion, retirement, and assignment regulations also contributed to collegial rule. Before 1965, the active-duty service of four-star generals in government was unlimited. In an explicit effort to reduce the opportunity for personalistic factions under senior officers, Castelo Branco passed a comprehensive reform in December 1965. Four-star generals were limited to four years active-duty service; advancement or forced retirement became mandatory at every subsequent step after an officer was promoted to general, admiral, or brigadier (the senior air force rank); all officers were limited to two years off-duty service before they were required to retire or be reactivated; and mandatory retirement ages were set (59 for colonels, 62 for brigadier generals, 64 for divisional generals, and 66 for four-star generals) (Bacchus 1990, 42; Schneider 1971, 324; Skidmore 1988, 48). The result was a systematic movement of senior officers so that by the early 1980s, each general rank averaged a turnover of about 25 percent (Wesson and Fleischer 1983, 126).

Other standards within the armed forces reduced the possibility of military *caudillos*. The president, as commander of the armed forces, had the authority to make promotions at the senior ranks, but was limited to the three-name lists prepared by the High Command. This procedure also

6. "Power to the President," *Latin America Political Report*, January 13, 1978, pp. 9–10. The centralization also disturbed many regime supporters in business. See "Brazil's Businessmen Score Geisel's Politics," *New York Times*, June 12, 1976, p. 29, Late city edition.

allowed for a limited amount of interservice oversight, given the interservice composition of the High Command. Finally, the educational requirements of senior officers maintained a merit-based environment. Officers entering the senior ranks were required to attend one or more highly competitive postgraduate schools. Indicative of the competition in these schools was the 75 percent failure rate on the entrance examination of the army's Major Command and Staff School (Bacchus 1990, 42).

The strict regulations guiding promotions, retirements, and assignments checked the actions of any individual senior officer wishing to concentrate authority. It became virtually impossible to exploit the institution of the military as a source of political power. Likewise, the merit-based attitudes instilled by educational requirements closed the institution to any such efforts.

The third dimension of power dispersion within the Brazilian regime was the growth of the legislature as a power base. At the onset of the regime, power was profoundly concentrated in the executive, and the division of authority carved out by military officers (and some civilian technocrats) within that branch maintained the collegial character of the regime. But over time, the legislature was granted more authority. This "redispersion" of authority helped in part to offset the concentration of authority within the executive office under Geisel.

At the time of the *golpe,* most officers looked upon the legislature with disgust and anger. They viewed the branch as a haven for petty politicking, greed, and corrupt patronage, and as the ultimate source of political instability in Brazil. For this reason, the Institutional Act was passed to allow a purge of the branch while it remained in a subordinate position to the president. A number of restrictive measures followed, including the prohibition of consecutive terms, the Act of Party Fidelity to prohibit cross-party voting, and severe limitations on the initiation of bills (Soares 1979).

The purges and restrictions placed on the legislature created a system dominated by the executive.[7] But the 1974 congressional elections represented a turning point. Geisel identified them as a symbol of his *distensão* (liberalization) policy and thus worked to ensure their integrity.[8] The opposition party MDB won several important victories, and from that point on, the legislature became a principle dynamic in the transition from military rule (Lamounier 1989). It became recognized as a viable arena by the

7. "Brazil's Military Regime Meeting Opposition," *Washington Post,* July 2, 1971, p. A18.

8. I discuss in greater detail the *distensão,* the manipulation of electoral rules, and the development of legislative power in the section on the controlled transition. Here I present only a few basic points to support the characterization of the regime as collegial.

opposition, and the regime looked to it as the primary mechanism to contain and mold regime opposition and support (Sarles 1982). Indeed, before 1974 the regime concentrated on regulations that transferred power from the legislature to the executive, but after the 1974 elections the regime became obsessed with tinkering with electoral rules.

This is not to argue that the legislature eventually balanced the power of the executive.[9] The point is that over time the legislature developed as a minor, albeit significant, check on executive dominance. Because the military identified elections (however limited) as a source of legitimacy, the manipulation of electoral rules emerged as an issue of contention between military factions. Soft-liners saw electoral changes as the first steps toward transition, while hard-liners viewed manipulations as a means to assuage the opposition and prolong rule. As the debate continued, legislative influence gradually crept forward.[10] The ultimate expression of legislative power came with the 1984 presidential election. By this time, the legislature had grown strong enough to achieve control over the electoral college, which chose the president. Although the military authorities were prepared to accept an opposition victory, they clearly lobbied against it.[11]

In sum, the dispersion of authority in the Brazilian regime had three dimensions: the collegial division of authority within the executive branch by senior military officers; the obstacles to personalism within the armed forces created by strict promotion, retirement, and assignment rules; and the development of legislative power as a minor but significant impediment to executive dominance.

Low Regime Investment

The intention of the Brazilian military to dominate, rather than replace, civilian political institutions was apparent in the language of the Institutional Act:

> In order to demonstrate that we do not intend to radicalize the process of revolution, we have decided to maintain the Constitution

9. For a 1982 update on executive dominance, see "The Real Battle Comes Later," *Latin American Weekly Report,* November 12, 1982, pp. 8–9.

10. As early as 1978 the legislature was successfully defying military authorities on significant issues. At this time, ARENA congressmen joined ranks with the MDB and snubbed the government with a refusal to approve a Figueiredo confidant as São Paulo governor. See "United Front," *Latin America Political Report,* June 9, 1978, p. 172.

11. The efforts of the military can be traced in *Latin American Monitor* 1 (1984): 1–10.

of 1946. We have limited ourselves to amending it in the part that deals with the powers of the president of the republic.... In order to further reduce the powers that rightfully belong to this victorious revolution, we have also decided to maintain the national Congress—only establishing certain limitations on its power. (Alves 1985, 32)

Eventually, the constitution of 1946 was replaced by the constitution of 1967, which itself was replaced by the constitution of 1969 (as the constitution of 1967 was known after it was heavily amended in October 1969). But civilian involvement in the regime never departed from the political formula imposed by Brazil's military leaders.

The most important base of civilian involvement was the legislature, which never contained more than a few military officers. As I detail later, representation in the Senate and Chamber of Deputies was blatantly manipulated to favor the government party. Similarly, legislative initiation came to be dominated by the executive. Specially created congressional joint committees considered legislation initiated by the executive branch, and debate was expressly limited by time, whereas legislation initiated by the legislative branch had to first be approved by two of three legislative committees before it could be voted on (Blume 1967–68, 206). But even more important was Institutional Act No. 5 (December 1968), which allowed President Costa e Silva to purge eighty-eight congressmen immediately and threaten the remaining congressmen into submission. Legislative initiative fell dramatically after this, and while the executive bill passage rate reached 100 percent, that of the legislature hovered around 7 percent (Soares 1979, 115–17). The specter of Institutional Act No. 5 would haunt Congress until late 1978. Finally, the legislature was closed in October 1966, from December 1968 to October 1969, and again in 1977, demonstrating the willingness of the president to recess it when it was uncooperative.

But the significance of the legislature to the regime should not be downplayed. First, the government viewed the legislature as an important source of legitimacy. The government originally desired to create a strong two-party system as the basis for the new political system, and the legislature served as the obvious locus of this development.[12] Also, when the junta declared Médici president in October 1969, Congress was reconvened specifically to sanction the choice. Second, the legislature provided a forum

12. New party regulations were first drafted under Complementary Act No. 4 (November 20, 1965). The original draft was stringent on party creation and was revised to reassure the government that a loyal opposition party would arise (Alves 1985, 65).

for the loyal opposition. Third, the importance of the legislature's role in the electoral college grew in the 1980s as it became more independent. And finally, the legislature served as a medium for inter-elite accommodation of the civilian allies of the regime. Many politicians, especially those of the UDN (União Democrática Nacional), had supported the *golpe* and continued their political careers in the legislature under ARENA and even under the opposition MDB (Jenks 1979).

Civilian involvement in the legislature was matched at the local level. Over four thousand municipalities had elected mayors and chambers of councillors.[13] Overall civilian involvement in elected posts is illustrated by the 1982 elections, when 49,133 posts were decided: 22 governorships, 25 senatorial seats, 479 federal chamber seats, 947 state chamber seats, 3,924 mayoralties, and 39,790 municipal chamber seats (Carlos de Medieros 1986, 149). The importance of elections, however manipulated, should not be underestimated. Research has demonstrated how even ritualistic participation in electoral procedures by the populace tends to legitimate a regime (Ginsberg 1982).

Civilian involvement in the executive was different in character from that in the legislature. Under Castelo Branco, UDN politicians found themselves in a number of ministry posts (Skidmore 1988, 22–23). But afterward, executive civilian participation took on a more technocratic flavor, a novelty in Brazilian politics (Ronning and Keith 1976, 236). The technocracy that developed under President Costa e Silva and his successors became the third pillar of the domestic alliance that supported the regime (the other two being certain traditional politicians and the military). Their power was most apparent in the Finance Ministry under President Médici, where Antônio Delfim Neto redesigned government policy to permit a more extensive use of state resources to guide the private sector (Frieden 1991, 115–18). Linkages between the state and private interests that had previously existed in the legislature had already begun to move to the administration, and this policy change intensified this move (Blume 1967–68).

A July 1971 study of the composition of executive ministries illustrates the extent of civilian participation. It identified 2,366 "key posts" in the thirteen nonmilitary ministries (i.e., excluding the Ministries of the Air Force, Navy, and Army, and the office of the chief of the military household) and found military personnel in only 50 of these posts (Ronning and Keith 1976, 239). Note that the date of the study falls under the Médici

---

13. At any given time, about 150 municipalities had mayors appointed by the respective state governors. These municipalities were designated as "national security areas" (under the Municipal Security Law of 1968) and always included the state capitals.

administration, when overt military influence in government was at its height. A compilation of ministry composition from 1964 to 1983 shows that of the 120 individuals holding ministerships, 44 were military officers (37 percent). And when one excludes the military ministries (which were always headed by military officers), the numbers drop to 20 of 96 (21 percent) (Huneeus and Olave 1987, 136). Overall, military participation in administration actually remained close to pre-*golpe* levels (Ronning and Keith 1976, 239). At no time did military participation in the cabinet reach a majority.

Civilian participation in the cabinet was important both because of the noted authority extended to cabinet members (especially under Costa e Silva, Médici, and Figueiredo), and because it gave civilians admission to the powerful NSC. In 1976, ten of the twenty-five NSC members were civilians (Ronning and Keith 1976, 239). Although military personnel were always in the majority in the NSC, it is notable that a military regime consistently allowed a significant civilian presence in such a powerful institution.

As in most military regimes, civilian participation remained in the judiciary, but the authority of the judiciary itself was significantly undermined. President Castelo Branco disturbed traditional judicial autonomy when he packed the eleven-member Supremo Tribunal Federal (STF—Supreme Court) with five compliant allies to ensure institutional cooperation.[14] The scheme proved inadequate in 1968 when the court declared sections of the National Security Law unconstitutional and released a number of students and other political prisoners. President Costa e Silva responded with the powers granted to him under Institutional Act No. 5 and forcibly retired three judges.[15] This led to protest resignations by two other judges. To ensure compliance in the future, Costa e Silva preserved the court membership at eleven and removed the appellate jurisdiction that the STF had had over the Superior Military Court for offenses against national security or the armed forces. The Superior Military Court, an independent court system originally designed to hear only those cases pertinent to offenses by military officers, thus became the highest court for these cases. This court remained powerful through the remainder of the regime. It consisted of fifteen judges, five of whom were civilians and who often acted more hard-line than did the ten officers on the court (each service contributed personnel). Nonetheless, it is again significant to note the role allotted to

14. This was done under the authority granted by Institutional Act No. 2.

15. "Brazil's Chief Ousts 3 Justices and 37 Federal Congressmen," *New York Times,* January 17, 1969, p. 12, Late city edition; "Purge, Protest and Politics," *Latin America,* January 24, 1969, pp. 30–31.

civilians on such a powerful military institution in a military regime (Skidmore 1988, 83; Wesson and Fleischer 1983, 83–86).

The institutional composition of the regime illustrates the extent of civilian participation. Certain regulations also demonstrate the lack of regime investment for the military. The president and the heads of the nonmilitary ministries were barred from active duty and appearing in public in uniform. Also, participation by military officers in civilian administration was limited to two years (Barros 1985, 33). Such regulations served to limit the identification of the military with the government.

Despite the extent of civilian involvement and a level of identification far from that found in Pinochet's Chile or the *Proceso*, there is no question that the Brazilian regime was a *military* regime. As noted, the president ruled as a delegate of the armed forces and thoroughly dominated the Congress. Likewise, the placement of an individual from the DSI in each ministry ensured that the civilians serving in the executive branch would be supervised. These security personnel scrutinized policy to assure its compatibility with the national security concerns of the military and were authorized to veto all significant appointments by the minister (Wesson and Fleischer 1983, 76–77; Ronning and Keith 1976, 242).[16] The military knew it was the most significant base of support for the regime, but at the same time, it stood apart from government, viewing it as something to be reformed and improved rather than subsumed.

Strategy Coordination in the Brazilian Military Regime

Strategy coordination refers to the capacity of a government to muster support for political and economic programs within both the military and society, and to deal with the growth of opposition during transition. A regime that lacks "lines of communication," or linkages to society or the military is likely to find itself without support. The *Revolución* in Argentina illustrates the ill-effects that come from the lack of linkages between the government and the military; the regime in Uruguay illustrates the difficulties that arise when a government fails to reach out to society. The *Proceso* illustrates what happens to a regime that is an abject failure in both directions.

16. Early administrative reforms under Castelo Branco initiated the growth of the intelligence apparatus. "Brazil's Reforms Sped by Castelo," *New York Times*, March 2, 1967, p. 20, Late city edition. For an overview of the intelligence apparatus and its penetration of government, see Alves 1985, 128–32. I return to the important role of the intelligence apparatus when I discuss the dynamics of the transition.

Collegial rule demands mechanisms of coordination among regime leaders to facilitate suitable strategies. As noted in the theoretical framework, strategy coordination is identified by the existence of institutions that either translate diffuse ideologies into political strategies or forge consensual strategies through such mechanisms as decision rules within the ruling group. Pinochet's concentration of authority created great certainty for decision-making in Chile, and he reached out to society for the ideology and expertise to justify his economic and political programs. Collegial rule lacking strategy coordination, even if buttressed by military unity, will find itself unable to impose a controlled transition. We should expect such regimes to be incapable of the coupling process described by Kingdon (the ability to blend problems, policies, and politics) and thus be unable to take advantage of environmental successes or to guard against environmental crises. Our identification of such a case will have to wait until Chapter 6, where the Uruguayan regime is examined. The Brazilian situation was somewhat different.

The Brazilian military eschewed the messianic role that so many military regimes grant themselves upon seizing power. Rather, the military presented themselves as mechanics intent only on repairing a political system gone awry and as having a practical approach to governing and a willingness to cooperate with civilian allies (Medina 1984). The goals the military established for the regime were pursued consistently and effectively. At the most fundamental level, the primary goals of the regime were "security and development." Such goals in no way distinguish the Brazilian regime from other military regimes under the influence of national security doctrine.[17] What does distinguish the Brazilian regime was the establishment of consistent guidelines to meet these goals. To meet the goal of security, the government sought to (1) eliminate leftist opposition; (2) decrease congressional deadlock; (3) and establish executive supremacy (Soares 1979, 114). Economically, three basic assumptions guided policymaking: (1) business and labor have complementary and compatible interests; (2) economic growth resolves social problems; and (3) the role of the state is to maintain order and guide the free market to better achieve economic growth (Ronning and Keith 1976, 229).

These guidelines and the effective pursuit of them can be closely linked to the curriculum of the Escola Superior de Guerra (ESG). The ESG was established in 1949 as a military school for senior officers. National security

---

17. On the National Security Doctrine in general and in the specific case of Brazil, see Arriagada 1981 and Pion-Berlin 1989b.

doctrine guided the ideology of the ESG, which was based upon the following values:

1. a sense of historical linkage with the West, which, nevertheless, is restricted when Brazilian interests clash with the interests of other Western countries;
2. anticommunism and anti-Marxism;
3. a formal belief in democratic institutions, with limitations, however, on the political positions allowed to participate;
4. the desire to build a political consensus excluding or neutralizing the left;
5. a religious culture expressed as a defense of certain Christian values;
6. a strong preoccupation with internal order and security as preconditions of development;
7. a belief that outside criticism is influenced by Marxism or does not understand the complexity and peculiarity of the nation's special problems;
8. a mode of development aimed at strengthening capitalism, which, nevertheless, depends on extensive government investment, planning, and stimulation of the economy;
9. the resolution of social problems through paternalism (Sanders 1971, 9; also see Stepan 1971, 178–83).

The ESG imparted its ideology directly to those prominent policymakers and senior officers in the high command who attended its courses (Bacchus 1990, 34–38). Beyond this impact at the peak of Brazilian politics, there existed a number of means by which the ideology was further disseminated throughout the military and society:

1. the ESG graduate division maintained a link between the college and graduates, created professional bonds between military and civilian graduates, and published the journal *Segurança e Desenvolvimento;*
2. the ESG maintained informal ties with civilian groups;
3. ESG ideology was disseminated into other military schools as early as the 1950s;
4. short ESG courses were offered outside the main school in Rio de Janiero;
5. ESG principles were incorporated into the 1967 constitution (and transferred to the 1969 constitution) (Selcher 1977, 8).

Markoff and Baretta (1985) question the significance of the ESG. They argue that the ESG provided more of a mentality than an explicit ideology, making it difficult to draw the link between ESG teachings and policy under the regime.[18] But no government works from a defined set of preestablished guidelines. The exigencies of governing demand areas of flexibility that cannot be predicted. Even communist regimes, which supposedly have been guided by the most encompassing of ideologies, have varied dramatically in their application of Marxist doctrine.

Indeed, arguably the more significant contribution of the ESG was the training, methodology, and orienting procedures it provided. ESG courses stressed structured detailed analysis on the economic, psychological, political, and security-related aspects of every problem. The impact of this global approach to problem-solving was found in the composition of the NSC, which included all cabinet members. The ESG also strongly emphasized the importance of planning. The Ministry of Planning, which was created under Castelo Branco, focused its efforts on the formation of a National Plan of Development (*Plano Nacional de Desenvolvimento*), while the NSC was charged with the formation of a National Plan of Security (*Plano Nacional de Segurança*).

And most important, the ESG created important linkages between civilian and military personnel. The Sorbonne faction, as military graduates of the ESG were known, maintained that "the Brazilian military needed to socialize civilians from such fields as education, industry, communications, and banking into the correct national security perspective," and therefore opened ESG classes to civilians. Indeed, by 1966, 690 of its 1,289 graduates were civilians (Stepan 1973, 54). The institutional linkages between the ESG and the IPES (Instituto de Pesquisas e Estudos Sociais — Institute for Research and Social Studies) and IBAD (Instituto Brasileiro de Ação Democrática — Brazilian Institute for Democratic Action) also facilitated civil-military interaction. Rio de Janiero and São Paulo businessmen founded these organizations to place pressure on the Goulart government and worked with the ESG to destabilize it. The IPES acted as a near shadow cabinet under Goulart, held a majority of ESG graduates on its secretariat, and recruited inactive military officers in the Rio de Janiero area for its staff. Many in the IPES would later find themselves in the new Ministry of Planning under Castelo Branco (Alves 1985, 6–8, 50–51; Schneider 1971, 88–89, 120).

Because of its experience with civilians at the ESG, the Sorbonne faction was able to ascertain the limitations of its own skills and recognize the need

18. The distinction drawn between a "mentality" and an "ideology" is drawn from Linz 1975, 266–69. While a mentality establishes only a set of general attitudes, an ideology specifies more detailed principles guiding behavior.

for civilian skills in the effective formulation and implementation of policies (Schneider 1991, 243). A second consequence of the ESG was the develop-ment of a sense of trust between civilians and the Sorbonne faction (Schnei-der 1971, 254–55). Indeed, a secret document released after the 1964 *golpe* specified unity among national elites as an ESG objective (Selcher 1977, 3). Flynn summarizes the influence of the ESG on civil-military interaction: "There were few other societies anywhere in the world where the inter-twining of military and civilian careers, debate, and politics was so marked, and where the military was so prepared, albeit with civilian help, to take over the running of a modern state and reshape it in accordance with an already highly developed theory of national development" (1978, 319).

Some might challenge the above argument by noting that the ESG declined in influence over time (Markoff and Baretta 1985). The response is that although the institution did decline, the ideological bent of the ESG lived on in the officers who had attended it (Stepan 1971); and perhaps more important, the institution set the framework for a regime that would grant civilian technocrats significant levels of autonomy (Alder 1987).[19] As I note below, these civilians maintained links to society and hindered the growth of isolation in the government, a shortcoming of many military regimes.

Thus, while the national security doctrine served as an inchoate source of strategy for other regimes (Pion-Berlin 1988), in Brazil it was translated into a political and economic program that allowed regime leaders to couple problems, policies, and politics. For the purposes of this analysis, it is important to stress the institutional basis of this success. In both Uruguay and Brazil civilian participation contributed to military unity, but only the latter was able to effectively use this participation to allow for a controlled transition. The critical difference is the level of trust and mutual respect between military and civilian personnel that enabled the government to act as a coherent unit. In the Brazilian case, the source of this trust and mutual respect rested in the linkages developed by the ESG. The attitudes fostered at the ESG facilitated the creation of institutional space for civilian tech-nocrats with a strategy of development conducive to military concerns. A shared general vision of nationalism, a shared faith in industrialization as a key to development, and a common quest for international status united military and civilian participants in government.[20] And although most politicians remained despicable in the eyes of the military, the ultimate

19. "Brazil's Policies Shaped at War College," *New York Times,* August 2, 1972, p. 10, Late city edition.

20. For the unifying role of ideology in Brazil, see Alder 1987; for the continuity in eco-nomic policy, see Skidmore 1988, 69, 105–6, 211–12.

value of civilian rule in the ESG ideology led the regime to maintain linkages with some traditional politicians and thereby utilize their patrimonial networks and skills to cultivate regime support (Carlos de Medeiros 1986, 119–27). Civil-military linkages, a consequence of the particular institutions found in Brazil, thus worked to ensure predictability in government values and in the expectations of policymakers, and therefore worked to allow strategy coordination.

Institutionalized decision-making processes also cultivated strategy coordination. One of these processes was the aforementioned design of executive power. That is, that although overall rule was collegial and the presidency and positions of power were staffed strictly according to promotion regulations, at any given time there was a single individual expected to handle day-to-day politics. The president was set in an arena that established general guidelines, within which he was allowed some flexibility in policymaking. This design served to diminish conflict. So long as a president remained within the designated "sphere of maneuverability" and so long as other chief decision-makers remained assured of their involvement in the most significant decisions, infighting was curtailed. Several examples of this decision-making design are documented in this chapter: the pressure placed on Costa e Silva to close Congress and forgo a political opening; the "election" of Médici; and the crisis caused by Geisel when he moved to undermine the system and step outside his designated sphere. The conception of this decision-making process explains in part why the Brazilian movement toward transition was so long. Early on, the decision to restore civilian rule was clearly outside the designated sphere of maneuverability, but an accumulation of decisions slowly moved the sphere to incorporate transition. Later presidents worked off the pokes and pushes (and sometimes fought against the retractions) of previous presidents to open new decision areas.

A second important institutionalized decision-making process involved the linkage between the regime and society. As I argued in Chapter 1, no regime can last long without linkages to society. But as a regime reaches to incorporate the necessary societal expertise, it encounters some risks. Societal actors may extract concessions for their expertise and thus lower government autonomy, and the rise of another significant actor may disrupt the balance of power within the regime as factions jockey for dominance. In Brazil, this problem was managed by the *conselho* system (Barros 1978, 254–64; also see Blume 1967–68). A *conselho* was a consultative council composed of government officials and civilians that met regularly to make policy prescriptions under the direction of a relevant ministry. Consultative councils are of course not a peculiarity of Brazil, nor of the regime—they were first used in the country in 1911. But their number multiplied under the regime (from thirty in 1964 to a hundred in 1974), and their use became much more specialized. Some examples are the National Monetary *Conselho*, the National *Conselho* of Tourism, the National Rubber *Conselho*, the National Sports *Conselho*, and the National Railroad *Conselho*. This particular institutional design—specialized, formally distinct committees, served to minimize the risks associated with societal linkages:

> The result is that the *conselhos* operate as functionally specialized mini-parliaments where the administration has the possibility of *listening* to demands and deciding in a relatively autonomous fashion about the adequate balancing of interests. It diminishes considerably the need to bow to pressures and demands while maintaining a simulacre of accountability and representation. The *Conselhos* [*sic*] allow for a casuistic administration in which the only institutional political actor that has a global view of the process and can coordinate its strategy is the government. Extra-governmental interests find themselves in a submissive position. (Barros 1978, 262)

The system effectively blocked "log-rolling" strategies. For example, whereas a comprehensive "agricultural exports council" might allow cattle, coffee, and rubber interests to coordinate pressure for export subsidies, having an independent council for each of these sectors allowed the government to strike separate arrangements and weaken their respective positions. The *conselho* system, the sphere of maneuverability granted to presidents, and the background influence provided by the ESG served to foster strategy coordination in the Brazilian military regime.

Strategy Coordination and Military Unity in the Brazilian Regime

The success the Brazilian military regime enjoyed in creating links to society and uniting regime leaders was due to its institutional bases of strategy coordination and the unity in the military itself.

Examples of the regime's links to society abound. Early on, interest groups quickly mobilized themselves for integration into the *conselho* system (Blume 1967–68, 210). And it is important to recognize that the link between the regime and society was not simply due to spaces in the regime that interests groups were able to manipulate. Rather, the government consciously worked to establish these links. For example, to select governors, the most hard-line of the presidents, Médici, sent representatives throughout the country to confer with aspirants and publicly discuss who ought to be selected (Sanders 1970a). Moreover, the incentive-laden economic policies established by the regime encouraged regime-society interaction. The distribution of foreign borrowing, infrastructural development, tariff reductions, and contract extensions for large state projects could all be manipulated to control economic development (Frieden 1991, 103–34). Sanders (1970b) presents an interesting case study of how the government used tax deduction incentives to increase stock purchases and thereby create a more diverse capital market. But perhaps the most conspicuous link between the regime and society was found in the Assessoria Especial de Relações Públicas (Special Advisory Staff on Public Relations—AERP), created under Costa e Silva. This institution headed massive advertising campaigns to tie the government to economic growth, national unity, and even the 1970 World Cup Soccer Championship. Its success, measured in government popularity, led many citizens to identify more closely with the government (Skidmore 1988, 110–12).

Civilian expertise allowed the regime to establish a strong base of support within society. Although the high rates of growth under the "economic miracle" could just as easily have been ignored in the face of growing income inequality and the damage to domestic business caused by the influx of foreign enterprises, the regime was able to use economic growth as a source of legitimacy.[21] The ideology of "growth now, distribution later" filtered down to the poorest sectors and impeded opposition based on redistributive demands (Cohen 1979; Geddes and Zaller 1989). The government also demonstrated its skill with its ability to undermine potential opposition movements. For example, Project Rondon was a program similar to the U.S. Peace Corps. By 1971 Project Rondon had sent over three thousand students to underdeveloped areas within the country. By challenging students to participate actively in the development of the most depressed areas, the government was able to undercut student calls for more equitable growth, as well as take some credit for distributive efforts. Also, the government initiated a number of labor policies, such as profit sharing, loan programs, and the financing of union nurseries, clinics, and sports facilities, to pacify the labor unions (Sanders 1970a).

The linkages created between the regime and society would not have been possible without military unity. Lacking unity, a regime cannot be expected to reach out to society coherently. The unity achieved by the regime

21. "Brazil's Economic 'Miracle' Appears of Little Benefit to Workers," *New York Times,* January 25, 1976, p. 3, Late city edition. An authoritative study on the Brazilian economy under the regime can be found in Baer 1989.

was not an established condition of the Brazilian military at the time of the *golpe*. Goulart supporters and other suspicious officers were dealt with swiftly through purges (Skidmore 1988, 27), but the remaining anti-Goulart forces contained significant political and economic splits. Politically, some officers pointed chiefly to defects in political institutions in need of reform, while others placed greater emphasis on the existence of "bad" politicians who contaminated the institutions with their corrupt patronage networks. Because the latter group had a fundamental mistrust of all politicians (and a concomitant vision of the military institution as the only capable representative of the nation), this faction found it much more difficult to return positions of authority to civilians (Schneider 1971, 143). Economically, the military was first divided on how much influence to grant to foreign enterprises. But after Castelo Branco, most of the military steered toward a relatively more nationalist stance, and the division shifted to how much government policy ought to be devoted to distribution as well as growth.

Of these factions in the military (which may have numbered as many as eight, if all combinations of political and economic dispositions are considered), four were more significant than the others were. Two of them were soft-line groups and two were hard-line groups. One already noted soft-line group, the Sorbonne faction, endorsed institutional reform, an internationalist economic stance, and growth before distribution. It was the dominant soft-line group at the beginning of the regime. But after Castelo Branco, ESG influence began to decline. Regime soft-liners also became more nationalist. Nonetheless, the soft-liners still identified themselves most strongly with the institutional-reformist approach of Castelo Branco, and for this reason were labeled *Castellistas*. The hard-liners in the regime also experienced a change in the dominant faction. Under Castelo Branco, a distrust of politicians distinguished the hard-liners. Although Costa e Silva originally positioned himself as a moderate between this group and the Sorbonne faction, the group grew in influence under him and thus became known as the *Costistas*. The economic stance of the *Costistas* was only slightly more nationalist than that of the *Castellistas*. By the end of the 1960s, this hard-line group was matched by another based principally in the security apparatus. This faction's interest in continued military rule was not primarily based on their view of civilian politicians, but rather on their fear of reprisals because of human rights abuses, their material gains from involvement in repression, and the concerns over subversion drawn from the national security doctrine. The "security hard-liners" overshadowed the *Costistas* over the course of the 1970s. Because this faction had no real economic program, it was open to alliances with other hard-line military factions opposed to the *Costistas*.

These factions existed for the duration of the regime, but failed to throw the regime into crisis. The institutional structure of the regime allowed it to mollify the disruptive potential of these divisions. The combination of collegial rule and low regime investment spurred unity in the Brazilian regime in two ways. First, civilian involvement helped defray politicization of the military by keeping it out of daily policy battles and by granting an air of neutrality to those officers in government. Second, collegial rule allowed rival factions access to government institutions. This helped contain their distrust, and also allowed factional alliances to form so that more radical military factions could be quelled.

As noted, civilians involved themselves in the regime both as politicians and as technocrats. Each of these groups played different roles in the regime and contributed to military unity differently. Although most officers distrusted the politicians at one level or another, both Castelo Branco supporters and hard-liners were reluctant to abolish the legislature. The soft-liners held firmly to their faith in institutional reform, the hard-liners feared adverse international opinion (especially from the U.S. military, whom they respected greatly), and both were unwilling to take any actions that stirred memories of the *Estado Nôvo* under Getúlio Vargas, the populist dictator of the 1930s (Skidmore 1988, 152).

The maintenance of representative institutions contributed significantly to the unity of the military. As Kinzo (1988, 8) notes, "The presentation of some form of party organization, Congress and elections, aside from maintaining favorable international opinion and the support of civilian politicians, would also serve to legitimate one faction, one soldier, as head of state, to the detriment of others within the institution." This analysis grants credence to the symbolic importance of the Congress in approving presidential policies. Potentially disgruntled officers would be faced with the fact that presidential initiatives were passed through an institution that represented the nation. Although such formalism would not sway the most antagonistic officers, it could affect those officers who were uncertain or uncommitted.

Politicians also maintained military unity by creating links with society as representatives of the regime. Although centralization increased tremendously under the regime, the implementation of policy remained in the grip of local and regional authorities (councillors, mayors, provincial deputies, and governors) (Collins 1985, 38–39). This allowed many local politicians to rekindle traditional patrimonial relations and identify their standing with regime maintenance (Carlos de Medeiros 1986, 119).[22] This meant that the military was able to avoid much of the isolation that affects so many military regimes.

The participation of technocrats in government also spurred military unity. Their technical and presumably nonpolitical approach to policy-making restrained any accusations that this or that policy was an attempt by the incumbent president to enhance his personal power. Moreover, the military had a natural affinity and respect for such an approach to policy-making (Sanders 1973, 8). The impact of technocrats was especially felt under the Médici administration, but it was an important factor under each president.

If civilian participation was important for subduing potential opposition, the collegial aspect of the regime was important for accommodating existing opposition. No single faction dominated the regime over time, let alone within any single presidency. Rather, the collegial setting of the regime afforded a number of institutional positions to be allocated so that significant factions could be pacified. A strong proponent of this argument is Bacchus (1990, 66–69), who goes so far as to argue that the position of the Army Ministry (army commander) played a primary role in a so-called "alternation agreement" between military hard-liners and soft-liners. This agreement called for a rotation of the presidency between the two groups, and for the out-group to be accorded the Army Ministry.

A more detailed examination of the power arrangement among regime hard-liners and soft-liners exposes a more intricate balance of power between the two groups. In table 2, I note factional dominance in three areas under each administration: the presidential office itself, the staff that surrounded the president, and the policies pursued under the administration. While "policy" is obviously not an institutional accommodation, it is important to recognize it as a method of placating factions not accommodated institutionally. A brief historical survey of each administration will support the table's characterization.

Castelo Branco entered office with solid ESG credentials. He had been a part of the Brazilian Expeditionary Force that had fought in Italy in World War II, and which provided an international experience around which future ESG associates would shape their ideology, an ideology that Castelo Branco himself had promoted as a professor at various military schools.

---

22. Roett 1984 stresses the maintenance of patrimonial relations throughout Brazilian history, regardless of regime change.

Table 2   Institutional Accommodation in the Brazilian Regime

	Castelo Branco	Costa e Silva	Médici	Geisel	Figueiredo
President	SL	HL	ML	SL	ML
Staff	SL	HL	HL/SL	SL/HL	HL/SL
Policies	SL/HL	HL	HL	HL/SL	SL/HL

SL: softline
HL: hardline
ML: mixed
/: denotes dominant tendency

Having been in the high-profile position of army chief of staff under Goulart, Castelo Branco's credentials were well known. But this was not the case for most officers, who found themselves competing for positions with officers whose ideological predispositions were basically unknown. In such a state of uncertainty, the Sorbonne faction, with its leader as president and as the most organized faction, was able to move itself into important staff positions with relative ease (Schneider 1971, 120).

This meant that Castelo Branco was able to fill his staff with Sorbonne associates. In the cabinet, two close military associates, General Ernesto Geisel and General Golbery, were placed as chief of the military household and director of the SNI. The Finance Ministry went to Octávio Gouvéia de Bulhões and the Ministry of Planning went to Roberto de Oliveira Campos. Traditional politicians found themselves in six of the remaining ten nonmilitary ministries (with the final four ministries headed by technocrats). Costa e Silva, the only real outsider, stayed on as army minister.

Castelo Branco wasted little time in implementing policies infused with ESG ideological precepts. Economic policy took a dramatic turn from the traditional import-substitution strategy that had guided it for decades. The government shied from its role as an economic stimulator, inflation became a primary concern, and most significant (given the internationalist perspectives of the Sorbonne), international capital was welcomed as a chief contributor to economic growth (Frieden 1991, 103–6). Politically, a number of measures were implemented to reform representative institutions. The minimum requirements to form a political party were raised (in hopes of diminishing their number), party coalitions were prohibited in elections, the electoral courts were granted greater control over party affairs, campaign spending was limited, ticket splitting was restricted, and incumbents were barred from campaigning for other posts. Notably, none of the reforms by themselves are incompatible with a liberal political system

(Rowe 1966c, 19). The presidential term was extended from November 1965 to March 1967, but it was declared that the initial unpopularity of economic stabilization was the cause and not a move toward long-term military rule (Skidmore 1988, 40). Castelo Branco's promise of a return to democracy (albeit limited) in the near future seemed to ring true.

But as the political bent of the administration became clear, regime hard-liners began to press their interests. They were more disturbed by the corruption that traditional politicians spread and especially by the potential power that nonsupportive parties in government might wield. The October 1965 gubernatorial elections served as a rallying cry, and when two opposition governors emerged victorious, the hard-liners found it opportune to threaten a *golpe*. A number of units in the Rio de Janiero area, the most important of which were the naval officers at the First Naval District Headquarters and troops from the *Vila Militar* garrison, mobilized for action from October 5 to 6. But Army Minister Costa e Silva intervened and worked out a compromise at the *Vila Militar*: the units would agree to retract their threat, and Castelo Branco would implement Institutional Act No. 2 (October 27)—a document that pushed the regime toward a decidedly long-term authoritarian solution.

IA2 increased presidential authority dramatically. It authorized him to remove government employees and elected officials and to suspend the political rights of individuals and granted him more control over the budget. Also, the act ended direct elections for president and extended the jurisdiction of military courts. Finally, the act abolished all existing parties. Complementary Act No. 4 (November 20) established new regulations that required all parties to have a minimum of 120 federal deputies and 20 senators. A number of right-wing parties soon allied as ARENA (Aliança Nacional Renovadora—National Renovating Alliance) and grabbed so many seats that room was left for just one other party, which assumed the name MDB (Movimiento Democrático Brasileiro—Brazilian Democratic Movement) and served as the "official" opposition party. Institutional Act No. 3 followed in February 1966. It required governors to be appointed by the president rather than elected. The policy changes issued by IA2 and IA3 represented significant concessions to the hard-liners, and Costa e Silva's exercise of the role of moderator guaranteed his succession to Castelo Branco.

The Congress elected Costa e Silva president on October 3, 1966. Before his inauguration on March 15, 1967, he took a tour of the country in which he softened his image as a hard-liner (Flynn 1978, 350). He spoke of "humanizing the Revolution" and did not contradict any of Castelo

Branco's policies while on tour (Rowe 1967). In this sense he entered office as neither hard-liner nor soft-liner (Alves 1985, 93).

But hard-line elements made a clear appearance in the cabinet. The Navy Ministry went to Admiral Rademaker Grünewald, who had pushed for more severe purges of Congress as a member of the Revolutionary Supreme Command and had criticized Castelo Branco as soft on subversion. The new air force minister, Marshal Marcio de Souza e Melo, was also a recognized hard-liner, as was Costa e Silva confidant Colonel Mário David Andreazza, who assumed the Transportation Ministry. Reserve army officers placed in Labor and Social Security, Mines and Energy, and Trade and Industry further highlighted the military presence. To wrest control of the Sorbonne-dominated SNI, General Garrastazú Médici was made director. This appointment was so vexatious to the soft-liners that General Golbery, ESG affiliate, creator and outgoing director of the SNI, refused to attend the swearing-in ceremony. The most obvious hard-line accommodation was the appointment of General Albuquerque Lima, a strong nationalist and proponent for development in the poor northeast of Brazil, as interior minister. The only concession to the soft-liners was the appointment of Aurélio de Lira Tavares, a known Sorbonne affiliate, to head the Army Ministry.

In the economic area, there was only a partial break with the Castelo Branco policies. Hélio Beltrão became minister of planning, and Antônio Delfim Neto minister of finance. Policy under the two stressed greater economic stimulation by the state, thus retreating from the more orthodox policies implemented under Castelo Branco, but international business was still viewed as a key to development (Frieden 1991, 115–18).[23]

The placement of a number of nationalist hard-line officers in government even as the pursuit of internationalist economic policies continued created tensions early on. Well-known traditional politician Carlos Lacerda attempted to take advantage of the tension to gain a support base within the military sufficient to allow his accession to the presidency. After mobilizing in Lacerda's favor, several officers were removed from their posts, including Colonel Boaventura Cavalcanti, commander at Fort São João and brother of the minister of mines and energy, and Colonel Amerino Raposo, SNI chief in Rio de Janiero (Flynn 1978, 399). Lacerda's mobilization of the nationalists largely defused itself when he reached out to Goulart to increase his civilian base and thereby alienated many officers (Schneider 1971, 237).

Despite Lacerda's failed mobilization, Costa e Silva soon grew more

---

23. For the disappointment exhibited by those who expected greater nationalism under Costa e Silva, see "Six Months of Costa e Silva," *Latin America*, September 29, 1967, pp. 180–82.

isolated. Through 1968, social unrest increased while the president did little even in the face of hard-line demands for greater repression.[24] The image of Costa e Silva as an idle ruler began to grow. Lacking Sorbonne ties or inclinations, he failed to view the political parties as potential bases of support and was unresponsive to them.[25] Within the military Albuquerque Lima (Flynn 1978, 425–33) rekindled the nationalist hard-line opposition.[26] Costa e Silva would reach the peak of his isolation in December 1968, when a federal deputy gave a speech calling for the populace to withdraw all support for the regime. Although Costa e Silva originally stated that he would not coerce Congress to lift the member's immunity when it refused to do so, he soon felt tremendous pressure from the hard-liners to do something.[27]

The December 1968 crisis led Costa e Silva to close Congress and decree Institutional Act No. 5 (December 13). IA5 gave the president unrestricted authority to close Congress and rule by decree, and to intervene in the states and municipalities without regard to the limitations established in the constitution (Flynn 1978, 418–25). IA5, beyond its dramatic extension of presidential authority, was important because it signified a change in regime factional alliances. Costa e Silva had come to power with a number of nationalists as junior partners. But without a real shift in economic policy, the nationalists began to withdraw support, as evidenced by the mobilizations led by Lacerda and Albuquerque Lima. IA5 appealed to the hard-line elements located in the security apparatus and thus allowed Costa e Silva to lean on their support. Indeed, Costa e Silva used the decree to shelter the economic initiatives of Delfim Neto, and Albuquerque Lima resigned as a consequence.[28] The lack of opposition from the Sorbonne faction also bolstered Costa e Silva. Significantly, at about this time the ESG began to shed its pro-U.S., orthodox economic teachings. And with increased social mobilization viewed as increased subversion and therefore spurring military unity, the Sorbonne faction began to lose its soft-line color (Schneider 1971, 257).

The perceived subversive threat allowed Costa e Silva to rule without accommodating soft-line elements and unified the *Costistas* and security hard-liners. Indeed, the only obstacle to a complete monopoly of power by the hard-line groups was Costa e Silva himself. Staff and the policies under

24. "Violence on all Sides," *Latin America*, October 18, 1967, p. 311.
25. "The Unflappable President," *Latin America*, August 23, 1968, pp. 269–70.
26. "Minister Joins the Critics," *Latin America*, November 22, 1968, pp. 370, 372.
27. "President or Figurehead?" *Latin America*, December 6, 1968, pp. 388–89.
28. "The Mask of Unity Cracks," *Latin America*, January 31, 1969, pp. 33–34.

Costa e Silva were solidly hard-line, but Costa e Silva actually reemerged as a moderate in mid-1969. "After issuing IA5 (Costa e Silva) was still at the helm of the state, but its direction was in the hands of hard-faced security men, telephone tappers, and torturers" (Skidmore 1988, 94). An April speech on the possible reopening of Congress and return to "political normality" provoked a stir in the army command, with General Alberto Ribeiro (commander of the Second Infantry Brigade) declaring that political normality could not be established until the revolutionary forces finish "clearing the ground on which they will do their revolutionary work."[29] On August 27, Costa e Silva was again warned, this time by the three military ministers, that a majority of the commanders opposed reopening Congress at that time and did not want to relinquish any of the powers gained under the institutional acts in the reedited constitution then in draft form (Skidmore 1988, 94–95).

Costa e Silva's efforts became moot when he suffered a stroke on August 29. The military ministers quickly moved to block the civilian vice president from the presidency, and formed a military junta to rule until a successor was chosen. During the selection process, a crisis began to brew from below as Albuquerque Lima roused the younger officers, where he had always found support, to promote his candidacy. Angered by this breach of hierarchy, *Castellista* and *Costista* senior officers closed ranks to choose the politically unknown Médici.[30] Although Médici was a clear *Costista,* "the team chosen by him reflected an attempt to conciliate the *Castellista* and *Costista* groupings, while acknowledging the more right-wing elements in the armed forces and firmly excluding the nationalist officers associated with Albuquerque Lima" (Flynn 1978, 442).[31] *Castellistas* Orlando Geisel and Antônio Carlos Muricy were appointed minister of war and army chief of staff, respectively. Admiral Rademaker was given the vice presidency to appease the right-wing elements dominant in the navy. And the *Costistas* not only saw one of their own assume the presidency but also were assured

29. "This Year ... Next Year?" *Latin America,* April 18, 1969, p. 126. Also see ""Back to the Melting Pot," ibid., August 1, 1969, pp. 246–47, on hard-liner pressures to stifle Costa e Silva's efforts to promote a civilian successor to the presidency.

30. Schneider (1971, 243) notes that the *Costista-Castellista* division was only meaningful for officers above the grade of lieutenant colonel. Also see "2 Generals Vying for Post in Brazil," *New York Times,* September 28, 1969, p. 27, Late city edition, and "Split in Military Widens in Brazil," ibid., October 6, 1969, p. 17, Late city edition.

31. Albuquerque Lima became less of a threat after November 1970, when he was passed over for promotion (Schneider 1971, 324). Afterward, Albequerque Lima made a number of speeches in an effort to mobilize a nationalist opposition in both the military and society. For government moves to counter his efforts, see "Signs of Panic?" *Latin America,* April 2, 1971, pp. 108–9.

continuity in economic policy with Delfim Neto staying on as finance minister. Finally, one should note that the number of technocrats in government grew under Médici. As noted, the use of such civilians helps to instill unity into distrustful factions.

Although Médici's staff contained a mixture of factions, his policies were clearly hard-line. Under him, the Brazilian state reached its repressive pinnacle, and the security forces gained a tremendous amount of autonomy (Alves 1985, 103–37). Although *Torture in Brazil* (Dassin 1986), a study directed by the Archdiocese of São Paulo, covers the period from 1964 to 1979, it recognizes that repression was most widespread under Médici. It presents a graphic and detailed account of the thorough penetration of the security apparatus and notes that by the end of the Geisel administration (1979), the regime had produced 10,000 political exiles, removed 4,682 persons from office and deprived them of their political rights, expelled 245 students from universities, left almost 300 dead or disappeared, and engaged in human rights violations that included the deprivation of civil liberties, torture, and disappearances.[32] The study depicts the Brazilian repressive apparatus as a brutally efficient machine that thoroughly penetrated Brazilian society; produced psychological, physical, and moral damage; and thereby spawned a culture of fear that left the populace passive and subdued.[33]

The level of repression under Médici created new tensions in the regime. Although economic growth spurred regime support, the rampant use of repression reinvigorated *Castellista* concerns over political institutionalization as a more legitimate base of regime maintenance (Dias David 1977, 32). General Ernesto Geisel had these concerns when he assumed the presidency in March 1974. By this time, the ESG had declined in influence and the *Castellistas,* with their less direct link to the ESG, had become the dominant soft-liners. In the hard-line, the security apparatus emerged as the dominant force, although the nationalist current that typically runs through most Latin American militaries remained an important factor.

Geisel's association with the ESG and the close friendship he had with Castelo Branco marked him as a clear soft-liner. But his connections to

32. The study produced a data set from 695 of the 707 legal proceedings held in the Superior Military Court between 1964 and 1979. It noted that of the 7,367 defendants in these proceedings, 1,918 mentioned torture in court records (pp. 77–80). With the relatively safe assumption that many were simply too fearful to mention torture, and given the widespread anecdotal evidence of torture documented in the study, we can safely presume that torture was widespread.

33. Dassin 1986, especially pp. 180–91. On "culture of fear," see Corrandi, Fagen, and Garretón 1992.

Médici, who appointed him to the Superior Military Tribunal and who had his brother Orlando Geisel as his army minister, somewhat lessened hard-line concerns. Likewise, nationalist officers recognized his tenure as director of the state oil industry, Petrobrás. But perhaps most of all it was his professional standing that dampened most opposition. He was recognized as an administrative perfectionist with a aversion to personalization and had held a number of governmental positions since the 1950s (Flynn 1978, 472–73; Skidmore 1988, 161).

Geisel's cabinet represented a clear break with the Médici administration. Two notable members were Justice Minister Armando Falcão and Education Minister Ney Braga. Falcão had held the same position under Kubitschek and was viewed as a potential negotiator with the traditional political leaders. Braga had deep roots in the UDN, but was also a retired general, and was thus viewed as a link between the military and politicians. The appointments of both these men made dialogue with the opposition seem a real possibility.[34] The appointment of recognized soft-liner General Golbery do Couto e Silva as the primary presidential adviser in the chief of the civilian household position also highlighted the bent of the cabinet. Nonetheless, there were two appointees more congenial to the hard-liners. These were General Adalberto Pereira dos Santos (Médici's original choice for president) as vice president and recognized hard-liner General Silvio Coelho da Frota as army minister. Most of the remaining positions went to technocrats (Flynn 1978, 472–75).

Geisel entered office with four goals: (1) to maintain military unity while reducing the role of the security hard-liners and reviving the professional role of the military; (2) to control the rise of any perceived subversion in order to deny the security hard-liners any justification for autonomy; (3) to restore a limited representative democracy; (4) and to maintain economic growth to ensure support for the regime (Skidmore 1988, 162–64).

Geisel's goals involved a careful mixture of soft-line and hard-line policies. Although his ultimate aim was reform, he had to rule with an iron hand to contain hard-line opposition.[35] Early on, the government worked toward opening dialogue with opposition groups and the proclaimed policy of *distensão* of the political system seemed promising. The 1974 congressional elections proved to be the most competitive and unhindered since 1964, and the government showed its willingness to accept significant victories by the MDB. Indeed, the MDB now controlled one-third of Congress,

---

34. "Political Pointers," *Latin America,* March 8, 1974, pp. 78–79.
35. "Brazilians Still Await Democracy," *Washington Post,* June 5, 1975, p. A16.

which meant that constitutional amendments it opposed could only be passed through an authoritarian recourse to IA5.

But those hoping for early liberalization would be disappointed by the end of the year, when Geisel declared in a New Year's speech: "The exceptional tools that I inherited [e.g., IA5] will not be surrendered. I shall use them whenever I see fit."[36] The March 1975 military appointments showed significant concessions from Geisel to the hard-liners, and rising human rights abuses undermined *distensão* pledges. By August it seemed that *distensão* had lost all its steam. In a nationally televised speech, Geisel lauded the security apparatus as an important element in the fight against subversion and portrayed democracy as a distant goal. The MDB leader in the Chamber of Deputies, Laerte Vieira, described it as a "Médici speech," and MDB chairman Ulysses Guimarães declared his total lack of confidence in the government's commitment to *distensão*.[37] Through 1976, repression increased under Geisel. In June, the "Falcão law" (named after the minister of justice) was passed to minimize future MDB victories. The law prohibited campaigning on radio and all but still shots on television, in an obvious response to the gains made by the MDB through the media (Skidmore 1988, 189). But while Geisel was growing more isolated from society, his control over the armed forces increased. He formed a purely military committee within the NSC in an attempt to better supervise the security apparatus, raised military wages to foster support, used the rekindled war against subversion to spur unity, and began a series of reassignments in the army to move his allies to stronger positions (Flynn 1978, 496–501).[38]

The peak of the hard-line Geisel policies came with the 1977 "April Package," which was implemented through a closure of Congress under the powers granted by IA5. The most significant portion of the package was a set of electoral reforms designed to prevent further MDB victories. The move to direct elections for governors in 1978, as called for in the constitution, was altered to election by electoral colleges, which would consist mainly of ARENA-controlled municipal councils. Representation in the Chamber, which was previously based on voter registration, was now to be based on total population. Because registration depended upon literacy, this reform was expected to increase representation of the ARENA-controlled

36. "Political Reality," *Latin America*, January 10, 1975, p. 12.
37. "An End to '*Distensão*,'" *Latin America*, August 5, 1975, pp. 247–48; "Fool I Was," ibid., August 15, 1975, pp. 250, 252.
38. "Geisel Recovers," *Latin America*, January 9, 1976, pp. 14–15; "Screwing Down the Lid," ibid., January 23, 1976, pp. 25–26; "Appeasing the Military," ibid., February 27, 1976, pp. 68–69; "Military Disorder," ibid., July 23, 1976, p. 231; "Military Two-Step," ibid., August 6, 1976, p. 247.

poorer states of the North and Northeast. In the Senate, one-third of the body was declared "bionic," to be elected by same electoral college that elected the governors. In reforms directed toward the president, the size of the electoral college was altered to increase the representation of the national Congress (over which the government now expected to have more control) relative to the number of the members appointed by the state legislature, and the president's term was extended to six years (Alves 1985, 148–51).

Not surprisingly, the April Package caused a stir in the MDB, who in their September convention essentially changed their platform from calling for reform to calling for an end to the regime.[39] Many ARENA members joined the criticism, angered by the damage done to the integrity of their representative institutions. The ARENA dissent was significant because it gave Army Minister Silvio Frota a source of frustration to exploit for his presidential bid. Geisel, having pointed to SNI director Figueiredo as his successor since his inauguration, acted swiftly and dismissed Frota in October 1977.[40]

Geisel's action against Frota initiated a new strategy of control. Whereas previously Geisel had dulled hard-line opposition by condoning repression, he would now move to establish control on his own terms. Within one week after the dismissal, two Frota associates were also dismissed, and Geisel began maneuvering to advantage *castellistas* in the next round of military promotions.[41] Geisel also began a full-scale attack on the most recalcitrant security agency, the Centro de Informacões do Exercito, through intelligence leaks of its involvement in human rights abuses.[42] Finally, Geisel broke protocol in the regime by naming General Figueiredo as his successor without allowing the high command to deliberate on the decision. The chief of the military household, General Hugo Abreu, resigned in protest, expecting to stir up controversy, but Geisel quickly made a number of personal contacts and secured statements of support from his ministers. That quelled any opposition, and Abreu was replaced with little fanfare (Dunbar 1979, 31–35).[43]

In 1978, Geisel used his newfound power to open a broad dialogue with the MDB, interest groups, and the Church, and then to push a number

39. "The Democratic Umbrella," *Latin America*, September 23, 1977, p. 294.
40. "Brazil's President Retires General Who, in Rare Move, Talks Back," *Washington Post*, October 13, 1977, p. A23.
41. "Changing Guard," *Latin America Political Report*, October 28, 1977, p. 335.
42. "Spying Scapegoats," *Latin America Political Report*, November 18, 1977, pp. 356–57.
43. "President Geisel of Brazil Names Intelligence Chief as His Successor," *New York Times*, January 6, 1978, p. A3.

of reforms directed at *distensão*. The most important of these reforms included the repeal of IA5 and the other institutional acts, the reestablishment of congressional immunity, and the reintroduction of habeas corpus for political prisoners. Although a number of authoritarian measures remained and the opposition was less than satisfied,[44] the reforms were an important step insofar as they opened more political space for the opposition (Alves 1985, 166–68) and reestablished the government's commitment to liberalization (Lamounier 1989).

Toward the end of Geisel's administration, the regime actually moved away from its collegial character as Geisel concentrated an unprecedented amount of power. As noted, at another level the move illustrated the underlying collegial expectations within the regime insofar as it created a crisis within the armed forces.[45]

Controlled Transition in Brazil

Like his predecessors, General João Baptista Figueiredo assumed the presidency in a faction-ridden environment and responded with institutional accommodation. But these contesting factions weakened over the first half of his administration, leaving him with few significant military challengers to the democratic transition. Nonetheless, Figueiredo himself also weakened, and the dynamics of the transition shifted to the civilian politicians in the legislature. This shift did little to threaten the controlled transition, since the politicians worked within institutions established by the military regime to restrain radical change. Institutional accommodation and strategy coordination show their significance for the transition insofar as Figueiredo was able to contain factional threats from the hard-line early on, and also insofar as both factors were necessary conditions for the establishment and stability of the institutions that would guide the politicians during the transition.

Although Figueiredo was basically handpicked by Geisel, his tenure as chief of the military cabinet and secretary-general of the NSC under the Médici administration widened his appeal in the military (Skidmore 1988, 210). And although his commitment to the *abertura* (political opening) was

44. "Fiddling While Rome Burns," *Latin America Political Report*, September 22, 1978, 292–93.

45. The MDB attempted to take advantage of this crisis by nominating General Euler Bentes Monteiro as its 1979 presidential candidate. Monteiro was a leading military critic of Geisel's concentration of power and gained a fair amount of support from military personnel. "Opposition Decides," *Latin America Political Report*, August 18, 1978, p. 172.

recognized from the start, so too was his commitment to stability in order to assuage hard-line critics. Figueiredo made this quite clear in his October 1978 acceptance speech when he asserted: "I will promote a political opening, and will have anyone who dares to oppose it jailed and beaten."[46] His cabinet assignments paralleled this accommodation of both hard- and soft-liners. Médici associates were found in Agriculture (Delfim Neto), Mines and Energy (César Cals), Transportation (Eliseu Rezende), and Interior (Mário Andreazza), and Geisel associates were found in Finance (Carlos Rischbieter), Planning (Mário Henrique Simonsen), and as secretary-general of the presidency (Major Heitor Aquino Ferreira), and chief of the civilian household (General Golbery do Couto e Silva). Other government officers partial to *abertura* were placed in Labor (Murilo Macedo) and Education (Eduardo Portela), and as navy minister (Brigadier Délio Jardim de Mattos) (Baloyra 1986, 37).

As many expected, Figueiredo's January 1979 inauguration speech contained both carrots and sticks. Promises for direct elections for governors and all senators were mixed with allusions to a limited political amnesty and a postponement of the 1980 municipal elections to 1982.[47] *Abertura* appeared to be on track with the Party Reform Law of 1979 and a 1979 amnesty. The former abolished the existing parties (essentially, ARENA changed its name to PDS while MDB changed its name to PMDB) and opened the system to other parties, while the latter released thousands of political prisoners (Kinzo 1988, 207–8). But in military promotions, assignments, and retirements, Figueiredo would favor hard-liners through mid-1981 (Baloyra 1986, 37). Indicative of the pressure Figueiredo would receive from these officers was the March 1979 statement to the press made by then army chief of staff General José Maria de Andrade Serpa: "Economic and political liberalism is outdated. Democracy must not be allowed to run along a suicidal path; the fight against communism and corruption must not be interrupted."[48]

Early on it seemed that the growth of the hard-line in the military would influence the political bent of the government. Delfim Neto, the economic czar who oversaw the "Brazilian Miracle" under Médici, replaced Simonsen as planning minister in August 1979. This move, along with the dismissals and resignations of recognized soft-liners through 1980 appeared

46. "The President's President," *Latin America,* October 20, 1978, p. 324. Also see "After 15 Years, Military Rule Dies Hard in Brazil," *Washington Post,* March 31, 1979, p. A23.
47. "Promises," *Latin America,* January 26, 1979, p. 30.
48. "Unchanging Guard," *Latin America Political Report,* March 16, 1979, p. 85. The rise of military hard-liners is documented in "Eyes Rights," ibid., March 23, 1979, p. 90, and "Brazil's Hardliners Gaining Strength," ibid., August 24, 1979, p. 259.

to presage a solidification of the hard line in the administration (Baloyra 1986, 38).[49]

Nineteen eighty-one proved to be critical for the political definition of the regime. In an attempt to deter an IMF austerity program in the wake of the debt crisis, the Figueiredo administration essentially carried out its own austerity program through a number of contractionary policies. As a result, GDP declined by 1.6 percent, activity in the industrial sector plummeted 5.5 percent, and total investment fell nearly 11 percent (Baer 1989, 114–18). The once vibrant Brazilian economy was now in a steep recession, and business leaders who applauded the return of Delfim Neto began to criticize the government and call not only for economic but also for political reform (Frieden 1991, 125–34). The political effect was a greater reliance by Figueiredo on his hard-line supporters, and a greater isolation of the principle architect of the *abertura*, General Golbery (Selcher 1986, 59). Golbery, seeing his recommendations for reshuffling the military hierarchy, reforming the election laws, and reining-in the perpetrators of human rights abusers largely ignored, finally tendered his resignation in August.[50] The November 1981 electoral reform package, although partly designed by Golbery to increase PDS chances in the 1982 elections and support for the government, seemed more authoritarian in the hands of an administration with solid hard-line credentials.[51]

But while the Figueiredo administration found itself becoming more reliant on the hard-liners, factors were at work that eventually undermined the strength of the hard-line forces. The first incident was the Riocentro bombing on May 1, 1981. This attempt to disrupt a benefit concert for the opposition failed when the bomb exploded in the car of two army officers working for the security forces. The incident gained wide press attention, and denials of involvement by the army were ignored. The increased speculation over connections between other terrorist activities and the security forces compelled the hard-liners to eschew terrorist tactics (Skidmore 1988, 227–29). Also, the intense public inquiry forced the army to investigate the incident, and for its investigation to be further reviewed by the Superior

49. "And Now for My Next Miracle," *Latin America Political Report,* August 17, 1979, pp. 249–50.

50. "Hardliners Strengthen Their Grip as Golbery Finally Bows Out," *Latin America Weekly Report,* August 14, 1981, pp. 1–2.

51. The "November Package" prohibited on-ballot party coalitions, demanded that each party contest every office in localities where they had a branch, and forbade ticket splitting among the parties (*voto vinculado*). The reforms were a recognition that the opening of the party system failed to splinter the opposition, and were done with the hope that the *voto vinculado* would feed off the strength the PDS held in many municipalities.

Tribunal Militar. Although the tribunal eventually accepted the white-washed army report, the political pressures involved in forcing them to do so alienated some in the military and added to the growing suspicions of the effects of governance on the integrity of the armed forces (Bacchus 1990, 122–23).[52]

Other factors that weakened the military hard-liners were the deepening of the economic crisis and the war in the Malvinas. The economic crisis led many officers to question the capacity of the military to govern and the proper role of the military in a modern state. The Malvinas war opened speculations over whether or not deficiencies in military *materiel* could lead to a similarly devastating defeat for Brazil (Barros 1985). The thinking of many officers was that the military could more effectively lobby for increases in the defense budget under a civilian president because under a civilian, successful lobbying would appear to be more legitimate. Indeed, under the military regime, the armed forces had seen their budget decline precipitously since the mid-1970s. By the mid 1980s, Brazil had the lowest defense budget in South America when measured as a percentage of GDP (Stepan 1988, 72–81).

These factors reinvigorated *abertura* sentiments in government. In 1982, military withdrawal and the government commitment to it became obvious. Ironically, the first sign of this came from further electoral rule manipulations through amendment no. 22 of the constitution. By early 1982, intelligence reports showed that the opposition would do very well in the coming elections. This was important because many of the officials elected would compose the electoral college due to elect the next president in 1985, and because an overwhelming opposition victory would allow it to amend the constitution. The reforms eliminated proportional representation in the electoral college to favor the PDS, and required two-thirds rather than simple majorities for constitutional amendments. The reforms were significant because they showed that the government was willing to accept electoral defeat and work from a position of reduced strength to retain the presidency (Kinzo 1988, 212–13).[53] Other significant events in 1982 included an August 1982 cabinet reshuffle that strengthened regime soft-liners (Carlos de Medeiros 1986, 96)[54] and indications that same month that the high

---

52. "Internal Criticism of Cover-Up Embarrasses Military Leaders," *Latin American Weekly Report*, June 12, 1981, p. 5; "Serious Split in the Armed Forces Comes into the Open," ibid., October 9, 1981, p. 2.

53. "The Government Is Willing to Lose Elections, but Not Power," *Latin America Regional Reports: Brazil*, July 2, 1982, p. 1.

54. Also see "Rival Army Groups Bury the Hatchet," *Latin American Weekly Report*, August 27, 1982, p. 5.

command was willing to accept a civilian as the next president. As stated by an aide in the Army Ministry, "We have done our job and it is now time for the army to withdraw from power a little and look after its own internal affairs."[55]

But if any single date marks the initiation of the transition, it would be the November 1982 elections. First, more offices in this election were contested than in any other election under the military regime (about 56,000). Governorships and all senatorial seats were now open to election. Second, in the elections, voters rewarded political moderates and punished extremists of both the left and the right. This isolated hard-line regime elements that had warned of a "dangerous radicalization" after the elections (Selcher 1986, 64). In all, the results of the elections satisfied both the government and the opposition.[56] The electoral reforms gave the PDS majority representation in the electoral college, and the opposition welcomed its growth in the Congress and its victories in ten of the twenty-two governorships. Ironically, while gubernatorial elections induced an authoritarian move in 1965, in 1983 they acted as a significant contribution to the transition. The military remained in their barracks during the March 15 inaugurations and stressed the professional duties of the armed forces. And when economic riots erupted in São Paulo in April, the call for law and order by the leading opposition governors gratified the military and further isolated regime hard-liners.[57]

The scenario described above would lead one to expect a strongly controlled transition. Regime hard-liners were isolated, and electoral rules contained the opposition. But one must not forget that the Figueiredo administration was also very weak. The noted economic crisis, increased probes into government corruption, and lack of political skill displayed by Figueiredo were anything but conducive to a controlled transition. Selcher notes:

> There was during 1983 and 1984 the widespread impression of a reactive government in disarray, a crisis of authority without economic, political, and financial control, and without new approaches.

55. "Presidential Candidates Get Ready for Tough Battle," *Latin American Regional Reports: Brazil,* August 6, 1982, p. 1.

56. "Both Sides Can Claim Victories in Brazilian Elections," *Los Angeles Times,* November 21, 1982, p. A7.

57. "Riots Change Power Balance," *Latin American Weekly Report,* April 15, 1983, pp. 6–7. Also see "Exit the Brass in Brazil and Enter the Civilians," *New York Times,* April 19, 1983, p. 5, National edition.

There was also the image of a government marking time until the end of its term, without the competency, public support, or power of decision to solve the mounting problems, a government that within a year frittered away the national image of responsibility vital to the country's economic future. (Selcher 1986, 68)

How can the controlled transition be explained? The answer lies in how institutions, not standing governments, affect the transition process. The Figueiredo *government* was weak, but the military *regime* was not. With the presidential election dependent upon the vote in the electoral college and Figueiredo weakening, the dynamics of the transition shifted to the civilian politicians. Nonetheless, politicians accepted the decision rules established by the military. In this sense, we can say that as the opposition politicians increased their participation in actual governance, they also accepted certain rules set down by the regime. These included a prohibition on radical party activity, close consultation with the high command during the transition process, military involvement in the new democracy, and military tutelage over certain policy areas.

Fissures in the PDS led to the opposition victory in the electoral college. When the caustic, but politically skillful, Paulo Maluf secured the PDS nomination, dissidents in the PDS broke to form the Partido da Frente Liberal (PFL) and ally with the PMDB to form the Aliança Democratica (AD). The alliance was more than enough for AD candidate Tancredo Neves to win the presidency in the electoral college with 70 percent of the vote. Nevertheless, the defeat of the official government candidate was far from a defeat for the military. Many in the military, including Figueiredo, scorned Maluf's political machinery, viewing it as far too reminiscent of the politics they had worked to remove, and found Neves's victory easy to accept. Indeed, Neves had met with Army Minister Walter Pires on at least two occasions before the election to promise that there would be no investigations into military repression and to allay any fears of radicalization.[58]

Even when the armed forces looked to other PMDB leaders, it found little to fear. Viewed as the most promising party as democracy was becoming a reality, the PMDB attracted many old political elites as well as previous members of the PDS. Most party leaders allowed their self-interest to take over and welcomed the new members to strengthen the party. The result was a dilution of the influence of its more radical members. A startling indicator of this infusion is presented by Hagopian, who notes

---

58. *Latin American Monitor,* November 1985.

that after the "overwhelming" victory by the PMDB in the 1986 congressional elections, a survey of congressional members showed that 217 had once been ARENA members, whereas only 212 had been members of the MDB (Hagopian 1990, 161). The ramifications of this dilution was demonstrated when Neves died before taking office and was replaced by his vice president, José Sarney, who built his political career under ARENA and as a national PDS leader. The preservation of over fourteen thousand retired military officers in state ministries and companies and active officers in six of twenty-two cabinet positions further assured conservatism in the composition of government.[59] A study of the Sarney administration showed that the chief of the SNI, the chief of the armed forces general staff, and the ministers of the army, navy, and air force played an integral role in moderating political activism in agrarian reform, human rights, and labor policy (Zirker 1991). The military was also able to maintain a substantial degree of autonomy in military affairs. The military blocked the extension of the political amnesty to those officers purged after the 1964 *golpe,* assumed near total policy control over the arms industry, communications, foreign affairs, defense technology and research, and the development of Amazonia (Stepan 1988, 103–14; Skidmore 1988, 269–73; Conca 1992; Hagopian 1990).[60]

In conclusion, it is interesting to note that in just under five years after the transition, a poll indicated that the military was more popular than the president, the various political parties, and the Congress (Zirker 1991, 72). While support for the military is not equivalent to support for the regime, it is illuminating when one considers that the military tightly controlled the democratization process, engaged in human rights abuses, and withdrew in the midst of extreme economic crisis, yet still was held in a favorable light. The finding corroborates the view that the Brazilian military had accumulated a great deal of political capital, and that the controlled transition had its roots in political factors.

Conclusion

Comparatively, the Brazilian transition ranks well above other contemporary regime transitions in terms of military control over the process (Zaverucha 1993). Indeed, like the Chilean transition, it appeared that there was

59. "Transition Orderly in Brazil: Military Retreating with Aplomb after 21 Year Rule," *Washington Post,* February 16, 1985, p. E3.
60. "A Democracy that Suits the Generals," *New York Times,* April 10, 1988, p. E2.

more a government transition than a regime transition. Even when the new democratic government passed a new constitution in 1988, it did little to decrease the role of the military in politics.[61] I see this controlled transition as linked to the institutional configuration established under the military regime. The combination of collegial rule and low regime investment sheltered the military institution from politicization. Politicization was hindered first and foremost through low regime investment, in so far as the military consistently defined its governing mission as one that required the input and participation of civilians and focused on the creation of a civilian-controlled party system. A process I defined as institutional accommodation, which is dependent upon the combination of both collegial rule and low regime investment, further dampened politicization. Through this process, the interests of regime factions were appeased in that even as such groups were denied substantial involvement in government positions, they saw their leaders placed in positions of significant influence. The result was a regime bolstered by military unity.

Institutional accommodation was also important to strategy coordination in that it prevented alienation within the military institution. Also important to the strengthening of the tie between the military institution and government was the devolution of day-to-day policymaking to the president and the general acceptance of a coherent national security doctrine to guide the political and economic ideology of the regime. On the other side of strategy coordination, that of creating links to significant economic and political groups within society, we found a number of supportive institutions. The legacy of the ESG led the military to view civilian input as integral to their own success. By 1964, Brazilian military elites knew that a certain portion of the expertise needed for governing could come only from civilians. During its rule, the regime maintained important links to civil and political society. Some of these links discussed in this chapter were the party system, the legislature, the *conselho* system, and the devolution of policy implementation to civilian elites at the local or regional levels.

Strategy coordination allowed the regime to accumulate political capital as military rule stabilized and the economy began to grow. In an environment that could have been defined in terms of authoritarianism and increasing economic inequality, the regime effectively "campaigned" to convince significant portions of society to view this environment instead as one of political stability and economic growth. One can recognize the persistence

---

61. "Brazil's New Constitution Must Pass the Military Muster," *Los Angeles Times,* May 8, 1988, p. 2

of military disagreement and growing criticisms from society, but twenty-one years of military rule, the positive view of the military held by many in society after transition, and the capacity of the military to protect its prerogatives cannot but leave one with the view that this regime succeeded in completing its mission. The Figueiredo government illustrates the institutional basis of this success. Although his government weakened over time, the institutions established under the regime were strong enough to confine the rising opposition within rules established by the military and allow for a controlled transition.

6

Institutional Accommodation, a Lack of Strategy Coordination, and Balanced Transition in Uruguay

As the future Commander in Chief I have
the responsibility of planning how the army
is going to exit from this situation, and this
preoccupies me excessively.
—General Hugo Medina

On June 27, 1973, the Uruguayan Congress was dissolved, and political activities were suspended. Uruguay had finally fallen to military rule. The infiltration of the Uruguayan armed forces into politics occurred over a long period of time and was aided by the deterioration of legitimacy and the decline of initiative from civilian political institutions. The divisions within the legislature, the acquiescence of the president, and the ease with which the judiciary was subjugated lead many observers rightly to portray the advent of military rule more as an *autogolpe* than a *golpe* proper. As I note below, this slow accretion of power provides important background to the military regime that ruled Uruguay from 1973 to 1985, insofar as it cultivated the factors that led the regime to its eventual balanced transition—military unity and the lack of strategy coordination.

Like Brazil, Uruguay found itself under a military regime that chose collegial rule and balked at staffing government institutions with military personnel. Likewise, the Uruguayan military had difficulty defining the political future of Uruguay outside the traditional framework of political parties, and this also contributed to low regime investment. Thus, like Brazil, the Uruguayan military was able to promote unity through institutional accommodation and effective coalition building, and consequently was able to endure longer than most military regimes. But the similarities between Brazil and Uruguay end there. For in Uruguay, the lack of strategy coordination prevented the regime from fully exploiting its military unity. The regime failed to build on moderate economic success or to implement its modest political goals, and found itself both unable to endure an economic crisis when one did arise and powerless to face a growing legitimacy crisis. Unlike the Brazilian military, the Uruguayan military had neither a strong ideological basis to its rule nor decision rules to allow for the formulation and implementation of any such program. This lack of strategy coordination prevented the regime from instituting a controlled transition and consigned it to a balanced transition.

The Accretion of Political Power by the Military

Before the military intervention, Uruguay stood as an anomaly in a region marked by military unrest. Although racked by civil war throughout the nineteenth century, a system of "coparticipation" between the rural Blanco Party and urban Colorado Party emerged in the 1870s (Weinstein 1975). Uruguay soon emerged as a model Latin American democracy by the early twentieth century.[1] The economy was founded upon import-substitution industrialization and a paternalistic state sector and remained healthy until the 1950s. The artificial boom created by the Korean War gave the economy its last gasp before it fell into a steady decline (Finch 1981; Macadar 1987, 1–37).

The declining economy had an important effect on the military during the 1960s. As state resources dwindled, the military found itself spending more and more time fighting for its portion of the budget. Dragged into the political arena to justify its budget allotment, the military soon viewed politicians as antagonists, and the professional self-image of the military began to deteriorate (del Huerto Amarillo 1984).[2] Social unrest created by economic stagnation also affected the military. The growth of the Tupamaro

1. Before 1973, the country had had just one experience with dictatorship (1933–38). Notably, the dictator was an elected civilian president (Gabriel Terra), who was supported, not by the armed forces, but by the police.
2. A small state buffered by two regional giants, the Uruguayan armed forces have never had a sense of external military mission. Moves to decrease their budget forced officers to ponder their purpose, an exercise that for many could only produce angst.

guerrilla movement during the 1960s gave the military a new mission, but because this mission concerned internal security, it only served to politicize the military even more.

Vice President Jorge Pacheco Areco assumed the presidency in 1968 after the death of President Oscar Gestido. A minor Colorado Party figure, Pacheco increased the presence of *tecnicos* in the executive branch and initiated the move away from the traditional political parties (del Huerto Amarillo 1986, 9). Pacheco also opened the path for greater military influence (López Chirico 1985, 145–72). Pointing to the subversive threat, on June 13, 1968, he instituted the "medidas prontas de seguridad," which granted the executive emergency powers and increased the role of the police.[3] The military saw the police as notoriously insubordinate and viewed their control over the campaign with anxiety (del Huerto Amarillo 1986, 20). In early 1971, General Gregorio Alvarez organized from within the Escuela de Armas y Servicios an ad hoc group to formulate antisubversive strategy and process intelligence. In reaction to growing military pressure, Pacheco transferred control of the antisubversive campaign from the police to the military in September 1971.[4] The armed forces responded with the creation of the Junta de Comandantes en Jefe (JCJ), the first ever joint body of service commanders the country had known, which represented the political views of the armed forces and separated the military hierarchy from its traditional chain of command through the Ministry of Defense. The Alvarez group evolved into the Estado Mayor Conjunto (ESMACO) to coordinate antisubversive strategy among the three forces.[5]

Unable constitutionally to succeed himself in the November 1971 elections, Pacheco coordinated the election of the politically obscure Juan María Bordaberry in hopes of continuing his own influence. The result was a weak executive with little legislative support. Lacking political skill in a climate of economic crisis and social unrest, Bordaberry looked to the military for support (Bruschera 1986, 77–78). Feeding the military appetite for control, on April 15, 1972, Bordaberry pressed the legislature to declare a "state of internal war," which placed all civilians apprehended in the "war" under the jurisdiction of military courts.[6] This greatly reduced

---

3. These measures initiated a chain of repressive moves against the media, universities, labor, and other sectors even before the overt military intervention. See McDonald 1975.

4. Decree No. 566/971 (September 9, 1971).

5. Indicative of military power, both bodies were recognized by civilian authorities in a March 1973 decree. See del Huerto Amarillo 1986, 20.

6. The original declaration called for a forty-five-day period. The legislature extended the declaration several more times. On July 10, 1972, the Ley de Seguridad del Estado y el Orden Interno (No. 14,068) extended the power of the military courts by defining a number of new

civil liberties and allowed the military to establish detention centers (Rama 1973, 11–13).

The antisubversive campaign initiated a new political conflict, this time between the armed forces and the legislature. Troubled by the restrictions on civil liberties and reports of human rights abuses, on June 22, 1972, the legislature decided to investigate allegations of torture. The military refused to cooperate (Rama 1973, 14) and turned its attention to the legislature itself as the guerrilla threat came under control. Interestingly, contact with the Tupamaros inspired the military to adopt their crusade against government graft and corruption (Kaufman 1979, 131). Bordaberry aided the military offensive by organizing the Comisión de Represión de Ilícitos Económicos to investigate corruption and gave each service a seat on its board (Minello 1976, 19–21).

Involvement in the antisubversive campaign produced an institutional drive to increase repression and encroach further upon civilian political institutions. Officers up to the rank of captain found themselves in positions of unaccustomed authority. Equipped with a vague definition of subversion, they found it easy to justify their new positions (López Chirico 1985, 174–78). An expansive definition of subversion also gave the military new ammunition in its attack on government officials, whom it increasingly viewed as sympathetic to subversives. Surprisingly, the legislature did little to counter these attacks. Even after the Tupamaros had been defeated in September 1972, the legislature extended the state of internal war in September 1972, November 1972, and March 1973. This is partly explained by the assault on the legislature. The "medidas prontas de seguridad" had transferred much decision-making authority to the executive at the expense of the legislature. Yet despite warnings of a military *golpe* or an executive motion to dissolve the legislature (del Huerto Amarillo 1986, 13–14), few legislators perceived this as a threat. Conservatives accepted the military definition of subversion, leftists were encouraged by signs of progressive tendencies in the armed forces, and many saw the military encroachment on legislative prerogatives as a problem for the executive (del Huerto Amarillo 1986, 47–52).[7]

Interestingly enough, military encroachment on civilian areas of authority soon emerged as a problem for Bordaberry. After years of complicity that began under Pacheco (McDonald 1972), in October 1972 Bordaberry,

---

crimes to be placed under military jurisdiction. See Weinstein 1975, 129. Also see "El verdadero conflicto," in Quijano 1989, 277–81, originally published in *La Marcha*, May 4, 1973.

7. On the growth of political infighting under Pacheco and Bordaberry, see "Tanto va el cántaro al agua," in Quijano 1989, 231–36, originally published in *La Marcha*, February 9, 1973.

for whatever reason, suddenly decided to reestablish executive authority. First, he demanded the transfer of an investigation of illegal currency transactions from a team of air force captains to civilian authorities (Handelman 1981b, 216). Second, he demanded the release of four physicians who had been arrested and tortured by military personnel. In response, General Estéban Cristi, commander of the powerful First Army Division, organized a meeting between members of the military hierarchy and Bordaberry on October 19. There the army presented Bordaberry with an eight-point program that included demands for the immovability of commanding officers, military participation in state enterprises, absolute independence for military corruption investigations, and greater military control over local police forces. Initiated by the military itself, the action was the first explicit intervention by the military into Uruguayan political institutions (Lerin and Torres 1987, 10). In protest at having their authority disregarded, Defense Minister Legnani and army commander General Gravina resigned.

Bordaberry folded in the face of military pressure, but again attempted to reassert his authority in February 1973. With the replacement of General Gravina by another *civilista* (an officer opposed to direct military rule), General César Martínez, Bordaberry felt that he could work within the military to reestablish civilian authority. To this end, General Antonio Francese (ret.) was appointed defense minister. Francese had held the Interior Ministry under Pacheco and strongly supported the antisubversive campaign, but he backed the police and special forces and saw the army as a force of last resort (Lerin and Torres 1987, 11). The move enraged the army and air force, who issued communiqué 737 on February 7 to declare that they would not recognize the defense minister, and occupied Montevideo and all media outlets. Although the navy initially supported Bordaberry, they were swayed the amount of force the army and air force had displayed and unimpressed by Bordaberry's failure to organize popular support. The navy's decision to ally itself with the army and the air force led to the Agreement of Boiso Lanza on February 12. The agreement allowed the replacement of each commander in chief by officers more sympathetic to the military agenda, replaced the ministers of defense and the interior and led to a more general purge, and called for the creation of a National Security Council (Consejo de Seguridad Nacional—COSENA) to project military influence directly into the executive.[8]

8. COSENA was created under decree 163/73, and later ratified in laws 14,157 and 14,227. "Uruguayan Crisis Eased by Accord," *New York Times*, February 13, 1973, p. 5, Late city edition; "Uruguay Pact Assures Military Control," ibid., February 14, 1973, p. 3, Late city edition; "Worth a Mass," *Latin America*, February 16, 1973, pp. 49–50.

Opportunistically, Bordaberry attempted to portray the agreement as his own accomplishment. In a public explanation of the agreement, he proclaimed: "Now, through these measures, the armed forces will have an open legal road to undertake the new mission the executive branch assigns them. In September of 1971 they received the assignment to assume management over the antisubversive struggle; now they receive the mission to give security to national development."[9]

Having successfully subdued the executive, the military revived the corruption and subversion charges against the legislature. In late April, the military began a crusade that would result in the definitive fall of democracy. Charges of subversion were leveled against Senator Enrique Erro for alleged encounters with known Tupamaros. For two months, the military pressed the legislature to remove Erro's congressional immunity so that the military courts could prosecute him.[10] When the request was denied, the military turned to its now acquiescent agent, President Bordaberry. On June 27, 1973, Bordaberry enacted decree 464/73, which dissolved Congress,[11] created the Consejo de Estado in its place, prohibited the press from dictatorial characterizations of the executive, and empowered the armed forces to adopt any "necessary measures" to ensure the continuation of public services (Lerin and Torres 1987, 93–95). The *autogolpe* was complete.

Institutional Bases of the Uruguayan Military Regime: Collegial Rule, Low Regime Investment, and the Lack of Strategy Coordination

The accretion of political power by the military had important consequences for the construction of the military regime and strategy coordination. First, because authority was accumulated gradually, the armed forces were not "structurally obliged" to develop a unifying ideology among the officer corps to explain the institutionalization of authoritarianism. Instead, the encroachment on civilian institutions was explained piecemeal and problems were faced on an ad hoc basis. Second, compromises both

9. "La era de los militares," in Quijano 1989, 237–48, originally published in *La Marcha*, February 16, 1973.

10. On the conflict between the military and legislature during this time, see "El verdadero conflicto," "Ruido de trebejos," and "La soledad de las armas," in Quijano 1989, 277–95, originally published in *La Marcha*, March 2, 1973, May 4, 1973, and May 11, 1973.

11. Article 148 of the 1966 constitution granted the president the power to dissolve the legislature. Nonetheless, the same article also demanded elections for a new legislature on the eighth Sunday after the motion.

within the military and toward outsiders were developed in terms of the "transitory" nature of military rule. While this maximized the number of supporters, it reduced the possibility of developing a discourse conducive to permanent institutional change (Aguiar 1985, 10). Finally, the gradual accretion of political power led the military to accept a civilian role in the regime. Attempts to manage public administration exposed the inexperience of the military in such matters and the fact that the military lacked an integrated political-economic program; these discoveries became more significant to the military as the antisubversive campaign sensitized it to legitimacy concerns (Torres 1984, 169). The first two factors affected the development of strategy coordination, whereas the last affected the level of regime investment.

The Dispersion of Authority

The impetus to disperse authority had three sources. First, the growth of a paternalistic state sector under President José Batlle y Ordóñez (1903–7 and 1911–15) increased concerns over the use of state resources for political purposes. The result was an expansive state sector with little centralized control (Solari and Franco 1983, 13–40).[12] Second, even before the *autogolpe* military regulations had been designed to prevent the rise of a *caudillo* (Rial Roade 1992, 116–17, 129). For instance, the two senior officers of each service faced retirement every two years (Kaufman 1979, 55), new commanders were appointed to the four army divisions every year (Finch 1985, 95), and no officer could remain in a command position longer than four years (Rial Roade 1992, 142). Consequently, by the time of the *autogolpe* there was no obvious central military figure (Maggiolo 1976, 75), and by early 1982, every senior officer involved in the *autogolpe* had retired.[13] Also, the fact that the JCJ and ESMACO represented the first coordinating bodies among the services meant that centralization was still a novelty to most officers. A final impetus toward the dispersion of military rule was the general fear within the officer corps of a charismatic

12. There are three types of Uruguayan state agencies: autonomous agencies, which hold all powers of administration and receive minimal oversight; decentralized services, which are given basic guidelines and come under greater oversight; and intervened businesses, which hold no administrative legal status. Notably, by constitutional imperative, all industrial and commercial state businesses (the most lucrative) must be autonomous agencies (Solari and Franco 1983, 33–34). By 1965, there were twenty-two autonomous agencies, representing about 30 percent of GDP and 40 percent of all salaries (Weinstein 1988, 35).

13. "Cambios militares en Uruguay," *Clarín*, January 20, 1982, p. 17. Kaufman wrote in 1979: "Many of the originators of the *autogolpe* have already retired" (p. 76).

populist military figure. The history of self-seclusion from politics and scarcity of central military figures produced a fear of the unknown that could be addressed with collegial rule.

The dispersion of authority was caused by an attempt to create a balance of power among the executive, legislative, and judicial branches. Power was thoroughly concentrated within the executive and its new military appendages; however, there existed no single office that could be used as a springboard to concentrate authority. The formal line of authority in the executive went from the president, to COSENA, to the Secretaría de Planeamiento, Coordinación, y Difusión (SEPLACODI) and the Consejo de Económico y Social (CES), and finally to the various ministries and state businesses. The formal line of authority in the administration of defense ran from the president, to COSENA, to the JCJ, to the Junta de Oficiales Generales (JOG), to ESMACO, and to both the minister of defense and the chains of command in each service. Although these hierarchies existed on paper, reality matched neither this hierarchy nor the division between the executive and military institutions. The president was no more than a puppet figure in the regime, and the JOG, fourth in terms of the formal military hierarchy, dominated critical military *and* government policy decisions.

Four individuals held the presidency during the regime. Bordaberry lasted until 1976, when he again began to show thought independent of the military. The reluctant Alberto Demichelli,[14] vice president of the Consejo de Estado, replaced him and was removed when he refused to sign a decree to withdraw the political rights of thousands of former politicians. His replacement, Aparicio Méndez, who held the office to September 1981, was routinely censored by the military and showed no great initiative. General Gregorio Alvarez (ret.) was allowed to assume the presidency and intended to concentrate power, but was made to agree upon a shortened tenure and a commitment to a withdrawal from military rule. And when he rebelled against the JOG transition plan, he was effectively isolated.

COSENA consisted of the three service commanders; the president; the ministers of the interior, defense, foreign affairs, and economics and finance; the director of SEPLACODI; and the chief of ESMACO, who also acted as its secretary. COSENA met weekly and addressed day-to-day decision-making (Rial Roade 1986, 32). It often dictated policies through the Ministries of Defense or the Interior.[15] With the consistent placement of

14. The day after his appointment, Demichelli made the following statement at a press conference: "I am not the new president of Uruguay, but the vice-president in exercise of the presidency ... as such my mandate will not exceed 70 days" (Lerin and Torres 1987, 61).

15. "Aspectos salientes de la dialéctica político-castrense," *Búsqueda*, August 8, 1984.

an active or recently retired officer as interior minister, the armed forces dominated the body with representation from five of its nine members. The secretary would prepare documents to be considered by the body and enforce COSENA resolutions.[16] Despite the gravity of this responsibility, the position never became a center of power. Alvarez, who sought political power from the start of the regime, originally held this position, and although it helped him maintain power, it did not allow him to centralize it.

SEPLACODI and the CES coordinated planning in public administration. SEPLACODI analyzed budget and investment proposals and advised the president.[17] It was the only body that approached a unifying council for state businesses. The CES was a collegial organ presided over by the president, the minister of economics and finance, the director of SEPLACODI, the minister of defense, and the service commanders. It largely (but not completely) displaced the advisory functions of SEPLACODI when it was created in June 1974 to oversee the implementation of proposals from ad hoc civil-military conclaves (discussed below). Finally, the Economics and Finance Ministry itself held a great deal of autonomous power. Important economic policies would normally be proposed by the Ministry of Economics and Finance, considered by the CES, and then approved by the president or Consejo de Estado (Solari and Franco 1983, 41–43).

The JCJ and ESMACO were important links between the military and the government. Both were legally recognized executive advisory bodies. The JCJ represented the political positions of the armed forces, while ESMACO advised on the tactics and strategies of security-related issues. For a regime driven by "national security doctrine," this meant that ESMACO placed representatives in most government agencies (Handelman 1981b, 226).

Despite the formal hierarchy within the government and the legal connections between the JCJ and the ESMACO and the government, the JOG was the true center of power. Generals in the army, brigadiers in the air force, and admirals in the navy sat on the JOG. At the start of the regime, twelve officers from the army and three from the other forces were members. The Armed Forces Organic Law of 1974[18] added two more from each force, and in 1977 the army received two more while the other two forces received one more, raising the membership of the body to twenty-eight. The JOG exerted greater power than the JCJ both because retirement rules

16. "Uruguay: Who Will Rule?" *Latin America,* March 2, 1973, pp. 69–70.
17. SEPLACODI had its origins in the Oficina de Planeamiento y Presupuesto, which was created under the 1967 constitution. Under Institutional Act No. 3 (September 1, 1976), the name of this agency was changed to SEPLACODI.
18. Promulgated under decree 14,157 (February 21, 1974).

greatly shortened the tenures of the commanders in chief, and because the JOG used its promotion powers to advance compliant and harmless officers to the commander in chief position (this also helped to reduce infighting) (Rial Roade 1986, 30–31). The body also exerted control over all ranks through clause G of the 1974 Organic Law of the Armed Forces,[19] which allowed the compulsory retirement of any officer, including its own members, "whose activities compromise the purposes which inspire their actions" (Rial Roade 1992, 141–42). The JOG established its authority early on when it pressured Bordaberry to dismiss army commander Chiappe Posse for his resistance to input from senior officers.[20]

JOG control over the government was equally impressive. Its role in the dismissal of Bordaberry and the authorization of the rise of Alvarez (both discussed below) are indicative. COSENA, given its daily involvement in government, stood as a potential power center. To contain this threat, the JOG was given responsibility to discuss all decisions "of a substantial strategic character" first (Rial Roade 1986, 32). In 1976, the body institutionalized its role in government by inserting itself within a newly designed upper chamber of the legislature. Institutional Act No. 2 (December 6, 1976) created the Consejo de la Nación by combining the Consejo de Estado with the JOG. The body was charged with selecting the president of the republic, the president and members of the Consejo de Estado, the members of the Court of Justice (the supreme court), and the members of the Electoral Court. With a membership of twenty-eight (by 1977) to the Consejo de Estado's twenty-five (raised to thirty-five in 1981), domination was ensured for some time through the fabrication of majority rule.

A final indication of JOG power is found in the legal policymaking structure. There were three legal instruments: presidential decree laws, *leyes fundamentales,* and institutional acts. Patterned upon the Brazilian model, the institutional acts were to be the basis of a constitutional reform and were drafted by the JOG.[21] The *leyes fundamentales,* while not of a constitutional status, were to be comprehensive laws directed toward a certain area (e.g., education or labor), and were enacted by the Consejo de Estado. Notably, most actions meriting *ley fundamental* status were enacted by presidential decree, where the JOG was able to inject influence more easily (Bruschera 1986, 97–99). Early on, Bordaberry had stated that the Consejo would have

---

19. Placed in article 192 of the document by law 14,157 (April 21, 1977).

20. "Desmiente el gobierno la renuncia de todo el elenco ministerial," *El Día,* May 23, 1974, p. 1; "Snakes and Ladders," *Latin America,* November 23, 1973, pp. 370, 372; "A Delicately Unbalanced Situation," ibid., May 31, 1974, pp. 166–67.

21. The Comisión de Asuntos Políticos prepared most institutional acts.

a significant role in the drafting of new comprehensive laws.[22] The military came to view the Consejo de Estado as a threat when it realized that Bordaberry intended to establish an authoritarian regime based on it and the presidency that would be independent of the military (Maggiolo 1976, 81).

If there was any center of power within the regime, it was the JOG. But because the body worked behind the scenes, it could never act as a clear agent of authority concentration. Moreover, it was eminently collegial. Although most important decisions were handled by majority vote, decisions considered to be fundamental issues required a two-thirds majority (Rial Roade 1986, 40). The description of the regime as a "truncated pyramid" by González (1983, 68) captures the essence of how authority was dispersed in the Uruguayan government.

Low Regime Investment

Given its lack of experience in government, it is little surprise that the Uruguayan military chose to fill most government positions with civilians. Moreover, the lack of a central military figure meant that any attempt to impose one would promote discord in the ranks (Maggiolo 1976, 76). Fear of how political involvement might affect military unity is indicated by the decision to maintain the historical prohibition on military voting with Institutional Act No. 2 (June 12, 1976) (The ban was repealed in July 1984 when it was clear that the military needed all the support it could muster).[23] Significantly, this detached approach did not apply to the judicial branch. Equipped with a complete system of military justice, the armed forces did not hesitate at uprooting civilian judicial institutions. The military had already undermined the judiciary with the *Ley de Seguridad* and declarations of internal war. Institutional Act No. 3 (September 1, 1976) was meant to weaken the autonomy of the judiciary with the creation of a ministry of justice. Previously, the lack of a clear institutional linkage to the executive had served judicial independence. Institutional Act No. 8 (July 1, 1977) completed the subjugation of the judiciary. Under IA8, the executive was granted authority to remove any judge in their first four years (sitting judges were declared "interim" for four years), and replacements came under the complete authority of the executive.[24] Since the Supremo Militar

22. "Dijo ayer Bordaberry: 'No dudo en afirmar que somos protagonistas de una revolución,'" *El Día*, December 20, 1973, p. 8.

23. "Directorio Blanco denunció que se procura influenciar el voto militar," *Búsqueda*, November 21, 1984, p. 4.

24. For an early criticism, see "El Acto Institucional N. 8," *Búsqueda*, July 1977, p. 42.

Tribunal was the court of final appeal, it was fitting that the Supreme Court had its name changed to the Court of Justice. The usurpation of power by the military courts was such that at least in this branch, there was in fact a high level of direct military participation (Canabal 1985; Berrutti 1985).[25]

In the legislative branch, military involvement grew through the Consejo de la Nación. But as noted, this body held appointive rather than strictly legislative powers. Nonetheless, the Consejo de Estado itself turned out to be a powerless body. Established in the same decree that dissolved the existing legislature, the body was given the following functions:

1. to independently carry out the functions specific to the general assembly;
2. to supervise the executive power, in respect to individual rights of persons and with the compliance of said powers to legal and constitutional norms;
3. to draft a proposal for constitutional reform that reaffirmed fundamental democratic and representative principles, to be voted upon by the electoral body within a reasonable period of time (Bruschera 1986, 94).

Despite the expressed supervisory powers, the body was recognized early on as a rubber stamp for executive decrees.[26] In regard to legislation, most of the councillors had little to no political experience, and the entire body worked in isolation from public input and never divulged information on internal debates (votes were always reported as unanimous).[27]

The executive branch, where real governmental power was found, was marked by an absence of military officers. As noted, an active military officer never held the presidency, and in the cabinet, only the Interior Ministry consistently had an officer on its staff. The only executive bodies with a substantial military presence were COSENA and the CES. COSENA represented a true insertion of the military into policy decisions, but the role of the CES is easily overstated. The body was designed to assure the implementation of the economic policy proposals formulated at periodic civil-military conclaves, which were held over several days at resort-like settings in the interior of the country (Lerin and Torres 1987, 50). The fact that the

25. For informative descriptions of the judicial system under the regime, see Washington Office on Latin America 1981 (appendix) and Pearce 1980.

26. "La determinantes culturales del Consejo de Estado," *Búsqueda*, March-April 1974, pp. 20–30. For a strained argument on the powers of the Consejo, see the *dictamen* issued by a special commission of the Consejo de Estado, printed in "Debe promulgar el ejecutivo los actos del Consejo de Estado con calidad de sancionados," *El Día*, January 3, 1974, p. 10.

27. "Historia de los consejos de estado," *La Democracia*, September 4, 1981, p. 11.

neoliberal policy implemented under the regime did not significantly break from pre-*golpe* strategy (Macadar 1987, 105), and that the populist rantings of many officers were effectively ignored, signifies the weight of civilians in economic policy.[28] Indeed, at the same time the CES was created, the Ministry of Economics and Finance was granted a host of new powers to coordinate policy planning and implementation among the ministries (Solari and Franco 1983, 42).

At the local and regional level, military involvement seems to have been subordinated to collegial rule within the military. Each of the commanders of Uruguay's four army divisions was granted extensive powers of appointment in their respective regions, which they used to appoint officers responsible to them as *intendentes*-governors and as departmental administrators (Rial Roade 1986, 39).[29] At the municipal level, the Juntas Departamentales were dissolved and effectively replaced by military-appointed Juntas de Vecinos. Granted the same nominal supervisory and legislative authority as the Consejo de Estado by a July 1973 decree and later under IA3 (November 1, 1976), these bodies had little actual authority (Bruschera 1986, 99).

The military refrained from greater involvement in government, not because it did not wish to govern, but rather because it did not know how. In the areas in which the military felt that it had an acceptable level of proficiency (e.g., the judiciary, police, and diplomatic services), it intervened with zeal. Moreover, ESMACO established itself as a placement service for officers in government. In almost every government agency, ESMACO placed an officer, usually a colonel, at the second or third tier of the hierarchy (significantly, the Ministry of Economics and Finance was the only ministry without an ESMACO officer). This allowed the military both to monitor civilians and give its officers experience in governing (Handelman 1981b, 226–27). Finally, the military did place officers as directors of many state businesses, including the Central Bank, UTE (electrical utilities), ANCAP (oil refining), ANTEL (telecommunications), and the postal service (Gillespie 1991, 53). In general, the army ran the railroads, the air force ran the state airline, and the navy ran the fishing terminals.[30] But the lack of expertise as well as the lack of effective coordinating bodies within the

28. For a report on the first conclave, see "After San Miguel," *Latin America*, September 7, 1973, pp. 284–85.

29. All officers serving in government positions remained answerable to the military hierarchy (López Chirico 1985, 198–99). This increased the power of the division commanders and made the JOG a more collegial institution.

30. "Uruguay Regime Considers Relaxing Grip," *New York Times*, February 12, 1976, p. 18, Late city edition.

executive bureaucracy kept most officers from being anything more than administrators. The military was intellectually capable of policy control only in security-related matters. In most all other areas, the armed forces gawked with envy, but felt comfortable exerting nothing more than a veto power.

Although the lack of military involvement in government was a primary reason why regime investment remained low, one must also recognize how regime institutions and the role of the military in them were defined. The intervention had not been the result of any grand strategy on the part of the military (Kaufman 1979, 68–69; McDonald 1975). The degeneration of civilian institutions largely drew the military into politics. This does not mean that the military were unwilling participants or oblivious to their own actions. Indeed, six days after its creation, on September 15, 1971, the JCJ drafted secret Resolution No. 1 to orient strategy toward two goals: (1) the dismantling of the subversive threat; (2) military participation in all decisions related to national security. Although the obtuse definitions imparted to "subversion" and "national security" in the document were hardly conducive to the formulation of a clear political strategy, the JCJ declared that the goals of Resolution No. 1 had been attained with the February 1973 establishment of COSENA (del Huerto Amarillo 1986, 30–31). Thus, the only document that provided a semblance of a political plan did not actually call for a *golpe*.[31] In the end, the intervention itself can rightly be portrayed as "defensive"—the military wished to defend political and economic institutions from "subversion," and over time, found that it needed to defend itself from a legislature that weakened its crusade with allegations of torture (López Chirico 1985, 197). This inability to focus the military role in the founding of a new political regime (as I document below, military elites found it difficult to speak of future Uruguayan politics without reference to traditional political parties) did little to promote regime investment for the military.

The Lack of Strategy Coordination

The discussion thus far highlights basic similarities between Uruguay and Brazil. In both cases authority was dispersed, and the distinction between the military and the government roles was maintained. But in the area of strategy coordination, the two cases stand far apart. The Uruguayan military did not pursue an "offensive project" because it lacked an institutional

---

31. Indeed, according to Resolution No. 1 one of the primary means toward containing subversion was the security of the November 1971 elections and subsequent March 1972 transfer of power (del Huerto Amarillo 1986, 30).

apparatus to translate the diffuse national security doctrine ideology into a political strategy. Moreover, institutionally, the regime was poorly equipped to develop a political program while in power. The military leaders inherited a disorganized bureaucracy, had few linkages with civilians, and failed to design accommodative decision rules that would allow its collegial ruling group to forge consensual strategies.

In the midst of the February 1973 *autogolpe,* the military did announce what appeared to be a political program in communiqués 4 and 7. The calls for land reform, government actions to increase exports and employment, a redistribution of income, and greater inquests into government corruption seemed to signify a *peruanista* inspired strategy.[32] But time proved these pronouncements to be a hoax, designed to inspire support for the new military role in COSENA (López Chirico 1985, 190).

Indeed, over the course of the regime, the most radical proposals to redesign Uruguayan politics came not from the military, but from the civilian presidents. Bordaberry was ousted for proposing a permanent reform of the state that would have concentrated power in a civilian executive and definitively suppressed all parties, while Demichelli, whose policy proposals were corporatist inspired, was simply ignored (Lerin and Torres 1987, 62–66).[33] The first official political program, the *Plan Político de las Fuerzas Armadas de 1977* (August 9, 1977) was never even released publicly in a coherent manner. Rather, several officers divulged it over time in a series of press conferences, and each gave it a personal spin. The contradictory and piecemeal statements did more to produce confusion in society than to specify regime intentions (Lerin and Torres 1987, 69). The proposed constitution of 1980 was an attempt to redesign Uruguayan politics, but it was essentially an amalgamation of the security-based institutional acts and depended greatly on participation from the traditional political parties. Like the *autogolpe* itself, the constitution was essentially "defensive." It was not so much a design for a new political order as a design to restrain the old political order.

As noted, the dearth of political initiative on the part of the military can be attributed partly to the gradual pace of the *autogolpe.* A more fundamental cause was the late professionalization of the Uruguayan armed forces and the paucity of institutions to formulate and disseminate political ideas. The development of an organized, professional military was slower in Uruguay than in the rest of the Southern Cone (English 1984, 426). Both

32. The communiqués can be found in *Clarín,* February 11, 1973, pp. 3, 24–25.

33. For an exposition of Bordaberry's political ideas, see Bordaberry 1980. For the corporatist thought of Demichelli, see Demichelli 1976.

civilians and officers recognized that the Brazilian and Argentine militaries dwarfed their own armed forces, and many politicians had advised severely reducing, or even completely disbanding, the armed forces. Military service was not compulsory and had little prestige in the eyes of the Uruguayan elite (Rial Roade 1986, 11). For these reasons, military education concentrated on purely military techniques and concerns. Not until the 1960s did courses for superior officers include sociology, economics, and international politics (López Chirico 1985, 91–95), and national security doctrine did not appear in standard military training until 1972 (Rial Roade 1986, 40 n. 45). Even so, the main school for superior officers, IMES (Instituto Militar de Estudios Superiores), did not approach the ideological push of such institutions as the Peruvian CAEM by the time of the *autogolpe* (Kaufman 1979, 60 n. 20; Ramírez 1971, 198). ESEDENA (Escuela de Seguridad y Defensa Nacional), which was expressly commissioned with diffusing a doctrine of national security that favored military tutelage over political institutions, was not created until 1978.[34]

Given the above, it should come as no surprise that scholars have found it difficult to identify any ideological predispositions within the Uruguayan military (Rama 1973; Sondrol 1992). Even those scholars who do distinguish between apparent ideological factions (e.g., the "Peruvian-populists" and "Brazilian hard-liners") (Handelman 1981b, 221–24; also see Kaufman 1979, 55–60) recognize that these divisions were more personal than ideological (Kaufman 1979, 56–57) and in fact differed very little ideologically (Handelman 1981b, 222–24). This is not to deny the impact of the national security doctrine that inspired military regimes throughout South America (Arriagada 1981; Martorelli 1984), but simply to note that it was not as well developed in Uruguay. Whereas the Brazilian military conflated security and development, the Uruguayan military submerged development within security, expecting it to flow freely in an environment absent of subversion. Because of this, national security doctrine did serve to unify the military (Rial Roade 1986, 40), but it could not serve as a catalyst for policy. And even in this partial form, the doctrine lacked the numerous avenues of dissemination found in the Brazil. Hence the first obstacle to the development of strategy coordination in Uruguay—the armed forces had no political strategy in the first place.[35]

34. ESEDENA was replaced by CALEN (Centro de Altos Estudios Nacionales).
35. The education policy manifests the lack of political initiative. Despite the absolute control exerted by the military, officers placed in teaching positions, and continuous expressions on the need to direct students toward patriotic, moral studies, school curricula reflected the effects of censorship more than they represented a program of indoctrination (Cayota 1985).

But the lack of an independently formulated political ideology does not necessarily mean that a regime will lack a coherent political program. The Brazilian military went a long way toward formulating a political program independently, but the Chileans borrowed an existing strategy from civilians (this was especially evident in the economic strategy developed under Pinochet). But even the Chilean course was denied to the Uruguayan armed forces for two reasons. First, the traditional disdain felt by the civilian elite toward the military furthered the divide between civilians and officers, thereby impeding interaction. For example, fellow officers usually reproached those officers that did attend civilian universities as part of their education, and these same officers often found themselves passed over for promotion (Rial Roade 1992, 174). Second, public administration in Uruguay was not conducive to the generation of a coherent, unifying ideology. Solari and Franco provide a comprehensive documentation of the paucity of coordinating bodies and advisory groups at the disposal of chief decision-makers. In specific reference to the state businesses, they write: "This dispersed network of communication with the executive impedes a continuous and earnest flow of information, having shown itself as not very adequate for conferring homogeneity and coherence to the management of business" (1983, 47). As highlighted by the *Revolución Argentina,* a regime's success in political strategy is closely linked to its success in economic strategy.

The periodic conclaves did little to help the regime. Unlike the Brazilian *conselho* system, which saw an ideologically equipped regime successfully extract expertise from sectoral groups as it maintained its autonomy and cohesion, the conclave design simply reinforced the lack of strategy coordination. It allowed interest groups to coordinate their own strategy and impose their policy preferences, as evidenced by the lack of military initiative in economic policy.

Finally, the Uruguayan regime lacked the decision rules conducive to strategy coordination in a collegial setting. In Brazil, power was dispersed — senior officers expressed their opinions and were involved in the most significant decisions. But these same officers recognized that the day-to-day decision-making of the regime was under the purview of the president. So long as the president did not move outside of a general sphere of policy-making expectations, he was let alone. On the other hand, in Uruguay, the JOG did not hesitate to involve itself in the daily decision-making process and was a strong presence in the operations of the JCJ and COSENA. The president was not so much a delegate as a closely observed puppet, controlled by the hands of numerous officers who spent much of their time debating just how to manipulate him.

The Uruguayan Military Regime: Bolstered by Military Unity but Ultimately Unsuccessful

A journalistic account of the Uruguayan case presents us with a puzzle. The regime displayed a significant level of cohesion, experienced moderate economic success, and had modest political goals. Nonetheless, in the end it was unable to elicit support from society and was thereby unsuccessful in its attempt to control the transition. This outcome can only be explained by the combination of military unity and the lack of strategy coordination.

Cohesion in the Uruguayan Military

Subordination to civilian rule and warm relations with the long-dominant Colorado Party (Rial Roade 1986, 11–17) stifled the growth of ideological divisions in the armed forces for much of the twentieth century. The election of a Blanco president in 1958, deepening economic problems, and budget reductions increased disgruntlement, but involvement in the antisubversive campaign rejuvenated military unity. The psychological impact of military operations generated an esprit de corps, and the need for interservice coordination produced coordinating institutions such as ESMACO, the JCJ, and the Servicio de Inteligencia de la Defensa (SID), which centralized the intelligence operations and many repressive programs of the three forces (López Chirico 1985, 198–203).

As in all instances of military rule, some unity is fabricated through the use of purges against *civilista* officers. The Uruguayan military was no exception (Kaufman 1979, 75–76). The Boiso Lanza accord allowed for the replacement of the army and naval commanders by more sympathetic officers, and called for the creation of new organic law. A secret disposition diminished the traditional use of coursework completion as a primary criterion for promotions, thereby allowing greater political discretion over the rise of officers (López Chirico 1985, 198). And the 1977 addition of clause G to the 1974 Organic Law of the Armed Forces legalized the purging of disobedient officers.[36]

But more than the antisubversive campaign or purges, it was the institutions found in government that maintained unity. Collegial rule allowed the military to incorporate potentially rebellious officers. Recognizing the contribution of collegial rule, in April 1977 the government reinterpreted

---

36. Soon after the law was passed, forty-six army and navy officers (including three generals) were retired. For details, see "Desperation," *Latin America Political Report,* April 1, 1977, p. 103; "Military Fixing," ibid., May 6, 1977, p. 135; and "Military Purge," ibid., May 27, 1977, p. 157. Rial Roade 1986, 28 n. 31, notes that the navy used the clause the most, followed by the army. The air force never applied it.

the 1974 Organic Law of the Armed Forces, which called for fourteen army generals, to call for "at least" fourteen generals and made some key promotions without subsequent retirements.[37] Although most civilian leadership roles were titular, their existence was critical. Civilian participation allowed the military to answer collectively critics who pointed to its lack of direct political experience and expertise in policy (Handelman 1986, 205–6). More important, by granting civilians nominal leadership titles, the regime was able to prevent politically ambitious officers from using government offices as positions of power. The mixture of collegial rule with civilian participation meant that most soldiers could identify politically with some superior officer who held significant decision-making power, while at the same time there was a safeguard against any officer gathering too much power. The possibility of alienation or politicization on the part of the armed forces was decreased considerably.

The rise and fall of military divisions during the regime illustrates the impact of these institutional features. Some divisions marked the first year of rule by driving the *civilistas* from their ranks. General Hugo Chiappe Posse, who had replaced General César Martínez as army commander, first quarreled with Colonel Ramón Trábal (chief of the Servicio de Inteligencia del Ejército and ally of General Gregorio Alvarez, who was commander of the Fourth Army Division by this time), over his continued inquiries into government corruption (Chagas and Tonarelli 1980, 62). Chiappe Posse's Colorado antecedents may have played a role in his defense of the Bordaberry administration, and given the Blanco past of most other generals of the time, his stand put him at odds with many in the JOG. The division deepened as his opposition to political input from the JOG became clear. When Chiappe Posse tried to dismiss Generals Eduardo Zubiá (commander of the Second Army Division) and Rodolfo Zubiá (commander of the Third Army Division) for criticizing government policy, Alvarez threw his support behind the Zubiás and called for Chiappe Posse's removal. When General Estéban Cristi, commander of the most powerful First Division, refused to take his side, Chiappe Posse stood down.[38]

Cristi's neutrality was politically motivated. His differences with Alvarez materialized quickly.[39] But a series of moves prevented these differences from generating a regime crisis. Cristi's power increased when Colonel

37. "Military Fixing," *Latin America Political Report,* May 6, 1977, p. 135.

38. "A Delicately Unbalanced Situation," *Latin America,* May 31, 1974, pp. 166–67.

39. While many scholars place Alvarez as a *peruanista* and Cristi as a hard-liner, at the same time they argue that their differences were essentially political posturing, and portray them as opportunists, simply vying for political power. See Kaufman 1979. Also see "Military Two Step," *Latin America,* June 20, 1975, pp. 185–86.

Trábal, an ally of Alvarez, as noted earlier, was reassigned to Paris as a military attaché (where he was "mysteriously" assassinated), and a Cristi partisan, General Julio César Vadora, was appointed army commander. This helped balance the power held by Alvarez and the Zubiá brothers, who were somewhat appeased because Vadora was essentially a political unknown. Because of collegial rule, each group was able to find multiple points of policy influence within the regime without threatening the prerogatives of the other.

Circumstances united the Cristi and Alvarez factions over the next few years. The transition toward collegial rule produced the perception of a power vacuum within the army. The security forces grew more factionalized and autonomous, and took the initiative in a ferocious onslaught against Communist Party members in late 1975. The move united the high command, who reinstated their authority (Chagas and Tonarelli 1980, 99). About this same time, tensions began to develop between the military and President Bordaberry. In a series of memos sent to the JOG, Bordaberry expressed his desire to extend his mandate past March 1976 and establish an authoritarian state. The military grew suspicious of his recommendation that the military completely remove itself from public administration and rejected his proposal to prohibit all party activity in any future regime. The military could not envision a regime completely devoid of the traditional parties and feared international repercussions from financial groups and the Carter administration (Maggiolo 1976, 79–82). Significantly, both Cristi and Vadora were due to retire in February 1976, but were allowed to stay on so as not to upset the balance of power as the military resolved the Bordaberry crisis by removing him from office.[40]

From 1977 to 1979, the collegially organized JOG effectively contained a series of retirements, promotions, and assignments that threatened military cohesion. The year 1977 seemed to portend the rise of Alvarez. Vice Admiral Hugo Márquez, who as navy commander led a massive purge of *civilista* navy officers and represented a hub of political power,[41] relinquished command of the navy in April, and Cristi retired in August. Alvarez especially welcomed the Cristi retirement, expecting a move from Fourth Division commander to First Division commander (the rotation was a tradition). Hesitant to assist Alvarez in his well-known quest for power, the JOG instead placed the less threatening General Rodolfo Zubiá in this powerful position.[42] Alvarez was set back, but his credentials assured him of the

40. "No Elections," *Latin America,* March 12, 1976, p. 82.
41. "Military Purge," *Latin America Political Report,* May 27, 1977, p. 157.
42. "Laying Down the Law," *Latin America Political Report,* September 16, 1977, p. 286.

army command in February 1978. Nonetheless, by this time, new opponents moved forward to check his rise. General Alberto Ballestrino, former head of the Montevideo Police and in 1978 the director of the Escuela de Armas y Servicos, and General Manuel Nuñez, former army chief of staff and in 1979 interior minister, moved forward as a new centers of hardline opposition to check Alvarez. The chief of army intelligence, General Amaury Prantl, also attempted to block any accumulation of power by Alvarez, who was trying to impose greater centralization on the intelligence services. However, Prantl overstepped his authority when he used a military publication, *El Talero*, to portray Alvarez as a powermonger with little regard for military professionalism. Alvarez used his authority as army commander to dismiss Prantl in June 1978.[43]

But it was the JOG itself that was Alvarez's greatest obstacle. Alvarez led calls for competitive elections in 1981, when the Aparicio Méndez presidential term would expire. The reality was that Alvarez was due to retire in February 1979; and knowing that he would thereupon lose much of his authority, he saw a quick movement away from strict military oversight as his only chance to contain his opponents in the military and gain the presidency (Lerin and Torres 1987, 104–6). Nineteen seventy-eight was thus a critical year for the regime as the balance of power was threatened. Although Alvarez was due to retire the following year, two expected promotions were likely to set supporters in positions to aid his quest for the presidency. First, in November 1978, the First Army Command position again opened with the retirement of Rodolfo Zubiá. General Abdón Raimúndez, a brother-in-law and supporter of Alvarez, held the Fourth Army Command. The JOG delayed its assignment decision and left the position open. Second, General Juan José Méndez, an Alvarez supporter, was due to follow Alvarez as army commander. In February 1979, the JOG made its move to maintain equilibrium. The First Army Command position was filled by a neutral officer (although he would soon oppose Alvarez)— the previous interior minister General Hugo Linares Brum, and José Méndez was passed over as army commander in favor of General Luis V. Quierolo. At the same time, four of the five colonels promoted to general and thereupon gaining membership in the JOG were recognized Alvarez supporters.[44]

The 1977–79 period illustrates the contribution of collegial rule and low regime investment (in so far as it implies military involvement primarily

43. "Top Dog Barks," *Latin America Political Report*, July 14, 1978, p. 213.
44. "More of the Same," *Latin America Political Report*, February 2, 1979, p. 37–38; "Filling Gaps," ibid., March 9, 1979, pp. 78–79.

for higher-ranking officers only) to military unity. With multiple points of authority and frequent turnover created by the retirement rules, it was difficult for any one individual to accumulate power. Likewise, the oversight provided by the JOG provided a check against any accumulation of power. Regime institutions explain why contemporary investigations of the regime at this time concluded that it was not seriously threatened by factional divisions (Maggiolo 1976, 75; Pearce 1980, 33–34).

Moderate Economic Success

Economic progress under the regime was unspectacular and mixed. But placed in the context of decades of economic decline, the military could legitimately claim some success. And as the cases of Chile and Brazil demonstrate, economic gains do not have to be evenly distributed across all groups to elicit regime support. So long as some important economic groups benefit, conditions are suitable for the development of political support.

The economic model under the regime did not vary considerably from the model already in place at the time of the *autogolpe*. The National Plan of Development for 1973–77 had been formulated in 1972. In conclaves at San Miguel (August 1973) and Nirvana (October 1973), the military attempted to exert some influence, but changes in the plan, designed now to guide policy from 1974 to 1978, did not reflect military pressure as much as they did the 1973 oil crisis (Notaro 1983, 114). The four main points of the plan essentially restated the neoliberal civilian plan: (1) reduce the public sector with private enterprise; (2) allow for economic concentration to facilitate the incorporation of modern technology; (3) induce foreign investment; (4) reduce protectionism. Inflation, considered a purely monetary phenomenon, was to be attacked through deficit reduction (Bruschera 1986, 137–38). The minister of economics and finance, Alejandro Vegh Villegas, implemented the plan from July 1974 to the moment that his close contact, Valentín Arismendi, replaced him in September 1976.

Under the plan, the Uruguayan economy showed its greatest vitality since the 1950s. An average annual rise in the GDP of 4.1 percent represented five straight years of growth for the first time in twenty years,[45] and investment increased from 11.6 percent to 16 percent of GDP. Nontraditional exports, the development of which was a central goal of the government, increased at an average annual rate of 32 percent, and overall

45. The years 1961–68 saw an average annual GDP growth rate of just 0.3 percent, and the 1968–73 rate rose to just 1.9 percent (Macadar 1982, 51).

exports increased from 14.1 percent to 17.9 percent of GDP (Favaro and Bensión 1993, 273). The fight against inflation found mixed success. While consumer price increases averaged 43.4 percent from 1968 to 1973, the average rose to 62.4 percent for the following five years. An assessment of the economic plan in 1978 by the liberal newspaper *Búsqueda* criticized the government for not following some of its own prescriptions, such reducing government intervention and liberalizing the financial sector, strictly enough.[46] A general assessment shows that from 1974 to 1980, Uruguay fared better economically than Argentina and Chile did (Macadar 1982, 50; Filgueira 1984, 5). Finally, in a detailed survey of industrial growth during the 1970s, Macadar (1987) illustrates the vibrancy of the sector, which experienced an average annual growth rate of 4.8 percent.

Despite the economic turnaround, labor found itself worse off. Although employment remained fairly stable, real salaries fell 43 percent during the 1970s (Macadar 1982, 228). The impoverishment of labor had repercussions in the retail sector, which saw the demand for its goods decrease (Handelman 1981a, 263). Another economic loser was the livestock sector, which saw its problems in the international economy (e.g., the closure of the European market) remain largely unaddressed by the government. The sector maintained a defiant position toward the regime, although it did benefit some from 1978 to 1980 after price controls were lifted on many of its products (Finch 1985). The clear beneficiaries of the regime's economic policies were nontraditional exporters and the financial sector (Pearce 1980, 38).

The period up to 1980 can be divided into two. From 1974 to 1978, the Uruguayan business sector reaped the rewards of socioeconomic calm, and exports drove the economy. In 1979 and 1980, the economy experienced its greatest boom, with GDP growth rates of 8.7 percent and 4.5 percent. During this time, high inflation and restricted credit rates created a negative real interest rate, and speculation increased dramatically. The construction sector boomed, but most loans were not used for investment purposes (although public investment picked up the slack). When inflation failed to achieve anticipated levels, a debt crisis ensued. The crisis deepened when the exchange rate began to fall, and foreign capital drawn to Uruguayan banks by the once favorable exchange rate began to retreat, driving up interests rates further and reducing the amount of capital available for refinancing. Despite the severe economic crisis of the 1980s, the picture presented by

---

46. "Objetivos del Plan de Desarollo: 1973–1977," *Búsqueda*, January 1978, pp. 22–23. Also see the editorial "Esto no es aquello," ibid., July 1977, p. 1.

most studies of the Uruguayan economy is one of stability and moderate success from 1973 to 1980. True, many structural problems, such as the lack of capital improvements and an impending consumption crisis, were not being addressed, but it cannot be denied that there were clear economic winners available to the regime as potential supporters.[47]

Modest Political Goals

The Uruguayan military wished not to transform Uruguayan politics, but to contain them. The limited nature of JCJ Resolution No. 1 and disregard of communiqués 4 and 7 meant that the military entered government without an established political plan. An early political statement released by the JOG on May 15, 1974, defined as the political intentions of the military the following: (1) a recess from political activities, during which time adequate social, economic, and moral conditions of the country would develop and the parties would restructure themselves around new leaders; and (2) a new constitution to institutionalize the security concerns of the armed forces.[48] The first evidence of a political plan did not come until 1975, when the Comisión de Asuntos Políticos (COMASPO—a JOG committee normally consisting of six officers from the army and two from each of the other forces plus any number of nonpermanent members) issued Memorandum No. 1/75 on February 4.[49] The short memo defines as the mission of the armed forces: "To give continuity through political measures to the process initiated by the armed forces in an adequate political, economic, and social environment, maintaining its competence in national security." The memo then recognizes the following "minimum conditions" for a transition:

1. a system of proscriptions;
2. the designation by the armed forces of a single candidate acceptable to the traditional parties for the first presidential election;
3. the prohibition of Marxist parties;
4. constitutional changes to create institutions that allow for military influence;

47. Good surveys of the economy under the regime can be found in Weinstein 1988, 55–68, Notaro 1983, Astori 1982, Macadar 1982, and Finch 1981.
48. A 1981 COMASPO report mentions this document as the first official political statement by the armed forces. See document in Achard 1992, 323.
49. The complete document is printed in Achard 1992, 233–35.

5. electoral laws to assure a majority in parliament for the winning party;
6. acceptance of these conditions by both domestic and international public opinion.

The memo goes on to define four transition stages. The "present" stage would be an interim period that would last until the constitutionally mandated change in government (in March 1977); a "pseudo-constitutional" stage, during which a new constitution would be formulated; a "pre-constitutional" stage, which would begin with the promulgation of the constitution and under which the new political parties would be restructured and general elections would take place, and finally a "constitutional" period, which would begin with the assumption of office by the new political authorities. None of the latter three stages were given dates.

On August 9, 1977, after a conclave at Santa Teresa, the president placed his rubber stamp on the *Plan Político de las Fuerzas Armadas de 1977*. The JOG-COMASPO document elaborated slightly on Memorandum 1/75. It set dates for elections to specific offices, for party internal elections, and for constitutional reform. The *cronograma*, as it became known, called for a constitutional plebiscite in November 1980, the rehabilitation of the political parties through 1981 and restricted elections (e.g., a single presidential candidate) in November 1981 with the transfer of office in March 1982, and unrestricted national elections in November 1986 with the transfer of office in March 1987. While the document said nothing of the content of the constitution, other than to emphasize military tutelage in national security matters, it was understood that the constitution would be based upon existing institutional acts and others currently under study.[50]

COMASPO, with the aid of outside military and civilian advisers, began elaborating specific principles of the constitution in December 1977. On March 21, 1980, suggestions were delivered to the JCJ, which scrutinized them and presented them to President Méndez in a COSENA meeting. On May 15, COSENA approved the guidelines and sent them to the Consejo de Estado to elaborate a final draft. After numerous consultations with COSENA, the Consejo de Estado produced a text of 239 articles on October 24, 1980. The draft then went to an ad hoc "constitutive assembly" (so named in hopes of garnering greater legitimacy) composed of the president, the ministers, the Consejo de Estado, and the JOG. After four days

50. The *Plan Político* is printed in Achard 1992, 261. Achard also reproduces JOG memos on proposed institutional acts (pp. 242–43, 247–51, 257–58).

of debate, the draft was finally made public on November 1, 1980, just four weeks before the plebiscite (Lerin and Torres 1987, 111–13). The document was an amalgamation of the institutional acts and numerous measures and was designed to instill military tutelage, centralize executive power, constrain civil liberties, facilitate the imposition of states of security, prohibit radical parties, and expand the jurisdiction of the military judicial system (Bruschera 1988, 70–82)

Compared to other cases of military rule, the original political objectives were modest. Many military regimes enter politics as regimes of exception, but they usually waffle on the establishment of a withdrawal date. The Uruguayan regime was quite deliberate in its self-portrayal as an interim regime.[51] In terms of the changes demanded in the political system, many politicians had already accepted the insertion of the military into government decision-making, and the recent political deadlock gave credence to the need to restructure the electoral system to produce majorities. Most important, the military did not demand the destruction of the traditional political parties and their replacement by some new mobilizing agent.[52] Leftist parties were to be excluded, but many politicians welcomed this. The essence of the military action was one of the restoration of stability and economic development by restricting the Uruguayan political system. The changes hoped for were more procedural than substantive, in that new rules of the games were to be introduced, but it was up to civil society to formulate the ideas to be played out within those rules.

The Lack of Strategy Coordination and Failure

Despite military cohesion, moderate economic success from which political capital could be cultivated, and relatively modest political expectations, by late 1980 it was clear that the military was isolated from society. The loss in the November 1980 constitutional plebiscite signified the definitive failure of the regime to impose a controlled transition (Handelman 1986). To

51. The revolutionary rhetoric of many military regimes means that anything less than a controlled transition must be viewed as an absolute failure. The image as a stabilizing, temporary regime allowed the Uruguayan military to claim victory even under a balanced transition. Comments by General Guillermo De Nava (chief of the Escuela de Especialidades del Ejército) in 1984 are illustrative—see "De Nava: 'Las fuerzas armadas vuelven a sus específicas fortalecidas ideológicamente y fuertemente unidas,'" *Búsqueda*, September 26, 1984, p. 6.

52. Indeed, the official explanation for the dismissal of Bordaberry was his desire to permanently dissolve the political parties. Although the extraction of military personnel from public administration was an equally important reason, by defending the traditional parties the military committed itself to their restoration.

explain this failure in spite of the auspicious conditions in which the regime found itself, I point to the absence of strategy coordination.

The first puzzle to be explained is why the beneficiaries of its economic policies failed to support the regime in its time of need. At the time of the *autogolpe* several principle business groups, such as the Cámara de Industrias, the Cámara de Comercio, and the Asociación de Bancos, declared support (Notaro 1983, 113). In interviews with several economic elites, Handelman (1981a, 249–50) found that most welcomed the intervention because it stifled labor strife and imposed order. And as evidenced by editorials in *Búsequeda*, many of those business elites which did not directly benefit applauded the neoliberal approach of the regime. But the problem was the lack of policy input by these groups. Economic groups could no longer lobby policies through the Congress or the political parties, the Consejo de Estado was inconsequential, and the Ministries of Agriculture and Industry, once important conduits for sectoral input, were incapacitated. Finally, those institutions which had real economic policymaking power, the Ministry of Economics and Finance and ESMACO, isolated themselves from external influence (Handelman 1981a, 258–59). Without effective lines of communication, economic beneficiaries were reluctant supporters because they could not be certain if present policies would continue, and economic losers saw outright opposition as their only form of pressure (Gillespie 1991, 108).

The inability to succeed with even modest political goals is also explained by the lack of strategy coordination. First, note the development of political objectives under the regime from the time of JCJ Resolution No. 1 and the May 15, 1974, JOG statement of political intentions to that of the proposed constitution of 1980. Without input from experienced conservative political leaders, the military largely confined its activities to that area it knew best, national security, and relentlessly expanded upon it. The result was perhaps the most Orwellian national security state of the Southern Cone dictatorships. Every adult citizen was assigned a letter to indicate faithfulness to democracy. "C" meant that the citizen was denied public employment and a passport. A "B citizen" was considered suspicious and watched carefully. Only "A citizens" were considered "safe." Although the number of disappearances, one hundred, was relatively low, it is estimated that one of every fifty Uruguayans was arrested (and often tortured) at some time by the regime (Amnesty International 1979). And while Brazil also imposed political proscriptions, the 15,000 proscribed in Uruguay represents a number proportionately 1,000 times that of the 500 proscribed in populous Brazil (Gillespie and González 1988, 222). To maintain the national security state, there was an inordinate increase in military personnel.[53] All this occurred in an environment lacking any threat from guerrillas, terrorist action, labor mobilization, or political protest (Handelman 1986).

Whereas the Brazilian military conflated security and development, the Uruguayan submerged development within security, expecting it to flow freely in an environment free of subversion. National security doctrine unified the military over time (Rial Roade 1986, 40), but it could not serve as a catalyst for policy. The constitution of 1980, then, was not so much a political plan as it was an expression of paranoia toward political mobilization. The document was replete with specifications on nocturnal home invasions, restrictions on habeas corpus, minimal civil liberties, an expanded military justice system, and military tutelage throughout government, but the traditional political parties were still expected to provide the substance of Uruguayan politics.

The lack of political vision was simply pathetic. Not only were economic elites isolated, but co-optable politicians were summarily disregarded (Aguiar 1985, 15). Rather than employ their political experience, as in Brazil, politicians became the most repressed group in Uruguayan society (González 1991, 65). Furthermore, a number of practical political tactics were left untested. No effort was made to create a political organization as an alternative to the political parties, no parallel workers organization was created to replace the dissolved unions, no attempt was made to gain the support of those who had replaced the thousands of purged government employees, and no effort was made to extend the franchise to the military.[54] Whether or not any of these tactics would have worked is debatable, but their feasibility is not important to the argument. What is significant is that no serious effort was made to garner support, and yet the regime expected society to accept a new constitution. There could be no better indicator of the lack of political vision.

As hypothesized above, the lack of strategy coordination makes a controlled transition difficult. In Uruguay, collegial rule and civilian participation served as a system of checks and balances to allow factions to gain a

53. A report in the popular press noted that if Argentina, Brazil, and United States had the same proportion of superior officers to population as that found in 1984 Uruguay, these countries would have 280, 1,180, and 2,310 superior officers, respectively. See "Uruguay: 1 oficial general cada 100.000 habitantes," *La Semana Uruguaya*, April 3, 1984, p. 5. From 1970 to 1978, military personnel increased from 21,269 to 38,545 (Rial Roade 1986, 25).

54. Institutional Act No. 4 (September 1, 1976) banned for fifteen years any political activity by citizens who had held elective office prior to the *autogolpe*. Institutional Act No. 7 (June 27, 1977) removed the tenure rights of all public servants. On labor relations, see Chagas and Tonarelli 1980.

sense of security in their government positions. But the lack of a recognized ideology in any faction prevented it from making explicit policy prescriptions. Thus, factions looked upon one another with mutual mistrust, and the regime as a whole was unable to couple problems, policies, and politics. Compelling circumstantial evidence corroborates the existence of overloading and unpredictability. For example, regime members valued the status quo: "The machinery of dictatorship amounted to terror as it functioned to instill fear, passivity, and compliant behavior in the general public, but stopped short of more transformative goals.... The regime's agenda concerned control, not transformation" (Sondrol 1992, 197–98). And just as overloading would lead officials to concentrate on familiar problems, the military concentrated on that area it knew best, security, and waffled on the elaboration of political and economic objectives. Likewise, existing rules and regulations of the military institution were conserved after the intervention; no attempt was made to accommodate governance by reorganizing them (González 1983, 69). In the area of uncertainty, the military's reluctance to allow the rise of leaders is indicative. It is quite rational to create obstacles to leadership positions when it is unpredictable who will assume leadership and the ideas that they will bring. Without ideology to impart factional intentions or to use as a vehicle of persuasion toward other factions, factions simply entrench themselves within government positions and guard them as vested interests. The consequent absence of coordination then precludes agenda setting and policy formulation (González 1983, 68–69; Solari and Franco 1983; Favaro and Bensión 1993, 291). And without the expertise of civilians to remedy military ineptness, political capital remains untapped, the regime grows isolated, and a controlled transition becomes impossible.

Balanced Transition

Although it was unable to implement a controlled transition under the constitution, the regime did not collapse. Bolstered by military unity, the regime stood intransigent toward the civilian opposition for four years before it finally exited under a balanced transition. By 1984 the military authorities had retreated from the goal of setting limits on civilian decision-making to the more modest, and attainable, goal of protecting military autonomy (González 1984, 42), which it largely achieved.

The transition process had four phases. The first ran from the constitutional defeat to the internal party elections of November 1982. The second phase was one of failed negotiation, ending with the breakdown of the Parque Hotel talks, and the third phase was one of successful negotiation, ending with the Club Naval pact in August 1984. The highlight of the final phase was the November 1984 elections, and it ended with the March 1985 transition of power.

The immediate reaction of most officers to the plebiscite defeat was one of denial. Admiral Márquez and General Manuel Núñez, the interior minister, initially argued that NO meant at worst a rejection of the method of transition and not the regime, and perhaps signified support for continued rule.[55] But the recognition of the defeat soon settled in and General Raimúndez, now chief of COMASPO, announced in February 1981 that the two immediate goals of the regime were the management of the presidential succession and the formulation of a new *cronograma*.

Although in early 1980 there was some speculation that the next president would be a civilian, either Pacheco Areco or Vegh Villegas, the push by Alvarez meant that only a rival officer could effectively contend for the position. The infusion of Alvarez supporters into the JOG in February 1979 was enough to prolong Alvarez influence even after his retirement, but collegial rule again provided the necessary check against any disruption of military unity. Through 1980, tension began to build between Alvarez and army commander Quierolo, as Alvarez made known his desire to succeed President Méndez. Quierolo feared that an Alvarez presidency would threaten military unity. In December 1980, he took a stand, announcing during a trip to the United States that any officer wishing to run for public office would have to be retired at least four years. Upon his return to Uruguay, Quierolo was summoned to a secret JOG meeting, and subsequently made public his "revised" position that any retired officer would be eligible for office.[56] The JOG was not simply acting as an agent of Alvarez, as the debate over Alvarez's placement as presidency and future tensions between the two would prove. Rather, the move was a reaction to the encroachment by Quierolo upon the absolute authority of the JOG to establish the rules of transition.

Alvarez was strongly challenged for the presidency by the now retired

55. "Uruguayans Reject New Constitution in Record Referendum Turnout," *Latin American Weekly Report*, December 5, 1980, p. 1; "Generals Ponder the Next Step as Opposition Sees Chances to Improve," ibid., December 12, 1980, pp. 5–6. To the officers' credit, the interpretation of the vote actually was viewed as ambiguous even before the plebiscite. See "Consulta ambigua, efectos efímeros," *Búsqueda*, October 1980, p. 2.

56. "Uruguayan Brass, Now Tarnished, Begins to Snipe at Each Other," *New York Times*, December 28, 1980, p. D4.

General Vadora, who had made his desire for the office public in 1978.[57] Recognizing that his ascension to the presidency was not certain, Alvarez maneuvered to weaken Vadora, Quierolo, and other opponents in early 1981. At this time, evidence of the involvement of Vadora and various superior officers in a number of scandals and corrupt activities led to numerous resignations of Alvarez opponents.[58] Alvarez engineered the exposé to bolster his power before the JOG began its debate over presidential succession in July 1981 (Chagas and Tonarelli 1980, 156; Gillespie 1991, 80). Although the ploy succeeded, the JOG worked to ensure that Alvarez would not usurp its authority. Institutional Act No. 11, which granted Alvarez the presidency, also shortened his term of office and increased the power of the Consejo de Estado vis-à-vis the executive. It was also understood that the JOG would have complete autonomy in military affairs, and that Alvarez would not announce government positions on fundamental issues without prior consultation with the JOG (Achard 1992, 16–18).[59]

The second goal during this first phase of the transition, the drafting of a statute for internal party elections, was contained in a list of proposals conveyed to the Colorados, the Blancos, and the Unión Cívica when they began negotiations with COMASPO in July 1981. Although Raimúndez, a clear soft-liner, was chief of the body, General Julio Rapela (who became First Army Division commander in August) led a hard-line push for *continuismo*. The proposals included participation by the parties in the Consejo de Estado, legitimation by the parties of the military's presidential selection, and dialogue with the parties over constitutional reform. The proposals were a clear attempt to co-opt the parties into the agenda already embodied in the constitution of 1980, and the parties quickly withdrew from the talks (Bruschera 1986, 131–32). Institutional Act No. 11, passed just after the breakdown, emitted mixed signals. On the one hand, the document unilaterally imposed a presidential choice. But on the other hand, the document removed the constituent authority held by the Consejo de Estado, and committed the regime to negotiations with the political parties.[60]

57. *El País*, April 30, 1978.
58. "Uruguayan Regime Shaken by Scandal," *New York Times*, May 29, 1981, p. A3; "Greedy Generals Come to Grief," *Latin American Weekly Report*, June 12, 1981, p. 6. The most important were General Núñez, Colonel Walter Arregui (Montevideo chief of police), and General Alberto Ballestrino (director of the Escuela de Armas y Servicios).
59. "General Alvarez Gets the Top Job After Years of Plotting," *Latin American Weekly Report*, August 7, 1981, pp. 4–5.
60. "The participation of the grand political groups in the future management of the state will have to be realized after the political parties function in a clear and defined legal framework, which makes indispensable the sanction of corresponding norms." Quoted in Bruschera 1986, 132.

Nonetheless, it should be noted that a statute on political parties had not yet been passed; many officers still assumed that they could manipulate the organization of parties to their advantage.

Toward the end of 1981, Raimúndez renewed the talks, but this time within ESMACO quarters rather than at COMASPO (Gillespie 1991, 81). Within this forum, Raimúndez was able to concentrate solely upon regulations for internal elections and convince military leaders that overly restrictive elections and conspicuous rules that advantaged sympathetic party sectors would jeopardize the legitimacy of the elections (Achard 1992, 18–19). In the end, the parties had very little influence over the regulations that were to guide internal party elections, which were publicized piecemeal through early 1982 and inserted into *Ley Fundamental No. 2* (June 6, 1982).[61] The February 1982 round of promotions brought Rapela to the leadership of COMASPO when Raimúndez retired. Nonetheless, the legacy of Raimúndez was in place—a framework for holding respectably open internal elections.

The first phase is distinguished by the acceptance of the parties as necessary partners in the transition. The second phase is distinguished by the reaction on the part of the military to what was a surprise only to it—the overwhelming victory of opposition sectors in the internal party elections. The period also saw a merger of interests between the two main factions in the military. As president, Alvarez led one faction, which included Interior Minister Yamundú Trinidad and *consejero* Colonel Nestor Bolentini (ret.). The second faction came to be dominated by Rapela, as well as by the Second Army Division commander General Julio C. Bonelli. The Alvarez faction favored an extension of the Alvarez presidency and would resort to populist measures and ranting more out of political opportunism than ideological commitment (Gillespie 1991, 111–12).[62] The Rapela faction essentially desired an imposition of the constitution of 1980.[63] The interests of the two coalesced insofar as Alvarez knew that a hard-line stance by Rapela would spoil negotiations, leading to the retention of the status quo—that is, the retention of Alvarez as president (Achard 1992, 23).

Even with thousands of politicians still denied their political rights, the

---

61. "La Ley de Partidos" *La Democracia,* May 7, 1982. For a comprehensive survey of the law, see "Importantes inovaciones en el nuevo texto de la Ley de Partidos," *Búsqueda,* May 27, 1982. Gillespie (1991, 81) suggests that Raimúndez and three Colorado leaders, including future president Julio María Sanguinetti, essentially drafted the statute.

62. "Alvarez Goes for the Rural Voters," *Latin American Regional Reports: Southern Cone,* October 9, 1981, pp. 5–6.

63. "Rapela anuncia creación de una comisión constituent y Bonelli expresó sus temores por acción de políticos," *Búsqueda,* July 7, 1982, p. 5.

1982 internal party elections saw an overwhelming victory for opposition candidates (Franco 1984, 113–32). The hard-line stance of the Alvarez and Rapela factions now seemed preposterous, but they nonetheless presented an impenetrable front to the political parties.[64] In December 1982, Alvarez attempted to take the initiative with a proposal to the JOG that he organize an official party to bolster the regime as it entered negotiations with the traditional parties. Fearful of both greater involvement in politics and growing populism on the part of Alvarez, the JOG denied the request. Defiantly, Alvarez went straight to the public on March 25, 1983, and called for the formation of a new political party in a speech at Aceguá (Achard 1992, 20, 28).[65] The constraints imposed by regime institutions forced the direct appeal, and these same institutions now worked to isolate him. Alvarez had broken the understanding that all significant political decisions would be made in consultation with the JOG, and this hardened opposition to him. From this moment on, Alvarez began to recede as a political force.[66]

Rapela now stood as the primary representative of the armed forces at the start of negotiations on May 13, 1983. To the dismay of the parties, the proposals forwarded by Rapela essentially restated the security-based concerns of the constitution of 1980.[67] COMASPO members met with leaders from the Colorado, Blanco, and Unión Civíca parties in seven meetings at the Parque Hotel in Montevideo. Facing complete intransigence, the parties declared a *sine die* suspension of negotiations on July 5.[68] Illustrating his

64. Sanguinetti stressed the intransigence of Rapela during the negotiations: "All of his arguments were arranged in the same way: the parties will not be able to control the situation, they will fall into the hands of the radical sectors, the radical sectors will be provoked from the outside by Marxist groups, and this will bring about an unmanageable situation given the force of the unions that would be reappearing, given the anarchy that would be produced." He also described Alvarez as "closed to almost any mechanism of dialogue in any way." See interview in Achard 1992, 207–8.

65. "Alvarez por nueva 'opción política,'" *La Democracia*, March 25, 1983.

66. Alvarez's actions became more desperate over time. In an effort to gain leverage in the face of contrary statements by several superior officers, in September 1982 he declared that the military would allow investigations into the antisubversive battle ("Alvarez: Armed Forces Have Nothing to Hide," *Foreign Broadcast Information Service-Latin America*, September 23, 1982, p. K1). During the Parque Hotel talks, he announced that the 1984 elections were contingent upon successful negotiations (Achard 1992, 61). And in early 1984, Alvarez allegedly provoked labor unrest in an effort to declare a state of emergency and cancel the elections. The JCJ prevented him from taking such action (Gillespie 1991, 126).

67. The proposals are published in "El Documento de las fuerzas armadas," *Búsqueda*, May 18, 1983, p. 6. Also see "Los puntos planteos por las fuerzas armadas que han sido objeto de debates con los políticos," *Búsqueda*, June 23, 1983, p. 5.

68. A comprehensive summary of each meeting that illustrates this intransigence is found in "Actas: una muestra reveladora del enfrentamiento de las posiciones sustenadas por políticos y militares," *Búsqueda*, August 10, 1983, pp. 24, 4–5, and "La interrupción del diálogo parecía inevitable ya en la penúltima sesión," ibid., August 17, 1983, pp. 6–9.

obstinacy, Rapela then portrayed party leaders as "criminal" for joining street protests in which "communist slogans" such as "The Military Dictatorship Will Come to an End" and "They Must Go" were used.[69] This second phase of the transition saw the swift rise and fall of the hard-line elements. By its end, "the military had the worst of both worlds: Negotiations had collapsed, but they could not agree on any alternatives" (Gillespie 1991, 124).

The JOG had some responsibility for the breakdown because the guidelines given to Rapela were not very flexible. But the anger expressed toward Rapela after the suspension of negotiations demonstrates than many officers felt he was too rigid (Achard 1992, 52).[70] Nevertheless, the regime reacted precisely as one would expect a regime lacking strategy coordination to react. It remained defensive and increased repression. On August 2, 1983, Institutional Act No. 14 and an executive decree placed severe restrictions on political activities and the press and mandated political proscription for violators of the new regulations.[71]

The regime soon found itself in a web of its own making. Under its own *cronograma*, elections were scheduled for November 1984. Cancellation was not an alternative simply because the regime did not have a viable alternative to the resumption of civilian rule—even the most stubborn officers finally realized that the constitution of 1980 simply could not act as a starting point for negotiations. From this point on, the tide of concern in the armed forces shifted from military oversight over a civilian regime to the protection of military autonomy under a civilian regime.

It is a mistake to view this twist simply as a retreat in the face of public pressure. Some analysts portray the change as a product of rising social protests that invigorated the political parties in late 1983 (e.g., Weinstein 1988, 80–82).[72] On its surface, the interpretation seems compelling. The Parque Hotel talks fail in July, repression is increased in August, and some officers begin to threaten the unilateral imposition of constitutional reform.

69. "Politicians Scored for Withdrawal from Dialogue," *Foreign Broadcast Information Service—Latin America*, August 4, 1983, p. 1.

70. In April, COMASPO submitted to the JOG a list of issues to be discussed at the Parque Hotel. The JOG returned the document and listed each issue as negotiable or nonnegotiable. Of the fifty issues, thirteen were marked negotiable, nineteen nonnegotiable, and eighteen to be considered in light of the political situation. For both documents, see Achard 1992, 341–60.

71. *La Semana Uruguaya*, August 8, 1983, p. 5: "Acto Institucional No. 14"; "Decreto del poder ejecutivo de 2 de Agosto de 1983."

72. See the reporting in *Latin American Weekly Report*, such as "Time is Running Out for Alvarez," December 9, 1983, p. 9. Also see Mercedes Lynn de Uriarte, "Uruguay: Broken Promises," *NACLA Report*, January/February 1984, pp. 43–44.

A small demonstration movement slowly builds and explodes on November 27 (the final Sunday in November and traditional election date), when up to 400,000 Uruguayans protested against the regime (an incredible number for a country of 2.8 million). A second massive protest on December 30 leads to police beatings and over a hundred arrests. In response, the military reduces its demands and concentrates on military issues in the Club Naval negotiations of July-August 1984.

It would be imprudent to deny the impact of the protests. They undoubtedly weakened the harder-line elements in the regime. The problem with this approach is that it fails to recognize movements within the regime well before the social explosion. In early August, the JCJ, working within the JOG, began to organize its own committee to study the resumption of talks. The informal committee, headed by General Angel Barrios, director of IMES and a recognized soft-liner, acted as a parallel body to COMASPO and initiated talks with leaders of the political parties.[73] At this time, the most important problem faced in the negotiations was the refusal of the Blancos to participate once it became clear that their leader, Wilson Ferriera, would remain proscribed, even while the proscriptions on most others were being lifted. The military held Ferriera responsible for the reduction of military aid from the United States because of his appearance at a congressional subcommittee investigating human rights abuses in Uruguay.[74] With negotiations already excluding the leftist Frente Amplio party, this left the Colorados, representing about 35 percent of the population (representation of the Unión Civíca Party was relatively insignificant), as the only participant. Through the Barrios group, the Colorados were able to communicate a proposal to substitute the Frente Amplio in place of the Blancos in order to preserve the legitimacy of the accord. Military leaders, driven more by vengeance than ideology, accepted the proposal, and to demonstrate good faith, reversed the August 2 executive decree, lifted more proscriptions, and offered greater civilian involvement in public administration. Finally, in what would be a defining institutional move, the JOG announced that the JCJ, and not COMASPO, would control future negotiations. The changes structured by the Barrios group occurred in early November, before the protests.[75]

73. "Military Group Set Up to Advance Democratization," *Foreign Broadcast Information Service—Latin America*, August 19, 1983, p. 1; "'Extra-official' Military-Political Dialogue," ibid., August 29, 1983, p. 2.

74. "Uruguayan Exile Faces Indictment," *New York Times*, July 25, 1976, p. 15, Late city edition.

75. "Políticos y militares: es inminente una segunda ronda de negociaciones," *Búsqueda*, September 7, 1983, p. 1; "Definición política de la Junta de Oficiales Generales," *La Semana*

One reason the JCJ was able to assume control over the negotiation process was that the political deadlock and growing social protests had weakened hard-line elements within the army. But another reason was due to the
regime institutions in the context of the November 1984 election deadline.
The fleeting tenure of Uruguayan service commanders had assured a weak
JCJ over the course of the regime. But with the end of the regime in sight,
members of this institution grew more powerful. It did not matter that the
commanders would not keep their positions very long if defining negotiations occurred within their term. This was precisely the position air force
commander Manuel Buadas and navy commander Rodolfo Invidio found
themselves in.[76] The failure of the army-dominated COMASPO, infighting
in the army spurred by Alvarez's revelations of corruption, and the growing sense of despondency in army hard-liners emboldened both services.
Turnover in the army command also invigorated them. In February 1984,
General Pedro Aranco replaced hard-line army commander Boscan Hontou. Aranco was more supportive of the reopening of negotiations,[77] but he
was ultimately inconsequential, as he reached the mandatory retirement
age of sixty just five months into his term. The subsequent rise of General
Hugo Medina on June 7 solidified the soft-line tone of the JCJ.[78] Medina
had worked within COMASPO from 1980 to 1984 where he strengthened
his contacts with the politicians, especially with Julio Maria Sanguinetti,
leader of the Colorado Party (Gillespie 1991, 144).

Thus the stage was slowly built for more flexible negotiations. Contacts
with the Frente Amplio leading to the March 19 release of their leader, Liber
Serengi, allayed some of the distrust between the officers and the Frente
Amplio, as did contacts between Sanguinetti and Serengi.[79] In February
COMASPO experienced a turnover of five of its ten members and, for the

---

Uruguaya, November 7, 1983, p. 6; "Military Seeks Rapproachment with Politicians," *Foreign Broadcast Information Service—Latin America,* November 22, 1983, p. 1; Achard 1992,
21, 53–56.

76. For soft-line lobbying by Invidio, see "Invidio y Linares confían que en 1984 militares
y políticos fijen las bases de la futura democracia," *Búsqueda,* January 4, 1984, p. 5. In a 1981
COMASPO meeting Buadas was allied with Raimundez, General Hugo Medina, and another
recognized soft-liner, General Jorge Borad, in a call for greater dialogue and elections as early
as November 1983. See meeting transcripts in Achard 1992, 295–304.

77. "'Contactos preliminares': quienes los mantuvieron?" *La Democracia,* March 2, 1984.

78. In his inaugural address, Medina emphasized: "As the future Commander in Chief
I have the responsibility of planning how the army is going to exit from this situation, and
this preoccupies me excessively." "El Gral. Medina nuevo Comandante en Jefe," *La Semana
Uruguaya,* June 5, 1984, p. 7.

79. "Military-Political Rappraochment Reported," *Foreign Broadcast Information Service—Latin America,* February 13, 1984, p. 1; "Secret Military Political Talks Reported,"
ibid., February 23, 1984, p. 1.

first time, was not presided over by an army officer (Brigadier General Herbert Pampillón from the air force became president).[80] COMASPO, however, lost most of its significance when the JCJ took primary responsibility for drafting the new military proposal. This new proposal, delivered to the parties on May 1, was openly referred to as a *borrador,* or rough draft, to convey flexibility.[81] Negotiations began on July 6, 1984, in ESMACO quarters, and were moved to the Club Naval later in the month. Quickly meeting some of the parties' demands, the military derogated Institutional Acts 7 (which removed tenure for civil servants) and 14 (which extended the proscription regime) on July 16. Although no document was signed when the talks ended on August 2, the agreements were embodied in Institutional Act No. 19, passed the following day. Agreements incorporated into the act included the following:

1. Institutional Act No. 1, which suspended elections, was repealed.
2. Army promotions to the rank of commander in chief would be made by the president from a list of three candidates provided by the generals; for the other services, from a list of only two candidates.
3. The National Security Council (COSENA) would survive in only an advisory capacity, meeting at the request of the president alone, and including a majority of cabinet ministers over the military.
4. At the initiative of the president, Parliament would have the right to vote a "state of insurrection" to suspend habeas corpus.
5. A new protective legal mechanism (*recurso de amparo*) would allow appeals against government decisions or military actions.
6. Military courts would continue to try civilians only when Parliament had voted a "state of insurrection."
7. The National Assembly elected in 1984 would act as a constituent assembly to consider permanent provisions of this last institutional act into the constitution.
8. If amended, the new text of the constitution would be submitted to a plebiscite in November 1985 (Gillespie 1991, 177–78).

The agreement represented a triumph for the JCJ. This does not mean that the regime became more centralized. The JCJ were expected to, and did,

---

80. "Los 10 oficiales generales de la Comisión Política Militar," *Búsqueda,* March 7, 1984, p. 3; "La Comaspo está en sesión permanente," ibid., April 10, 1984, p. 1.

81. "La propuesta de las fuerzas armadas," *La Semana Uruguaya,* May 8, 1984, p. 5; the complete text is found in "Texto de la propuesta militar entregada a los partidos el 1 de Mayo," *Búsqueda,* July 11, 1984, p. 6.

report to the JOG to inform them of events.[82] The transfer of negotiating power to this small body indicates that most officers were demoralized over the lack of a political plan and accepted a stricter concentration on military affairs—issues that the commanders could be expected to push more effectively than other officers. Furthermore, without a comprehensive agenda, negotiation concerns shifted to how an agreement could be best expedited. The three-member JCJ was much more conducive to this goal than was the ten-member COMASPO. Finally, one should not omit the skill and preferences of the commanders themselves, especially Medina and Invidio, both of whom saw transition as integral to military professionalism.

The civilian achievements in the transition are clear: military tutelage over the democratic regime was not institutionalized; civilian issues were removed from the jurisdiction of the military courts; and constitutional reform was completely delegated to the democratically elected Congress. Military achievements were also meaningful in both areas of political decision-making and especially in purely military affairs. Military achievements in political decision-making were informal and transitory, but they did represent significant constraints on the new democracy in its early years. Frequent meetings between Sanguinetti and the commanders after the transition were understood to involve discussions of critical policies, such as labor unrest and legislative investigations into the regime.[83] Most important in this area was the understanding that human rights cases against officers would not be pursued. A second achievement was the proscription of Ferriera from the presidential elections. In military affairs, success was more formalized. The promotion process was strongly internalized, much to the dismay of activists who criticized the repeated promotions of known human rights violators.[84] Likewise, although ESEDENA was dissolved, the content of education in the other schools was left largely untouched. The armed forces also detached the command structure from the Ministry of Defense. Before the transition, a new November 1984 Organic Law of the Armed Forces removed ministerial control over the Servicio de Información

82. Medina notes that while the JOG gave the JCJ a blank check to negotiate, they were expected to report back to the JOG often. Interview in Achard 1992, 182, 186. For an early reference to JOG oversight, see "Para las fuerzas armadas el tema constitucional tiene que estar en la mesa de negociones," *Búsqueda*, February 28, 1984, p. 1.

83. "Apaciguando a los militares," *La Democracia*, July 12, 1985.

84. "La cuestión militar y los derechos humanos," *Paz y Justicia: Sumario de Derechos Humanos*, September-December 1989, pp. 25–30. For the submissive human rights policy approach of the Sanguinetti administration, see "Ley de Caducidad: crónica de un 'Punto Final' largamente anunciado," *Paz y Justicia: Sumario de Derechos Humanos*, January-March 1987, pp. 15–29. Also see Pion-Berlin 1994.

de Defensa, and after the transition, officers claimed that command went directly to the president rather than through the Ministry of Defense.[85] The portrayal of the transition as balanced is supported by a 1986 poll of Montevideans, the majority of whom stated that the military continues to influence significantly political power.[86]

Conclusion

The Uruguayan regime was advantaged by military unity, but ultimately paid the price for its lack of strategy coordination as it found itself able to do no better than a balanced transition. The mixture of collegial rule and low regime investment allowed military unity to be sustained. The primacy of the JOG in the regime instituted collegial rule. Also, the historical lack of coordinating military bodies (such as the JCJ and ESMACO) contributed to the reluctance to allow centralization. Finally, strict military codes on retirement, assignment, and promotions hindered politically ambitious officers. The low level of regime investment, a consequence of significant civilian participation and the difficulties the military had in defining for itself a ("offensive") role in the future of Uruguayan politics, allowed the regime to walk the line between granting officers involved in decision-making too much power, while at the same time appeasing their supporters. Unlike the *Proceso*, military elites did not find subordinate officers below them in government, and this dulled most inclinations to forcefully push personal political interests. Hence, as in Brazil, regime factions were accommodated and military unity sustained.

Despite a level of military unity that supported the regime for twelve years, the lack of strategy coordination spoiled the prospects of a controlled transition. From the outset, the military was disadvantaged in this area because of its inexperience in politics, limited educational institutions, and lack of ties to civilian elites. The slow pace of the *autogolpe* stimulated tactical rather than ideological discussion, and thus did not contribute to the foundation of a political program. The regime also had little success

85. An excellent analysis of the maintenance of military autonomy just after the transition can be found in Rial Roade 1986. A perusal of *El Soldado* (Montevideo), a publication from the Centro Militar, illustrates the defiant position of the military. Early articles after the transition are filled with justifications of military rule, warnings of subversion, and portrayals of the Argentine human rights trials as an act of Marxist vengeance.

86. Twenty-six percent stated that the military co-governs, and 44 percent stated that the military holds power in specific areas. See "La mayoría de los Montevideanos considera que los militares son un factor de poder político," *Búsqueda*, September 18, 1986, p. 1.

in reaching out to society in order to develop a coherent political program and maintain links to significant economic groups. While the conclave system did provide a potential line of communication similar to Brazil's *conselho* system, it suffered from a lack of regime guidance and coordination. In Brazil, *conselhos* were placed under the direct authority of individual ministers and thus were more specialized. Interests could be confronted more individually, and, in addition, the Brazilian regime had the expertise to respond to interests. In Uruguay, the meetings were more ad hoc, and the body under which the conclaves acted, the CES, was more a consultative body than an initiating body in the regime. The institutional apparatus made it difficult for economic groups to feel as if they played a significant role in policymaking.

The only area of substantial engagement with society was in the realm of security matters—the only area in which the military had some level of expertise. In economics and in politics, the regime found itself neither able to formulate its own programs nor able to reach out to society for expertise. Even as the economy showed some positive signs, economic winners saw little reason to support a regime that refused their input. While this lack of strategy coordination limited the military government in its attempt to impose a controlled transition, the military unity engendered by regime institutions allowed it to excel in the defense of corporate interests. The result was a balanced transition.

7

Conclusion: From Transition Control to Democratization

Each of the five cases of military rule examined in this study illustrates the importance of political institutions. Whether through opening opportunities, impeding certain avenues of action, or disseminating ideologies that mold preferences, institutions stand between actors and outcomes. Students of democratic regimes have long accepted the importance of institutions, as evidenced by the plethora of studies on electoral rules, parliamentary versus presidential forms of government, and federal relations. On the other hand, the military regime has traditionally been viewed as a one-dimensional phenomenon, with institutional differences among cases considered to be of little consequence. Military intervention itself is a denial of the rules of the game, so why should we expect a military, once in power, to accede to a set of rules?

The facts belie such reasoning, and it is not difficult to understand why. Institutions reduce uncertainty in a world of infinite possibilities. To rule outside any institutional apparatus is to invite anarchy. Indeed, it is curious that institutional variance in military regimes has been so neglected—

a fixation on rules and regulations is inextricably tied to the development of a professional military.

Thus, institutions matter in the military regime just as they do in any other regime. In this study, I have argued that military unity and strategy coordination, two variables that allow us to predict transition control, find their roots in institutions. A regime endowed with both military unity and strategy coordination is well equipped to stage a controlled transition, while a military regime with neither is prone to collapse. The combination of military unity and a lack of strategy coordination is most likely to result in a balanced transition.

Case studies from the Southern Cone and Brazil corroborate these expectations, and also illustrate some differences within their more general similarities. For example, although Chile, Brazil, Uruguay, and the *Revolución Argentina* were supported by military unity, the cases demonstrate the variety of means by which it can be produced. In Chile, the military institution solidified as Pinochet forged unity repressively, through a process I have termed institutional aggrandizement. The acquisition of control over advisory organizations aided Pinochet's path from army commander, to president of the Junta, to president of the republic, and finally to *generalissimo* of the armed forces. The power of information allowed Pinochet to repress dissent. And with direct control over the intelligence apparatus and multiple mechanisms of control over each military service, Pinochet was able to deal with potential rivals masterfully.

Compare this to the experiences of Brazil and Uruguay. In these countries, rivals within the regime were less likely to be repressed and more likely to be incorporated into the ruling center through a process I have labeled institutional accommodation. The institutional basis for this accommodation was the placement of rival leaders in official positions of significant authority. This both helped to placate their desire for power and political input and linked their partisans to the regime. With their leaders in positions of importance, members of different factions could be reassured that the decision-making process would include their values and goals to some extent. In Brazil, this was achieved mainly through incorporation into the "military electoral college," rotations in access to the president and army minister, and divisions within the executive cabinet. In Uruguay, involvement in the JOG, rotations among the division commanders, positions in various state institutions (e.g., SEPLACODI, CES, ESMACO, IMES, and ESEDENA), and, ultimately, placement in the presidency, served this same purpose of institutional accommodation. The variety of institutional positions in Brazil and Uruguay provided numerous sources of input into the regime to mollify factional aspirations, in stark contrast to the repression of factional aspirations found in Chile.

The *Revolución Argentina* also exhibited military unity, but this unity was not the result of interaction across the military as government-military as institution divide, as in Chile, Brazil, and Uruguay, but rather the result of the lack of interaction. This lack of interaction left the military hierarchy intact. Superior officers were able to stave off factional growth through the powers granted to them within the military, and the armed forces were not greatly disrupted. Subordinates continued to answer to their superiors, and the services grew united in their opposition to the disregard displayed by the government. The consequent alienation indicated disunity in the regime between the military and government, not within the military.

The determinants of military unity can be found within two institutional dimensions—the centralization of authority and regime investment. In Chile, authority was centralized and regime investment was high. In Brazil and Uruguay, authority was dispersed and regime investment was low. And in the *Revolución*, authority was centralized and regime investment was low. The final combination, collegial rule and regime investment, breeds politicization in the military and thus undermines military unity. This combination was found in the Argentine *Proceso*, where factions were given not only representation in government but also significant power because the numerous lines of authority in the military were transferred to the government apparatus. At the peak of the regime hierarchy, each service commander could face off against the other in the Junta Militar with support from lower-ranking officers in positions throughout government. This also allowed each to counter the power afforded to the president and minister of economics. Infighting invited deeper factional growth as aspiring leaders sought to impose their own answers to disunity. The military then grew more politicized as formal lines of authority were undermined.

Military unity alone is an important determinant of transition control. Its presence means that the move away from military rule is unlikely to fall below a balanced transition, and its absence is likely to produce a collapse. Nonetheless, military unity is essentially a defensive device. It allows a regime to present a united front and fend off opponents. But transition control entails, not the suppression of the opposition, but their incorporation into the transition plans of the regime. For this reason, military unity is a necessary, but not sufficient, condition for a controlled transition. Strategy coordination is also required for adequate strength and security. This variable centers on the relationship of the government toward both the military institution and society as it attempts to administer coherent political and economic programs.

On the one hand, these tasks demand that a government create meaningful links with the military. Here, a fine line must be walked between alienation and politicization. Alienation means that the military, which is the primary pillar upon which the government rules, is a reluctant supporter of government. Society is thus more likely to lose confidence in whatever political or economic programs are proposed. Politicization is the result of uncontrolled military involvement, such that political debate disrupts the military hierarchy and the military loses its capacity to support the government because it has turned inward to resolve its own problems.

On the other hand, the implementation of coherent political and economic programs also demands linkages with significant groups within society. No government can rule as a completely autonomous agent, and military government is no exception. Often the military finds that it needs expertise that can only be found in society, that the legitimation of programs is aided by supportive members of the *intelligentsia,* academics, or interest groups, and that the implementation of policy is dependent upon civilian bureaucrats and local bosses, many of whom may have no official position with the government. And only with lines of communication can a government take advantage of economic growth or interest in a political program and accumulate political capital. Those advantaged by a given economic or political program are unlikely to display support if they remain uncertain of future policy, and those on the fringes of advantage see no hope in swaying policy when they are shut out of the decision-making process.

This second variable, strategy coordination, distinguishes Brazil and Chile from Uruguay and the *Revolución,* and was the determining difference for controlled transition in the former cases and balanced transition in the latter. The Uruguayan armed forces lacked the educational institutions found in Brazil that encouraged strategy development in officers and created links to civilians. Likewise, in Brazil, strategy coordination was facilitated by the empowerment of a single individual, the president, for more mundane decisions, while in Uruguay, the collegial JOG demanded day-to-day involvement in decision-making. Uruguayan officers could unite behind the principle to repress opposition, but when it came time to develop a transition strategy, the regime waffled and weakened to the level of a balanced transition. Given the lack of strategy coordination toward society, it comes as no surprise that the regime was unable to gain support from those groups advantaged during the period of economic growth and suffered electoral defeat of its constitution.

In the *Revolución,* alienation meant that the government failed in its relations with the military, and this undermined its efforts toward society. The institutional arrangement was such that the military was held responsible for a government that it could not completely control. In good times this would not have been a problem, but the economic and political downturns that all regimes periodically suffer were especially damaging in the context of such alienation. The military fretted as criticisms were directed toward it and as it was dissuaded from suggesting its own policy solutions. The result was a military that had grown isolated from government. And because the regime had left the military essentially intact as an institution, military grievances were expressed through the chain of command (and military unity was not disrupted). Thus, in the *Revolución* we found a regime that seemed to lose its footing suddenly and suffer irreversible damage after the 1969 *cordobazo.* The uprising solidified military opposition to the government, and Onganía, in near denial of the military basis of his rule, found himself unable to implement his corporatist policies in the face of military resistance. The military, realizing that the regime structure provided it no formal means to enforce its own policy proposals, broke the very rules of the game that it had established and tried again with Levingston.

We should take note of a minor distinction between how strategy coordination developed in Brazil and in Chile. That is, while the impetus for strategy coordination largely developed within the officer corps in Brazil, in Chile, Pinochet reached out to civilians more deliberately and borrowed from civilian ideas as he developed strategy. Lacking an institution like the ESG, Pinochet took responsibility for developing strategy and reached out to neoliberal economists and traditional politicians for help in developing economic and political programs. And when the economic program provided by the Chicago Boys faltered, Pinochet surveyed the problem and replaced them with the pragmatic neoliberals.

Strategy coordination is integral to the development of political credit and regime support. Without it, a regime is unable to translate environmental advantages, such as economic growth or social stability, into successes linked to the regime. This "primacy of politics" argument disputes the popular contention that regimes rise and fall in conjunction with variations in economic well-being (e.g., Frieden 1991). The cases studied here challenge this assertion. The Uruguayan regime was experiencing economic growth well before and even during the 1980 constitutional plebiscite, yet suffered a humiliating defeat. The *Revolución Argentina* similarly failed to follow economic exigencies experienced to mid-1969. The *cordobazo* was in part a response to the economic shortcomings of some groups, but this week-long event was no more threatening than the mobilizations that struck Chile from 1982 to 1985, and the Pinochet regime survived another four years and instituted a controlled transition. The dubious impact assigned to economic swings is even evidenced by the Brazilian case, where the regime was able to accrue political credit during the boom years and effectively expend that credit, while instituting a controlled transition under economic crisis. The *Proceso* regime perhaps most closely followed its economic path, but the evidence presented in this study highlights how politicization within the military disrupted economic policymaking, thus further evidencing the primacy of politics.

The result is a model comprised of two variables—military unity and strategy coordination—each of which has its roots in institutions. Together, the two variables impart insight into how military rule will unfold in a given case, and how successful the regime will be in its attempt to exert transition control. To conclude, I assess the significance of this work with comments on two questions: (1) How will a better understanding of the dynamics behind military rule aid our understanding of the future of Latin America—a region that has taken a dramatic turn away from military rule? And (2) Of what significance is this study of transition control to democratic consolidation?

Military Rule and the Future of Latin America

With the retreat of military rule in Latin America through the 1990s, a study of military government might seem irrelevant to the political future of the region. Indeed, the disruptive experience with rule for the military, pressures from international organizations and states, the strengthening of human rights groups and other supportive actors in civil society, and the greater reluctance of politicians and societies to rap on the barrack doors signal a watershed in Latin American political history. The metaphor of a pendulum swinging from military to civilian rule and back may no longer be applicable.

But it would be equally imprudent to view the recent wave of democratic transition as an endpoint in Latin American political development. We ought to be just as adamant in our dismissal of the view that the region is likely to cycle back and forth, as of the view that the region will stabilize on the side of democracy. History has shown that as waves of democracy pass over regions, over time we find that some democracies consolidate, others revert back to authoritarianism, and still others develop into some form of limited democracy (Huntington 1991). Speculations on the prospects for democratic consolidation must take into account the cultural diversity, economic contrasts, and variety of political tradition found in the region and accept that there is no universal answer applicable to the region. And in Latin America, whether a democracy consolidates, reverts, or stalls, history tells us that the armed forces will play a significant role.

Given that military rule is likely to reappear sometime, someplace, it is interesting to speculate on the form military intervention may take in the future. There are two tendencies currently prevalent throughout Latin America. One tendency is the pressure to centralize decision-making within government, and the second is the hesitancy most militaries now display toward direct involvement in government. Should these two tendencies come to fruition in the context of weakening democratic institutions, the result could be a military regime with historical precedent, one similar to the Rojas Pinilla regime in Colombia (1953–57), the Pérez Jiménez regime in Venezuela (1948–58), and the Argentine *Revolución* regime examined here. In the conceptual language of this study, these were regimes characterized by centralized authority and low regime investment. Why should we expect such military regimes in the future?

Presidentialism, although simply one aspect of regime configuration in Latin America,[1] easily opens itself to greater centralization. Unlike in the United States, many executives in Latin America have long had the power to dismiss congress, issue special legislative decrees, and exercise special vetoes. And Mainwaring (1990) notes that when the multipartism found in many countries of Latin America is combined with presidentialism, presidents are often encouraged to weaken other branches of government. Because presidentialism does not demand party coalitions before a government is formed, governments are often stricken with a paralysis that encourages this behavior. And the standing weakness of most legislatures in terms of staff support and investigative funding, and the propensity of most citizens to target general political criticisms on this body, facilitates moves by presidents to centralize power (Vial 1993).

Pressure to centralize also comes from the status of Latin American countries as developing countries. Because political and economic crises are

---

1. The presidential-parliamentary distinction simplifies and distorts regime distinctions. Regimes are distinguished on many other bases, such as electoral laws, party systems, federal-state relations, and constitutional restrictions on policy power (Lijphart 1999).

endemic to most of these countries, there is greater pressure to process decisions quickly than to build consensus (Lambert 1969, 257–365; Huntington 1968, 1–32, 93–139). Indeed, the economic crisis of the 1980s favored the technocratic concentration of decision-making in the executive (Conaghan 1988). And the consequent privatization of functions formerly performed by the state leads to an "elitization" of democracy (Smith 1993). One should also recognize pressures inflicting all states in the new world economy. Pressures to negotiate economic treaties, pass economic stabilization legislation, refinance debt, and coordinate monetary policy all point toward a concentration of authority in the executive. Finally, the possible resurgence of guerrilla movements such as the Zapatistas in Mexico and the security threats posed by narcotics trafficking may lead to a greater use of executive emergency powers, as in Colombia and Peru.

While it is certain that many Latin American countries will have to deal with political and economic crises in the future just as they had to in the past, it is not certain that the military will play the same role it once did. In the wave of military governments that beset the region from the 1960s to the 1980s, officers in most countries did not hesitate to place themselves in government positions. Soldiers acted not only as presidents and legislators but also as directors of state businesses, cabinet ministers and secretaries, ambassadors, judges, and local level representatives. The experience scarred many militaries. The economic crisis of the 1980s forced them to face the cold realities of governing and problem solving, and most failed the test (Baloyra 1987; Haggard and Kaufman 1995, 45–74). National security concerns allowed security forces to run rampant, and the consequent rash of human rights abuses damaged military prestige (Stepan 1988, esp. 58–59). The crises raised by economic difficulties and human rights abuses created divisions within the ranks as groups pushed independent solutions and thus led to a general politicization of the forces which threatened the ultimate military value, corporate unity (Farcau 1996).

The recent experience with military rule demonstrated the lack of military expertise in governing. The exigencies of the new world economy, including knowledge of new computer-based technologies and the need for deft legal expertise as trade relations grow, present an even more formidable barrier. Gone are the days when a military could blend its nationalist proclivities with import-based substitution policies and thumb its nose at outside pressures. Finally, one should recognize the repugnance of international opinion toward military rule. This is not to argue that the United States and Western Europe will place democratization at the top of their foreign policy agendas, but that political and economic pressures are likely to be advanced toward the more egregious movements away from democratic rule, as illustrated by the attempted military coups in Paraguay (1996) and Ecuador (2000).

Hence, wherever pressure builds for military intervention, the military of the country in question will be less likely to replace civilian officials with soldiers and will probably shy away from identifying itself too closely with any authoritarian moves that the government initiates—low regime investment will be more likely than high regime investment. This reluctance toward direct involvement, when combined with centralized decision-making means that military governments similar to the *Revolución* are most likely to arise. The case thus holds relevance for the political future of some countries.

Indeed, the *Revolución* presents several insights into the future of military rule in Latin America, wherever and whenever it may occur. The dominant approach to democratic transition, as enunciated by O'Donnell and Schmitter (1986), argues that democratic transition is likely to be initiated as splits develop within the regime between hard-liners and soft-liners. The descriptive nature of this approach is not very helpful (Remmer 1991a). A more complete understanding of democratic transition demands that we explain, not only that regime splits contribute to authoritarian breakdown, but also how, why, and where these splits occur (Farcau 1996). The argument presented here suggests that these dynamics may vary according to specific authoritarian regime types.

For a military regime, splits do occur, but they do not occur randomly. In a case of low regime investment, the military hierarchy can remain largely intact. Because this helps to insulate the military from politicization and to maintain military unity, we should not expect consequential splits to begin from within the military. Rather, we should expect these splits to occur between the military and the government, represented by the president. Government administration then becomes a battleground between the two, as the military attempts to whittle away at presidential power. The likelihood for military opposition to the government that it put in place is significant to democratic opposition movements, because this means that the military itself may become an important ally. This potential is demonstrated by the Colombian and Venezuelan cases. In both countries, the democratic opposition eventually worked closely with the military to establish civilian rule.[2]

2. On Colombia, see Martz 1962 and Hartlyn 1986. On Venezuela, see Burggraaff 1972 and Karl 1986b.

The type of regime exemplified by the *Revolución* is distinct in this regard from the more recent Latin American military regimes of the 1970s and 1980s. The greater involvement of military personnel in government in these regimes disrupted the military hierarchy and allowed military factions to gain independent centers of power. As a result, the consequential splits developed within the military itself (Farcau 1996). Should military rule return, *Revolución*-like military regimes are a very real possibility due to the pressures to centralize decision-making and the reluctance of most militaries to involve themselves directly in government. For this reason, the study of historical cases of this form of rule is an important endeavor. Further historical investigations and comparative studies will deepen our understanding not only of Latin American history, but perhaps its future as well.

The Significance of Transition Control

But why study transition control in the first place? The countries examined presently feature relatively stable democracies. This raises a question of significance. If variation in transition control is independent of democratic consolidation, why examine it in the first place? Before addressing the linkage between the two, it should be noted that transition control is important in itself. How much control a military regime wields during the period of transition establishes patterns of conflict and cooperation among all political groups, and could mean the difference between freedom and imprisonment for opposition members. Given that transition can last for some time, for instance, roughly five years in Brazil and Uruguay, this period of time is worthy of study in itself.

Transition control has relevance to democratic consolidation, but its impact must be placed within the context of other modes of transition, as well as new factors that arise and influence consolidation. The pace of transition, the bottom-up or top-down dynamics of transition, authoritarian attitudes toward democracy, and a host of stochastic factors particular to an individual case must all be considered part of the "transition package." These, plus factors that may arise after transition such as corruption scandals, economic crisis, or international events (e.g., involvement in war), will influence democratic consolidation, and it would be foolish to argue that they are all likely to point in the same direction. Thus, while civilians may find a low level of transition control to be opportune for democratic consolidation, there is always the possibility of mitigating factors.

To better appreciate the significance of transition control under military regimes, one ought to focus on civil-military relations, rather than the more multifarious phenomenon of democratic consolidation. Civil-military relations play an obvious role within democratic consolidation, and by examining the impact of transition control here first, its significance is clearly revealed.

First, one should note that the establishment of civilian control over the military consists of two processes—disengagement and neutrality (Welch 1975; Finer 1988). Disengagement refers to the exit of a military regime and its replacement by a civilian regime. Neutrality is a longer process that occurs as the armed forces recognize their proper role within a democratic regime and accept civilian supremacy. The distinction is important because it highlights the fact that a military withdrawal from government is not the same as a military withdrawal from politics. There exists a continuum of military influence from outright rule to legitimate lobbying under civilian supremacy (Welch 1987; Colton 1979). By viewing neutrality as a process that occurs over time, we open a field of inquiry that examines the positions, interactions, and movements of civilian and military authorities. Transition control is important here in so far as it establishes the initial positions of conflict in which civilians and officers find themselves (Hunter 1997a). The prerogatives expected by officers, and the level of contestation civilians feel comfortable with are both originally set by transition control.[3]

How transition control allows a military to influence these initial positions of conflict brings us again to institutions. As most clearly illustrated here by the Pinochet regime, a controlled transition allows a military to establish institutions that establish military tutelage and a significant intrusion into civilian affairs. Agüero (1998) notes that those military regimes which most clearly established their prerogatives in constitutions and other institution-defining documents have had the greatest success in sustaining their political influence.

Nonetheless, we should not expect militaries to have complete success through the use of institutions. Pion-Berlin and Arceneaux (1998, 638) recognize why this is so. First, political regimes contain a multitude of institutions, and these institutions in turn contain a manifold collection of procedures and rules. The reality of time limitations, incomplete information, and uncertainty means that we should expect some oversights and errors even when a relatively unhindered military designs the forthcoming

3. See Stepan 1988 for a framework of civil-military relations based upon prerogatives and contestation.

democracy. Second, institutions cannot be created out of thin air. Their design is influenced by a particular historical-cultural context to which even de facto military rulers must answer (Meyer and Scott 1983). And finally, it must be recognized that democratic institutions contain inherent limitations that reduce the extent to which they can be effectively manipulated. By definition, democracy entails some level of indeterminacy. Przeworski (1986, 5) notes that although democracy demands certainty in procedures, it also requires uncertainty in outcomes. Democratic procedures can only be manipulated to make outcomes more likely; they cannot be designed such that outcomes are assured. A military on its way out of government may gerrymander district lines or set electoral thresholds to assist favored parties, but ultimately these parties must win votes on their own.[4]

In sum, transition control in military regimes should not be analyzed as a direct determinant of democratic consolidation. This area is overdetermined by a multitude of factors, many of which are difficult to predict. On the other hand, transition control is more immediately relevant to civil-military relations during the period of democratic consolidation, and these relations are central to the establishment of a solid democratic order.

The linkage between civil-military relations and democratic consolidation is a further area of inquiry. Future studies in this area will complement this work.[5] Following the arguments set in this study, discerning inquiries will be based on institutional dynamics. How stable are the institutions bestowed under the transition? How can they be changed? How can new institutions be stabilized? And, of course, which institutions best contribute to democratic consolidation, and do they vary from case to case? Just as the militaries in the Southern Cone and Brazil found their missions to be bounded by institutional design, the new democracies must work to assure that they are bounded by institutions that point toward greater democratic empowerment.

4. Chile's binomial electoral system exemplifies the limitations of institutional manipulation. In the most recent electoral results (1997), the right-wing Union for Chile Pact was able to translate 36 percent of the vote into 39 percent of the chamber seats (47 of 120 seats), but the Concertación was able to gain 58.3 percent of the chamber (70 of 120 seats) with just 50.55 percent of the vote. While the system forces alliances, it is not at all clear that the electoral format works as the military regime had expected, and one could even argue that the Concertación may be its most ardent supporter.

5. Important institutional or transition-based investigations of civil-military relations and democratic consolidation include Agüero 1995, Hunter 1997b, and Pion-Berlin 1998.

REFERENCES

Published Sources

Abós, Alvaro. 1982. *Las organizaciones sindicales y el poder militar (1976–1983)*. Buenos Aires: Centro Editor de America Latina.

Abrahamsson, Bengt. 1972. *Military Professionalism and Political Power*. Beverly Hills, Calif.: Sage Publications.

Achard, Diego. 1992. *La transición en Uruguay*. Montevideo: Ingenio en Servicios de Comunicación y Marketing.

Agüero, Felipe. 1998. "Legacies of Transitions: Institutionalization, the Military, and Democracy in South America." *Mershon International Studies Review* 42:383–404.

Aguiar, César A. 1985. *La transición Uruguaya: balance y perspectivas en el campo teórico*. Working paper no. 28, Centro Interdisciplinario de Estudios Sobre el Desarrollo, Montevideo.

Agüero, Felipe. 1988. "La autonomía de las Fuerzas Armadas." In Felipe Agüero et al., *Chile en el umbral de los noventa: quince años que condicionan el futuro*. Santiago: Editorial Planeta de Chile.

———. 1991. "Political and Military Elites in the Transition to Democracy: Chile since the 1988 Plebiscite." Paper presented at the Sixteenth Congress of the Latin American Studies Association, Washington, D.C.

———. 1995. *Soldiers, Civilians and Democracy: Post-Franco Spain in Comparative Perspective*. Baltimore: Johns Hopkins University Press.

Alder, Emmanuel. 1987. *The Power of Ideology: The Quest for Technological Autonomy in Argentina and Brazil*. Berkeley and Los Angeles: University of California Press.

Almond, Gabriel A. 1988. "The Return to the State." *American Political Science Review* 82 (3): 853–74.

Almond, Gabriel A., and G. Bingham Powell, Jr. 1966. *Comparative Politics: A Developmental Approach.* Boston: Little, Brown.

Alvarez, Edwin. 1992. "Criminalidad y abuso de poder: el caso argentino (1976–1983)." *Revista Cultural Lotería* 51 (388): 5–33.

Alvarez, Julio. 1966. "Presidencialismo." In *La "Revolución Argentina": análisis y prospectiva,* ed. Universidad del Salvador, Instituto de Ciencia Política. Buenos Aires: Ediciones Depalma.

Alves, María Moreira. 1985. *State and Opposition in Military Brazil.* Austin: University of Texas Press.

Amin, Samir. 1977. *Imperialism and Unequal Development.* New York: Monthly Review.

Amnesty International. 1979. *Political Imprisonment in Uruguay.* London: Amnesty International.

Angell, Alan, and Benny Pollack. 1990. "The Chilean Elections and the Politics of the Transition to Democracy." *Bulletin of Latin American Research* 9 (1): 1–23.

Anzorena, Oscar R. [1988.] *Tiempo de violencia y utopía (1966–1976).* Buenos Aires: Editorial Contrapunto.

Arceneaux, Craig L. 1997. "Bounded Missions: An Institutional Approach to Military Rule and Democratic Transition in the Southern Cone and Brazil." Ph.D. diss., University of California, Riverside.

Arriagada, Genaro Herrera. 1981. *El pensamiento político de los militares: estudios sobre Chile, Argentina, Brasil y Uruguay.* Santiago: Centro de Investigaciones Socioeconómicas de la Compañía de Jesús en Chile.

_____. 1986. *El pensamiento político de los militares.* Santiago: Editorial Aconcagua.

_____. 1991. *Pinochet: The Politics of Power.* Boulder, Colo.: Westview.

_____. 1992. "Despues de los presidencialismos ... que?" In *Cambio de régimen político,* ed. Oscar Godoy. Santiago: Ediciones Universidad Católica de Chile.

Astori, Danilo. 1982. *Neoliberalismo: critica y alternativa.* Montevideo: Ediciones de la Banda Oriental.

Babini, Pablo. 1991. "La caída de Viola." *Todo es Historia* (Buenos Aires) 25 (294): 8–42.

Bacchus, Wilfred A. 1990. *Mission in Mufti: Brazil's Military Regimes.* New York: Greenwood.

Baer, Werner. 1989. *The Brazilian Economy: Growth and Development.* New York: Praeger Publishers.

Baloyra, Enrique. 1986. "From Moment to Moment: The Political Transition in Brazil, 1977–1981." In *Political Liberalization in Brazil,* ed. Wayne A. Selcher. Boulder, Colo.: Westview.

_____, ed. 1987. *Comparing New Democracies: Transition and Consolidation in Mediterranean Europe and the Southern Cone.* Boulder, Colo.: Westview.

Baran, Paul. 1957. *The Political Economy of Growth.* New York: Monthly Review.

Barros, Alexandre de Souza Costa. 1978. "The Brazilian Military: Professional Socialization, Political Performance, and State Building." Ph.D. diss., University of Chicago.

_____. 1985. "Back to the Barracks: An Option for the Brazilian Military?" *Third World Quarterly* 7:63–77.

Bemis, George W. 1964. *From Crisis to Revolution: Monthly Case Studies.* Los Angeles: International Public Administration Center, School of Public Administration, University of Southern California.

Bermeo, Nancy. 1992a. "Democracy and the Lessons of Dictatorship." *Comparative Politics* 24 (3): 273–91.

_____. 1992b. "Surprise, Surprise: Lessons from 1989 and 1991." In *Liberalization and Democratization: Change in the Soviet Union and Eastern Europe,* ed. Nancy Bermeo. Baltimore: Johns Hopkins University Press.

Berrutti, Azucena. 1985. "Justicia militar." In *Coloquio sobre Uruguay y Paraguay: la transición del estado de excepción a la democracia,* ed. El Secretariado Internacional de Juristas por la Amnestía en Uruguay. Montevideo: Ediciones de la Banda Oriental.

Bertelsen Repetto, Raúl. 1988. "Antecedentes electorales en la elaboración de la Constitución de 1980." *Revista de Ciencia Política* (Edición Especial): 21–31.

Blume, Norman. 1967–68. "Pressure Groups and Decision-Making in Brazil." *Studies in Comparative International Development* 3 (11): 205–23.

Bordaberry, Juan María. 1980. *Las opciones.* Montevideo: Imprenta Rosgal S.A.

Botana, Natalio R., Rafael Braun, and Carlos A. Floria. 1973. *El régimen militar, 1966–1973.* Buenos Aires: Ediciones La Bastilla.

Bova, Russell. 1991. "Political Dynamics of the Post-Communist Transition: A Comparative Perspective." *World Politics* 44 (1): 113–38.

Bra, Gerardo. 1985. *El gobierno de Onganía: crónica.* Buenos Aires: Centro Editor de America Latina.

Bratton, Michael, and Nicolas van de Walle. 1992. "Popular Protest and Political Reform in Africa." *Comparative Politics* 24 (4): 419–42.

_____. 1994. "Neopatrimonial Regimes and Political Transitions in Africa." *World Politics* 46 (4): 453–89.

Bruneau, Thomas. 1992. "Brazil's Political Transition." In Higley and Gunther 1992.

Bruschera, Oscar H. 1986. *Las decadas infames: análisis político, 1967–1985.* Montevideo: Libreria Linardi y Risso.

_____. 1988. *Evolución institucional del Uruguay en el siglo XX.* Montevideo: Ediciones del Nuevo Mundo.

Burggraaff, Winfield J. 1972. *The Venezuelan Armed Forces in Politics, 1935–59.* Columbia: University of Missouri Press.

Burkhart, Ross E., and Michael S. Lewis-Beck. 1994. "Comparative Democracy: The Economic Development Thesis." *American Political Science Review* 88:903–10.

Campero, Guillermo. 1984. *Los gremios empresariales en el periodo 1970–1983: comportamiento sociopolítico y orientaciones ideológicas.* Santiago: Instituto Latinoamericano de Estudios Transnacionales.

Canabal, Rodolfo. 1985. "Persistencia de la violación de los derechos humanos." In *Coloquio sobre Uruguay y Paraguay: la transición del estado de excepción a la democracia,* ed. El Secretariado Internacional de Juristas por la Amnistía en Uruguay. Montevideo: Ediciones de la Banda Oriental.

Canessa Robert, Julio. 1992. "Significado y proyecciones de la reforma constitucional para las fuerzas armadas." *Política* 30:345–56.

Canitrot, Adolfo. 1980a. "Discipline as the Central Objective of Economic Policy: An Essay on the Economic Programme of the Argentine Government Since 1976." *World Development* 8 (11): 913–28.

_____. 1980b. *Teoría y práctica del liberalismo: política antiinflacionaria y apertura económica en la Argentina. 1976–1981.* Buenos Aires: Centro de Estudios de Estado y Sociedad, Estudios CEDES, vol. 3, no. 10.

Cardoso, Fernando Henrique, and Enzo Faletto. 1979. *Dependency and Development in Latin America.* Berkeley and Los Angeles: University of California Press.

Carlos de Medeiros, Antônio. 1986. *Politics and Intergovernmental Relations in Brazil, 1964–1982.* New York: Garland Publishing.

Castello, Antonio Emilio. 1986. "Onganía y la caída de Illia." *Todo es Historia* 19 (230): 8–27.

Cavallo Castro, Ascanio, Manuel Salazar Salvo, and Oscar Sepúlveda Pacheco. 1990. *La historia del régimen militar.* Mexico City: Editorial Diana.

Cavarozzi, Marcelo. 1992a. "Beyond Transitions to Democracy in Latin America." *Journal of Latin American Studies* 24 (3): 665–84.

_____. 1992b. "Patterns of Elite Negotiation and Confrontation in Argentina and Chile." In Higley and Gunther 1992.

Cayota, Victor. 1985. "La enseñanza." In *Coloquio sobre Uruguay y Paraguay: la transición del estado de excepción a la democracia,* ed. El Secretariado Internacional de Juristas por la Amnestía en Uruguay. Montevideo: Ediciones de la Banda Oriental.

Chagas, Jorge, and Mario Tonarelli. 1980. *El sindicalismo Uruguayo bajo la dictadura.* Montevideo: Ediciones del Nuevo Mundo.

Chaparro N., Patricio, and Francisco Cumplido C. 1982. "El proceso de toma de decisiones en el contexto político militar-autoritario Chileno: estudio de dos casos." In *Chile 1973–198?,* ed. Revista Mexicana de Sociologia and FLACSO. Mexico City: Revista Mexicana de Sociologia and FLACSO.

Chehabi, H. E., and Juan J. Linz. 1998. *Sultanistic Regimes.* Baltimore: Johns Hopkins University Press.

Cheresky, Isidoro. 1985. "Hacia la Argentina postautoritaria." In *Crisis y transformación de los régimenes autoritarios,* ed. Isidoro Cheresky and Jacques Chonchol. Buenos Aires: Editorial Universitaria de Buenos Aires.

Coelho, Eduardo Campos. 1988. "Back to the Barracks: The Brazilian Military's Style." In *The Decline of Military Regimes: The Civilian Influence,* ed. Constantine Danopoulos. Boulder, Colo.: Westview.

Cohen, Youssef. 1979. "Popular Support for Authoritarian Governments: Brazil Under Médici." Ph.D. diss., University of Michigan.

Collins, Charles. 1985. *Military Rule and the Reform of Local Government in Latin America: The Case of Brazil, 1964–1980.* Norwich, U.K.: Geo Books.

Collier, David, ed. 1979. *The New Authoritarianism in Latin America.* Princeton: Princeton University Press.

Colton, Timothy J. 1979. *Commissars, Commanders, and Civilian Authority: The Structure of Soviet Military Politics.* Cambridge: Harvard University Press.

Conaghan, Catherine. 1988. "Capitalists, Technocrats, and Politicians: Economic Policy-Making and Democracy in the Central Andes." Working Paper no. 109, Helen Kellog Institute for International Studies, Notre Dame.

Conca, Ken. 1992. "Technology, the Military, and Democracy in Brazil." *Journal of Interamerican Studies and World Affairs* 34 (1): 141–77.

Corrandi, Juan E., Patricia Weiss Fagen, and Manuel Antonio Garretón, eds. 1992. *Fear at the Edge: State Terror and Resistance in Latin America.* Berkeley and Los Angeles: University of California Press.

Cotta, Maurizio. 1990. "The 'Centrality' of Parliament in a Protracted Democratic Consolidation: The Italian Case." In *Parliament and Democratic Consolidation in Southern Europe: Greece, Italy, Portugal, Spain and Turkey,* ed. Ulrike Liebert and Maurizio Cotta. New York: Pinter.

Cuevas Farren, Gustavo. 1989. "Chile 1989: las coyunturas de un proceso político." *Política* 21:11–27.

_____. 1990. "Las fuerzas armadas y transición a la democracia en América Latina." *Política* 22–23:83–99.

Cutright, Phillips. 1963. "National Political Development." *American Sociological Review* 28:253–64.

Dabat, Alejandro. 1984. "El durrumbe de la dictadura." In *La década trágica,* ed. Alberto J. Pla et al. Buenos Aires: Editorial Tierra del Fuego.

Dahl, Robert A. 1971. *Polyarchy: Participation and Opposition.* New Haven: Yale University Press.

Dassin, Joan, ed. 1986. *Torture in Brazil.* Translated by Jaime Wright. New York: Vintage Books.

de Dromi, María Laura San Martino. 1988. *Historia política Argentina (1955– 1988).* 2 vols. Buenos Aires: Editorial Astrea de Alfredo y Ricardo Depalma.

del Huerto Amarillo, María. 1984. "Participación política de las fuerzas armadas." In *Uruguay y la democracia: volume I,* ed. Charles Gillespie, Louis Goodman, Juan Rial, and Peter Winn. Montevideo: Ediciones de la Banda Oriental.

_____. 1986. *El ascenso al poder de las fuerzas armadas.* Montevideo: Servicio de Paz y Justicia.

Delich, Francisco. 1974. *Crisis y protesta social: Córdoba, 1969–1973.* Buenos Aires: Siglo Veintiuno Editores.

Demichelli, Alberto. 1976. *Reforma constitucional: democracia participative, representación del trabajo, del capital, y la cultura.* Montevideo: Barreiro y Ramos.

Di Palma, Giuseppe. 1990. *To Craft Democracies: An Essay on Democratic Transitions.* Berkeley and Los Angeles: University of California Press.

Diamond, Larry. 1999. *Developing Democracy: Toward Consolidation.* Baltimore: Johns Hopkins University Press.

Diamond, Larry, Juan Linz, and Seymour Martin Lipset. 1989. *Democracy in Developing Countries.* Boulder, Colo.: Lynne Rienner.

Dias David, Mauracio. 1977. "El control militar-corporativo en Brasil y Chile." *Desarrollo Indoamericano* 12 (39): 29–35.

Dix, Robert. 1994. "Research Note: History and Democracy Revisited." *Comparative Politics* 27 (1): 91–106.

Dunbar, Layton G. 1979. *State-Military Relations in Brazil.* Alexandria, Va.: Army Military Personnel Center.

Dunlavy, Collen. 1993. *Political Structure and Industrial Change: Early Railroads in the United States and Prussia.* Princeton: Princeton University Press.

Ekiert, Grzegorz. 1991. "Democratization Processes in East Central Europe: A Theoretical Reconsideration." *The British Journal of Political Science* 21 (3): 285– 313.

Elster, Jon, and Rune Slagstad. 1988. *Constitutionalism and Democracy: Studies in Rationality and Social Change.* New York: Cambridge University Press.

English, Adrian J. 1984. *Armed Forces of Latin America: Their Histories, Development, Present Strength, and Military Potential.* London: Jane's.

Ethier, Diane. 1990. "Processes of Transition and Democratic Consolidation: Theoretical Indicators." In *Democratic Transition and Consolidation in Southern Europe, Latin America, and Southeast Asia,* ed. Diane Ethier. London: Macmillan.

Ethington, Philip J., and Eileen L. McDonagh. 1995. "The Common Space of Social Science Inquiry." *Polity* 28 (1): 85–90.

Evans, Peter B. 1979. *Dependent Development: The Alliance of Multinational, State and Local Capital in Brazil.* Princeton: Princeton University Press.

Evans, Peter, Dietrich Reuschmeyer, and Theda Skocpol, eds. 1985. *Bringing the State Back In.* New York: Cambridge University Press.

Farcau, Bruce. 1996. *The Transition to Democracy in Latin America: The Role of the Military.* Westport, Conn.: Praeger.

Favaro, Edgardo, and Alberto Bensión. 1993. "Uruguay." In *The Political Economy of Poverty, Equity, and Growth: Costa Rica and Uruguay,* ed. Simon Rottenberg. Oxford: Oxford University Press.

Fayt, Carlos S. 1971. *El Político armado: dinámica del proceso político Argentino (1960/1971).* Buenos Aires: Ediciones Pannedille.

Fernández Jilberto, Alex, and Fernando Polle. 1988. "Burocracia militar y transición a la democracia en Chile." *Boletín de Estudios Latinoamericanos y del Caribe* 45:3–28.

Ferrer, Aldo. 1981. *Nacionalismo y orden constitucional.* Buenos Aires: Fondo de Cultural Económica.

_____. 1982. "Monetarismo en el cono sur: el caso Argentino." *Pensamiento Iberoaméricano* 1:109–15.

Filgueira, Carlos. 1984. *Restauración o cambio: el dilema de la democratizacón en el Uruguay.* Working paper no. 66, CIESU, Montevideo.

Finch, M.H.J. 1981. *A Political Economy of Uruguay Since 1870.* New York: St. Martin's.

_____. 1985. "The Military Regime and Dominant Class Interests in Uruguay, 1973–1982." In *Generals in Retreat: The Crisis of Military Rule In Uruguay,* ed. Philip O'Brien and Paul Cammack. Manchester: University of Manchester Press.

Finer, S. E. 1988. *The Man on Horseback: The Role of the Military in Politics.* Boulder, Colo.: Westview.

Floria, Carlos A. 1983. "El régimen corporativo y la Argentina corporativa (1966–1973)." In *Historia política Argentina: 1943–1982,* ed. Ricardo del Barco et al. Buenos Aires: Editorial de Belgrano.

Flynn, Peter. 1978. *Brazil: A Political Analysis.* Boulder, Colo.: Westview Press.

Fontaine, Juan Andrés. 1993. "Transición económica y política en Chile: 1970–1990." *Estudios Publicos* 50:229–79.

Fontana, Andrés. 1985. "Fuerzas armadas e ideologia neoconservadora: el redimensionamiento del estado en la Argentina, 1976–1981." In *Privatización: Del Hecho al Hecho,* ed. Horacio Boneo. Buenos Aires: El Cronista Comercial.

_____. 1986. *De la crisis de Malvinas a la subordinación condicionada: conflictos intramilitares y transición política en Argentina.* Working paper no. 74, Helen Kellog Institute for International Studies, Notre Dame.

_____. 1987. "Political Decision Making by a Military Corporation: Argentina 1976–1983." Ph.D. diss., University of Texas at Austin.

Foxley, Alejandro. 1983. *Latin American Experiments in Neo-Conservative Economics.* Berkeley and Los Angeles: University of California Press.

Fraga, Rosendo. 1988. *Ejército: del escarnio al poder.* Buenos Aires: Grupo Editorial Planeta.

Franco, Rolando. 1984. *Democracia "a la Uruguaya."* Montevideo: Editorial El Libro Libre.

Frank, Andre Gunder. 1967. *Capitalism and Underdevelopment in Latin America.* New York: Monthly Review.

Frieden, Jeffrey A. 1991. *Debt, Development, and Democracy: Modern Political Economy and Latin America, 1965–1985.* Princeton: Princeton University Press.

Fruhling, Hugo. 1983. "Stages of Repression and Legal Strategy for the Defense of Human Rights in Chile: 1973–1980." *Human Rights Quarterly* 5:510–33.

Garretón, Manuel Antonio. 1978. "De la seguridad nacional a la nueva institucionalidad." *Foro Internacional* 19 (1): 103–27.

_____. 1989. *The Chilean Political Process.* Boston: Unwin Hyman.

_____. 1991. "The Political Opposition and the Party System under the Military Regime." In *The Struggle for Democracy in Chile, 1982–1990,* ed. Paul Drake and Iván Jaksic. Lincoln: University of Nebraska Press.

Geddes, Barbara. 1994. *Politician's Dilemma: Building State Capacity in Latin America.* Berkeley and Los Angeles: University of California Press.

_____. 1999. "Authoritarian Breakdown: Empirical Test of a Game Theoretic Argument." Presented at the annual meeting of the American Political Science Association, Atlanta, September 1999.

Geddes, Barbara, and John Zaller. 1989. "Sources of Popular Support for Authoritarian Regimes." *American Journal of Political Science* 33 (2): 319–47.

George, Alexander L., and Timothy J. McKeown. 1985. "Case Studies and Theories of Organizational Decision Making." In *Advances in Information Processing in Organizations,* ed. Lee S. Sproull and Patrick D. Larkey. Greenwich, Conn.: JAI.

Geywitz, Carlos Andrade. 1991. *Reforma de la Constitución Política de la República de Chile.* Santiago: Editorial Jurídica de Chile.

Gillespie, Charles. 1991. *Negotiating Democracy: Politicians and Generals in Uruguay.* New York: Cambridge University Press.

Gillespie, Charles, and Luis E. González. 1988. "Uruguay: The Survival of Old and Autonomous Institutions." In *Democracy in Developing Countries — Volume 4: Latin America,* ed. Larry Diamond, Juan J. Linz, and Seymour Martin Lipset. Boulder, Colo.: Lynne Rienner.

Gillespie, Richard. 1982. *Soldiers of Perón: Argentina's Montoneros.* Oxford: Clarendon Press; New York: Oxford University Press.

Gills, Barry, Joel Rocamora, and Richard Wilson, eds. 1993. *Low Intensity Democracy: Political Power in the New World Order.* Boulder, Colo.: Pluto.

Ginsberg, Benjamin. 1982. *The Consequences of Consent: Elections, Citizen Control, and Popular Acquiescence.* Reading, Mass.: Addison-Wesley, 1982.

González, Luis E. 1983. "Uruguay, 1980–1981: An Unexpected Opening." *Latin American Research Review* 18 (3): 63–76.

_____. 1984. *Political Parties and Redemocratization in Uruguay.* Working Paper no. 83, CIESU, Montevideo.

_____. 1991. *Political Structures and Democracy in Uruguay.* Notre Dame: University of Notre Dame Press.

Goodwin, Jeff, and Theda Skocpol. 1989. "Explaining Revolutions in the Contemporary Third World." *Politics and Society* 17 (December): 489–509.

Groisman, Enrique I. 1984. "El 'Proceso de Reorganización Nacional' y el sistema jurídico." In *"Proceso," crisis y transición democrática,* ed. Oscar Oszlak. Buenos Aires: Biblioteca Política Argentina.

_____. 1987. *La Corte Suprema de Justicia durante la dictadura.* Buenos Aires: Centro de Investigaciones Sociales Sobre el Estado y la Administración.

Haggard, Stephan, and Robert R. Kaufman. 1995. *The Political Economy of Democratic Transitions.* Princeton: Princeton University Press.

Hagopian, Frances. 1990. "'Democracy by Undemocratic Means'? Elites, Political Pacts, and Regime Transition in Brazil." *Comparative Political Studies* 23 (2): 147–70.

Hall, Peter A. 1992. "The Movement from Keynesianism to Monetarism: Institutional Analysis and British Economic Policy in the 1970s." In Steinmo, Thelen, and Longstreth 1992.

Hall, Peter A., and Rosemary C. R. Taylor. 1996. "Political Science and the Three New Institutionalisms." *Political Studies* 64:936–57.

Handelman, Howard. 1981a. "Economic Policy and Elite Pressures." In *Military*

Government and the Movement Toward Democracy in South America, ed. Thomas G. Sanders. Bloomington: Indiana University Press.

———. 1981b. "Military Authoritarianism and Political Change." In *Military Government and the Movement Toward Democracy in South America,* ed. Thomas G. Sanders. Bloomington: Indiana University Press.

———. 1986. "Prelude to Elections: The Military's Legitimacy Crisis and 1980 Constitutional Plebiscite in Uruguay." In *Elections and Democratization in Latin America,* ed. Paul W. Drake and Eduardo Silva. San Diego: Center for Iberian and Latin American Studies, Center for US-Mexican Studies, and Institute of the Americas.

Hartlyn, Jonathan. 1986. "Military Governments and the Transition to Civilian Rule: The Colombian Experience of 1957–58." In *Armies and Politics in Latin America,* ed. Abraham F. Lowenthal and J. Samuel Fitch. New York: Holmes and Meier.

Hattam, Victoria C. 1993. *Labor Visions and State Power: The Origins of Business Unionism in the United States.* Princeton: Princeton University Press.

Higley, John, and Michael G. Burton. 1989. "The Elite Variable in Democratic Transitions and Breakdowns." *American Sociological Review* 54:17–32.

Higley, John, and Richard Gunther, eds. 1992. *Elites and Democratic Consolidation in Latin America and Southern Europe.* New York: Cambridge University Press.

Horowitz, Irving Louis. 1985. "Militarism and Civil-Military Relationships in Latin America: Implications for the Third World." *Research in Political Sociology* 1:79–99.

Huneeus M., Carlos. 1985. "La Política de la apertura y sus implicancias para la inauguración de la democracia en Chile." *Revista de Ciencia Política* 7 (1): 25–83.

———. 1988. "El ejército y la política en el Chile de Pinochet: su magnitud y alcances." *Opciones* 14:89–136.

———. 1997. "La autodisolución de la 'democracia protegida' en Chile." *Revista de Ciencia Política* 19:61–86.

Huneeus M., Carlos, and Jorge Olave. 1987. "La participación de los militares en los nuevos autoritarismos: Chile, en una perspectiva comparada." *Opciones* 11:119–62.

Hunter, Wendy. 1997a. "Continuity or Change: Civil-Military Relations in Democratic Argentina, Chile, and Peru." *Political Science Quarterly* 112 (3): 453–75.

———. 1997b. *Eroding Military Influence in Brazil.* Chapel Hill: University of North Carolina Press.

Huntington, Samuel P. 1957. *The Soldier and the State: The Theory and Politics of Civil-Military Relations.* Cambridge: Belknap Press of Harvard University Press.

———. 1968. *Political Order in Changing Societies.* New Haven: Yale University Press.

———. 1984. "Will More Countries Become Democratic?" In *Political Science Quarterly* 99:193–218.

———. 1991. *The Third Wave: Democratization in the Late Twentieth Century.* Norman: University of Oklahoma Press.

———. 1994. "Democratic Development in the Post-Cold War Era." Presented at the International Political Science Association Roundtable, Kyoto.

Ikenberry, G. John. 1988a. "Conclusion: An Institutional Approach to American Foreign Economic Policy." *International Organization* 42 (1): 219–43.

———. 1988b. *Reasons of State: The Oil Shocks of the 1970s and the Capacities of American Government.* Ithaca: Cornell University Press.

Immergut, Ellen M. 1992. "The Rules of the Game: The Logic of Health Policy-Making in France, Switzerland, and Sweden." In Steinmo, Thelen, and Longstreth 1992.

Isaacs, Anita. 1993. *Military Rule and Transition in Ecuador, 1972–92.* Pittsburgh: University of Pittsburgh Press.

Iturriaga Ruiz, Osvaldo. 1983. "La Controlaria General de la República: funciones importantes para el estado de derecho." *Política* 15:425–41.

Jackman, Robert W. 1973. "On the Relation of Economic Development to Democratic Performance." *American Journal of Political Science* 17:611–21.

Janowitz, Morris. 1960. *The Professional Soldier.* New York: Free Press.

Janowitz, Morris, and Roger W. Little. 1974. *Sociology and the Military Establishment.* Beverly Hills, Calif.: Sage Publications.

Jenks, Margaret S. 1979. "Political Parties in Authoritarian Brazil." Ph.D. diss., Duke University.

Jepperson, Ronald L. 1991. "Institutions, Institutional Effects, and Institutionalism." In *The New Institutionalism in Organizational Analysis,* ed. Walter W. Powell and Paul J. DiMaggio. Chicago: University of Chicago Press.

Joaquín Brunner, José. 1990. "Chile: claves de una transición pactada." *Nueva Sociedad* 106:7–12.

Johnson, John J. 1964. *The Military and Society in Latin America.* Stanford: Stanford University Press.

Karl, Terry Lynn. 1986a. "Imposing Consent: Electoralism vs. Democratization in El Salvador." In *Elections and Democratization in Latin America, 1980–1985,* ed. Paul W. Drake and Eduardo Silva. San Diego: Center for Iberian and Latin American Studies, Center for U.S.-Mexican Studies, and Institute of the Americas.

_____. 1986b. "Petroleum and Political Pacts: The Transition to Democracy in Venezuela." In *Transitions from Authoritarian Rule: Latin America,* ed. Guillermo O'Donnell, Philippe Schmitter, and Laurence Whitehead. Baltimore: Johns Hopkins University Press.

_____. 1990. "Dilemmas of Democratization in Latin America." *Comparative Politics* 23 (1): 1–22.

Karl, Terry Lynn, and Philippe C. Schmitter. 1991. "Modes of Transition in Latin America, Southern and Eastern Europe." *International Social Science Journal* 128:269–84.

Katzenstein, Peter, ed. 1978. *Between Power and Plenty: Foreign Economic Policies of Advanced Industrial States.* Madison: University of Wisconsin Press.

Kaufman, Edy. 1979. *Uruguay in Transition: From Civilian to Military Rule.* New Brunswick, N.J.: Transaction Books.

King, Desmond S. 1992. "The Establishment of Work-Welfare Programs in the United States and Britain: Politics, Ideas, and Institutions." In Steinmo, Thelen, and Longstreth 1992.

Kingdon, John W. 1984. *Agendas, Alternatives, and Public Policies.* Glenview, Ill.: Scott Foresman.

Kinzo, Maria D'Alva G. 1988. *Legal Opposition Under Authoritarian Rule in Brazil: The Case of the MDB, 1966–79.* London: Macmillan.

Kirchheimer, Otto. 1965. "Confining Conditions and Revolutionary Breakthroughs." *American Political Science Review* 59:964–74.

Krasner, Stephen D. 1984. "Approaches to the State: Alternative Conceptions and Historical Dynamics." *Comparative Politics* 16 (2): 223–46.

_____. 1988. "Sovereignty: An Institutional Perspective." *Comparative Political Studies* 21 (1): 66–94.

LADH (Liga Argentina por los Derechos del Hombre). 1969. *Acta de acusación al régimen de llamada Revolución Argentina.* Buenos Aires: Liga Argentina por los Derechos del Hombre.

Lambert, Jaques. 1969. *Latin America: Social Structure and Political Institutions.* Berkeley and Los Angeles: University of California Press.

Lamounier, Bolivar. 1989. "Authoritarian Brazil Revisited: The Impact of Elections on the Abertura." In *Democratizing Brazil: Problems of Transition and Consolidation,* ed. Alfred Stepan. New York: Oxford University Press.

Lanusse, Alejandro A. 1977. *Mi testimonio.* Buenos Aires: Lasserre Editores.

Lawson, S. 1993. "Conceptual Issues in the Comparative Study of Regime Change and Democratization." *Comparative Politics* 25 (2): 183–205.

Lazara, Simon. 1988. *Poder militar: origen, apogeo, y transición.* Buenos Aires: Editorial Legasa.

Lerin, François, and Cristina Torres. 1987. *Historia política de la dictadura Uruguaya (1973–1980).* Montevideo: Ediciones del Nuevo Mundo.

Lerner, Daniel. 1958. *The Passing of Traditional Society: Modernizing the Middle East* Glencoe, Ill.: Free Press.

Lijphart, Arend. 1971. "Comparative Politics and the Comparative Method." *American Political Science Review* 65:682–93.

————. 1999. *Patterns of Democracy: Government Forms and Performance in Thirty-Six Countries.* New Haven: Yale University Press.

Linz, Juan J. 1975. "Totalitarian and Authoritarian Regimes." In *Macropolitical Theory,* vol. 3 of *Handbook of Political Science,* ed. Fred I. Greenstein and Nelson W. Polsby. Reading, Mass.: Addison Wesley.

————. 1981. "Some Comparative Thoughts on the Transition to Democracy in Portugal and Spain." In *Portugal Since the Revolution,* ed. Jorge Braga de Macedo and Simon Serfaty. Boulder, Colo.: Westview.

Linz, Juan J., and Alfred Stepan. 1996. *Problems of Democratic Transition and Consolidation: Southern Europe, South America, and Post-Communist Europe.* Baltimore: Johns Hopkins University Press.

Linz, Juan J., Arend Lijphart, Arturo Valenzuela, and Oscar Godoy Arcaya. 1990. *Hacia una democracia moderna: la opción parlamentaria.* Santiago: Ediciones Universidad Católica de Chile.

Lipset, Seymour Martin. 1960. *Political Man.* Garden City, N.Y.: Anchor.

————. 1967. "Values, Education, and Entreprenuership." In *Elites in Latin America,* ed. Seymour Martin Lipset and Aldo Solari. New York: Oxford University Press.

López Chirico, Selva. 1985. *El estado y las fuerzas armadas en el Uruguay del siglo XX.* Montevideo: Ediciones de la Banda Oriental.

Lousteau Heguy, Guillermo A. 1966. "El sistema instituticional Argentino." In *La "Revolución Argentina": análisis y prospectiva,* ed. Universidad del Salvador, Instituto de Ciencia Política. Buenos Aires: Ediciones Depalma.

Loveman, Brian. 1986. "Military Dictatorship and Political Opposition in Chile." *Journal of InterAmerican Studies and World Affairs* 28 (4): 1–38.

————. 1991. "Misión Cumplida? Civil-Military Relations and the Chilean Political Transition." *Journal of InterAmerican Studies and World Affairs* 33 (3): 35–74.

Loveman, Brian, and Thomas M. Davies, Jr. 1997. *The Politics of Antipolitics: The Military in Latin America.* Wilmington, Del.: Scholarly Resources.

Luttwak, Edward. 1968. *Coup d' Etat—A Practical Handbook.* London: Penguin.

Macadar, Luis. 1982. *Uruguay 1974–1980: un nuevo ensayo de reajuste económico?* Montevideo: Ediciones de la Banda Oriental.

_____. 1987. *Industrialización, apertura externa, y reestructura productiva: una reseña del proceso de industrialización en Uruguay durante los años setenta.* Montevideo: Centro de Investigaciones Económicas.

MacHale, Tomás. 1979. "Poder político y libertad de expresión en Chile (1976–1978)." *Revista de Ciencia Política* 1 (1): 41–51.

Maggiolo, Oscar J. 1976. "Uruguay, tres años de dictadura." *Nueva Sociedad* 27:74–84.

Mainwaring, Scott. 1990. "Presidentialism in Latin America." *Latin American Research Review* 25 (1): 157–79.

_____. 1992. "Transitions to Democracy and Democratic Consolidation: Theoretical and Comparative Issues." In *Issues in Democratic Consolidation: The New South American Democracies in Comparative Perspective,* ed. Scott Mainwaring, Guillermo O'Donnell, and J. Samuel Valenzuela. Notre Dame: University of Notre Dame Press.

Maira, Luis. 1988. *La Constitución de 1980 y la ruptura democrática.* Santiago: Editorial Emision.

March, James G. 1989. *Rediscovering Institutions.* New York: Free Press.

March, James G., and Herbert Simon. 1958. *Organizations.* New York: John Wiley and Sons.

March, James G., and Johan P. Olsen. 1984. "The New Institutionalism: Organizational Factors in Political Life." *American Political Science Review* 78:734–49.

_____. 1989. *Rediscovering Institutions: The Organizational Basis of Politics.* New York: Free Press.

Markoff, John, and Silvio R. Duncan Baretta. 1985. "Professional Ideology and Military Activism in Brazil: A Critique of a Thesis of Alfred Stepan." *Comparative Politics* 17 (2): 175–91.

Martorelli, Horacio. 1984. *Transición a la democracia.* Montevideo: Ediciones de la Banda Oriental.

Martz, John D. 1962. *Colombia: A Contemporary Political Survey.* Chapel Hill: University of North Carolina Press.

Masterson, Daniel M. 1991. *Militarism and Politics in Latin America: Peru from Sánchez Cerro to Sendero Luminoso.* New York: Greenwood.

Matsushita, Hiroshi. 1987. "Democratización Argentina en 1983." *Cuadernos Americanos* (new edition) 1 (5): 138–63.

McDonald, Ronald H. 1972. "Electoral Politics and Uruguayan Political Decay." *Inter-American Economic Affairs* 28 (1): 25–45.

_____. 1975. "The Rise of Military Politics in Uruguay." *Inter-American Economic Affairs* 28 (4): 25–43.

McSherry, J. Patrice. 1997. *Incomplete Transition: Military Power and Democracy in Argentina.* New York: St. Martin's Press.

Medina, José María F. 1984. "Argentina y Brasil: redemocratización y poder militar." *Nueva Sociedad* 73:135–44.

Meyer, J. W., and W. R. Scott. 1983. *Organizational Environments: Ritual and Rationality.* Beverly Hills, Calif.: Sage.

Midlarsky, Manus I. 1995. "Environmental Influences on Democracy: Aridity, Warfare, and a Reversal of the Causal Arrow." *Journal of Conflict Resolution* 39 (2): 224–62.

Minello, Nelson. 1976. *El militarización del estado en América Latina: un análisis de Uruguay.* Mexico City: Centro de Estudios Sociológicos, El Colegio de Mexico.

Modelsky, George, and Gardner Perry III. 1991. "Democratization in Long Perspective." *Technological Forecasting and Social Change* 39 (1–2): 23–34.

Molina Johnson, Carlos. 1990. "La Constitución Política, la obediencia y la no deliberancia militar." *Memorial del Ejército de Chile* 434:20–31.

Moore, Barrington, Jr. 1967. *Social Origins of Dictatorship and Democracy: Lord and Peasant in the Making of the Modern World.* Boston: Beacon.

Morlino, Leonardo. 1987. "Democratic Establishments: A Dimensional Analysis." In Baloyra 1987.

Munck, Gerardo L. 1994. "Democratic Transitions in Comparative Perspective." *Comparative Politics* 26 (3): 355–75.

———. 1998. *Authoritarianism and Democratization: Soldiers and Workers in Argentina, 1976–1983.* University Park: Pennsylvania State University Press.

Niosi, Jorge. 1974. *Los empresarios y el estado argentino (1955–1969).* Buenos Aires, Siglo Veintiuno Editores.

Notaro, Jorge. 1983. *La política económica en Uruguay, 1968–1982.* Montevideo: Centro Interdisciplinario de Estudios Sobre el Desarrollo Uruguay.

Nordlinger, Eric A. 1977. *Soldiers in Politics: Military Coups and Governments.* Englewood Cliffs, N.J.: Prentice-Hall.

———. 1987. "Taking the State Seriously." In *Understanding Political Development: An Analytic Study,* ed. Myron Weiner and Samuel P. Huntington. Boston: Little, Brown.

Nunn, Frederick M. 1976. *The Military in Chilean History: Essays on Civil-Military Relations (1810–1973).* Albuquerque: University of New Mexico Press.

———. 1983. *Yesterday's Soldiers: European Military Professionalism in South America, 1980–1940.* Lincoln: University of Nebraska Press.

O'Brien, Phil, and Jackie Roddick. 1983. *Chile: The Pinochet Decade.* London: The Latin American Bureau.

O'Donnell, Guillermo A. 1972. *El "juego imposible": competición y coaliciones entre partidos políticos en la Argentina, 1955–66.* Buenos Aires: Instituto Di Tella.

———. 1973. *Modernization and Bureaucratic Authoritarianism.* Berkeley and Los Angeles: Institute of International Studies.

———. 1988. *Bureaucratic Authorianism: Argentina, 1966–1973, in Comparative Perspective.* Berkeley and Los Angeles: University of California Press.

———. 1992. "Transitions, Continuities, and Paradoxes." In *Issues in Democratic Consolidation: The New South American Democracies in Comparative Perspective,* ed. Scott Mainwaring, Guillermo O'Donnell, and J. Samuel Valenzuela. Notre Dame: University of Notre Dame Press.

O'Donnell, Guillermo A., and Philippe C. Schmitter. 1986. *Transitions from Authoritarian Rule: Tentative Conclusions about Uncertain Democracy.* Baltimore: Johns Hopkins University Press.

Ollier, María M. 1988. "El imperio de la violencia." *Todo es Historia* 22 (253): 80–97.

Orren, Karen, and Stephen Skowronek. 1993. "Beyond the Iconography of Order: Notes for a 'New Institutionalism.'" In *The Dynamics of American Politics: Approaches and Interpretations,* ed. Lawrence C. Dodd and Calvin Jillson. Boulder, Colo.: Westview.

———. 1996. "Institutions and Intercurrence: Theory Building in the Fullness of Time." In *Political Order: Nomos 38.* New York: New University Press.

Ortega Frei, Eugenio. 1992. *Historia de una alianza.* Santiago: CED-CESOC.

Oxhorn, Philip. 1994. "Where Did All the Protestors Go? Popular Mobilization and the Transition to Democracy in Chile." *Latin American Perspectives* 21 (3): 49–69.

Paoletti, Alipio. 1986. *Con los Nazis, como en Vietnam: los campos de concentración en la Argentina*. Buenos Aires: Editorial Contrapunto.
Pearce, Jenny. 1980. *Uruguay: Generals Rule*. London: Latin American Bureau.
Perina, Rubén M. 1983. *Onganía, Levingston, Lanusse: los militares en la política argentina*. Buenos Aires: Editorial de Belgrano.
Philip, George. 1984. "The Fall of the Argentine Military." *Third World Quarterly* 6 (3): 624–37.
Pion-Berlin, David. 1987. "Military Breakdown and Redemocratizaton in Argentina." In *Liberalization and Redemocratization in Latin America*, ed. George Lopez and Michael Stohl. Westport, Conn.: Greenwood.
_____. 1988. "The National Security Doctrine, Military Threat Perception, and the 'Dirty War' in Argentina." *Comparative Political Studies* 21 (3): 382–407.
_____. 1989a. *The Ideology of State Terror: Economic Doctrine and Political Repression in Argentina and Peru*. Boulder, Colo.: Lynne Rienner.
_____. 1989b. "Latin American National Security Doctrines: Hard- and Softline Themes." *Armed Forces and Society* 15:411–29.
_____. 1992. "Military Autonomy and Emerging Democracies in South America." *Comparative Politics* 25 (October): 83–102.
_____. 1994. "To Prosecute or to Pardon? Human Rights Decisions in the Latin American Southern Cone." *Human Rights Quarterly* 16:105–30.
_____. 1995. "The Armed Forces in Politics: Gains and Snares in Recent Scholarship." *Latin American Research Review* 30 (1): 147–62.
_____. 1998. *Through Corridors of Power: Institutions and Civil-Military Relations in Argentina*. University Park: Pennsylvania State University Press.
Pion-Berlin, David, and Craig Arceneaux. 1998. "Tipping the Civil-Military Balance: Institutions and Human Rights Policy in Democratic Argentina and Chile." *Comparative Political Studies* 31 (5): 633–61.
Pírez, Pedro. 1986. *Coparticipación federal y descentralización del estado*. Buenos Aires: Centro Editor de América Latina.
Portantiero, Juan Carlos. 1987. "La transicion entre la confrontación y el acuerdo." In *Ensayos sobre la transición democrática en la Argentina*, ed. Jose Nun and Juan Carlos Portantiero. Buenos Aires: Puntosur Editores.
Potash, Robert A. 1996. *The Army and Politics in Argentina, 1962–1973: From Frondizi's Fall to the Peronist Restoration*. Stanford: Stanford University Press.
Pozzi, Pablo. 1988. "Argentina 1976–1982: Labour Leadership and Military Government." *Journal of Latin American Studies* 20 (1): 111–38.
Pridham, Geoffrey. 1984. "Comparative Perspectives on the New Mediterranean Democracies: A New Model of Régime Transitions?" In *The New Mediterranean Democracies: Régime Transition in Spain, Greece and Portugal*, ed. Geoffrey Pridham. London: Frank Cass.
_____, ed. 1991. *Encouraging Democracy? The International Context of Regime Transition in Southern Europe*. London: Leicester University Press.
Pridham, Geoffrey, Eric Herring, and George Sanford, eds. 1994. *Building Democracy? The International Dimension of Democratisation in Eastern Europe*. London: Leicester University Press.
Przeworski, Adam. 1986. "Some Problems in the Study of the Transition to Democracy." In *Transitions from Authoritarian Rule: Comparative Perspectives*, ed. Guillermo O'Donnell, Philippe C. Schmitter, and Laurence Whitehead. Baltimore: Johns Hopkins University Press.
_____. 1991. *Democracy and the Market: Political and Economic Reforms in*

Eastern Europe and Latin America. Cambridge: Cambridge University Press.

_____. 1992. "The Games of Transition." In *Issues in Democratic Consolidation: The New South American Democracies in Comparative Perspective,* ed. Scott Mainwaring, Guillermo O'Donnell, and J. Samuel Valenzuela. Notre Dame: University of Notre Dame Press.

Pye, Lucian. 1966. *Aspects of Political Development.* Boston: Little, Brown.

Quijano, Carlos. 1989. *Los golpes de estado.* República Oriental del Uruguay: Cámara de Representantes.

Quiroga, Hugo. 1989. *Autoritarismo y reforma del estado.* Buenos Aires: Centro Editor de América Latina.

Ragin, Charles C. 1987. *The Comparative Method: Moving Beyond Qualitative and Quantitative Strategies.* Berkeley and Los Angeles: University of California Press.

Raggio, Ezequiel. 1986. *La formación del estado militar en la Argentina, 1955/1979.* Buenos Aires: Editorial Losada.

Rama, Carlos M. 1973. "Uruguay: de los Tupamaros a los militares?" *Cuadernos Americanos* 189 (4): 7–26.

Ramírez, Gabriel. 1971. *Las fuerzas armadas Uruguayas y la crisis continental.* Montevideo: Tierra Nueva.

Ramseyer, J. Mark, and Frances M. Rosenbluth. 1995. *The Politics of Oligarchy: Institutional Choice in Imperial Japan.* Cambridge: Cambridge University Press.

Remmer, Karen. 1980. "Political Demobilization in Chile, 1973–78." *Comparative Politics* 12 (2): 275–301.

_____. 1991a. *Military Rule in Latin America.* Boulder, Colo.: Westview.

_____. 1991b. "New Wine or Old Bottlenecks? The Study of Latin American Democracy." *Comparative Politics* 23 (4): 479–95.

_____. 1992/93. "The Process of Democratization in Latin America." *Studies in Comparative International Development* 27 (4): 3–24.

Rial Roade, Juan. 1986. *Las fuerzas armadas: soldados-políticos garantes de la democracia?* Montevideo: CIESU-CLADE-EBO.

_____. 1992. *Estructura legal de las fuerzas armadas del Uruguay: un análisis político.* [Montevideo]: CIESU.

Ribera Neumann, Teodoro. 1987. "Función y composición del Tribunal Constitucional de 1980." *Estudios Publicos* 27:77–112.

Ricci, María Susana, and J. Samuel Fitch. 1990. "Ending Military Regimes in Argentina: 1966–73 and 1976–83." In *The Military and Democracy: The Future of Civil-Military Relations in Latin America,* ed. Louis W. Goodman, Johanna S.R. Mendelson, and Juan Rial. Lexington, Mass.: Lexington Books.

Richards, Gordon. 1986. "Stabilization Crises and the Breakdown of Military Authoritarianism in Latin America." *Comparative Political Studies* 18 (4): 449–85.

Rickard, Steven, and Cynthia Brown. 1988. *Chile: Human Rights and the Plebiscite, An Americas Watch Report.* Washington, D.C.: Americas Watch.

Roett, Riordan. 1984. *Brazil: Politics in a Patrimonial Society.* New York: Praeger.

Ronning, C. Neal, and Henry H. Keith. 1976. "Shrinking Political Arena: Military Government in Brazil Since 1964." In *Perspectives on Armed Politics in Brazil,* ed. Center for Latin American Studies. Tempe: Center for Latin American Studies, Arizona State University.

Roth, Roberto. 1980. *Los años de Onganía.* Buenos Aires: Ediciones la Campana.

Rouquié, Alain. 1986. "Demilitarization and the Institutionalization of Military-dominated Polities in Latin America." In *Transitions from Authoritarian Rule: Comparative Perspectives,* ed. Guillermo O'Donnell, Philippe C. Schmitter, and Laurence Whitehead. Baltimore: Johns Hopkins University Press.

_____. 1987. *The Military and the State in Latin America.* Berkeley and Los Angeles: University of California Press.

Rowe, James W. 1966a. "Onganía's Argentina: The First Four Months, Part I: The Golpe in Retrospect." *American Universities Field Staff: East Coast South America Series* 12 (7).

_____. 1966b. "Onganía's Argentina: The First Four Months, Part II: Men, Words, and Deeds." *American Universities Field Staff: East Coast South America Series* 12 (8).

_____. 1966c. "The 'Revolution' and the System: Notes on Brazilian Politics—Part III: The 'Revolution'—Generals and Technocrats." *American Universities Field Staff Reports: East Coast South American Series* 12 (5).

_____. 1967. "Brazil Stops the Clock—Part 1: 'Democratic Formalism' before 1964 and the Elections of 1966." *American Universities Field Staff Reports: East Coast South American Series* 13 (1).

Rueschemeyer, Dietrich, Evelyn H. Stephens, and John D. Stephens. 1992. *Capitalist Development and Democracy.* London: Polity.

Rustow, Dankwart A. 1970. "Transitions to Democracy: Toward a Dynamic Model." *Comparative Politics* 2:337–63.

Sáenz Quesada, María. 1986. "Onganía: el amargo final." *Todo es Historia* 19 (230): 72–82.

_____. 1989. *Dos transiciones a la democracia: de Lanusse a Alfonsín.* Buenos Aires: Universidad de Belgrano.

Sanders, Thomas G. 1970a. "Institutionalizing Brazil's Conservative Revolution." *American Universities Field Staff Reports: East Coast South American Series* 14 (5).

_____. 1970b. "Making Money: From Animal Game to Stock Market." *American Universities Field Staff Reports: East Coast South American Series* 14 (4).

_____. 1971. "Development and Security Are Linked by a Relationship of Mutual Causality." *American Universities Field Staff Reports: East Coast South American Series* 15 (3).

_____. 1973. "The Brazilian Model." *American Universities Field Staff Reports: East Coast South American Series* 17 (8).

_____. 1978. "Chile: The 'New Institutionality' and the 'Consultation.'" *American Universities Field Staff Reports* 5.

_____. 1981. "Decompression." In *Military Government and the Movement Toward Democracy in South America,* ed. Howard Handelman and Thomas G. Sanders. Bloomington: Indiana University Press.

Sarles, Margaret J. 1982. "Maintaining Control through Parties: The Brazilian Strategy." *Comparative Politics* 15 (1): 41–72.

Schmitter, Philippe C. 1973. *Military Rule in Latin America: Function, Consequences, and Perspectives.* Beverly Hills, Calif.: Sage Publications.

_____. 1992. "The Types of Democracy Emerging in Southern and Eastern Europe and South and Central America." In *Bound to Change: Consolidating Democracy in East Central Europe,* ed. Peter M. E. Volten. New York: Institute for East-West Studies.

Schmitter, Philippe C., and Terry Lynn Karl. 1991. "What Democracy Is ... And Is Not." *Journal of Democracy* 2 (3): 75–88.

Schneider, Ronald M. 1971. *The Political System of Brazil: Emergence of a "Modernizing" Authoritarian Regime, 1964–1970*. New York: Columbia University Press.

Selcher, Wayne A. 1977. *The National Security Doctrine and Policies of the Brazilian Government*. Carlisle Barracks, Pa.: Strategic Studies Institute of the U.S. Army.

———, ed. 1986. *Political Liberalization in Brazil: Dynamics, Dilemmas, and Future Prospects*. Boulder, Colo.: Westview Press.

Selser, Gregorio. 1986a. *El Onganiato (I): la espada y el hisopo*. Buenos Aires: Hyspamerica Ediciones Argentina.

———. 1986b. *El Onganiato (II): Lo llamaban Revolución Argentina*. Buenos Aires: Hyspamerica Ediciones Argentina.

Share, Donald. 1987. "Transitions to Democracy and Transition through Transaction." *Comparative Political Studies* 19 (4): 525–48.

Share, Donald, and Scott Mainwaring. 1986. "Transitions through Transaction: Democratization in Brazil and Spain." In *Political Liberalization in Brazil*, ed. W. Selcher. Boulder, Colo.: Westview.

Shepsle, Kenneth A. 1986. "Institutional Equilibrium and Equilibrium Institutions." In *Political Science: The Science of Politics*, ed. Herbert Weisberg. New York: Agathon.

Shils, Edward. 1962. "The Military in the Political Development of the New States." In *The Role of the Military in the Underdeveloped Countries*, ed. John J. Johnson. Princeton: Princeton University Press.

Shin, Doh Chull. 1994. "On the Third Wave of Democratization: A Synthesis and Evaluation of Recent Theory and Research." *World Politics* 47 (1): 135–70.

Shugart, Matthew Soberg, and John M. Carey. 1992. *Presidents and Assemblies: Constitutional Design and Electoral Dynamics*. Cambridge: Cambridge University Press.

Silva, Eduardo. 1993. "Capitalist Coalitions, the State, and Neoliberal Economic Restructuring: Chile 1973–88." *World Politics* 45 (4): 526–59.

Simmel, George. 1955. *Conflict and the Web of Group Affiliation*. Trans. Kurt H. Wolff and Rheinhard Bendix. New York: Free Press.

Skidmore, Thomas E. 1988. *The Politics of Military Rule in Brazil: 1964–1985*. New York: Oxford University Press.

Skocpol, Theda. 1985. "Bringing the State Back in: Strategies of Analysis in Current Research." In Evans, Reuschmeyer, and Skocpol 1985.

Skocpol, Theda, and Margaret Somers. 1980. "The Uses of Comparative History in Macrosocial Inquiry." *Comparative Studies in Society and History* 22 (2): 174–97.

Skowronek, Stephen. 1995. "Order and Change." *Polity* 28 (1): 91–96.

Smith, William C. 1989. *Authoritarianism and the Crisis of the Argentine Political Economy*. Stanford: Stanford University Press, 1989.

———. 1993. "Neoliberal Restructuring and Scenarios of Democratic Consolidation in Latin America." *Studies in Comparative International Development* 28 (2): 3–21.

Snow, Peter G. 1972. "Desarrollo económico y seguridad nacional en el régimen militar Argentino." *Desarrollo Ecónomico y Seguridad Nacional* 5 (20): 67–74.

Soares, Gláucio Ary Dillon. 1979. "Military Authoritarianism and Executive Absolutism in Brazil." *Studies in Comparative International Development* 14 (3/4): 104–26.

Solari, Aldo, and Rolando Franco. 1983. *Las empresas públicas en el Uruguay.* Montevideo: Fundación Cultura Universitaria.

Sondrol, Paul C. 1992. "1984 Revisited? A Re-examination of Uruguay's Military Dictatorship." *Bulletin of Latin American Research* 11 (2).

Spagnolo, Alberto, and Oscar Cismondi. 1984. "Argentina: el proyecto económico y su carácter de clase." In *La década trágica,* ed. Alberto J. Pla et al. Buenos Aires: Editorial Tierra del Fuego.

Spitta, Arnold. 1983. "El 'Proceso de Reorganización Naciónal' de 1976 a 1981: los objetivos basicá y su realización práctica." In *El poder militar en la Argentina, 1976–1981,* ed. Peter Waldmann and Ernesto Garzón Valdéz. Buenos Aires: Editorial Galerna.

Starr, Harvey. 1991. "Democratic Dominoes: Diffusion Approaches to the Spread of Democracy in the International System." *Journal of Conflict Resolution* 35 (2): 356–81.

Steinmo, Sven. 1993. *Taxation and Democracy: Swedish, British and American Approaches to Financing the Modern State.* New Haven: Yale University Press.

Steinmo, Sven, Kathleen Thelen, and Frank Longstreth. 1992. *Structuring Politics: Historical Institutionalism in Comparative Analysis.* New York: Cambridge University Press.

Stepan, Alfred. 1971. *The Military in Politics: Changing Patterns in Brazil.* Princeton: Princeton University Press.

――――. 1985. "State Power and the Strength of Civil Society in the Southern Cone of Latin America." In Evans, Reuschmeyer, and Skocpol 1985.

――――. 1986. "Paths Toward Redemocratization: Theoretical and Comparative Considerations." In *Transitions from Authoritarian Rule: Comparative Perspectives,* ed. Guillermo O'Donnell and Philippe Schmitter. Baltimore: Johns Hopkins University Press.

――――. 1988. *Rethinking Military Politics: Brazil and the Southern Cone.* Princeton: Princeton University Press.

――――, ed. 1973. *Authoritarian Brazil: Origins, Policies, and Future.* New Haven: Yale University Press.

Stephens, John. 1989. "Democratic Transition and the Breakdown in Europe, 1870–1939: A Test of the Moore Thesis." *American Journal of Sociology* 94 (5): 1019–77.

Thelen, Kathleen, and Sven Steinmo. 1992. "Historical Institutionalism in Comparative Politics." In Steinmo, Thelen, and Longstreth 1992.

Tomic, Esteban. 1988. *1988 ... y el general bajò el llano.* Santiago: Ediciones Chile América CESOC.

Torres, Cristina. 1984. "Las Fuerzas Armadas Uruguayas en la transición hacia democracia." *Uruguay y la democracia: volume II,* ed. Charles Gillespie, Louis Goodman, Juan Rial, and Peter Winn. Montevideo: Ediciones de la Banda Oriental.

Trindade, Hélgio. 1991. "Presidential Elections and Political Transition in Latin America." *International Social Science Journal* 128 (2): 301–14.

Troncoso, Oscar. 1984. *Cronología y documentación: el Proceso de Reorganizacion Nacional.* Vols. 1–5. Buenos Aires: Centro Editor de América Latina.

Ugalde, Alberto. 1984. *Las empresas públicas en la Argentina.* Buenos Aires: El Cronista Commercial.

Vacs, Aldo C. 1987. "Authoritarian Breakdown and Redemocratization in Argentina." In *Authoritarians and Democrats: Regime Transition in Latin America,* ed. James Malloy and Mitchell Seligson. Pittsburgh: University of Pittsburgh Press.

Valdés, Juan Gabriel. 1989. *La escuela de Chicago: operación Chile.* Buenos Aires: Grupo Editorial Zeta.

Valenzuela, Arturo. 1991. "The Military in Power: The Consolidation of One-Man Rule." In *The Struggle for Democracy in Chile, 1982–1990,* ed. Paul W. Drake and Iván Jaksic. Lincoln: University of Nebraska Press.

Valenzuela, J. Samuel. 1992. "Democratic Consolidation in Post-Transitional Settings: Notion, Process, and Facilitating Positions." In *Issues in Democratic Consolidation: The New South American Democracies in Comparative Perspective,* ed. Scott Mainwaring, Guillermo O'Donnell, and J. Samuel Valenzuela. Notre Dame: University of Notre Dame Press.

Varas, Augusto. 1982. "Fuerzas armadas y gobierno militar: corporativazación y politización militar." In *Chile 1973–198?,* ed. Revista Mexicana de Sociologia and FLACSO. Mexico City: Revista Mexicana de Sociologia and FLACSO.

Vásquez, Enrique. 1985. *PRN la última: origen, apogeo y caída de la dictadura militar.* Buenos Aires: EUDEBA.

Vergara, Pilar. 1982. "Las transformaciones del estado Chileno bajo el régimen militar." *Revista Mexicana de Sociología* 44 (2): 413–52.

Vial, Alejandro S. 1993. "Poder Legislativo y Reforma del Estado en el Cono Sur." *Revista Paraguaya de Sociología* 87:71–84.

Viola, Eduardo, and Scott Mainwaring. 1985. "Transitions to Democracy: Brazil and Argentina in the 1980s." *Journal of International Affairs* 38 (2): 195–219.

Walton, Gary M., ed. 1985. *The National Economic Policies of Chile.* Greenwich, Conn.: JAI.

Washington Office on Latin America. 1981. *"Uruguay after the Plebiscite: Prospects for Democracy": Proceedings from the June 12, 1981 Symposium at American University.* Washington, D.C.: Washington Office on Latin America.

Weinstein, Martin. 1975. *Uruguay: The Politics of Failure.* Westport, Conn.: Greenwood.

——. 1988. *Uruguay: Democracy at the Crossroads.* Boulder, Colo.: Westview.

Weir, Margaret. 1992. "Ideas and the Politics of Bounded Rationality." In Steinmo, Thelen, and Longstreth 1992.

Weiss, Linda. 1998. *The Myth of the Powerless State.* Ithaca: Cornell University Press.

Welch, Claude E., Jr. 1975. *Civilian Control of the Military: Myth and Reality.* Buffalo: Council on International Studies, State University of New York at Buffalo.

——. 1987. *No Farewell to Arms? Military Disengagement from Politics in Africa and Latin America.* Boulder, Colo.: Westview.

Wesson, Robert, and Davis V. Fleischer. 1983. *Brazil in Transition.* New York: Praeger.

Whitehead, Laurence, ed. 1996. *The International Dimensions of Democratization: Europe and the Americas.* New York: Oxford University Press.

Williams, Philip J. 1994. "Dual Transitions from Authoritarian Rule: Popular and Electoral Democracy in Nicaragua." *Comparative Politics* 26 (2): 169–86.

Wynia, Gary W. 1992. *Argentina: Illusions and Realities.* New York: Holmes and Meier.

Zapata, Francisco. 1979. "Las relaciones entre la Junta Militar y los trabajadores Chilenos: 1973–1978." *Foro Internacional* 20 (2): 191–219.

Zaverucha, Jorge. 1993. "The Degree of Military Political Autonomy During the

Spanish, Argentine, and Brazilian Transitions." *Journal of Latin American Studies* 25 (2): 283–99.

Zhang, Baohui. 1994. "Corporatism, Totalitarianism, and Transitions to Democracy." *Comparative Political Studies* 27 (1): 108–36.

Zirker, Daniel. 1991. "The Civil-Military Mediators in Post-1985 Brazil." *Journal of Political and Military Sociology* 19 (1): 47–73.

Newspapers and Wire Services

Análisis (Santiago)
Búsqueda (Montevideo)
Carta Política (Buenos Aires)
Chile-America (Rome)
Clarín (Buenos Aires)
Convicción (Buenos Aires)
Democracia, La (Montevideo)
Día, El (Montevideo)
Epoca, La (Santiago)
Ercilla (Santiago)
Foreign Broadcast Information Service—Latin America (Washington, D.C.)
Hoy (Santiago)
Latin America (London)
Latin American Monitor (London)
Latin American Political Report (London)
Latin American Regional Reports: Southern Cone (London)
Latin American Regional Reports: Brazil (London)
Latin American Weekly Report (London)
Los Angeles Times (Los Angeles)
Marcha, La (Montevideo)
Mensaje (Santiago)
Mercurio, El (Santiago)
Nación, La (Buenos Aires)
NACLA Report on the Americas
New York Times (New York City)
Opinión, La (Buenos Aires)
País, El (Montevideo)
Panorama (Buenos Aires)
Prensa, La (Buenos Aires)
Primera Plana (Buenos Aires)
Qué Pasa (Santiago)
Realidad (Santiago)
Redacción (Buenos Aires)
Semana Uruguaya, La (Montevideo)
Vigencia (Buenos Aires)
Washington Post (Washington, D.C.)

INDEX

Abi Ackel, Ibrahim, 148
Abreu, Gen. Hugo, 173
Aceguá, 215
Africa, 16
Agosti, Brig. Gen. Orlando, 114 (Table 1)
Agüero, Felipe, 233
Aguilar, Francisco R., 46
Aleixo, Pedro, 146
Alfonsín, Raúl, 124, 140
Allende, Salvador, 72, 78, 81, 86, 89, 95, 96
Alsogaray, Alvaro, 47, 52, 54
Alsogaray, Gen. Julio, 21, 41, 47, 48, 53, 57
Alta Gracia, 56
Alvarez, Gen. Gregorio, 185, 190, 191, 201–3, 212–13, 214, 215, 218
Alvarez, Brig. Gen. Teodoro, 33
Amadeo, Mario, 51
Anaya, Adm. Jorge, 114 (Table 1), 129, 137
Andreazza, Col. Mário David, 167, 175
antipolitics, 7
Aramburu, Gen. Pedro, 40, 60, 61
Aranco, Gen. Pedro, 218
Arceneaux, Craig, 233
Archdiocese of São Paulo, 170
Argentina, 29 n. 21, 198, 205. See also Argentine Proceso; Revolución Argentina
Argentine Proceso, 2, 4, 6, 16, 19, 20, 21, 22, 25, 26, 28, 29, 109–42, 154, 221, 225, 228, 229
   antisubversive war, 111, 113–14, 116, 117, 118, 118–19, 120, 121, 122–23, 124–25, 126, 130, 132, 136, 137, 138, 139, 140, 141
   collapse of, 109–10, 136–41, 141–42
   dispersion of authority, 109, 110, 110–15, 120, 126, 128, 130–34, 141, 155
   documents (selected): *Acta para el Proceso de Reorganización Nacional*, 115, 120; *Los bases politicos de las fuerzas armadas para el Proceso de Reorganización Nacional*, 126–27; *Bases para la intervención de las fuerzas armadas*, 121; *Documento final de la Junta Militar*, 140; *Estatuto para el Proceso de Reorganización Nacional*, 111, 112, 120; *Ley de Pacificación Nacional*, 140; *La Proclama*, 120; *El proposito y objetivos básicos del Proceso de Reorganización*, 120–21; *Nacional Reglamento para el funcionamiento de la Junta Militar, Poder Ejecutivo Nacional y Comisión de Asesoramiento Legislativo*, 111; Orientations No. 2, 128; *Proyecto Nacional*, 124
   economic interests, 127, 129–35; agriculture, 123, 129, 130, 134–35; business,

Argentine *Proceso* (*continued*)
129, 130, 131, 134; labor, 115, 116, 123, 128, 130, 131, 132–33, 136, 137, 139, 140, 141
economic policy, 110, 116, 120, 123, 127, 129–35, 141
human rights abuses in. *See* antisubversive war
institutions (selected): Comité Militar, 112; Comisión Nacional de Responsabilidad Patrimonial, 116; Consultation Staffs Designated by Area (PADA), 117; Junta Militar, 110, 111, 112, 112 nn. 7, 9, 112–13, 113 n. 12, 115, 116–17, 118 n. 22, 120, 123, 124, 127 n. 46, 128, 129, 131, 138–39; Legislative Consultation Commission (CAL), 111, 112, 112 n. 7, 113, 115, 116–17; interservice harmonization team (ECI), 117
judiciary, 112, 115, 139, 140
Malvinas Islands, invasion of. *See* Malvinas Islands
military disunity, 109, 110, 119, 120, 124–25, 127, 136, 137, 138, 140, 141, 142
policymaking in, 112–13, 116–17, 129–34
political parties in, 109, 118, 122, 123, 124, 125, 126, 127, 128, 136, 137, 138, 139–40; Multipartidaria, 136, 138
political program, lack of, 110, 119, 120–29, 133, 138, 136, 141
politicization of the military. *See* military disunity
popular protests, 137, 139
regime investment, 109, 110, 112, 115–18, 120, 132, 136, 141
strategy coordination, lack of, 109, 110, 119, 120, 127, 129, 135, 136, 141, 142
Arismendi, Valentín, 204
Arregui, Col. Walter, 213 n. 58
Arriagada, Genaro, 8
Ateneo de la República, 51
Aylwin, Patricio, 88, 103, 106

Balbín, Ricardo, 58, 118
Ballestrino, Gen. Alberto, 203, 213 n. 58
Bacchus, Wilfred, 147, 164
Baretta, Silvio R. Duncan, 156
Barrios, Gen. Angel, 217
Batlle y Ordóñez, José, 189
Beagle Islands, 84 n. 28, 123

Beltrão, Hélio, 167
Benjamín, Gen. Luciano, 113
Bignone, Gen. Reynaldo, 114 (Table 1), 120, 135, 138, 139, 140 n. 77
Bolentini, Col. Nestor, 214
Bonelli, Gen. Julio C., 214
Borad, Gen. Jorge, 218 n. 76
Borda, Gen. Guillermo, 42, 51, 53, 54, 59
Bordaberry, Juan María, 185, 186–88, 190, 192, 193, 197, 201, 202
Boscan Hontou, Gen., 218
Braga, Gen. Ney, 171
Bratton, Michael, 17
Brazil, 1, 2, 4, 6, 10, 16, 20, 21, 24, 25, 26, 28, 69, 143–82, 183, 184, 192, 196, 198, 199, 204, 210, 221, 224, 225, 226, 227, 228, 232, 234
civilian participation, 151–54, 157–58, 163–64, 179, 181
controlled transition in, 143, 158, 174–82
dispersion of authority, 143, 144–50, 163, 164, 181; institutional accommodation, 163, 164–74, 175, 181
distensão, 149, 159, 171–74
documents (selected): 1977 "April Package," 172–73; Falcão Law, 172; Institutional Act, 145, 149, 150–51; Institutional Act No. 2, 166; Institutional Act No. 3, 166; Institutional Act No. 5, 151, 153, 168, 169, 172, 174
economic policy, 155, 156, 158, 161, 162, 165, 166, 167, 168, 170, 171, 175, 176, 181
economic interests: business, 155, 157, 160, 161, 176; labor, 145, 155, 161
elections, manipulations of, 151, 152, 165–66, 172–73, 175, 176, 177, 178
human rights abuses in, 162, 169, 170, 172, 173, 176, 180
institutions (selected): Centro de Informacões do Exercito, 173; *conselho* system, 159–60, 160, 181, 199, 222; electoral college, 150, 152, 177, 179; Revolutionary Supreme Command, 143, 144–45, 151, 167; military electoral college, 148; National Information Service (SNI), 145, 146, 165, 167, 173; National Security Council (NSC), 145–46, 153, 157, 172, 174, 180
judiciary, 153–54, 166, 171, 176–77

legislature, 144, 145, 148, 149–50, 151–52,
154, 155, 159, 163, 165, 166, 167, 168,
169, 171–73, 174, 178, 180, 181
military factions: *Castellista* faction,
162–63, 169, 170, 173; *Costista* faction,
162–63, 168, 169–70; Geisel softliners,
175 (*see also* Geisel, Gen. Ernesto); security apparatus, as a faction (security
hardliners), 154 n. 16, 162, 163, 168–69,
170, 171, 172, 175, 176–77; Sorbonne
faction, 157–58, 162, 165, 167, 168. *See
also Castellista* faction
military unity, 147, 148–49, 150, 158, 160,
161–64, 168, 170, 171, 181
policymaking, 145, 147–48
political parties, 149, 150 n. 10, 152,
158–59, 162, 163, 165, 166, 168, 171,
172–73, 174, 175, 176, 177, 178,
179–80, 181
political reform, 150–51, 165–66. *See also*
elections: manipulations of, controlled
transition in
politicians. *See* political parties
popular protests, 168, 178
regime investment, lack of, 143, 150–54,
163, 181
security policy, 154, 155, 167, 168, 169,
170, 171, 172, 173. *See also* National
Security Council, human rights abuses;
security apparatus, as a faction
strategy coordination, 143, 150, 152,
154–61, 174, 181
Buadas, Brig. Gen. Manuel, 218
Búsqueda (Montevideo), 205, 209

Caballero, Carlos, 59
Cáceres, Carlos, 105
Cals, César, 175
Cámpora, Héctor, 68
Campos, Roberto de Oliveira, 165
Carcagno, Gen. Jorge R., 68
Carter, Jimmy, 202
Casa Rosada, 137
Castelo Branco, Marshal Humberto, 145,
147, 148, 152, 153, 154 n. 16, 157, 162,
163, 164–67, 170
Catholic Church, 32, 46, 51, 98, 156, 170,
173
Cavalcanti, Col. Boaventura, 167
Cavarozzi, Marcelo, 22
Central America, 16, 26

Centro de Altos Estudios Militares (CEAM)
(Peru), 198
Chiappe Posse, Gen. Hugo, 192, 201
Chile, 1, 2, 4, 6, 8, 19, 20, 21, 22, 25, 26, 27,
28, 32, 71–108, 123, 144, 154, 155, 180,
199, 204, 205, 224, 225, 226, 227, 228,
234 n. 4
antisubversive war, 72, 73, 75, 76, 78–79,
81, 86, 88–89, 90, 91, 93, 94, 99, 103, 104
Armed Forces Organic Law, 103
civilian participation, importance of, 84–85
concentration of authority, 71, 73–80, 84,
107
constitution of 1925, 89
constitutional reform, 89, 90, 92–93,
101–2, 103, 104–7
controlled transition in, 71–72, 100–107
documents (selected): *actas nacionales*,
88–89, 90, 91, 107; Chacarillas speech,
90–93; Constitution of 1980, 71, 79, 80,
86, 93, 94, 100, 101; *Declaración de Principios del Gobierno de Chile*, 86, 87–88, 89;
La Imagen de un Chile Nuevo, 86–87, 88;
New Institutionality, *see* Chacarillas
speech; *Objetivo Nacional de Chile*, 88
economic interests: labor, 95–99; business,
95–99, 108
economic policy, 84–85, 88, 94–100, 107;
Chicago Boys, 84–85, 94–95, 96, 108;
pragmatic neoliberalism, 96–99, 108
historical lack of civil-military interaction
in, 72
human rights abuses in. *See* antisubversive
war; 1978 Amnesty
institutions (selected): Central Nacional de
Inteligencia (CNI), 79, 94, 99 n. 57;
Comisión Nacional de la Reforma
Administrativa (CONARA), 77–78, 81,
82; Comité Asesor de la Junta de Gobierno (COAJ), 76, 82; Comité Asesor
Presidencial (COAP), 82; Consejo de
Estado, 85, 88, 89, 92; Dirección
Nacional de Inteligencia (DINA),
78–79; Estado Mayor Presidencial
(EMP), 78, 82; Junta de Gobierno, 72,
73, 75–77, 78, 79, 80, 81, 82, 83, 85, 87,
88, 89, 90, 91, 92, 93, 98, 100–101, 102,
105; National Security Council (NSC),
104, 105, 107; Officers' Extraordinary
Assessment Board, 74; Secretaría Ejecutiva Nacional de Detenidos (SENDET),

Chile (*continued*)
78–79; Secretaría General de la Presidencia (SGP), 82–83, 94
judiciary, 79, 81, 102, 103, 107
liberalism in, 32
military unity, 71, 72, 83, 84, 85, 86, 99, 106, 107
1978 Amnesty Law, 103, 104
1978 *consulta*, 79, 91, 92, 100
1988 plebiscite, 92, 93, 100–101
policymaking, 75–83, 84–85
political parties, 86–87, 88, 89–90, 96, 97–99, 102, 103, 104, 107: Acuerdo Nacional, 98–99; "Agreement for the NO," 100; Alianza Democrática, 97–98; Concertación, 103, 105, 106; Renovación Nacional, 104, 105, 107; Unión Democráta Independiente, 104, 107; Unidad Popular, 72, 89
political program, 86–94, 107
popular protests in, 97, 98, 99, 100
regime investment in, 72, 80–85, 106, 107
strategy coordination in, 71, 85, 86–100, 106, 107–8
civilian control, 233, 234
Collados, Modesto, 98
Colombia, 21, 229, 231
comparable cases approach, 26–27
Córdoba, 59, 65
Cordón Aguirre, Arturo, 64, 65
Correia de Melo, Brig. Francisco de Assis, 144
Corrientes, 59
Costa Méndez, Nicanor, 51
Costa e Silva, Gen. Artur, 144, 146, 147, 151, 152, 153, 159, 161, 165, 166–69
Cristi, Gen. Estéban, 187, 201–2

Dalla Tea, Gen. Carlos, 132
Delfim Neto, Antônio, 147, 148, 152, 167, 168, 175, 176
Demichelli, Alberto, 190, 197
democracy, 5, 10, 223, 230–31
democratic consolidation, 229, 232–34
democratic transition, 13–14, 15–16, 22–23, 228–29, 231
dependency theory, 7
Díaz Bessone, Gen. Genaro, 122, 123–25, 131, 132
Díaz Colodrero, Mario, 51, 53, 54

Eastern Europe, 16
Ecuador, 231

El Mercurio (Santiago), 84
El Talero (Montevideo), 203
Erro, Enrique, 188
Escobar, Luís, 98
Escuela de Armas y Servicios (Uruguay), 185, 203, 213 n. 58
Escuela de Seguridad y Defensa Nacional (ESEDENA) (Uruguay), 198, 220, 224
Escola Superior de Guerra (ESG) (Brazil), 69, 155–59, 162, 164, 165, 167, 168, 170, 181, 227
Estado Nôvo, 163

Fabricaciones Militares, 131
Falcão, Armando, 171
Falkland Islands. See Malvinas Islands
Farcau, Bruce, 29
Ferreira, Maj. Heitor Aquino, 175
Ferriera, Wilson, 217, 220
Ferrer, Aldo, 64, 135
Figueiredo, Gen. João Baptista, 28, 143, 147, 148, 153, 165 (Table 2), 173, 174–80, 182
Filho, Gen. Olympio Mourão, 145
Finer, S. E., 22–23
Fitch, J. Samuel, 29
Fontana, Andrés, 130
Francese, Gen. Antonio, 187
Franco, Rolando, 199
Franco, Adm. Rubén, 114 (Table 1)
Frei, Eduardo, 81
Frondizi, Arturo, 58, 60, 130, 131
Frota, Gen. Silvio Coelho da, 171, 173

Galimberti, Rodolfo, 46
Gallino, Gen. Oscar Bartolomé, 131
Galtieri, Gen. Leopoldo, 114 (Table 1), 116 n. 18, 120, 127, 128–29, 135, 136–38
Garretón, Manuel Antonio, 23
Geddes, Barbara, 17 n. 15
Geisel, Gen. Ernesto, 147, 148, 149, 159, 165, 170–74, 175
Geisel, Gen. Orlando, 147, 169, 171
Gestido, Oscar, 185
Gilardi, Enrique, 63
Gnavi, Adm. Pedro J., 62
Golbery de Couto e Silva, Gen., 24, 147, 165, 167, 171, 175, 176
González, Luis E., 193
Goulart, João, 143, 144, 145, 162, 165, 167
Gouvéia de Bulhões, Octávio, 165
Graffigna, Brig. Gen. Omar, 114 (Table 1)

Gravina, Gen., 187
Guimarães, Ulysses, 172
Guido, José María, 130
Guzman, Jaime, 73

Hagopian, Frances, 179
Harguindeguy, Gen. Albano, 118–19, 125–26, 127, 141
historical institutionalism, *see* institutional theory
Hughes, Brig. Gen. Augusto Jorge, 114 (Table 1)
Huntington, Samuel, 7, 8, 16, 17, 17 n. 13

Ibáñez, Gen. Carlos, 72
Ikenberry, G. John, 1
Illia, Arturo Umberto, 31, 40, 46, 58
Imaz, Gen. Francisco, 42, 59
institutional theory, 9–13, 19, 21, 223–24
    institutional manipulation and change, 233–34
Instituto Militar de Estudios Superiores (IMES) (Uruguay), 198, 217, 224
International Monetary Fund, 50, 176
Invidio, Adm. Rodolfo, 218, 220
Italy, 164

Jarpa, Sergio, 97, 105
Justicialista Party. *See* peronism

Kingdon, John W., 23, 25, 155
Kinzo, Maria D'Alva G., 163
Korean War, 184
Krasner, Stephen, 11, 21
Krieger Vasena, Adalbert, 48–50, 53, 55, 56, 58, 59
Kubitschek, Juscelino, 171

La Gaceta Marinera (Puerto Belgrano), 131
Lacerda, Carlos, 167, 168
Lacoste, Gen. Carlos A., 114 (Table 1)
Lambruschini, Adm. Armando, 114 (Table 1), 127, 129
Lami-Dozo, Brig. Gen. Basilio, 114 (Table 1)
Lanusse, Gen. Alejandro Agustín, 21, 33, 57, 60, 61, 62, 65, 65–67, 69
Lanusse, Antonio, 43 n. 24
legitimacy, 11
Legnani, Augusto, 187
Leigh, Gen. Gustavo, 73, 75, 77, 79–80, 86, 95
Leitão de Abreu, João, 147, 148

Letelier, Orlando, 91
Levingston, Gen. Roberto M., 21, 33, 61, 62–65, 67, 69, 227
Liendo, Gen. Horacio Tomás, 114 (Table 1), 131, 132
Lima, Gen. Albuquerque, 167, 168, 169
Linares Brum, Gen. Hugo, 203
Linz, Juan, 16, 17
Llerena, Moyano, 64
Los Olivos, 56
Ludwig, Gen. Rubens, 148

Macedo, Murilo, 175
Mainwaring, Scott, 229
Maluf, Paulo, 179
Malvinas Islands, invasion of, 2, 110, 120, 136–38, 177
Markoff, John, 156
Márquez, Hugo, Vice Adm., 202, 212
Martínez, Gen. César, 187, 201
Martínez Paz, Enrique, 51, 52, 53
Martínez de Hoz, José Alfredo, 123, 129–35, 136, 141
Massera, Adm. Emilio, 111 n. 2, 114 (Table 1), 122–23, 124, 125, 131, 136
Masterson, Daniel, 8
Matthei, Gen. Fernando, 80, 98, 105
Mattos, Brig. Délio Jardim de, 175
Mazzilli, Ranieri, 144
McLoughlin, Eduardo, 63, 64
Medeiros, Gen. Octavio, 148
Médici, Gen. Emilio Garrastazú, 147, 151, 152–53, 159, 161, 164, 165 (Table 2), 167, 169–70, 171, 172, 174, 175
Medina, Gen. Hugo, 183, 218, 220
Méndez, Aparicio, 190, 203, 207, 212
Méndez, Gen. Juan José, 203
Menéndez, Gen. Luciano, 119, 122, 126
Meoli, Roberto, 63
Merino, Adm. José Torino, 73, 94–95, 99 n. 57
military legacies, 1–2
military regimes, 17–23, 223–24
    alienation of the military in, 3, 20, 27, 29, 226, 231
    as regimes of exception, 4–5
    in Latin America, 6–9, 230, 232
    military unity in, 3, 4, 6, 17–23, 25–29, 155, 224, 225, 231
    politicization of the military in, 3, 20, 28, 29, 225, 226
    reappearance of, 228–32

military regimes (*continued*)
  regime investment by the military, 18–22, 26, 27–28, 231
  societal linkages in, 3–4, 11, 21, 25, 155, 226
  strategy coordination in, 23–29, 155, 199, 224, 225–28
  studies of, 7–8, 29–30
modernization theory, 7
Monteiro, Gen. Euler Bentes, 174 n. 45
Montevideo, 187, 215
Munck, Gerardo, 17, 17 n. 13, 23
Muricy, Gen. Antônio Carlos, 169

national security doctrine, 8, 24, 38, 40, 42, 88, 107, 118–19, 145, 155–59, 162, 181, 191, 197, 198, 210
Neves, Tancredo, 179
Nicolaides, Gen. Cristino, 138
Nirvana, 204
Nordlinger, Eric, 5
Nuñez, Gen. Manuel, 203, 212, 213 n. 58

O'Donnell, Guillermo, 15, 21, 58, 231
Onganía, Gen. Juan Carlos, 19, 21, 31, 32, 33–36, 39–49, 51–61, 63 n. 82, 69, 227
Ongaro, Raimundo, 55, 56
Orren, Karen, 12

Pacheco Areco, Jorge, 185, 186, 187, 212
Pampillón, Brig. Gen. Herbert, 219
Paraguay, 231
Paris, 202
Pastore, Diego, 59
Peace Corps, 161
Pereira dos Santos, Gen. Adalberto, 171
Pérez Jiménez, Gen. Marcos, 21, 44, 229
Perina, Rubén M., 39
Perón, Isabel, 128
Perón, Juan. *See* peronism
peronism, 2, 31, 32, 40, 42, 46, 53, 55, 56, 58, 59, 64, 67–68, 69, 118, 122, 127, 128, 132, 136
Peru, 8, 32, 198
Petrobrás, 171
Pinochet Ugarte, Gen. Augusto, 8, 13, 19, 22, 27, 32, 71–108, 144, 154, 155, 224, 227, 228, 233
Pion-Berlin, David, 233
Pires, Gen. Walter, 179
Pírez, Pedro, 36
Pistarini, Gen. Pascual, 21, 33, 45, 48, 53
Plaza de Mayo, 137

Portela, Eduardo, 175
Portugal, 32
Prantl, Gen. Amaury, 203
professionalization of the military, 7, 8
Przeworski, Adam, 234

Quierolo, Gen. Luis V., 203, 212, 213

Rademaker Grünewald, Adm. Augusto, 144, 167, 169
Raggio, Adolfo, 46
Raimúndez, Gen. Abdón, 203, 212, 213, 214, 218 n. 76
Rapela, Gen. Julio, 213, 214, 215–16
Raposo, Col. Amerino, 167
rational choice theory, 9, 12 n. 6, 13 n. 7
Remmer, Karen, 8, 18, 19, 20, 91
Repetto, Gen. Héctor, 37, 41, 42, 49
Resistencia, 59
Revista de la Escuela Superior de Guerra (Buenos Aires), 119
Revolución Argentina, 2, 4, 6, 19, 21, 22, 25, 26, 27, 28–29, 31–69, 110, 115, 154, 199, 224, 225, 226, 227, 228, 231, 232
  alienation of the military, 32–33, 43, 44–45, 58, 61, 65, 66–67, 68
  azul-colorado split, 40–41, 57 n. 70
  balanced transition in, 61–69
  concentration of authority in the executive branch, 31, 32, 33–40, 44, 45; movement toward collegial government, 65–66
  documents (selected): *Acta de la Revolución Argentina*, 34, 62; "*cinco puntos*," 68; *Estatuto de la Revolución Argentina*, 34, 35, 36, 37, 62, 65; "*gran acuerdo nacional*," 66–68; *Las Políticas Nacionales*, 62; *Mensaje de la Junta Revolucionaria al Pueblo Argentino*, 34; *Objetivos Políticos*, 34–35, 52; *Tres Tiempos* doctrine, 54
  economic policy, 31–32, 34, 38–39, 44–50, 53, 54, 55, 58, 64, 65, 66, 69
  economic interests: business, 32, 44, 45, 46–47, 48–50, 52, 56, 60, 64; agriculture, 32, 44, 46, 48–50, 64; labor, 32, 44, 46–47, 49, 50, 53–54, 55, 56–57, 58, 59, 60, 64
  guerrilla movement, 58, 61
  institutions (selected): Casa Militar, 38; Central Nacional de Inteligencia (CNI), 39, 42; Comisión Coordinadora del Plan Política, 66; Comisión Nacional de

Zonas de Seguridad, 38–39; Consejo Nacional Asesor, 39; Consejo Nacional de Ciencia y Técnica (CONACYT), 39; Consejo Nacional de Desarrollo (CONADE), 38–39, 41, 48, 60; Consejo Nacional de Seguridad (CONASE), 38–39, 41, 42, 53; Junta Revolucionaria, 33, 34, 35, 40, 41; Presidencia de la Nación, 37, 41; Secretaría de Informaciones de Estado (SIDE), 42, 62; Secretaría General, 36, 37; Secretaría de Prensa, 38; Secretaría Privada, 38; Sistema de Planeamiento y Acción para el Desarrollo y la Seguridad, 38, 41
judiciary, 34, 36–37, 43, 67 n. 95, 68; "rebellion of the court," 36
liberal-corporatist split, 31–32, 41, 44–61, 63–65, 69
military unity, 58, 61, 69
policymaking, 34–40, 42, 62–63, 66
political parties, 34, 52, 53, 55–56, 58, 59, 60, 63–64, 66, 67; La Hora del Pueblo, 64
political program, 34, 44–45, 50, 51–61, 62, 63–64, 65, 66–68, 69
regime investment, lack of, 32, 33, 40–43, 44, 61
security: security policy, 35, 38–39; security apparatus, 38–39
social unrest, 47, 53, 60–61, 64, 68; cordobazo, 31, 43, 47, 50, 59, 227, 228; viborazo, 65
strategy coordination, lack of, 32, 44–45, 46–47, 51–61, 67, 68
university relations, 47, 52–53, 59
Rey, Brig. Gen. Carlos A., 62, 65
Rezende, Eliseu, 175
Ribeiro, Gen. Alberto, 169
Ricci, María Susana, 29
Rio de Janiero, 144, 157, 166, 167
Riocentro, bombing of, 176–77
Rischbieter, Carlos, 175
Rojas Pinilla, Gen. Gustavo, 21, 44, 229
Rosario, 59
Roth, Roberto, 39
Rouquié, Alain, 5

Salimei, Jorge Nestor, 45, 48, 49, 51
San Miguel, 204
San Sebastián, Rubens, 55
Sanguinetti, Julio María, 214 n. 61, 215 n. 64, 218, 220
Santa Teresa, 207

São Paulo, 157, 170, 178
Saravia, José M., Jr., 51
Sarney, José, 180
Serpa, Gen. José Maria de Andrade, 175
Schmitter, Philippe, 15, 21, 231
Schneider, Ronald, 146
Segurança e Desenvolvimento (Rio de Janeiro), 156
Señorans, Gen. Eduardo, 42, 51
Serengi, Liber, 218
Share, Donald, 16
Simonsen, Mário Henrique, 175
Skowronek, Stephen, 9, 12
Smith, Oscar, 123
Solá, Hidalgo, 123
Solari, Aldo, 199
Southern Europe, 16
South America, 16, 177
Souza e Melo, Marshal Marcio de, 167
Spain, 32
Stepan, Alfred, 8, 16, 17, 23
strategy coordination, 3–4, 6. See also military regimes, strategy coordination in
Suárez Mason, Gen. Carlos, 122

Tami, Felipe, 46, 47
Tavares, Gen. Aurélio de Lira, 167
Thedy, Horacio, 58
Torture in Brazil, 170
Trábal, Col. Ramón, 201, 201–2
transition control, 2–3, 4, 6, 13–25, 26–29, 224, 225, 227, 228, 232–34
as a mode of transition, 14, 14 n. 9, 232
Trindade, Hélgio, 16
Trinidad, Yamundú, 214
Tucumán, 47, 59
Tupamaros, 184–85, 186, 188

United Kingdom, 136, 137
United Nations, 46
United States, 40 n. 13, 43 n. 24, 47, 90, 91, 129, 137, 161, 168, 217, 229, 230
Uriburu, José Camilo
Uruguay, 2, 4, 6, 16, 19, 20, 21, 22, 24, 24, 25, 26, 28–29, 154, 155, 158, 183–222, 224, 225, 226, 227–28, 232
accretion of power by the military, 184–89, 197, 221
antisubversive campaign, 185–86, 187, 188, 189, 193, 196, 200, 202, 207, 208, 209–10, 211, 215–16, 222
balanced transition in, 211–22

Uruguay (*continued*)
civilian participation, importance of, 201, 210, 221
constitutional reform, 192, 194, 197, 207–8, 209, 210, 213, 219, 220
dispersion of authority, 183, 189–93, 195, 197, 199, 200–201, 202, 210, 212, 221. *See also* military unity, institutional accommodation
documents (selected), Agreement of Boiso Lanza, 187, 200; Club Naval pact, 212, 219–20; communiqués 4 and 7, 197, 206; *Ley Fundamental No. 2*, 214; Memorandum No. 1/75, 206–7; *Plan Político de las Fuerzas Armadas de 1977*, 197, 207; Resolution No. 1, 196, 206, 209
economic interests: agriculture, 205; business, 191, 209; labor, 205, 209, 210, 215 nn. 64, 66, 220
economic policy, 184, 189, 191, 195, 199, 204–6, 208, 222
human rights abuses, 186, 187, 217, 220. *See also* antisubversive campaign
institutions (selected): civil-military conclaves, 191, 194, 199, 204, 207, 222; Comisión de Asuntos Políticos (COMASPO), 192 n. 21, 206, 207, 212, 213, 214, 215, 217, 218–19, 220; Consejo de Económico y Social (CES), 190, 191, 194–95, 222, 224; Consejo de Estado, 188, 190, 191, 192–93, 194, 195, 207, 209, 213; Consejo de la Nación, 192, 194; Estado Mayor Conjunto (ESMACO), 185, 189, 190, 191, 195, 200, 209, 214, 219, 221, 224; Junta de Comandantes en Jefe (JCJ), 185, 189, 190, 191–92, 196, 199, 200, 206, 207, 215 n. 66, 217, 218, 219–20, 221; Junta de Oficiales Generales (JOG), 190, 191–92, 193, 199, 201, 202, 203, 204, 206, 207, 212, 213, 215, 216, 217, 220, 221, 224, 226; National Security Council (COSENA), 187, 190–91, 192, 194, 196, 197, 199, 207; Secretaría de Planeamiento, Coordinación y Difusión (SEPLACODI), 190, 191, 224; Servicio de Inteligencia de la Defensa (SID), 200
judiciary, 183, 185, 190, 192, 193–94, 208, 210, 219, 220
late professionalization of the armed forces in, 197–98
legislature, 183, 185, 186, 188, 196, 209,

219, 220; created by military. *See also* Consejo de Estado *and* Consejo de la Nación
military factions, 198, 201–4, 211; security forces, as a faction, 202, 203
military unity, 183, 184, 193, 200–204, 208, 211, 212, 221; institutional accommodation, 184, 200–201, 221
Parque Hotel talks, 212, 215–16
plebiscite, of November 1980, 207, 208, 211, 212
policymaking, 192–93, 194, 198, 199
political parties, 183–84, 185, 196, 197, 200, 201, 202, 206, 207, 208, 209, 213–16, 217, 218–19
political program, 183–84, 189, 197, 198–99, 206–8, 212, 213–16, 220, 221–22
regime investment, lack of, 184, 193–96, 203, 221
social unrest, 184, 185, 209, 210, 216–17, 218, 220
strategy coordination, lack of, 183, 184, 188, 196–99, 200, 208–11, 221
traditional politicians. *See* political parties

Vadora, Gen. Julio César, 202, 213
Valenzuela, J. Samuel, 14–15
Van de Walle, Nicolas, 17
Vandor, Augusto, 46
Varela, Adm. Benigno, 33
Vargas, Getúlio, 163
Vegh Villegas, Alejandro, 204, 212
Venezuela, 21, 229, 231
Videla, Gen. Jorge, 112 n. 9, 113, 114 (Table 1), 118, 119 n. 27, 120, 122–27, 132, 134
Vieira, Laerte, 172
Villegas, Gen. Osiris, 38, 42, 53
Villarreal, Gen. José, 125, 128
Viola, Gen. Roberto, 111 n. 1, 114 (Table 1), 116 n. 18, 120, 126, 127–29, 133, 135, 136, 137, 141

Washington, D.C., 54
Western Europe, 230
World Bank, 47

Yofre, Ricardo, 125

Zubiá, Gen. Eduardo, 201, 202
Zubiá, Gen. Rodolfo, 201, 202, 203